GLADSTONE, HOME RULE AND THE
ULSTER QUESTION, 1882-93

JAMES LOUGHLIN

Gladstone,
Home Rule and the
Ulster Question
1882-93

Humanities Press International, Inc.

First published in 1987
in the United States of America
and Canada by
Humanities Press International, Inc.,
Atlantic Highlands, NJ 07716

© James Loughlin, 1987

Library of Congress Cataloging-in-Publication Data

Loughlin, James.
Gladstone, Home Rule and
the Ulster Question, 1882-93.

1. Ireland — Politics and Government — 1837-1901.
2. Gladstone, W. E. (William Ewart), 1809-1898.
3. Home Rule (Ireland)   4. Ulster (Northern Ireland and
Ireland) — Politics and Government.   5. Nationalism —
Ireland — History — 19th Century.   I. Title.
DA951.L68 1987   941.5081   86-27832
ISBN 0-391-03503-7

Printed in Great Britain

To Caroline, Carmen, Jacinta
and my parents

Contents

Tables

Acknowledgments

MY FIRST debt of gratitude is to Dr W. E. Vaughan, of Trinity College, Dublin, who supervised the doctoral thesis on which this work is based and who taught me a great deal about historical inquiry.

I have also incurred debts to many other people and am especially grateful to the staffs of the following institutions: Public Record Office of Northern Ireland; Linenhall Library, Belfast; Belfast Public Library (Irish section); library of Queen's University, Belfast; National Library of Ireland; Manuscripts Room, Trinity College, Dublin; Berkeley and Lecky Libraries, Trinity College, Dublin; State Paper Office, Dublin Castle; Royal Irish Academy; Public Record Office, London; British Library; British Museum Newspaper Library at Colindale, London.

Thanks are also due to the Department of Education for Northern Ireland for the major state award which enabled me to carry out my research. Financial assistance was also forthcoming from the Trinity Trust Travel and Research Fund, and from my parents, who contributed generously, both financially and materially. For their generosity and helpfulness I would like to thank Dr Greta Jones and Dr Paul Bew, and also the following custodians and owners of papers, who gave me permission to publish materials in their possession: Deputy Keeper of Records, Public Record Office of Northern Ireland; Board of Trinity College, Dublin; Keeper of State Papers, Dublin Castle; Council of Trustees, National Library of Ireland; Keeper of Public Records, Public Record Office, London; Miss A. G. G. Brown; Captain Peter Montgomery, Miss Sylvia M.

Duffin, John Saunderson, and William Johnston Esq. For his helpful advice in the course of preparing the manuscript for publication, I would like to thank Mr Colm Croker.

Finally, there is the enormous debt I owe to my wife, who typed this work through the several stages of its development and who performed this task in addition to many other pressing demands on her time.

Preface

THE judgment on the Home Rule struggle of the 1880s and 1890s, traditionally accepted, is one that assesses it, essentially, as a contest between the forces of enlightenment and reaction. In its broad outlines the picture painted depicts the Irish nation earnestly desiring Home Rule, being responded to by Gladstone, influenced by his 'European sense' and sympathy with struggling nationalities. His Home Rule proposals, however, eagerly accepted by the Irish and promising to put an end to the strife of centuries, are defeated by Unionists, incapable of understanding Irish problems and motivated by aggressive imperialism and/or anti-Irish prejudice.

Paradoxically, this view of the struggle for Home Rule has been established by an historiography not primarily concerned with testing its validity. For instance, it is remarkable that in his massive tribute to Gladstone's attempts at solving the Irish question, *Gladstone and the Irish Nation*, J. L. Hammond provides no analysis of Gladstone's concept of Irish nationality and how it influenced his expectations for Irish political developments. Similarly, his treatment of Gladstone's Home Rule schemes fails to examine their all-important and contentious fiscal provisions. The central weakness of Hammond's approach to his subject was his tendency to assume that the *fact* of Gladstone's sympathy with struggling nationalities was itself a vindication both of his insight into Irish nationalism and of the Home Rule schemes he devised. Nor has Hammond been entirely alone in his approach. A succession of historians, including Nicholas Mansergh, Philip Magnus and E. D. Steele, have noted the importance of Gladstone's sympathy with European nationalism in moving him to take a constructive attitude to Irish nationalism; however, they have also failed to provide full and critical analyses of his concept of Irish nationality and his Home Rule plans. This has also been true even of those who have distanced themselves from the Hammond tradition and sought to explain Gladstone's involvement with Home Rule primarily in terms of a power struggle within the Liberal Party.

As for the nationalist dimension to the Home Rule issue, a similar historiographical weakness is observable. As exemplified by the work of Conor Cruise O'Brien in *Parnell and his Party* and F. S. L. Lyons in *Charles Stewart Parnell* respectively, the main trends of analysis on the Parnell movement have been either organisational or biographical, and these have led not only to inadequate assessments of Gladstone's Irish plan but also to questionable assumptions about the Irish desire for Home Rule and the extent to which the acceptance of Gladstone's proposals by the Parnellite leadership was representative of Irish public opinion.

Many of the inadequacies of Home Rule historiography would appear to stem from an excessive concentration on party conflict, with the result that the ideas and proposals which provoked it have become subsidiary concerns. This study is intended as a contribution towards redressing that imbalance. Chapter 1 begins with an account of the developments in historical literature that provided — especially for Gladstone — material for the nationalist and Home Rule case. It also examines how nationalist propaganda changed with the demotion of agrarian struggle in favour of constitutional agitation for Home Rule from 1882, and the extent to which the new policy found support. Consequently the traditional view of Irish support for Home Rule is significantly modified.

In dealing with Gladstone's public conversion to Home Rule, in the winter of 1885-6, this study has departed from the practice of accounting for his actions in terms either of a reaction to Parnellite electoral successes or the exigencies of a Liberal Party power struggle. Instead, in Chapter 2, Gladstone's ignorance of Ireland is emphasised, as well as the extent to which he was influenced by disturbing information on the state of Ireland from apparently reliable sources. This discussion is followed, in Chapter 3, by a detailed examination of the Home Rule and land bills of 1886. It is important to see these proposals not as un-connected projects but as two closely related elements of a single quite sophisticated and massive operation aimed at solving the Irish question. It was intended that the land bill would not only remove the land issue as a source of social tension in Ireland but through the method of its operation contribute substantially to the finances of an Irish government. Particular attention is paid to the financial clauses of the Home Rule plan and how far they would have determined its viability.

The failure of historians generally to deal adequately with this aspect of Gladstone's scheme has, moreover, led to quite dis-torted views of Unionist objections to Home Rule. Notwith-standing the often racist sentiments of many Unionists, it is shown, in Chapter 4, that their objections to Gladstone's proposals were more solidly based. Unionists made a detailed critique of the Home Rule bill, emphasising especially its financial limitations. This chapter, moreover, also greatly modifies the accepted view of Irish nationalist reaction to the Home Rule and land bills. Following Conor Cruise O'Brien, it has been widely believed that the Parnellite leadership con-stituted an accurate barometer of local nationalist feeling in Ireland on the Home Rule plan. This view is shown to be erron-eous: a critical examination of local nationalist opinion reveals the extent to which Parnellite leaders were seriously out of touch with Irish opinion.

The central figure of this study, of course, is Gladstone, and Chapter 7 provides a critical examination of his concept of Irish nationality. In particular it assesses the extent to which insights drawn from European nationalism could be applied to the Irish situation; the chief sources on which Gladstone's ideas on Irish nationalism depended, and how far his perception of it reflected an enlightened understanding of Irish problems or provided a realistic guide to political developments in Ireland. One of the most important issues which tested the strengths and weaknesses of Gladstone's concept of Irish nationality was the Ulster question. This issue, in the period 1886-93, has usually been regarded by historians as a mere prelude to the dramatic events of 1911-14. The treatment presented in this study is very different. It examines in detail the attitudes and policies of both Gladstone and the nationalists to the Ulster issue and the

Ulster Unionist reaction to Gladstone's Home Rule plans. In particular it demonstrates that, contrary to popular belief, Unionists devised a significantly different strategy for meeting the implementation of Home Rule in the period 1886-93 than the armed rebellion planned in 1911-14.

In sum, then, this study, by examining the Home Rule campaign in its Gladstonian phase from a wider perspective than has usually been the case, is intended to contribute both to a clearer estimate of its dimensions and a better appreciation of the factors preventing its successful conclusion.

1

Nationalism
and the Home Rule Movement,
1882-6

WITH the end of the land war in 1882, the primacy of agrarian agitation in nationalist politics was replaced by a constitutional programme directed towards the restitution of an Irish parliament; the change of direction was marked by the establishment of the Irish National League in that year. The new policy required a significantly different method of operation than hitherto, emphasising political propaganda rather than action. It was also a more difficult task, for while the degree of popular support for agrarian agitation, with its promise of tangible benefits to be gained, could be easily estimated, the success of a programme that, in practice, divorced the land question from the national question and relied instead on establishing the psychological reality of the national idea, was of its nature less easy to assess. The difficulties of this task were compounded by the reluctance or inability of Parnellites to define specifically what Home Rule meant.

The nature of nationalist thinking in this respect will be more fully examined below, but at this time the public attitude taken by leading Home Rulers was that the term 'Home Rule' was virtually self-explanatory. While on a fund-raising tour of Australia in 1883 John Redmond gave a speech at Melbourne entitled 'Home Rule — Its Real Meaning'. He declared that Home Rule simply meant Irish self-government and that its specific content could safely be left to 'the collective wisdom of Englishmen, Irishmen and Scotchmen in the imperial parliament'. Similarly, and perhaps more surprisingly given his strong social-reforming outlook, Michael Davitt, in a speech at Draperstown, defined Home Rule as 'simple self-government'.

When Parnell was asked by John Redmond at this time how he would make Ireland prosper under Home Rule, he merely replied that English government was excessive and that 'an Irish government could keep down expenses'; it would 'save a million' on the police alone.[1]

Instead of defining practically what Home Rule would entail, Home Rulers sought generally to establish the psychological reality of the nationalist idea by identifying the Home Rule campaign with the centuries-old struggle for Irish freedom — a policy usually promoted by focusing the indignation at past English 'atrocities' in Ireland onto contemporary political issues. Simultaneously a campaign of militant propaganda by *United Ireland* sought to sustain a high level of popular indignation towards England, while efforts were made both to widen the social basis of support for the National League and to increase local branch formation. By examining these aspects of nationalist politics this chapter will attempt to assess the progress of the Home Rule movement in the period 1882-6.

NATIONALIST IDEOLOGY:
THE HISTORICIST BACKGROUND

In his almanac of nationalist arguments, *The Home-Ruler's Manual*, R. Barry O'Brien asked:'What is a nation?' The answer he supplied was a 'people bound together by historical associations'. There were, of course, other factors to consider, such as race, religion, language, geography and population; nevertheless, 'history is the determining factor'. That he should emphasise history is not surprising. The process of national emancipation, a dominant feature of nineteenth-century European history, was accompanied and stimulated by a great upsurge in historical studies. More specifically, the relationship between history and nationalism lay in the material that historical studies provided for the construction of legends of ethnic or racial struggle — essential elements in most movements for national emancipation.[2] The historical legend consisted of a record of grievances to be either avenged or removed, and, as will be seen in Ireland's case, often included an ideal vision of 'national' society before the oppression of the invader.

The developments on which such constructions were based affected several disciplines and were felt as much in Great Britain as elsewhere. The influence of Leopold von Ranke and later German scholars produced a significant shift away from the 'Whig religion of progress' represented by Macaulay to an empirical analysis of facts: a development which harmonised easily with the empiricist tradition that was the dominant strain in British philosophy. Germany was also an important centre for the study of racial origins, which, as the century progressed, widened in meaning from the general study of classical literature to include ethnology, history and geography. J. W. Burrow has written of this aspect of Victorian thought:

> Comparative philology, as the maturest and apparently most precise of the disciplines by which in the nineteenth century men were attempting to trace modern phenomena in an unbroken line to a remote or prehistoric past, naturally appealed as an example to scholars working along these lines in biology, in legal and social history, and in folklore.

Certainly historical inquiry at Oxford under Dr Arnold followed this approach. E. A. Freeman learned there 'the unity of European history', and the importance of geography, language and geology to an understanding of that history; most important of all, he learned from Arnold to 'regard the essence of history as consisting in the record of man's political being'.[3] But how did these developments affect Ireland?

Their influence being generally most considerable in the study of law, it was perhaps natural that this would be reflected in Irish land legislation; however, they also had an important influence on popular religious attitudes, which in their Protestant aspect had tended to view Catholic persecution of Protestants during the Reformation as events occurring but a few days previously. For example, the noted Protestant theologian George Salmon attributed the influence of the new historical inquiry to the decline among his students of interest in the 'controversy' with Rome:

> Modern conceptions of the proper attitude of mind of an historian require him to enter impartially into the feelings of his characters. We can now find apologies even for the magis-

trates who shed the blood of the first Christians, and whom their victims regarded in no other light than as the instruments of Satan.... No wonder, then, that we can find apologies, too, for Roman Catholic persecutors, and believe that many a judge who sent a heretic to the stake may have been a conscientious good man, fulfilling what he regarded as an unpleasant duty.[4]

Salmon's comments on the change in popular religious attitudes provides a succinct indication of the gradual demise of the general tradition of anti-Catholic prejudices prevalent in Victorian Britain. This tradition combined grotesque notions about the dominating temporal designs of the papacy with equally grotesque beliefs as to the evil influences of Catholicism in Ireland's history. One commentator, A. S. G. Canning, struck by the prevalence of these views, considered that a large part of the blame for this state of affairs rested with influential writers who had embodied such prejudices in their work. Singling out Macaulay's treatment of the 'aboriginal' Catholics involved in the 1798 rebellion for its gross generalisations and racial slurs, he concluded that the ignorance of the general public was 'less surprising when even learned historians write about it [the rebellion] without sufficient authority for the conclusions they both form for themselves and convey to others'. Canning's criticism is very much to the point, for this tradition, emphasising Irish racial and religious backwardness, and endorsed by Carlyle, Froude and even, at an early stage of his career, Lord Acton,[5] was to produce an Irish historiographical reaction that would supply Home Rule propagandists with an 'authentic' historical basis for their arguments. Indeed, the development of an historical approach denying the view that Irish grievances arose from a congenital racial and religious backwardness in the face of progress could not but have this effect.

Perhaps most symptomatic of the new objectivity being brought to bear on historical inquiry is the fact that two of the most talented critics of the ethnocentric view against the Irish were both Protestants and Unionists: J. P. Prendergast and W. E. H. Lecky. In particular the Irish historiographical battle of the 1870s and 1880s, when J. A. Froude's anti-Celtic and anti-Catholic work, *The English in Ireland*, was answered by Lecky's historicist *History of Ireland in the Eighteenth Century*, created a great public controversy in Ireland, Britain and America. Both writers cited English misgovernment as being responsible for Irish troubles. It was, however, Froude's claims of Irish religious and racial backwardness that contributed most to the emotional atmosphere of the controversy. Lecky's refutation of Froude's prejudiced treatment of Irish history was forceful and penetrating:

> By selecting simply such facts as are useful for the purpose of blackening a national character; by omitting all palliating circumstances; by suppressing large classes of facts... by keeping out of sight the existence of corresponding evils in other countries; by painting crimes that were peculiar to the wildest districts and the most lawless class as if they were common to the whole country and to all classes; by employing the artifices of a dramatic writer to heighten, in long, detailed, and elaborate pictures, the effects of the crimes committed on one side, while those committed on the other are either wholly suppressed or ... dismissed ... by these methods... it is possible... to carry the art of historical misrepresentation to a high degree of perfection.[6]

Lecky denounced also the racial theories which characterised Froude's work: 'Without denying that there are some innate distinctions of character between the subdivisions of the great Aryan race, there is... abundant evidence that they have been enormously exaggerated.' It was to be hoped that contemporary thought would make an effort to emancipate itself from the habit of 'adopting theories of race'.[7] More importantly, though, in his Irish history Lecky focused attention on the period of Grattan's Parliament, 1782-1800, a subject he had earlier publicised in Volume I of his *Leaders of Public Opinion in Ireland* — consisting of biographies of Henry Flood and Henry Grattan. This work, published during a youthful 'nationalist' phase in 1861, associated Irish problems with English interference and portrayed Grattan's Parliament as a model of Irish self-government, concomitant with economic prosperity, increasing religious tolerance and a keen sense of nationality on the part of Ireland's Protestant leaders. Such a vision of Ireland under self-government was ideally suited to the purposes of nationalist propagandists during the Home Rule struggles of the 1880s and 1890s.

Lecky's views on nationalism, however, began to change with the advent of Fenianism, and by the early 1880s he lost his desire to see the return of an Irish parliament. Being a landlord himself, his desire was for a parliament controlled by the aristocracy and landlords. He had no wish to encourage Parnellite 'Jacobins' who associated Home Rule with an agrarian campaign to remove that very class of Irish society. Consequently he not only refused permission for a cheap edition of the book, but also toned down much of its 'nationalist' emphasis in later editions:

> I carefully revised these biographies, adding a good deal of new information, excising some manifest exaggeration, and toning down a rhetoric which savoured too much of a debating society. . . . Some of the worst specimens of its [the first edition's] boyish rhetoric were, indeed, frequently quoted — usually without the smallest intimation that they had been suppressed by the author in his later edition. . . . Conditions in Ireland had profoundly changed since it was [first] written, and . . . some portions of its introduction were no longer applicable.

These modifications were necessary, he argued, because the book was originally written without an examination of the great manuscript collections of confidential government correspondence that exist in London and Dublin: 'This exploration had now begun. . . . It was impossible that such an investigation should not in some respects modify earlier judgments.'[8]

Lecky's priorities as an historian, however, were not synonymous with those of nationalist propagandists, and both his *Leaders of Public Opinion* and *History of Ireland* were used extensively to validate their arguments. Indeed, so important did they rate Lecky's contributions to their cause that even his strenuously Unionist politics were, as the Home Rule propagandist J. A. Fox informed him, never alluded to by nationalists except in the 'kindest and most respectful terms'. He continued: 'You have certainly done more than any living man to keep alive the spirit of nationality amongst Irish Catholics . . . and your name is never, so far as I know, mentioned amongst Home Rulers but with respect if not affection.'[9] While Fox's claim is certainly exaggerated, it nevertheless affirms the fact that Lecky's work provided some of the most influential texts for Irish nationalists in this period.

Of the Irish historiographical debate, generally, it is a reasonable assumption that most rank-and-file Home Rulers were ignorant of its detailed nature. Nevertheless, there were many able propagandists willing to illustrate the essential political point of the issue. For example, T. D. Sullivan, a specialist at putting party propaganda into verse and credited by other leading Home Rulers with great influence among the peasantry, celebrated J. P. Prendergast's condemnation of Froude thus:

> When Froude with bigot fury blind,
> To strike at Ireland felt inclined,
> He wrote a book to ease his mind,
> Crammed full of lies of every kind —

> But though his venom thus was cast,
> Old Ireland's answer followed fast,
> Rung out as if with trumpet blast,
> By gallant John P. Prendergast.[10]

In reality, however, given the intensity of Froude's Unionist views, the criticisms he did make of English government in Ireland provided excellent propaganda for nationalists and were especially used by extreme Irish-Americans, while Prendergast and other writers of the new historical school were, like Lecky, unhappy with the political uses nationalists made of their work. Nothing illustrates better the political relevance of Irish history in this period than Prendergast's reaction to this practice. He wrote to Lecky: 'The organisation of the English has always been superior to the Irish: so that the Irish could not meet them without defeat. I see all this clearly now, and regret my essay on the Cromwellian settlement.' A. G. Richey warned against the 'half-knowledge of history which enables political intriguers to influence the passions of their dupes by misleading them with garbled accounts of the past'. Nevertheless, once published, their work was largely out of their control. But though Lecky himself came to take a more sympathetic view of

Froude's work during the political battles of the 1880s and 1890s, his correspondence with T. H. Huxley at this time shows that his attitude to historical inquiry in general was not materially affected; and in any event, the fact remains that arguments made by Home Rulers in this period could draw on the work of both writers. Indeed, L. M. Cullen has shown how considerably the nationalist economic critique of English government in Ireland depended on the resuscitation, by Lecky and Froude, of the work of eighteenth-century writers such as John Hely Hutchinson.[11] More specifically, it will be seen that Lecky's work had an important influence on Gladstone's outlook as to what Home Rule could be expected to achieve in Ireland.

Irish nationalist ideology, however, needed to appeal to several constituencies; and while Lecky's work had an obvious appeal for the 'constitutional' agitation for Home Rule in Ireland and Britain, a less compromising version was needed for those of a more militant frame of mind. Here again Froude's work was important. While in the United States in 1872 on a lecture tour designed to counter the damage done to England's good name by the recently released Fenian, Jeremiah O'Donovan Rossa, his book and lectures created a considerable stir, not only there, but in Britain and Ireland. Moreover, the debate was maintained because Ireland's foremost contro-versialist, Father Tom Burke, also happened to be there and was persuaded to reply formally to Froude.[12] But unlike Lecky, whose work was inspired by a contemporary historicism and regard for accuracy, Burke simply moved to the other end of the spectrum occupied by Froude, and where the latter sought to locate the source of Ireland's ills in a congenital racial and religious backwardness, Burke drew a picture of a people formed in the likeness of gods, whose shortcomings could be traced to the evil policy of an oppressing neighbour. Consequently in the Burke/Froude controversy the history of Anglo-Irish relations was reduced to a series of black and white images, manipulated to suit the needs of their particular audiences. By investing nations with personal characteristics and reducing the complexity of the issues involved, Burke elucidated the moral rather than the his-torical issues at the heart of Anglo-Irish relations.

History so represented was a moral tale of a Catholic nation united as one man, always at the mercy of English tyranny. Not less important was the timing of the controversy: publicly conducted and extensively reported, it helped to crystallise the idea of Catholic nationalism in the Irish-American mind at the very time when the forces of Irish nationalism and Catholicism there — mutually antagonistic since the late 1840s — were coming together in support of Home Rule. In Ireland, moreover, the historiographical background against which the Froude controversy took place was one of a steadily increasing growth of nationalist literature. This process had begun with the Young Ireland movement, whose task, notwithstanding some element of exaggeration on the part of Sir Charles Gavan Duffy, must indeed have been formidable:

> Irish history was rather less known than Chinese. . . . One man out of ten thousand could not [*sic*] tell whether Owen Roe followed or preceded Brian Boru; in which hemisphere the victory of Benburb was achieved; or whether the O'Neill who held Ireland for eight years in the Puritan wars was a naked savage armed with a stake, or an accomplished soldier bred in the most adventurous and punctillious service in Europe.[13]

In much the same manner as contemporary movements in Europe, Young Ireland promoted a romantic concept of nationalism, invoking the spirit and memories of Celtic militarism, as well as that of more recent revolutionaries like Wolfe Tone and Robert Emmet, and presented a vision of Ireland that nationalists would appeal to in the succeeding struggles of later decades. Moreover, the visual symbols of ancient 'national' Ireland — the harp, round tower, shamrock and wolfhound — became well established in these years, while Young Irelanders also designed membership cards for the Repeal Association, illustrating a succession of Irish leaders from Brian Boru through to Grattan and O'Connell.[14]

The contribution of Young Irelanders to nationalist literature can be gauged by the abundance of such material — largely written by them and cheaply produced by nationalist firms — in the 1880s. Cameron & Ferguson of Glasgow had a list of at least fifty-seven Irish publications: biographies of Wolfe Tone, John Mitchel's *History of Ireland*, accounts of the 1798 rebellion,

Thomas Clarke Luby's biography of O'Connell and many others, as well as historical romances, songs and ballads. A similar service was provided by the publishing houses of T. D. Sullivan and M. H. Gill in Dublin. The debt that nationalists in the 1880s owed to Young Ireland in this respect was well explained by William O'Brien when he lamented the lack of knowledge of the Irish language among the country's youth, noting that, because of this, Irish nationality was an affair of 'the day before yesterday' and the stock of Irish literature 'the songs and essays of Young Ireland'. The steady growth of this literature and its political implications were described by *The Irishman* in 1868, in the course of reviewing an addition to the list:

> Twenty-five years ago Ireland had no history. There were scanty records.... They were dull and little interesting. It required the fire of patriotism to undertake the task of studying their details, for no glow of genius had illumined the archives of a generous, a brave, and indomitable race....
>
> But the fervid enthusiasm of an ardent nationality kindled by a holy fire ... was destined to light up all the dark passages, all the glorious reminiscences of the transit of Ireland through the ages.... Irishmen with their heart and soul in their work arose to do justice to their native land.
>
> By their efforts and their genius Ireland grows into history.[15]

The significance of the phrase 'Ireland grows into history' lay in the extent to which the historiographical basis of Irish nationalism was being established in these years. Indeed, in 1870 John Denvir, a Fenian agent living in Liverpool, established a printing and publishing business and proceeded to issue a series of Irish histories, biographies, stories and songs, which ultimately sold over a million copies. Two of the most important publications at this time arose out of the researches of John O'Donovan and Eugene O'Curry into the laws and social life of ancient Ireland. On the basis of their work Irish-Americans were to construct a Celticist myth extolling the spiritualist nature of the Celt against the materialist greed of the Saxon. Furthermore, the steady growth of nationalist literature in these years was stimulated by the increasing development of Irish education. Between 1850 and 1900 the number of National Schools rose from 4,500 to 9,000, while between 1851 and 1911 the proportion of the population unable to read and write fell from 47 per cent to 12 per cent.[16] At the same time government policy in regard to the teaching of Irish history also assisted the popularity of nationalist literature.

Government policy forbade the study of Irish history in National Schools, and the following verse composed by Archbishop Whately was used by generations of nationalists to show that government policy in this respect aimed at nothing less than the destruction of Irish nationality:

> I thank the goodness and the grace
> That on my birth have smiled,
> And made me in these Christian days
> A happy English child.

But, like so much English policy in Ireland, if the intention was to eliminate Irish nationalist consciousness, it was a policy only partly pursued. Both the schools under the control of Christian Brothers and sermons in Catholic chapels provided a highly charged version of the Catholic view of the country's history. A perceptive contemporary critic in the conservative *Graphic* explained the adverse political consequences of government policy: it was one of the many 'blunders' of English policy in Ireland. The mere fact of the exclusion of Irish history created in the minds of a fretted and suspicious people

a conviction that the government did not do so without good reason, that Irish history must tell a tale of unrelenting cruelty and oppression on the part of the conquerors, of an ancient civilisation ruthlessly trampled under foot, and of the most heroic virtues of courage and race-faithfulness to the cause of Ireland on the part of the conquered. The mere fact ... of the exclusion of Irish history from Irish schools was in itself enough to excite such a conviction, and did excite it. Nor did a class of writers fail to arise, capable of giving full and ardent expression to the conviction generally entertained.[17]

NATIONALIST IDEOLOGY:
IDEOLOGUES AND THE HISTORICAL LEGEND

In his essay on nationalism Sir Isaiah Berlin argues that essential to the progress of any nationalist movement is the lack of opportunity for the use of the skills of a group of men 'psychologically unfit' to enter the established bureaucracy: 'artists, thinkers, whatever their professions — without an established position'. There is then an effort to create 'a new synthesis, a new ideology, both to explain and justify resistance to the forces working against their convictions ... and to point in a new direction and offer them a new centre for self-identification'. As a general description, this passage might well apply to the leading propagandists of Home Rule nationalism in the 1880s:[18] Justin McCarthy, John Dillon, J. Huntley McCarthy, Michael Davitt, T. P. O'Connor, T. M. Healy, William O'Brien, T. D. Sullivan, Sir Charles Gavan Duffy and, occasionally, Parnell.

Almost without exception these were men who had engrossed themselves in Irish history, and also in many cases were motivated by a sense of personal or family grievance. Justin McCarthy had the experience of a father preoccupied with Irish history and personal knowledge of the famine and Young Ireland movement. Michael Davitt had bitter experiences of his own family's eviction as a child, which he described in his evidence before the Special Commission in 1889:

> I remember distinctly the eviction — the cottage being set fire to and we having to go to a workhouse, from the doors of which establishment we were turned because my mother refused to part with me for the purpose of proselytism.

This experience was much dwelt on by Davitt's parents during his childhood. T. P. O'Connor, hypersensitive and prone to fits of depression, was converted to nationalism on hearing his father's account of the famine and subsequent 1848 rebellion; his nationalist conviction was reinforced through his personal sense of 'shock' at the execution of the Fenians Allen, Larkin and O'Brien in 1867. William O'Brien had an intense sense of his family's lineage and wrote that when, as a schoolboy, he was compelled to read Hume's *History of England*, with its glorification of English military successes, the experience merely drove

him to 'find out for myself all about...our Benburbs, and
Yellow Fords, and Races of Castlebar'.[19]

Similarly, T. M. Healy's daughter wrote of him: 'He was born
on the 17 May 1855, and almost from his cradle he was conscious
of that sense of past greatness and present oppression, and of that
dim expectation of future resurrection.' According to her, the
family kept a record of how their forebears had lost their lands
through the confiscations of succeeding centuries. More recent
and lasting impressions were created by tales of the famine, and
of proselytisers refusing food to those who would not listen to
them. John Dillon had his own family experience of the Young
Ireland movement, of which his father was a leading figure,
while a similar connection with that movement inspired T. D.
Sullivan and Sir Charles Gavan Duffy, another of its leaders. As
for Parnell, his personal experience of rejection and alienation as
a Cambridge undergraduate, manifesting itself in the belief that
'These English despise us because we are Irish', is well known.
He too was 'extremely conscious of the historical dimension of
the Irish question'. These men, then, were well placed to propa-
gate an ideology based on a tradition of historic struggle.[20]

A classic example of the kind of militaristic vision employed
by nationalists was contained in the leading article of the first
issue of *United Ireland*: it sought to establish firmly the Parnellite
movement as the legitimate inheritor of the ancient struggle for
Irish freedom:

> We are the inheritors of all the ages that have fought the fight
> after their several ways. We are proud of the Volunteers of
> 1782 though they were a caste; we do not fear to speak of '98,
> though in those days they did not fear to wave some bloody
> pikeheads in the sun. We stand under Robert Emmet's
> scaffold; we see O'Connell's giant figure looming over the
> monster meetings far and wide; we read Davis's kindling
> pages; we behold Mitchel rising up like a titan to cross the
> path of tyranny; we see Fenianism as it springs from what
> seems the ashes of national spirit, and girds up our youth to a
> pitch of heroism that did not blanch upon the scaffold nor on
> the threshold of the more dreadful penal hell. We listen to the
> shout of the Manchester rabble when three Irishmen lay dead
> before them; we hear the hardly more decent yell of exul-

tation that went up in the English commons house when it was announced that the great British government had succeeded in waylaying, gagging, and kidnapping and consigning to prison again, Michael Davitt, the man who taught Mr Gladstone there was a land question to be settled.

We remember them all and see in each of them the workings of the self-same sacred, self-sustaining, unquenchable spirit — only that each cycle of persecutions and hangings brought us nearer to the vantage-ground on which we stand today.[21]

More generally, though, in the form in which it was usually presented to Irish and Irish-American audiences, the historical vision in Home Rule propaganda entailed the view of the Irish people on a great circular march: the ideal image of Irish society before 1169 was both a starting-point and the eventual goal of the historical march of the Irish people. The golden age of Irish history had been destroyed by rapacious English invaders, who had brought untold suffering to the native population, robbed them of their lands, and persecuted their religion. The message of nationalist propaganda was that this or a similar golden age would return when Home Rule was enacted. Implicit also in this message was the notion of Catholicity and Celtic ethnicity as essential ingredients of Irish nationality. This vision was explicitly stated by the Parnellite party's leading propagandist, William O'Brien, in his presidential lecture, 'The Irish National Idea', to the Cork Young Ireland Society in January 1886:

I do not envy the mental structure of the man who could read a page of Irish history, or even cast his eye over an Irish landscape, without understanding that the Irish cause is not a mere affair of vulgar parish interests, but is woven so inextricably around the Irish heart as the network of arteries through which it draws its blood and the delicate machinery of nerves by which it receives and communicates its impulses. . . . It is invested with something of the mysterious sanctity of religion. . . . The passion of Irish patriotism is blent with whatever is ennobling and divine in our being. . . . It is the weird voice we hear from every graveyard where our fathers are sleeping, for every Irish graveyard contains the bones of uncanonised saints and martyrs. When the framers of the penal laws deprived us of our books, and drew their thick black veil over Irish history, they forgot the ruins they themselves made were the most eloquent schoolmasters, the most stupendous memorials of a history and a race that were destined not to die.

Having established the emotional, historical and spiritual bases of Irish nationality, O'Brien went on to urge that it was the small nations that contributed most to the moral worth of civilisation in opposition to the selfishness and greed of empires. Pursuing this line of argument, he continued by making a strong claim for the racial equality of Celt and Teuton:

> The Celtic race today is, in fact, as conspicuous a factor in human society as the Teutonic. It is little less in numbers; it is as distinct in type; it has as rich a range of capacities, sympathies, and ideals of its own; its fine susceptibilities and aerial genius are capable of exerting a potent influence upon an age which seems only too ready to accept this world as a gross feeding-trough at which happiness consists in greedy gorging.

Making reference to the movement in England towards Home Rule for Ireland, O'Brien exclaimed: 'There are signs that the genius of the Celtic race is about to be restored to its natural throne, and to receive its natural development. God grant it!' But the real question was: was Ireland ready to take her place among the nations? Despite 'seven centuries of wasting bondage' that had 'mutilated' the growth of the nation, the

> Irish . . . today . . . take . . . up the mission [to advance national greatness] just where the English aggression cut it short seven centuries ago, and leap to their feet as buoyantly as though the hideous tragedy of the intervening ages were but the nightmare of an uneasy sleeper. (*Applause*). The same sanguine blood flows in their veins; the same hopes, here and hereafter inspire them. . . . The same faith that once inhabited the ruined shrines is rebuilding them.[22]

O'Brien's speech is an example of nationalist propaganda at its most effective. Attention was focused on the idea of a chosen people in an historic struggle for freedom, which, it was suggested, was soon to end in victory; a militaristic rhetoric enjoined a spiritual imagery of the morality of their cause and endorsement of their racial characteristics. In short, it was an ideological view pitched at a sufficiently high level of abstraction to be capable of satisfying any element in the heterogeneous consciousness of the Home Rule movement. Indeed, this was a very necessary consideration given the several ingredients which made up the movement. Dr Conor Cruise O'Brien has succinctly described it thus: the Home Rule movement was 'the association in one great national movement of the agrarian agitation, the progressive (or opportunist) elements in Fenianism both in England and in Ireland, a strong Irish-American section led by Devoy, in association with a determined and aggressive parliamentary party'. It is worth pointing out, though, that the balance of forces within the parliamentary party and the movement in Ireland shifted considerably to the right in the years 1882-6. A police report on 83 Parnellite M.P.s in 1887 listed 18 who could be classed as Fenians or of Fenian sympathies, 12 as being 'advanced nationalists' or strong and 'violent' speakers, while 53 were described mainly as moderates and non-Fenians. Moreover, following the alliance of the Catholic church with the party in 1884, the movement in Ireland came more and more under clerical influence. The number of local National League meetings presided over by priests rose from 13.5 per cent in 1883 to 50 per cent in 1886. However, the clergy were 'fellow-travellers' rather than 'coachmen': 'The churchmen left political initiatives to the laity, confining themselves to encouraging political activities which they believed to be commendable and to discouraging excesses (notably the agrarian outrages and dangerous defiances of authority) which they took to be lacking in prudence or even morality.'[23]

Nevertheless, the drift to the right in the Irish movement contrasted sharply with the militancy of the Irish-American section, though both were held together ideologically by a rhetoric that conceptualised in militaristic terms the constitutional tactics of the parliamentary party. This was an essential part of the task of establishing the psychological reality of the nationalist idea; and it was all the more necessary given the subordinate role agrarian struggle played to constitutional agitation in nationalist politics from the formation of the National League in 1882.[24] The tactics employed were of two broad types. First, there were efforts to identify contemporary political manouevres and issues with specific historical events, in order to enhance the legitimacy of the Parnellite movement as the inheritor of the ancient struggle for Irish freedom, to illustrate the long ancestry of English oppression in Ireland, or to show how a central historical grievance had been remedied by action in the present. Secondly, a nationalist consciousness and code of conduct was encouraged through the medium of serialised historical tales and political verse.

For instance, following the enactment of the 1881 land act, Parnell referred to the disbandment of the Volunteers in 1783 as an example of what could happen were the act accepted uncritically by the Irish people. He had advised that the act be tested rather than used, and consequently incurred the condemnation of Gladstone, who compared him disparagingly with O'Connell for wanting to create hatred and discord between England and Ireland. Parnell, however, when replying in a speech at Cork, was careful to conceptualise his action in historicist terms and declared that the bill was only a little of what Irish farmers were due, and that 'The Irishman who thinks he can now throw away his arms, just as Grattan disbanded the Volunteers in 1783, will find to his sorrow and destruction when too late that he has placed himself in the haven of the perfidious and cruel and relentless English enemy.' Again, at the general election of 1885 several Parnellite M.P.s appealed in similar terms to the voters. Matthew Harris, in a speech at Athenry on 26 October 1885, declared that going into parliament was going into the citadel of the enemy:

I shall always keep in my mind first the independence of my country.... Keep a strong determined animus against England in your hearts and do not mind Englishmen for they are your enemies. They have destroyed and are every day endeavouring to destroy you, so ... it behoves you as Irishmen, to keep a firm front against these men, and join together in an organisation throughout the country [the National League] in every possible way; ... as long as it is against England it has good in it.

At the same meeting John Dillon declared:

> We are not electing ordinary members of parliament, we are electing members of an army, who are to go under a special discipline to carry out the work under enormous difficulty.

In reality this kind of rhetoric masked the fact that many party members were closely involved in English life; indeed, not a few supported British imperialism. Yet this should not underestimate the importance of the ideology the party propounded in Ireland. For the great mass of its supporters who would never see the inside of parliament or know anything of the inner workings of party politics at the higher levels, nationalism existed entirely in the state of consciousness that the party's rhetoric was designed to inculcate; and this was especially the case once agrarian agitation was dropped in favour of constitutional propaganda. Given that that consciousness depended on a sense of historic grievance, it is hardly surprising to find Parnellites attempting to reinforce it through what was often a simple appeal to national hatred. As William O'Brien informed his audience during a speech in the Phoenix Park in 1885, 'They [the English] hate us and we hate them in return.' Nor is it surprising to find an ambivalent attitude being taken to physical force: it was praised as a morally legitimate means of achieving Irish freedom, though given the balance of forces between England and Ireland, it was recognised as being practically impossible.[25]

Apart from the speeches of party leaders, the work of sustaining the building of a nationalist consciousness was carried on chiefly in serialised historical tales. A good example of this genre is one featuring historic Dublin buildings in *The Nation*. Describing the history of Dublin City Hall, it noted that during the 1798 rebellion this building was turned into a 'torture chamber' where 'poor innocent people were taken in ... tortured and violated'. Their screams caused 'many a passerby to shudder, and in the Castle of Dublin ... they caused many a smile of satisfaction'. The same 'smile of satisfaction is still to be seen in the Castle of Dublin when sorrow and suffering are scourging the Irish people'. Similar stories, seeking to concentrate the indignation felt at past English 'atrocities' onto contemporary institutions, groups, or aspects of the political struggle, can be found in virtually all nationalist papers in this period.[26] Such tactics were, however, perhaps best employed in relation to the question of landlordism and nationality. The centrality of the land question to nationalist politics in general, and Parnellite commitment to the tenants' cause, necessitated an unambiguous statement of the position of landlords in Ireland and their relation to the Irish nation.

Unlike the Young Ireland movement, which always hoped to attract the landlords' support, nationalists in the 1880s — with the exception of Parnell and Protestant Home Rulers — generally had no such desire. Moreover, they made it explicitly obvious, well before 1886, that neither was there any place in the culture of Home Rule nationalism for the Irish gentry. This attitude was strongly expressed during the redrawing of the Irish constituency boundaries in 1884-5. F. H. O'Donnell had received the sanction of both Liberal and Tory parties to revive in the new constituencies some of the most famous of Gaelic place-names. He proposed several changes:

> West Galway or the Connemara Division, South Cork or the Carbery Division... North Antrim or the Dunluce Division.... I sought to revive Thomond, and Desmond, and Ossory, Oriel and Masserene, Clandeboy and Oneilland. The united mass of the Parnellites rejected the ancient place-names. The nearest to an intelligent explanation which I could obtain for this ostracism of the Irish past was that many of the ancient place-names had become the titles of Irish peers.[27]

Thus, essential to the exclusion of the gentry from membership of the nation was their discrediting in the nationalist historical legend; and this policy — which usually took the form of identifying the landlords as a racially and religiously alien element intent on persecuting the native Irish people — was vigorously pursued.[28]

But while much of the nationalists' historically infused rhetoric was given over to heightening indignation and diverting animus towards England and the landlord class, it could also be employed to more peaceful ends. The parish priest of Firies, Co. Mayo, informed the Special Commission that he cautioned against 'moonlighting' by urging his congregation:

'Look at what happened in '48...'67...'98. Spies and traitors and informers rose from...[secret societies] and brought destruction on the people.' This, he argued, was 'the most forcible means there was' for deterring such activities. Moreover, it should also be remembered that the policy which Home Rule propaganda sought to legitimise was one that urged the people to rely on their parliamentary leaders to obtain benefits from parliament — a fact attested to by police witnesses during the Special Commission proceedings. Indeed, William O'Brien was to argue at the Special Commission that the function of 'strong language' by *United Ireland* was simply to give people confidence in themselves and in their representatives.[29] But notwithstanding the efforts party propagandists put into establishing the psychological reality of the nationalist idea, what degree of success did they achieve?

CONSCIOUSNESS AND COMMITMENT: THE NATURE OF NATIONALIST SUPPORT

Certainly leading Home Rulers at the Special Commission sought to show that their movement was not manufactured by agitators, as critics argued, but rested on enduring ideas and anxieties of the people; but the evidence either way tended to vary with the nature of the witness under examination. Davitt's attempt to establish — from the testimony of Garrett Tyrrell, a land agent from King's County — that uppermost in the minds of the peasantry in his district during the crop failure of 1878-9 were fears of a repeat of the famine and the disturbances which followed it, was unsatisfactory. Tyrrell claimed never to have heard such fears expressed and was ignorant of whether or not they were held.[30]

Sir Charles Russell, however, did have some success in this respect when Head Constable William Irwin, who had been stationed in Co. Galway during the Land League agitation, substantially agreed that such fears loomed large in the peasants' thinking. Timothy Harrington, examining John Keen, a seventy-year-old peasant, obtained the most explicit confirmation that memories drawn from the famine period heightened anxieties in 1879 when the crop failed; while John Loudon, a Land leaguer of the period, had no hesitation in going much further:

The people of Ireland always looked upon the land as their own, and as long as I remember they looked upon the land-lords as robbers. They remember that the land of Ireland belonged to the Celts, and not the adventurers that came in with different parties.[31]

The question of the role of the peasants' historic memory of persecution and plantations during the land war and after has been a subject of dispute among historians. T. N. Brown has argued that it was not the folk memory of a collectivist golden age but 'fears inherited from the past mixed with hopes for better days that seem to have motivated Irish tenant farmers'. This view is substantially supported by Joseph Lee, who argues that the Land League not merely articulated but largely created the aspiration for tenant proprietorship, legitimising it with an 'immaculate' pedigree 'by which tenants acquired retrospective shares in a mythical Gaelic garden of Eden'. E. D. Steele, however, has based his argument on the 'enduring animosity' between landlords and peasants arising from the plantations and religious persecutions of the sixteenth and seventeenth centuries. The evidence given at the Special Commission was not such as to endorse specifically any one view. The most reasonable conclusion seems to be that the peasants were afraid of famine, while agitators relied on rhetoric appealing to historicist ideology. On the nature of peasants' consciousness during the land war, it is worth bearing in mind Davitt's opinion:

> The mass of small tenants, who were the main support of the movement, understood very little of the land problem beyond the question of rent and the dread of eviction. There could be no ignorance upon these powers of landlordism in Ireland, but otherwise the people generally were the enemies of the system by force of Celtic instinct more than by any process of independent thought or conviction.[32]

It is, however, important to make a distinction between the period before and after the establishment of the National League in 1882. During the land war, historicist arguments, while propagated by nationalist agitators, were subordinate to specific agrarian grievances and demands. The dropping of agrarian agitation in 1882 and the subsequent concentration on parliamentary activities produced a reversal of this position. The question was: would peasants adequately support a purely constitutional movement? The great attraction of agrarian agitation was that the objectives aimed for were tangible and could be expected to entail concrete benefits; what specific benefits Home Rule would entail were far less clear. The fact was, as we have seen, that little thought had been given to what this specific demand would entail. Party leaders neither defined what it meant, or what it could be expected to achieve for Ireland. Probably the best example of general party propaganda on this subject is provided in the popular verse of T. D. Sullivan:

> The laws conceived in days of shame,
> That closed, as with a sword of flame,
> The paths to knowledge, wealth and fame,
>   Are torn to shreds and cast aside;
> The road is free to one and all,
> Where'er they start from, hut or hall;
> To work and worth henceforth shall fall
>   The bright rewards so long denied.

Or, as F. H. O'Donnell put it in his highly coloured prose,

> The cheap pages of *United Ireland* under the influential proprietorship of Messrs Parnell, Justin McCarthy, and company, descended upon every rural household; and the peasantry learned . . . that 'Home Rule would abolish everything and give everybody five shillings a day.'[33]

The real significance of the change from agrarian to constitutional agitation was to shift the basis of nationalist propaganda from the economic grievances of the people to their sentimental aspirations. Moreover, where the tendency of agrarian agitation was essentially forward-looking — directed towards concrete benefits to be obtained — that of Home Rule was retrospective: Home Rule was an abstract concept, portrayed as the *fulfilment* of centuries of struggle. Of course, at one level this was an advantage. A heterogeneous movement will always fight better for an undefined ideal than for a specific set of proposals on which all might not be agreed. Indeed, the very term 'Home Rule', the master-symbol of the movement, was adopted purely because of its abstract nature: it could be invested with whatever meaning, by extremist and moderate alike. Michael McDonagh has aptly described it thus:

> There was a transfiguring vagueness about the phrase which enabled the most extreme nationalists, as well as the most moderate, to accept it. To moderate men 'Home Rule' meant nothing more than an Irish parliament for the management of Irish affairs in subordination to England. Fenians . . . saw in Home Rule the beginning of a movement which might possibly end in the establishment of an Irish republic.[34]

The ambiguity inherent in the term 'Home Rule' provides an important key to the general nature of nationalist ideology, but its strength lay not just in the fact that this term could appeal simultaneously, and with apparently equal intensity, to both militants and moderates. It lay also in how the historical legend at the centre of nationalist ideology integrated the revolutionary and constitutional images with which both extremes invested it, and in the fact that in Parnell the Home Rule movement was dominated by a leader whose true significance lay in his ability to pose simultaneously as a revolutionary and a con-stitutionalist. Yet notwithstanding the importance of ambiguity to the Home Rule campaign, Parnellite unwillingness, or inability, to define specifically what Home Rule was intended to achieve was a decided handicap: there was certainly nothing to show how, for example, it could satisfy a frustrated 'revolution in rising expectations', such as has been argued was the mainspring of the land war in 1879. Nor was the fact lost on Parnellite leaders that their agitation now rested on a more tenuous basis than hitherto. M. J. F. McCarthy, then on the staff of the *Freeman's Journal*, argued that in founding the National League Parnell aimed at bringing professional men, traders, artisans and labourers into the movement, fearing that rent reductions made by the land courts would constantly tend to make the farmers indifferent.[35]

Similarly, Matthew Harris testified before the Special Commission that he believed farmers cared little about Irish independence, and that if they were to get their lands, they would look on the boundary of their property as the boundary of their country. This view was supported by Jasper Tully, editor of the *Roscommon Herald*, one of the most radical journals in Ireland. He informed Wilfrid Blunt that the people in his area did not care much for Home Rule apart from the land question. Michael Davitt at this time expressed the fear that if the Liberals were defeated on Home Rule, and the Tories were elected pledged to establish a peasant proprietary, they could well succeed and the Home Rule demand disappear; this view was shared by E. D. Gray.[36]

John Dillon, indeed, had retired from politics in 1882 because the party had refused to reject totally the land act of 1881, which he believed would effectively kill the nationalist agitation. It is against this background of fear for the success of the agitation that the highly inflammatory journalism of *United Ireland* in the period 1882-5 has to be seen: as an attempt to sustain a high level of popular indignation or sense of grievance — the elementary basis of nationalism — against the 'English oppressor'. In this respect it is worth describing the experience of J. H. Tuke, whose activities in relieving Irish economic distress went back to the famine. Engaged in relieving distress caused by crop failure in the west of Ireland in 1886, he inquired of a prominent Home Ruler: 'Why is it you political Home Rulers never once lifted a finger to help us when we were working in a purely philanthropic spirit to help those people in the west?' The reply was: 'Well, you see Mr Tuke, the fact is, these districts and people furnish us with a very good *raison d'être*.'[37]

An important factor in sustaining Parnell's popularity in Ireland in this period was the attempts of the government in 1883 to connect him with the Phoenix Park murders, and the Roman letter of that year urging bishops and priests to refrain from supporting the Parnellite movement. In addition, William O'Brien kept *United Ireland* the focus of attention by an extremity of language that incurred several libel writs: 'It mattered little that literary grace had to be sacrificed to the exigencies of fighting journalism, to the temptation to the picture-writing which is best understanded [*sic*] by the multitude, to the tendency towards an excess of emphasis... which is all but inevitable in a country where strong language is the only weapon available.'[38]

An ideal occasion for this type of propaganda was the visit of the Prince of Wales to Ireland in 1885, which was boycotted by the nationalist population under *United Ireland*'s leadership. Moreover, O'Brien also sought to retain the support of extreme nationalist opinion by keeping in circulation *The Irishman*, a Fenian paper acquired from Richard Pigott in conjunction with two others in 1881.[39] At a more general level, the number of papers supporting Home Rule greatly increased in these years, as is shown in Table 1. These figures indicate that a quarter of the Irish Home Rule press came into existence in the first half of the 1880s, which must have added significantly to the influence of the National League. In order to consolidate the nationalist consciousness of the people in these years, an attempt was made

Table 1.   Number and decade of origin of Irish newspapers supporting Home Rule in 1886[40]

1770s	1
1810s	1
1820s	2
1830s	7
1840s	4
1850s	11
1860s	8
1870s	7
1880-86	14
Total	55

to persuade Irish children to read Irish, and not English, boys' newspapers, while a 'home manufacture' movement inspired by the Exhibition of Irish Arts and Manufactures of 1882 in Dublin — directing the Irish public towards buying Irish-made goods — was also made part of the propaganda of the National League. On a more subtle and coercive note, the national press worked to enforce obedience and membership of the League by publishing the names of those who had joined its local branches — a policy which William O'Brien admitted could be 'objectionable' as it tended to highlight, with the obvious implications, those who had not. A similar criticism could be made of the 'courts' held under the auspices of the National League, in which offenders against League rules were subjected to fines or 'worse'.[41]

Nevertheless, the progress of the Parnellite movement in the years between the formation of the National League and the Liberal conversion to Home Rule in 1886 was far from being one of unalloyed success. It is true that in these years the movement succeeded in one of its foremost aims — widening the basis of its support among the population. The national organiser, Timothy Harrington, argued that the executive of the National League contained only eight people who were on, or had anything to do with, the executive of the Land League, and there was no shortage of witnesses willing to testify to the 'respectable' nature of the movement. T. J. Condon, M.P. and Mayor of Clonmel, declared of the League in his area: 'Every class of the Clonmel community is represented in the Clonmel branch... priests, professional men, merchants, traders, artisans, farmers, labourers, all classes are included.' At a more local level, 'anti-landlord forces' had by 1886 succeeded in obtaining control of 50 per cent of the Poor Law boards in Ireland. But perhaps the most significant achievement of the movement was to maintain the revolution in national consciousness among the people. There are several indications of this revolution, from the demise of deferential attitudes towards landlords to the changing of street names commemorating English sovereigns to 'Brian Boru, Wolfe Tone, or Parnell streets'. In the north, Protestant Liberals, anxious to retain the support of Catholics, complained: 'All the popular histories read by the Irish Catholic peasantry at the present hour are from the pens of *Young Irelanders*.' F. S. L. Lyons has probably best described this 'consciousness' phenomenon in his succinct assessment of Parnell's achievement: '*He gave his people back their self-respect.*'[42]

'Consciousness', however, can be a rather nebulous commodity and is not necessarily synonymous with political commitment. For example, despite the fact that in the period 1882-5 the number of meetings held by the National League was greater than during the land war, there was no corresponding progress in local branch formation. Timothy Harrington admitted that up to 1885 there were 'very few' branches of the League. In 1883-4 they were not a third of the number they eventually reached in 1886, which he put at 1,700. This situation changed, however, following the electoral reforms of

1884-5, which trebled the Irish electorate and undoubtedly stimulated the interest in politics of many who previously could exert no political influence. Harrington declared that a massive increase in local branch formation took place in 1885, but it did not apparently represent any great upsurge of popular commitment to Home Rule, but rather the desire in every county 'to qualify for its [parliamentary] representation' in the months preceding the general election of that year.[43] Indeed, the onset of the election was bound to stimulate a great increase in local branch formation, given that the National League entrusted the selection of parliamentary candidates, nominally at least, to county conventions organised mainly around local League branches.

As to the number of branches existing in the period 1882-5 and their distribution, Patrick Egan claimed at a meeting in Buffalo, New York, on 8 April 1883 that 371 existed: 119 in Leinster, 96 in Munster, 86 in Connaught, and 70 in Ulster. Another index of the progress of the movement in the period up to 1886 is the circulation statistics of *United Ireland*, the movement's chief press organ. In the period 1886-90 it was to increase its sales to 90,000 per week. However, William O'Brien informed the Special Commission that its circulation was very small in 1882: 'something under 30,000'. In 1883 it was still under 50,000. No profits were made until 1884, and, in addition, O'Brien claimed that since 1883 he had received only £200 per year, half his agreed salary as editor.[44] The sales of *United Ireland* and the slow progress of local branch formation suggest that, notwithstanding the changed consciousness of the people and the exhortations of platform rhetoric, widespread active participation in nationalist politics was only forthcoming when substantial issues were at stake: parliamentary representation in 1885, Home Rule — briefly — in 1886, and the Plan of Campaign thereafter. Moreover, the effect of maintaining the extreme tone of nationalist politics in the period 1882-5 was to alienate much moderate nationalist and uncommitted opinion.

The establishment of *United Ireland* itself and the means by which control of the leading nationalist press organs was obtained are examples. Parnell was inspired to start *United Ireland* as a party organ after T. D. Sullivan's *The Nation* dissented from his approach to the land act of 1881. Sullivan was naturally concerned; his paper was for a long time the only leading journal consistently supporting Parnellite policies — as he forcefully informed Parnell, 'I said it was absolute treachery towards myself, ungrateful towards a national journal which had stood by the cause in all weathers, and which had helped to make the Land League, and to defend it and its leaders when they needed help very much.' His criticisms, however, went further and were more substantial: 'Newspaper journalism is a fair and open field for all who wish to embark their money and their talent in it, but it is quite a different thing to run against the existing journals one which shall be worked with funds which these journals helped to obtain for other purposes.' E. D. Gray, proprietor of the *Freeman's Journal*, had a similar experience. He informed F. H. O'Donnell that Davitt had threatened to have the *Freeman* burned on a hundred platforms if it did not support the League: 'I could not afford to beggar my family by opposition or resistance. Davitt could put £100,000 of American money into an anti-Freeman.'[45]

The views of Sullivan and Gray were shared by Alfred Webb, who not only resigned from the treasurership of the National League in 1883 but attempted to forestall the extremism of *United Ireland* by establishing, albeit unsuccessfully, 'a small monthly paper' like *The Athenaeum* to express 'the desire and necessity for some form of Irish nationality on the basis of friendliness and union with Great Britain'. In addition, W. J. O'Neill Daunt, the lifelong Repealer, claimed that 'Parnell and his followers', by 'attacking all landlords, good and bad indiscriminately', had 'totally widened the severance of classes which has always been the curse of Ireland'. Home Rule administered by Parnell, he informed W. E. H. Lecky, could be expected to result in 'bloodshed and chaos'.[46]

A similar impression was produced on Andrew Dunlop, a journalist with experience of writing for both Unionist and Home Rule papers in Ireland. Dunlop's refusal to put a nationalist slant on his writings incurred the wrath of William O'Brien, who, he claimed, forced his removal from the staff of the *Freeman's Journal* and the English *Daily News*. Dunlop also alleged that O'Brien's verbal abuse caused him to be physically attacked. As a result of his experience and those of others similarly placed, Dunlop contributed to the Home Rule debate in 1886 a pamphlet in which he declared: 'There can be no true estimate of public opinion — no one can tell what "the views of the majority are" when a penalty is attached to the expression of any opinion save such as have received the sanction of those who have assumed the position of dictators of the people.' Ironically, William O'Brien was to make exactly the same complaint when he fell foul of official party opinion many years later and sought to publicise his own views.[47]

CONCLUSION

In looking back on the limited scheme for Irish autonomy that Gladstone proposed in 1886 it is difficult to understand why it aroused the passions that it did. But to understand this phenomenon it is necessary to look beyond the details of the plan and to comprehend what kind of meaning was invested in the term 'Home Rule' by contemporaries; and it would be difficult to underestimate in this respect the role of nationalist propaganda in general, and of *United Ireland* under William O'Brien's editorship in particular. Appeals to a violent history of struggle to justify and conceptualise political actions in the present could not but strike fear into those sections of society, whether in the north or south, who were not part of the agitation; and given its supporters' reluctance, or inability, to define what exactly Home Rule meant, it was only to be expected that critics would invest the term 'Home Rule' with the violent and highly charged images of party propaganda. Herein lay the great negative aspect of nationalist ideology.

'People', as Karl Deutsch perceptively argues in his study of nationalism, 'are marked off from each other by communicative barriers, by "marked gaps" in the efficiency of communication.' While nationalist propaganda was an excellent medium for uniting those with a stake in identifying with dispossessed and persecuted ancestors, it could hardly be expected to make converts among those sections of Irish society stigmatised in nationalist legend as the descendants of the dispossessors and persecutors, and whose own awareness and interpretation of the Irish past was very different from the nationalist view. The comments of the Earl of Courtown on the Parnellite move-ment — at a time when its leaders were anxious to stress the 'constitutional' nature of the demand for self-government, its compatibility with membership of the empire and the authority of the Queen — would have been endorsed by Unionists, north and south:

> It suits the purposes of their leaders to disclaim any intention of separation from England; but the title of 'nationalist' alone connects them inseparably with the rebels of 1798, with James II's Irish parliament, with the nationalist and ultra-montane factions of the Confederates of Kilkenny, with the rising of 1641, and with the many futile attempts to expel the English from Ireland.[48]

The police, who had a better idea of the actual political practice of the National League up to 1886, were aware that the movement had worked to prevent the commission of crime in these years and strongly urged the Conservative government in January 1886 against suppressing the League. But in the popular imagination the organisation had unmistakable connotations of revolution and violence — reinforced by such well-publicised utterances as Parnell's declaration that no man had a right to fix the *ne plus ultra* to the march of a nation.[49] It is against this background that much of the hostile reaction to Home Rule in 1886 has to be seen, for fixing the *ne plus ultra* to the march of a nation was precisely what Gladstone intended when he proposed Home Rule as a 'final settlement' of the Irish question. Moreover, as will be seen, the scheme Gladstone formulated was not such as to inspire confidence that this objective would be secured.

2

Gladstone
and the Liberal Conversion
to Home Rule

THE question of Gladstone's conversion to Home Rule has long been a subject of debate among historians. His was a mind imbued with both an acute moral and political sense, and his attempts to synthesise the dictates of morality with the necessities of party politics have offered much scope for argument as to whether his conversion to Home Rule was determined chiefly by moral or political motives. Essentially this debate has focused on two opposing views of Gladstone. The first, emphasising his profoundly moral and religious frame of mind, charts his views on Irish autonomy as being in the process of development over a considerable period of time: how every attempt of the Westminster parliament to govern Ireland efficiently and fairly had failed, leaving Home Rule as the only satisfactory moral and political solution once it became certain, after the general election of 1885, that this was the wish of the great majority of Irish people.[1]

The opposing view, while accepting that Gladstone was inspired with great moral fervour, contends that his conversion to Home Rule was, nevertheless, effected as much for party political reasons: to diminish 'the independence and strength of Irish nationalism, so as to benefit the Liberal Party and his position in it'.[2] Thus there is, not surprisingly, a considerable amount of published material on the subject of Gladstone's taking up of the Home Rule question. However, while it is important to explain the nature of Gladstone's commitment to Home Rule in general, and while bearing in mind the material which already exists on this subject, of equal importance is the allied question of why Gladstone, once having declared for

Home Rule, proceeded with such haste to implement a Home Rule scheme in circumstances which were anything but congenial and in which his government depended on the support of the Parnellite party — an eventuality which he had previously declared to be of 'vital danger to the country and the empire'.[3] In examining this question attention will be focused on Gladstone's views of the state of Ireland in the period from the general election of 1885 until April 1886 and his sources of information on the Irish question.

Despite their differences, both schools of thought on Gladstone's conversion to Home Rule agree on one important point: that before 1885 he did not practically consider Home Rule as a solution to the Irish question. However, once he was convinced of its necessity, his commitment was real. Herbert Gladstone has argued that when the Whig element in the Liberal government rejected Joseph Chamberlain's 'central board' scheme on 9 May 1885, his father privately accepted that as a matter of practical politics a separate parliament for Ireland 'in some form or other' would eventually have to be conceded. In fact in March 1885 Gladstone accepted the moral case for Home Rule: that self-government should be conferred on Ireland as an act of atonement for decades of misrule under the Union. Asked in 1890 by Lee Warner, headmaster of Rugby School, if he could identify 'the crucial moment' at which he determined to adopt the Home Rule policy, Gladstone replied:

> Yes; I had been reading a speech of Mr William O'Brien [Dublin, 1 March], and I put it down and said to myself — what is there in this speech that I must get to realise before I put it aside? And I saw then that there never was and never could be any moral obligation to the Irish race in the Act of Union.[4]

Thus Gladstone's personal commitment to Home Rule was apparently settled some months before it was necessary to make a public declaration in favour of Irish autonomy. His conversion to Home Rule, nevertheless, was always considered a likelihood by some. Following his public declaration in favour of Irish autonomy, Lord Hartington remarked: 'I think no one who has read or heard, during a long series of years, the declarations of Mr Gladstone on the question of self-government in Ireland can be surprised at the tone of his present declaration.'[5]

Writing in July 1886 of his own mental evolution towards public acceptance of Irish Home Rule, Gladstone argued that there had been several paramount conditions which had to be met before a Home Rule scheme could be considered ripe for implementation. It was essential that the failure of the Westminster parliament as a satisfactory 'legislative instrument for Ireland' should be demonstrated; that the demand for Home Rule should be 'made in obedience to the unequivocal and rooted desire of Ireland expressed through the constitutional medium of the Irish representatives'; that Irish Home Rule must not endanger the unity and security of the empire; that any Irish Home Rule scheme should be of such a nature as to apply to Scotland if so desired; that the Home Rule question should, so far as possible, be kept out of the arena of party politics. On the fulfilment of these conditions, he argued, it was essential that 'the question... be promptly and expeditiously dealt with', otherwise it would gravely dislocate the British political system by changes of government, dissolutions of parliament, obstruction, 'and derogating further from the character of the House of Commons'.[6] Clearly Gladstone was concerned as much for the stability of the British political system as he was for the peculiar needs of Ireland. But how far does Gladstone's explanation for his actions of the previous months adequately account for the course he took?

Certainly some of the conditions Gladstone stipulated had indeed been met. Ireland had endorsed the nationalist demand at the 1885 general election; the Westminster parliament had, arguably, failed to govern Ireland as well as a domestic legislature might have done; nationalists were prepared to accept a measure of autonomy which did not endanger imperial unity. But one important condition was not met. It rapidly became clear in the aftermath of the 1885 general election that the Tories were not prepared to concede Home Rule to Ireland, and that the subject, if taken up by Gladstone, dependent for support on the Parnellite party, would be very much at the centre of party politics. Moreover, an equally important consideration for the successful implementation of a Home Rule scheme was the necessity of allowing enough time for educating the British public on the justice and necessity of Irish autonomy.

Gladstone, however, though he had formed his government

ostensibly on the basis of an inquiry into the subject of Home
Rule in general,[7] moved rapidly to formulate and implement a
Home Rule scheme in the teeth of stiff opposition from a considerable section of his own party and from the Tories — a combination which would guarantee that his attempt would fail. His
argument that the threat to the British political system necessitated such a course is inadequate, for, as will be seen, the
Parnellite leadership was prepared to move in the direction of
Home Rule at a much slower pace than Gladstone.

To some extent the speed with which Gladstone took up the
Home Rule case is explicable in terms of his personal make-up.
Lord Selborne, who parted company with him over the Home
Rule issue, gave a perceptive and not unsympathetic analysis of
his motives. Whether wise or unwise, he wrote, they were nevertheless 'higher and more honourable than those of mere personal ambition'. Gladstone had an impatient spirit allied to a
strong distaste for coercion, which blinded him to the necessity
of firm government and maintenance of existing laws.
Moreover,

> The sands of his life were fast running out; whatever there
> might be still to do must be done quickly. 'The time',
> especially in Ireland, 'was out of joint'; he was 'born to set it
> right'.... When he determined to run any great risk in
> politics it was not his nature to feel doubt or misgiving; if
> one experiment failed he was so much the readier for
> another.... It is to this state of mind that I trace his new
> departure in politics at the age of seventy-six, a departure not
> new as to Ireland only but ... to many other questions also.[8]

Certainly Selborne highlights characteristics of Gladstone's per-
sonality which historians have commonly noted as influencing
his political actions: his distaste for coercion, sense of justice, historical sense, belief in a personal mission, and an excessively
optimistic frame of mind once having settled on a course of
action. However, there were far more concrete reasons for
Gladstone to have dealt with the Home Rule question in the way
that he did, and these are to be sought in an examination of what
Gladstone believed to be happening in Ireland following the Parnellite successes in the 1885 general election and the sources on
which his information depended.

Gladstone, while anxious to assist in a solution to the Irish question, was unwilling to appear to be soliciting Parnellite support at a time when the Tories seemed prepared to confer Home Rule on Ireland. As a result, his facilities for obtaining accurate information on Irish affairs in the autumn of 1885 were severely restricted. The problem, he informed Lord Rosebery, was that

> The unfriendly relations between the party of Nationalists and the late government in the expiring parliament, have of necessity left me and those with whom I act in great ignorance of the interior mind of the party, which has in parliament systematically confined itself to very general declarations.

Gladstone had virtually no practical experience of Ireland himself on which he could draw, and his sources of information on Irish affairs were to remain scanty, being confined to 'two or three colleagues'. Thus the reports on Ireland he received were prone to assume greater significance than they might otherwise have done had his sources been more numerous. As it was, the context in which they had meaning was one of rumour and supposition as to what the Nationalists were likely to do having swept the board at the general election of 1885, and following Parnell's vow that the chief task of his party was now to obtain the restoration of a native Irish parliament.[9]

Highly important in shaping Gladstone's mind on Irish affairs following the general election was an extensive memorandum on the Irish question drawn up by James Bryce. Bryce had made a tour of Ireland after the election, with the express purpose of taking the political temperature of the country, and his report, entitled 'Irish Opinions on the Irish Problem', was not calculated to calm Gladstone's mind on the Irish question. Emphasising the authority of his inquiry by pointing out that his sources were 'several of the leading judges and higher officials, leading professional men, prominent merchants and influential Nationalists', Bryce proceeded to paint a picture of Ireland on the verge of social dissolution. The general opinion among educated men, he remarked, was that 'things could not go on much longer the way they were. The sentiment of uncertainty and insecurity is telling injuriously in commerce and industry.' Moreover, the land market did not operate:

Very many estates are in the hands of receivers. It is feared that the difficulty in collecting rent will soon become very serious. The fall in the price of agricultural produce, especially cattle, has heated a widespread demand for a revision of judicial rents before the expiry of the fifteen years fixed by the land act of 1881. The success of the Parnellite candidates coupled with the conduct of the present ministry has given rise to a feeling of contempt for the authority of parliament. One is told everywhere that many persons, especially young men of education, are going over to the Nationalist Party.

Two possible solutions to this state of affairs had been suggested to Bryce from his Unionist and Nationalist sources. The former rejected the desirability of a domestic Irish parliament and suggested instead a reform of the existing administration; among their proposals were the substitution of a Secretary of State for the Lord Lieutenant, the abolition of the grand jury system and its replacement by the creation of elective boards, and the reform of the police administration. Significantly, Bryce recorded, many of those who suggested these reforms reluctantly admitted that if they could not be effected, 'legislative independence' was preferable to the existing state of things.

The solution to the Irish problem emanating from Nationalist sources was more predictable. A domestic parliament for Ireland based on the Westminster model was suggested, to deal with purely Irish affairs; to have no control over foreign affairs or imperial matters, the appointment of judges or the military forces; and with a power of veto over acts of the Irish parliament to rest with the imperial parliament at Westminster. All parties in Ireland agreed, Bryce noted, that the land question would have to be settled before the existing constitutional arrangements were interfered with. He concluded by urging: 'It is essential to obtain as soon as possible a statement from Mr Parnell on what he would accept.'[10] In sum, the general impression of the state of Ireland presented in Bryce's memorandum was of a country moving steadily, for various reasons, towards a situation approaching anarchy, but at the same time being capable of pacification if resolute action was promptly taken.

The threat of social dislocation conveyed by Bryce was again impressed on Gladstone a short time later by Lord Richard Grosvenor, the strongly anti-Parnellite Liberal chief whip, who informed him that he had it on good authority that a move was afoot among Parnellites to withdraw completely from the Westminster parliament. Gladstone replied:

> I should regard the withdrawal *en bloc* as by far the most formidable thing that can happen. It will be followed by an assembly in Dublin, which brings into view very violent alternatives. If Parnell is wise he will keep to the game he has been upon heretofore, viz, the ejecting of govts.[11]

Historians, where they have noticed this communication, have tended to minimise its significance. Hammond, though he acknowledges that 'Gladstone had been haunted by the fear that Parnell might take his eighty-five men to Dublin, and set them up as a parliament defying England', assumes that he only considered the possibility in terms of the detrimental effect it would have on England's international image: 'England the mother of free institutions... the nation that had read the tyrants of Europe so many a lesson'. Cooke and Vincent regard the threat to withdraw from Westminster as merely a 'madcap' possibility that Gladstone had to allow for. Dr Conor Cruise O'Brien regards Gladstone's fears on this issue as 'speculations in the dark. ... There is no evidence on the Irish side that the idea of secession was ever seriously considered.'[12] However, the real significance of this communication is only apparent when considered in the context of a flow of information, all of which generally supported the view of Ireland as being on the verge of revolution.

Coming just a few weeks after Bryce's report, Grosvenor's letter preceded by only a week what was perhaps the most serious and influential report of this nature. In a letter written for the attention of both Gladstone and his son Herbert, Edward Hamilton, lately one of Gladstone's private secretaries, described a conversation he had with Sir Robert Hamilton, Under-Secretary at Dublin Castle. Hamilton had replaced the unfortunate T. H. Burke, who was murdered in the Phoenix Park in 1882, and was known to favour Home Rule. He was not given to hysterical outbursts on Irish politics. As Edward Hamilton reminded Gladstone, 'His opinion on the situation in Ireland is entitled to great weight, not only because of the official position he occupies, but because his judgment is singularly sound and calm.' He then detailed exactly what Under-Secretary Hamilton had to say on Irish affairs:

> We are . . . approaching a crisis of no ordinary kind. Unless the dreadful policy of *drift* is superseded by some statesman taking a bold line the difficulties all round will become intolerable. *We are in the throes of a revolution* [my italics]. There is no use blinking the fact, and the press is a poor guide in such a case unless directed.

Clearly Ireland, according to apparently reliable sources, was approaching a state of social chaos that only rapid and radical action could forestall. It was an impression endorsed by at least one leading Parnellite, T. M. Healy. Henry Labouchere, who throughout this period acted as a political intermediary between all parties and especially as a source of information on Ireland for Gladstone, informed Joseph Chamberlain of Sir William Harcourt's belief that 'if the Irish found that they could get nothing, they would resort again to dynamite'. Having communicated Harcourt's views to Healy, with whom he was in close and frequent contact, Labouchere received the following reply:

> Harcourt's views quite interest me, and he is quite right, for if the people are disappointed after the visions held out to them, they cannot be held in. This country could easily be made ungovernable so far as the collection of rent and legal process is concerned, and the obstructers would find that they were not dealing with playboys but with resolute men. It is because I am for peace and feel the necessity for it that I am willing to accept any reasonable settlement, as things could not go on as they are for very long. If prices next year are as bad as this the country will not be habitable in any case for rackrenters.[13]

Indeed, on the rent question, Lady Cowper had already gone much further than Healy on 14 December 1885, when she told Gladstone that *no* rents were being paid in Ireland, even those judicially settled.[14] The broad consensus of opinion on the state of Ireland exhibited by Gladstone's informants was supported by a new development in Irish politics in the period from the autumn of 1885 to the summer of 1886. This was the emergence and rapid development of the House League.

Originating in Co. Longford in the summer of 1885, the movement had a fivefold objective; to reduce 'rack-rents' in town dwellings; improvement of dwellings; fostering of sanitation; encouragement of home industry; and legislation in favour of house-owners in towns. With the avowed intention of applying the methods of the Land League against rack-renting landlords in the towns, the movement found widespread support and had considerable success. By October 1885 branches had been organised in many parts of nationalist Ireland, including Donegal, Cavan, Sligo, Carlow, Wexford and Kerry. Indeed, so widespread did House League branches become in Kerry that the R.I.C. were of the opinion, based on 'excellent authorities', that 'in the event of the National League being proclaimed illegal, it is intended in Kerry to utilise "The House League" for all its purposes'.[15] Official endorsement of the movement by the Parnellite party was only prevented by the prorogation of parliament.

The emergence of an organisation like the House League, raising up visions of the strife of the land war being repeated in towns all over Ireland, was just the kind of tangible indication of impending revolution that gave substance to the fears expressed by Gladstone's sources on Irish affairs. The following report by *The Times* on the affairs of the League would have adequately expressed the apprehensions of British opinion, whether Liberal or Conservative:

> Leagury of all kinds is flourishing in Ireland. The National League is practically a Land League, and closely associated with it is the House League, an institution which has already assumed formidable proportions, not only in Kerry, but in the midlands and in the north.... At present it is not too much to say that the owners of houses in towns in Ireland are on the eve of being attacked in precisely the same way as were the owners of land.

In the event, however, the House League did not prove to be the agency of urban revolution predicted by *The Times*, but seems to have disappeared as quickly as it arose, some time in the summer of 1886, presumably a victim of the Liberal/Parnellite alliance and the efforts then under way to prove that Ireland was peaceful and ready to accept the boon of Home Rule. What is important, though, is its emergence and rapid expansion at a crucial stage in Anglo-Irish relations. The particular effect the emergence of this organisation had in moving Gladstone to take up Home Rule as a policy requiring immediate implementation is, of course, difficult to ascertain, but what is clear is that fear of social disorder in Ireland and consequent violence in England were the prime factors in determining his approach to the Tory Party on the Home Rule issue in mid-December 1885. Gladstone contacted A. J. Balfour, who described their conversation some months later in a letter to the press which is worth quoting extensively for the indication it provides of Gladstone's frame of mind:

> The conversation, entirely informal . . . consisted chiefly . . . of statements made by Mr Gladstone to me respecting the serious condition of Ireland, and the urgency of the problem which it presented to the government. He told me that he had information of an authentic kind, but not from Mr Parnell, which caused him to believe that there was a power behind Mr Parnell which, if not shortly satisfied by some substantial concession to the demands of the Irish Parliamentary Party, would take the matter into its own hands, and resort to violence and outrage in England for the purpose of enforcing its demands. 'In other words,' I said to Mr Gladstone, 'we are to be blown up and stabbed if we do not grant Home Rule by the end of the next session.' 'I understand', answered Mr Gladstone, 'that the time is shorter than that.'[16]

Following this meeting, Gladstone wrote to Balfour promising his support for any Tory Home Rule scheme and emphasising the 'stir in men's minds' and the 'urgency of the matter, to both of which every day's post brings me new testimony'. Balfour replied in a conciliatory tone, but highlighted the difficulty in keeping the Home Rule issue out of party politics and on a national plane, given that Ireland was an integral part of the United Kingdom and not a remote region such as Afghanistan or Roumelia. Gladstone replied stressing the urgency of the matter and hoping that the government would act, as 'time is precious, and is of the case'. As is well known, Gladstone's attempts to persuade the Tories to take up the Home Rule issue failed, but the value of his correspondence with Balfour lies in indicating the frame of mind with which he took up the Home Rule question. To Gladstone's mind the Irish question ceased to be just a serious problem facing the Westminster parliament: it became an emergency. As he put it in a letter to Sir William Harcourt, the 'Irish emergency at the present minute dominates and overshadows every other emergency'.[17]

However, to emphasise this point is not to detract from the extent to which Gladstone sympathised with the Irish demand for Home Rule *per se*, but rather to point out that his belief that Ireland was on the verge of massive social disorder had a determining influence in setting the pace with which he would deal with the question once having decided that it was 'ripe' for settlement. This is a crucial point, for the haste with which Gladstone proceeded to construct and implement a Home Rule scheme must have been an important factor making for the failure of his attempt to confer a domestic parliament on Ireland in 1886. Given the suddenness with which the Home Rule question came to the fore and the total lack of preparation on the part of the British public and political parties to consider the question, the most effective course to have taken would have been to declare in principle for Irish autonomy and then to proceed to investigate the problem by means of a parliamentary inquiry. Indications, moreover, were not wanting from Parnellite sources that this would have been acceptable. T. M. Healy inquired of Labouchere with characteristic sarcasm: 'Is it not plain that if we plunge into Home Rule plans just now before your intelligent public apply their enlightened minds to it that we shall get far less than what we should get by waiting and worrying you for a few years?' Michael Davitt, in like manner, informed Labouchere that both he and Parnell were agreed that the resolution of the land question should proceed with a 'representative commission' to fix the amount of compensation that should be given to landlords, and that if, while the land question was in the process of being settled, 'a parliamentary committee' was appointed 'to inquire into what amount of self-government could be given to Ireland without endangering the unity of the empire, this country would *immediately* settle down'.[18]

However, as was noted, although Gladstone had formed his government ostensibly on the basis of a general inquiry into the subject of Irish Home Rule, he chose to pursue a contrary course of action, moving to construct a Home Rule scheme with breath-taking speed. Defending his actions in the period immediately following the Home Rule debate, Gladstone metaphorically dismissed the view that he should have proceeded more prudently to deal with the Home Rule question:

> For England, in her soft arm-chair, a leisurely, very leisurely consideration, with adjournments interposed, as it had been usual, so also would have been comfortable. But for Ireland, in her leaky cabin, it was of consequence to stop out the weather. To miss the opportunity would not have been less clearly wrong than to refuse waiting until it came. The first political juncture which made action permissible also made it obligatory.

The 'weather' Gladstone refers to was the apparently very real threat of revolution in Ireland; and indeed, there was an early development which he might well have taken as proof of the rectitude of his Home Rule policy. Gladstone was much encouraged by the fact that the statistics of Irish agrarian crime for February 1886 — the first to emerge since he took office — were 'decidedly favourable... as compared with previous months'.[19]

Nevertheless, fear of revolution in itself was a very negative reason for wishing to admit the nationalist claim for self-government. This was, of course, recognised as such by a considerable section of British political opinion, which refused to be 'coerced' into accepting Home Rule. Gladstone, however, believed himself to be well equipped to deal with the Home Rule question: 'He said it was exactly because he was an old man that he felt he could deal with the subject. Everyone was violent about it. But everyone would pay respect to age and him.'[20] Moreover, there were positive indications that seemed to suggest that if a scheme for the solution of the land and autonomy questions were proposed, it would stand a good chance of success.

First, in the autumn of 1885, there was the increasing recognition in Gladstone's mind that Parnell could be trusted to accept and work a moderate measure of Home Rule enforced by Westminster. His speech on the address in January 1886 had supported that view, while at the end of the month Mrs O'Shea informed Gladstone that 'Some days ago Mr Parnell sent Mr Harrington to Ireland, with directions to overhaul the doings of the branches of the National League and with power to dissolve any that would not keep within bounds.' Enclosed with her letter were cuttings of Irish newspapers giving reports of local League branches that had been dissolved.[21] Secondly, and more important, were the indications coming from Irish landlords themselves that they would be prepared to accept major land and political reforms in Ireland.

Henry Villiers Stuart, a substantial landowner, informed Gladstone that only a solution to the land question would make Home Rule possible. Lord Midleton, although declaring himself against Home Rule, said he was willing to sell out on 'reasonable terms'. W. D. Webber, writing for himself and Lady Kingston, argued that the land question, not Home Rule, was the important one, and that 'The proprietors are still anxious to avail themselves of any fair terms for sale that would leave them the power of fulfilling their duties as residents as they have hitherto done.' Lord Powerscourt wrote urging state aid to assist some degree of buying out of the owner's interest in land and provision for private bills to be dealt with by committee in Dublin. Also, in early January 1886, Parnell communicated to Gladstone, through Mrs O'Shea, a plan he claimed had been submitted to him by 'the representatives of the chief landlord political organisations in Ireland', designed to secure the resolution of the land and Home Rule questions.[22]

Encouraging as these communications were in indicating at least a willingness to accept some major changes in Irish administration, much more influential were the efforts made in this direction by Lord Hartington. Hartington is known primarily for his strenuous Unionism and aversion to Home Rule, but, surprisingly, he played a major role in arranging contacts between Gladstone and representative sections of Irish landlord opinion in March 1886. Hartington arranged for his father's former land agent in Ireland, William Currey — 'a reasonable cultivated man who never took an extreme line in Irish politics' — to 'obtain the views of the most representative class of Irish landlords in regard to land purchases'. Currey saw, for example, T. C. Trench, Major Robert Perceval-Maxwell, H. H. Townsend (A. H. Smith-Barry's agent), Sir Richard Keane, Percy Smith and Sir Robert Paul. The general feeling entertained by this group and by another conference of owners and agents was that 'if land purchase became inevitable', a large scheme to effect a complete solution of the land question was preferred.[23] The details of their proposals will be covered when examining Gladstone's land bill; what is important to note at this stage is that when Gladstone decided to formulate his land and Home Rule bills in 1886 he had good reason to expect that they would, as a whole, be acceptable to most shades of Irish political opinion. If his reading of the political state of Ireland impressed on him the need to devise some large measure to settle the Irish question, his Irish contacts suggested that it would to a great extent succeed. But having decided to construct a Home Rule scheme, how far was Gladstone able to effect a conversion to Irish autonomy in the Liberal Party?

For many sections of British opinion the question of Home Rule in 1886 was considered primarily as an imperial question rather than an issue of local devolution within the United Kingdom. Gladstone's second ministry had presided over a series of imperial disasters, especially in Egypt and South Africa, and his conversion to Home Rule was interpreted as another aspect of imperial feebleness: 'The Irish question was to broaden its significance as it came to be seen as a domestic outbreak of a general epidemic which threatened the existence of the international order.'[24]

The English business class, it has been argued, was intensely patriotic and resented violence in Ireland as a threat to England; 'and as the affront — with others, e.g. Majuba and the loss of Gordon — occurred under a Liberal government, it withdrew its allegiance from the Liberal Party'. Certainly there was a steady stream of deserters from Liberal ranks: Matthew Arnold, A. V. Dicey, Goschen, Chamberlain, Bright, Sir John Seeley and Hartington. There was little enthusiasm for Home Rule in general in Liberal ranks, and thus it is not surprising to find a distinct lack of enthusiasm for the question among the leading Liberals who supported Gladstone. At the same time, though, it was important for Gladstone to have their support.

For example, the support of Lord Spencer was essential. His influence in the party was, as John Morley records, second only to Gladstone's: 'His unrivalled experience of Irish administration... powers of fixed decision in difficult circumstances, and the impression of high public spirit... gave him a force of moral authority in a crisis that was unique.' Morley wrote elsewhere that his conversion gave driving force to general arguments for Home Rule, and that without his 'earnest adhesion to the revolutionary change in the principles of Irish government, the attempt would have been useless from the first, and nobody was more alive to this than Mr Gladstone'. Yet Spencer's support for Home Rule was determined not by a belief in the justice of the Nationalist demand but by the fact that the Tory action is reversing the stern 'law and order' policies he had pursued in Ireland led him to believe that Ireland could not be governed 'successfully' by the Westminster parliament since it allowed such sharp changes of policy. This development was also influential in moving Sir William Harcourt to support Home Rule even though he despised the Parnellites and had virtually no faith in Home Rule as a solution to the Irish question.[25]

Similarly, Morley, who was to become deeply committed to Irish Home Rule, argued that a settlement of the Home Rule and land questions was necessary both to prevent a collapse of British political institutions and to prevent the peasants seizing landlord property. Even Hugh Childers, who alone of leading Liberals declared for Home Rule at the 1885 general election by actually producing a Home Rule scheme, was not prepared to go as far as Gladstone originally intended in his Home Rule plan. James Bryce, who was also to play a leading role in publicising the Home Rule cause, was a 'Home Ruler *in despair,* adopting it as the least of a choice of evils and being far from hopeful as to its results'. He also saw the Irish problem as an obstacle to Anglo-Saxon unity, which could be achieved if it were settled. The general feeling among leading Liberals towards the Home Rule question was accurately described by Bryce when he said that though Home Rule was not desirable, it 'would come and must come'. In a perceptive note Henry Ponsonby wrote:

Today I talked to Lord Spencer.... What makes me uncomfortable is that he does not seem keen. In all great reforms the leaders are always keen. . . . But those who talk of Home Rule talk more in the 'What else can you do?' tone.[26]

However, while the conversion of leading Liberals to Home Rule was motivated mainly by negative reasons, their views were to condition the character of the Home Rule scheme in some important respects.

As for the Liberal parliamentary party at large, the extent to which any specific process of 'conversion' to the view that the demand for Home Rule was a just one actually took place is difficult to determine. It is likely that, for many, Gladstone's influence carried the day, though he was to remark:

> Although our Home Rule bill was eventually supported by more than 300 members, I doubt whether, if the question had been prematurely raised on the night of the address, as many as 200 would have been disposed to act in that sense.

Certainly most of the Liberal candidates at the 1885 general election did not commit themselves on Home Rule. It has been estimated that of 321 Liberals who voted on 8 June 1886 on the Home Rule bill, 48 during the election were favourable to Home Rule, 29 were 'at least sympathetic in some degree towards the concept of Irish nationalism', 28 were opposed or unsympathetic, and 216, or two-thirds, did not commit themselves. During the course of the Home Rule debate, however, significant changes of attitude seem to have taken place. R. A. Hufford argues: 'It would seem that an estimate that 1 of every 3 Liberals who opposed Gladstone before the Home Rule debates was won over during the debates, was approximately correct.' The Liberal Party conversion to Home Rule, however, does not appear to have prompted any great interest in the Irish problem among individual party members. Alfred Webb was to complain that the Liberals who came to Ireland to support the Nationalists during the Plan of Campaign 'did so because Ireland was the fashion. . . . [They] never took the trouble to really understand what the problem was in its essentials.'[27]

As to how far Liberal supporters in the country supported Home Rule *per se*, a useful source of information is the survey conducted by the *Pall Mall Gazette* on this question. Several investigators were sent to the chief areas of Liberal support in the north of England and Scotland. In the north of England it was found that Gladstone's influence, rather than any real interest or concern for Home Rule, was the determining factor among supporters of the Liberal Party:

> 'People don't personally feel these Irish questions as they have felt other questions' explained an intelligent Liberal, 'But the great body of the population retain their faith in Mr Gladstone, a faith which is responsible for the conviction that he will not deliberately mislead them.'

In Glasgow it was also felt that 'an intense devotion to Mr Gladstone, combined with a strong reliance on [his] judgment, formed by an unexampled national service' would influence a large body of Liberals to vote for the Home Rule scheme 'in opposition to their own sympathies and desires'. It was also reported that in Leeds the local Liberal acceptance of Home Rule was really an act of faith in Gladstone: 'in his earnestness and sincerity of purpose'. This feeling also prevailed in Manchester.[28]

In an interesting assessment of local Liberal association attitudes to Home Rule throughout the country, the *Pall Mall Gazette* concluded that the local associations supported Gladstone to a far greater degree than either the parliamentary party or rank-and-file Liberals:

> The Liberal associations throughout the country are much more in favour of Mr Gladstone than the members whom they return to support him in the House of Commons. . . . The caucus exists in a large measure to win elections, and anything and everything which threatens success at the next electoral combat is hateful in the eyes of the thorough-going Liberal association. . . . Neither the members of parliament at the top nor the rank and file at the bottom are so keen in support of Mr Gladstone as the members of the Liberal hundreds who stand between the two. . . . Nearly all the resolutions of Liberal associations reported within the last ten days accept the principle of Home Rule.

However, the report continued:

While this is a somewhat remarkable phenomenon, it is perhaps less significant than the fact that, with all their devotion to Mr Gladstone, the Liberal managers are wonderfully unanimous in expressing their acceptance of his bills in very guarded terms.[29]

Gladstone was, it seems, in the intensity of his commitment to Home Rule, very much alone among Liberals.

3

The Home Rule Scheme of 1886

Whatever be its fate in the present parliament, everyone must recognise that the introduction of this measure [Gladstone's Home Rule bill] did one great irrevocable service to the cause of Irish nationality: it defined it.

C. H. Oldham, 'The Prospects of Irish Nationality',
Dublin University Review, ii (June 1886)

SHAPING THE IRISH LEGISLATURE

In moving to formulate his Home Rule scheme early in 1886 Gladstone had considerable scope for manoeuvre. As we have seen, Parnellites as a group gave little time either to studying the question in general or to formulating a scheme of their own. Only in the autumn of 1885 did a committee, including Thomas Sexton and T. P. O'Connor, meet to study formally federations, but since Parnell 'hardly spoke to his followers upon political matters', there was not much enthusiasm for the endeavour.[1] Thus there was no collective party view of what Home Rule for Ireland should be, though some leading Home Rulers now had their own individual ideas of what should be the basis of a solution to the problem.

Parnell spoke at this time in general terms of a 'unicameral legislature unencumbered by a House of Lords', and with varying degrees of emphasis on the need for Ireland to have powers to impose protective tariffs. More privately, he provided Gladstone, through the agency of Mrs O'Shea, with a Home Rule constitution that included special proportionate representation for the large Protestant minority in Ireland and left the definition of what 'matters did or did not come within the province of the local legislature' to the imperial parliament. The scheme was carefully designed with a view to propitiating

English prejudice 'and to effect those guarantees against hasty legislation, interference in extraneous matters and unfair action against particular classes apprehended by many people as the result of an Irish parliament'. His scheme, Parnell stressed, did not involve a repeal of the Act of Union — 'an irrevocable step' — and while 'it was not one I could undertake to suggest publicly myself', he would work to have it accepted in Ireland as a 'final settlement'. Michael Davitt rejected totally Parnell's views on protection and claimed that he had taken 'his one-chamber idea' from his own book, *Leaves from a Prison Diary*. In the concluding chapter of the book Davitt sketched a scheme of local and national self-government for Ireland: local government would be managed by elective county boards which would supersede the grand jury system and be invested with powers to manage all aspects of local government, including schemes for arterial drainage, tramways, railways, canals, docks, harbours and similar enterprises. The enactment of such schemes would be dependent on the ultimate approval of a national assembly, that would operate in much the same way as the British colonial legislatures except for 'the substitution of one for two chambers'.[2]

The expression of often different ideas on Home Rule by leading Nationalists, however, was hardly politically advantageous. By late December 1885 Parnell was worried that the public discussion of the details of Home Rule by Davitt, T. P. O'Connor and Justin McCarthy was supplying 'too many points for criticism to the English mind before it had grown used to the principle' of Home Rule and also 'tending to show that we ourselves are not agreed upon what we want'. But unco-ordinated as individual views among Nationalists on Home Rule tended to be, something close to a collective view on the subject did emerge in January 1886, and that it did so was largely due to Gladstone's instigation. Gladstone had set about sounding Nationalists on 'the Irish case' in August 1885, using as an intermediary John Knowles, editor of the *Nineteenth Century*, who was instructed to ask the Parnellite R. Barry O'Brien to write an article on the history of the Irish question. He followed this with a request to get 'Mr Parnell's mind on paper', regarding what he would accept as Home Rule for Ireland. O'Brien's article appeared in January 1886 and sought to represent the views, not just of Parnell, but of the 'five most influential men in Ireland ... Mr Parnell, Mr Davitt, Mr Healy, Archbishop Croke and Archbishop Walsh'. O'Brien outlined a scheme that resembled Gladstone's Home Rule bill of April 1886. Ireland should have a parliament for purely domestic affairs; the questions of exactly what sort of chamber it should be, and whether there should be Irish representation at Westminster or not, were essentially subordinate. The subject reserved to the imperial parliament should include 'foreign policy, peace or war, the army and navy, matters relating to the crown ... the currency, the post office'. Irish questions should include 'education, land, police, trade and commerce, customs and excise'. In a passage clearly designed to allay British fears O'Brien declared:

> Fortifications should be erected, harbours built, and garrisons established in any part of Ireland, irrespective of the views of the Irish legislature, and the question of the purse, so far as these matters are concerned, should be an imperial one. The appointment of the commander-in-chief of the forces in Ireland, and other military officers, should be at the disposal of the imperial parliament.

O'Brien concluded by emphasising that while it was important for an Irish parliament to have control of land and the police, and that the refusal of these subjects would lead to a 'rupture of negotiations', Nationalists did not regard customs control as ultimately essential, as 'There are few industries in the country which can be fostered by protective tariffs and little support for such a policy.' Moreover, they would also accept a veto on the endowment of any religion.'[3] O'Brien's article contained probably the most comprehensive statement then obtainable of the Parnellite view of an acceptable Home Rule scheme; and its credibility in this respect would have been enhanced in Gladstone's mind by the fact that it was both broadly synonymous with the scheme communicated to him by Parnell himself and consistent with the nationalist views contained in the report on the state of Ireland submitted by James Bryce in the autumn of 1885.

Satisfied that the Irish demand was compatible with imperial unity, Gladstone informed Mrs O'Shea that a full 'interchange of ideas' with Parnell was indispensable to any examination of the 'autonomy' question. Discussions with Parnell, however, were to be conducted chiefly through the agency of John Morley, who has claimed that Gladstone 'was never fond of direct personal contentions, or conversations when the purpose could be well served otherwise'. The question is: was the purpose well served otherwise? Although the general Nationalist view of an acceptable Home Rule plan was clearly enough expressed, the actual details of Ireland's relations with Great Britain as defined by that scheme involved important matters, particularly concerning finance, and, as will be seen, these were to provide fertile ground for disputes between Liberals and Parnellites.[4] Moreover, any disagreement between these two parties on the Home Rule scheme was sure to give ammunition to the Tory and Liberal Unionist argument that Home Rule would fail to solve the Irish question. Why, then, did Gladstone fail to consult Irish opinion more fully on the details of his Irish plan?

Apart from the reason given by Morley, it is likely that he was influenced in this course of action by Harcourt, who professed disbelief in the feasibility of an Irish parliament but had accepted cabinet membership. Harcourt, however, was most anxious that the Home Rule question should be discussed fully by the cabinet, and not just a set plan. In this respect he urged that

> no communication should be made to Mr Parnell which in any way involved *the idea of an Irish legislature* until the cabinet had a full opportunity of considering the question. In short, that Mr Parnell should receive no information as to your views on this point other than those publicly made by you already, until the basis of action has been settled by the cabinet. For of course if Mr Parnell was made acquainted with your views on this matter there could no longer [be] any freedom of judgment left to the cabinet.

In his anxiety to maintain cabinet unity, Gladstone may well have decided to follow this advice, especially since R. Barry O'Brien's article had already provided the 'basis of action'. In the event he was to keep the evolution of his scheme very much to himself. His private secretary, Edward Hamilton, noted: 'He ... keeps the construction of the measure entirely in his own hands with occasional reference to Lord Spencer and John Morley and consultation with the Lord Chancellor and Attorney-General.'[5] In some respects this course was unavoidable: there was no great enthusiasm for Home Rule among most cabinet ministers, and Gladstone, having great fears for social order in Ireland and inspired by a personal sense of mission, felt the necessity to produce a plan for Irish autonomy as quickly as possible.

Moreover, given the problems that had to be overcome, such drive and enthusiasm as Gladstone brought to the subject were essential if a Home Rule plan was to make headway. John Morley has emphasised the difficulties that surrounded the formulation of the Home Rule scheme in the short period between the formation of the government in mid-February and the introduction of the bill to parliament on 8 April:

> Considering the enormous breadth and intricacy of the subjects, the pressure of parliamentary business all the time, the exigencies of administrative work...and the distracting atmosphere of party perturbation and disquiet that daily and hourly harassed the work, the despatch of such a task within such limits of time was at least not discreditable to the industry and concentration of those who achieved it.[6]

It is in the context of the very difficult conditions that surrounded the formation of his scheme that Gladstone's contribution to Home Rule nationalism has to be sought.

Formidable as the problems he encountered were, Gladstone's communications with Nationalists at least provided the basis from which to build an acceptable Home Rule plan. From this basis he set about producing a detailed scheme for Irish autonomy, and a supporting view of Irish nationalism that sought to obviate objections to Home Rule by demonstrating that Irish nationalist sentiment had always been compatible with imperial unity. As will be seen, in both cases his ideas had been the product of very recent and sustained study of local constitutions and Irish history. Consequently, what was to emerge when he introduced his plan in parliament was a scheme for Irish self-government complete with an historical pedigree emphasising the essentially 'constitutional' character of Irish demands for self-government. Aware that both public opinion and parliament were largely unprepared to consider the Home Rule issue, Gladstone was concerned to present his bill not as something new or revolutionary but as an essentially conservative measure: it would restore to Ireland a parliament that she had possessed for five centuries before the Act of Union. However, owing to his profound sense of history as the expression of the Christian spirit in world affairs, Gladstone's need to provide an historical pedigree for his Home Rule scheme cannot be considered only as a tactic for calming British fears of Irish autonomy. Home Rule would also be a means of repaying the debt owed by England to Ireland for the misgovernment of the past: 'a sad exception to the glory of our country'.[7] But most importantly, Gladstone's historicist outlook was influential in colouring his view of what Home Rule could be expected to achieve.

It might not always have been at the centre of Irish history, but Irish parliamentarianism provided Gladstone not only with a 'pedigree' for his Home Rule scheme but also with the inspiration for a theory of Irish nationalism that he was to develop during his crusade for Home Rule in the period 1886-93. Gladstone focused primarily on the history of Grattan's Parliament and used that institution both as a point of comparison in the explanation of his Home Rule scheme and as a portent of the benefits that would result from self-government. He emphasised the moderate nature of his proposed Irish legislature by declaring that, unlike Grattan's Parliament, it would not be co-ordinate with Westminster, and referred to Ireland's imperial position in Grattan's time to demonstrate th 'absurdity' of the Unionist argument that Home Rule would disrupt the empire. Indeed, at a later stage of the Home Rule debate he argued that in any future war involving Great Britain an Irish legislature could be relied on to support her by freely voting money and supplies, since such action had already taken place in Grattan's Parliament during the Anglo-French war in 1795. But for all its virtues, Gladstone admitted that the chief fault of Grattan's Parliament was the ease with which British politicians could interfere with its executive government; had it been free of this interference, it could have worked 'out a happy solution to every Irish problem'. His own scheme, by removing that interference, would thus be 'a real settlement'.[8]

Gladstone's preoccupation with the late eighteenth century was enhanced by his reading of Edmund Burke, who apparently also favoured Irish local autonomy, with control of all imperial affairs remaining with the Westminster parliament. However, inspiring as these historical studies undoubtedly were, they were nevertheless open to the objection of being of little relevance in the very changed political climate of the 1880s. But when G. J. Goschen made the relevant point that the loyalty of Grattan's Parliament was due to its being a Protestant and landlord parliament, very unlike the institution being proposed under Home Rule, and that therefore no analogy between the two could be drawn, Gladstone seems to have entirely missed the point and practically accused him of being anti-democratic and approving of government by 'placemen and pensioners'. His reply to Goschen illustrates an attitude of mind that was often noted by contemporaries: 'When he has convinced himself . . . of some view, he thinks everyone else ought to see it at once as he does, and can make no allowance for difference of opinion.'[9] This characteristic made for a powerful combination when allied with the high degree of optimism with which Gladstone approached the subject of Irish autonomy, and it provides an important perspective from which to examine the provisions of his Home Rule bill.

Gladstone began the formulation of his Irish scheme with a consideration of those aspects of the Irish question in which he felt most competent, 'namely . . . land and finance'. It was mid-March before he earnestly set about getting his materials on Irish government into order. From that time on he worked rapidly to produce a specific scheme in order to bring to a head discussion on the plan to be adopted. Undoubtedly the speed with which the Home Rule bill was produced — its main provisions were established by 1 April — was greatly facilitated by the fact that Parnell was, with the exception chiefly of finance, prepared to leave the formulation of the plan in Gladstone's hands. Fearing the collapse of social order in Ireland, Gladstone felt that his immediate necessity was to produce a plan that would be the basis of a settlement, whether or not he got the final credit for its enactment. As Edward Hamilton wrote, 'He will be content to have laid the foundation of a settlement. He does not care who gets the credit of eventually effecting it.'[10] The question was: how far was Gladstone's scheme likely to provide a settlement of the Irish question? Some of the most important clauses of the Home Rule bill exhibit the twofold influence of Gladstone's optimism as to the political acceptability of Home Rule and of colonial precedents; however, it is questionable how far these reliably provided guidelines for the construction of a workable scheme.

The clause defining the executive government of the Irish legislature, for example, a highly important element of the Home Rule bill, was both extremely brief and generalised in its definition of the powers to be exercised by the Lord Lieutenant:

> The executive government of Ireland shall continue vested in Her Majesty and shall be carried on by the Lord Lieutenant on behalf of Her Majesty, with the aid of such officers and councils as to Her Majesty may from time to time seem fit.

Explaining this part of the bill in parliament, Gladstone argued that it was 'most requisite that our act should be as elastic as possible'. While it was important that a legislative body should be established 'by a single stroke', the executive transition 'must necessarily be gradual':

> We propose, therefore, to leave everything as it is until it is altered in the regular course; so that there shall be no breach of continuity in the government of the country, but that by degrees, as may be arranged by persons whom we feel convinced will meet together in a spirit of co-operation, and with no great, much less insurmountable, difficulty in their way, the old state of things shall be adjusted to the new.

Gladstone also vaguely referred to a Privy Council 'in a certain form' that would be established to 'aid and advise' in the government of the country.[11] In addition to his Irish intelligence, Gladstone's optimism as to the 'spirit of co-operation' which he believed would enable this part of his scheme to function satisfactorily was based on the experience of self-government in the colonies.

Lord Thring, the chief parliamentary draftsman of both the land and Home Rule bills in 1886, was to point out that the enumerating of the specific powers of the Lord Lieutenant would have been impractical, as 'The mode in which a governor ought to act under the endless variety of circumstances which may occur in governing a dependency . . . never have been and never can be expressed in an act of parliament.' Moreover, in practice there existed no examples in Britain or in any of her dependencies where 'any vital collision' had arisen between the executive and legislative authorities, and it was also demonstrable that all the 'Home Rule' colonies had managed to surmount the obstacles which opponents of Home Rule argued would be fatal to their existence.[12] But to what extent did colonial precedents apply to Ireland's case in 1886? In these examples the fact of distance alone made impractical any close scrutiny and working involvement on the part of Westminster in the affairs of local assemblies. In addition, in the great majority of cases the only important link between the local assemblies and Westminster was that of the crown. Ireland's case was very different. Not only was she close to Great Britain, but, as will be seen, it was intended that Ireland would also remain closely enmeshed in the affairs of Great Britain in many important respects. Again, the Home Rule question came to the fore in a climate of great imperial fervour and aroused depths of passion which the granting of autonomy to far-flung dependencies in former times had not. It is highly questionable whether, if Gladstone's Home Rule scheme had been enacted in 1886, those who had been its opponents would have settled down to work it in the 'spirit of co-operation' he had envisaged, especially since ambiguity in its framing would have made possible interference in Irish government without the necessity of having to repeal the Home Rule act.

J. H. Morgan, commenting on this part of the Home Rule scheme, drew attention to such legislative anomalies: the freedom given to the crown to determine exactly what powers the Lord Lieutenant should possess; the fact that these would be vested in the *person* of the Lord Lieutenant rather than the Lord Lieutenant in Council; the undefined nature of the Privy Council which was to advise on Irish government both in terms of its constitution and powers; and 'the extent to which the Lord Lieutenant was bound to act on its advice' — all of these considerations offered scope for a quite legal interference in Irish government by a Westminster administration so inclined. Thus, argued Morgan,

It would have been quite possible for a Unionist government coming into power immediately after the Home Rule bill had passed into law and an Irish parliament had met at Dublin, to retain in their own hands the executive authority in Ireland without breach of statutory obligations.

Supplementary legislation and the 'tacit adoption of the unwritten convention of the English constitution that the advisers of the governor must command the confidence of the legislature' would, Morgan continued, have resolved these issues as they had in the colonies. Nevertheless, given that British Unionists were encouraging Ulster Protestants to rebel should Home Rule be enacted, that many British peers had extensive land holdings in Ireland,[13] and that the southern landlord community was strenuously Unionist, the possibility of British interference in Irish affairs had Home Rule been conferred certainly cannot be dismissed lightly.

But in noting the faults of the scheme it is important to remember that one of the most serious difficulties associated with its construction was the sheer lack of adequate information. Lord Welby, who played an influential role in drafting the financial clauses, wrote many years later:

> It must be remembered that there had been no sufficient time for the collection of data on which an effective measure could be founded, and the collection of this data was a task of great difficulty, for the departments did not possess them. The government came into power in February and the bill was introduced on April 6 [*sic*]; thus there was no real opportunity for testing the value of the data collected in that short interval, or for gauging beforehand objections both to the principles and details of the scheme adopted.

The state of Gladstone's thinking in mid-February 1886 about a Home Rule legislature can be gauged from a letter he wrote to Lord Granville:

Please ask (as for yourself)
1. Whether the general rule of our chief colonies is to have dual legislative chambers.
2. Whether the second is in some cases nominated, in some

elective — what are the examples of each — and which is found preferable.

3. If elective — is it by a different constituency? for a longer term?

4. What are the cases if any [are] of one chamber only and is the system found to work well?[14]

In fact it will be seen that Gladstone's scheme can be identified with no single constitutional model, but, reflecting perhaps the anxiety of having to produce an adequate plan without proper materials, would incorporate features of both single- and dual-chamber models with a combination of nominated and elected representatives sitting for different periods of time.

Deliberately avoiding the term 'parliament' — presumably because of its separatist connotations — the scheme proposed an Irish assembly consisting of one legislative chamber divided into two 'orders' that would debate and vote together,

> except that if any question arises in relation to legislation, or to standing orders or rules of procedure, or to any other matter in that behalf in this act specified, and such question is to be decided by vote, each order shall, if a majority of the members present of either order demand a separate vote, give their votes in like manner as if they were separate legislative bodies, and if the result of the voting of the two orders do not agree the question shall be resolved in the negative.

A negative decision by the first order, however, was only to be in force until either a dissolution or the lapse of three years, whichever occurred first.[15]

Gladstone's Irish assembly, thus, was to be neither of a bicameral or unicameral type, but rather a hybrid of the two. The experience of deliberating as one body, it was hoped, would have a harmonising effect when the assembly voted in its separate orders:

> Each order shall have ample opportunity of learning the strength and hearing the arguments of the other order. They will therefore, each of them, proceed to a division with a full sense of the responsibility attaching to their action.

As reflected in their conditions of membership, the orders were

intended to give representation to the most important classes of
Irish society. The second, a wholly democratic order, was to
consist of 204 members, to be elected on the existing franchise
and electoral divisions. After the first dissolution the Irish legislature could change the second order, with the exception of
laws affecting the ratio of members to population, and the
number of members in the order.[16] In so far as this order would
have included the majority of nationalist representatives, it was
to find no great objection among Parnellites. As to the first
order, however, a willing acceptance by those whom it was
intended to represent was highly questionable.

This part of the legislature was to consist of 103
representatives: 75 elected members and 28 Irish peers. It was
intended that ultimately the first order would be totally elective,
as the peerage membership, consisting of the Irish representative peers in the House of Lords, was to end after thirty
years. Indeed, the peers were not to be compelled to take their
seats in the Irish legislature, but to have the option of either
doing so or remaining in the House of Lords: vacancies in the
first order due to peers refusing their seats were to be filled by
election. The 75 elected members were to be elected on a high
property qualification of an annual income of £200 or the
possession of £4,000 free of debt. Moreover, the electorate which
would send these representatives to the assembly would itself
consist only of those who were 'the owner or occupier of some
land or tenement within the [electoral] district of a net annual
value of twenty-five pounds or upwards'. Taken as a whole, the
legislative body would give political power to the most
important classes of Irish society, from the aristocracy to the
small farmer. In this way the 'social order' of Ireland, which
Gladstone believed was undermined, would be restored, both in
the sense that the threat of social chaos would be removed, and
the landed gentry, removed from their predominant role in Irish
affairs by militant nationalism, could once again come to the
fore in the political life of the country. In the process not only
would the 'natural' balance of Irish society be restored, but the
very nature of Irish nationalism itself would be transformed,
from a potentially revolutionary sentiment supported by men
of mostly low social origins into a safe constitutional idea
influenced by the propertied classes.[17]

In his speech introducing the land purchase bill Gladstone expressed the belief that even the Irish nationalists 'may desire' that those marked out by leisure, , wealth and station for attention to public duties, and for exercise of influence, may become 'the natural, and effective, and safe leaders of the people'. This view was expressed more forcefully in Herbert Gladstone's unauthorised statement of his father's Home Rule opinions in December 1885 — the 'Hawarden Kite' — and repeated in the Commons by an Ulster Tory M.P.:

> As soon as the question is settled — the question of an Irish legislature — the unity will vanish, and all the sectional differences of the Irish people will re-appear. The forces of intelligence, the wealth and interests of every class of the population will assert themselves *and the members returned to parliament in Dublin will be very different in all respects to those who represent Ireland now* [my italics].

This is what Gladstone meant when he ridiculed Lord Salisbury's intention of suppressing the National League by repression, and argued instead: 'I trust that we shall be the suppressors of the National League. That, if it comes about, will certainly be by a different process.' In one of the rare press reactions to Gladstone's Home Rule bill that correctly diagnosed his intentions, the *Daily News* declared: 'So far from handing Ireland over to the National League, this scheme may, on the contrary, be charged with handing the National League over to the middle classes and the aristocracy.' Gladstone's confidence that his Home Rule plan would find substantial acceptance among the Irish peers was demonstrated in subsection 7 of clause 10 of the bill, which declared that membership of the peerage body was to be voluntary and Irish representative peers would not be compelled to join it.[18]

His optimism, however, does not seem to have been widely shared in cabinet. When informed by Gladstone of his intention to give the 28 representative Irish peers the choice of either taking their places in the Irish assembly or remaining in the House of Lords, Harcourt replied that he did 'not think Irish peers would be fool enough to exchange voluntarily their seats in the H. of Lords for the . . . Irish parliament where they could be mobbed out of existence'. Harcourt, admittedly, was the least sympathetic to Home Rule of Gladstone's cabinet colleagues but his views were widely shared. Gladstone, however, believed the Irish peers would take their seats in the first order, and substantiated his case by reference to the part Irish peers played in Grattan's Parliament: Irish peers had 'an Irish as well as an imperial patriotism', and if the Home Rule bill passed under happy circumstances, 'one of its effects will be a great revival of the local as well as a great confirmation and extension of imperial patriotism'. Moreover, he went on to declare that Irish peers would be enabled to sit in both the Irish assembly and the House of Lords: 'Since they did so in Grattan's time we certainly see no cause for putting an end to the double qualification which was thus enjoyed, and which, I think, worked beneficially.' However, this intention was not followed up and did not find expression in the Home Rule bill when it was printed on 13 April.[19] Nevertheless, it does underline the extent to which Gladstone's hopes for Irish self-government were based on the precedent of Grattan's Parliament — a precedent which would have been enhanced by his communications with Irish Nationalists and Unionists.

Through Mrs O'Shea, Gladstone was made aware of Parnell's hopes of conciliating the landlords, and of a compulsory land purchase plan allegedly submitted to Parnell by a group of Irish landlords. More important, though, were the memoranda by Irish landlords on their terms for selling their estates, communicated to Gladstone by Lord Hartington.[20] Their apparent willingness to accept a comprehensive solution to the land question, and to stay in Ireland if the imperial government retained control of the police, would have removed in Gladstone's mind the chief obstacle to local autonomy. However, in his enthusiasm for Home Rule Gladstone apparently overlooked an important consideration attached to their views: they were describing the terms they would accept for the sale of their estates *if* land purchase became inevitable. At the time their views were ascertained the political situation was uncertain and rather confused: the breadth of Gladstone's bills and the extent of their support had yet to be determined.

With the experience in 1885 of Lord Ashbourne's land purchase act, which marked the first important step toward a solution of the land question, it was certainly not unlikely that a major undertaking on the land question might become inevitable in 1886. With the publication of Gladstone's Irish bills, however, and the linking of land purchase with Home Rule, the political situation clarified in a way adverse to his hopes. But despite evidence to the contrary, Gladstone was highly optimistic that the House of Lords would support his Home Rule scheme, and to some extent his confidence was not entirely without foundation. Early in January 1886 the Central News Agency carried the following report:

> We have authority for stating that the Earl of Kilmorey, a Conservative Irish representative peer, who has intimated his intention of bringing forward a motion in favour of the abolition of the Lord Lieutenancy of Ireland, has received promises of support from a number of Irish, Scotch, and English peers on both sides of the house.

Reports such as this may well have accounted for Gladstone's highly optimistic frame of mind regarding the attitude of the Lords to his scheme. At the end of January 1886 he informed the Duke of Argyll that in their attitude to Home Rule 'The peers of the late government are generally, I think, in a very reasonable frame of mind.' Towards the end of March he was confident that Lord Hartington would take an attitude of 'benevolent neutrality' to the Home Rule scheme, even though it was by then clear that Hartington was likely to oppose Home Rule.[21]

Lord Derby noted his reaction when it was put to him that the Lords would throw out his Home Rule bill: 'He had his answer at once. Why should the peers reject it? Who could tell that they would? and if once, would they do it a second time?' What is clearly in evidence here is Gladstone's power of self-deception, noted by more than one of his contemporaries as often being in evidence whenever he was engaged in a project of great moment.[22] But notwithstanding his errors of judgment, Gladstone's faith in the political acceptability of his Irish bills drew also on the belief that, in formulating the balance of powers and restrictions to be invested in the new Irish legislature, he had taken into account many of the major objections to Home Rule.

There were basically two ways in which Gladstone could have defined the powers of the Irish legislature: he could have defined specifically what subjects would fall within its purview, or, alternatively, he could have cited the range of restrictions on its powers and left authority over all other matters in its hands. Gladstone chose the latter course. Clauses 3 and 4 of the Home Rule bill detailed a considerable number of exceptions and restrictions on the powers of the Irish legislature. It was to have no powers to make laws affecting the crown, peace or war, any matter affecting the forces of the crown or defence of the realm, treaties or relations with foreign states. These first four cases of exception were most important in defining the rights of Westminster and in maintaining Ireland's position as a portion of the empire. There followed a range of subsidiary exceptions: titles of honour, war booty, offences against the law of nations, treason, alienage, naturalisation, and, more importantly, trade, navigation and quarantine. Other exceptions included matters affecting the postal and telegraph service, beacons, lighthouses, the coinage, copyright and patent rights.[23]

The chief restrictions on the powers of the Irish legislature related to matters of religion, education and customs and excise. Religious endowment was specifically banned, and the unde-nominational character of the National School system was to be maintained. A ban on the making of laws affecting customs and excise duties would be necessary, as will be seen, to carry into effect the financial scheme of the bill. Additionally, the Dublin Metropolitan Police was to remain under imperial control for two years, as was the R.I.C. while it existed, though the Irish authority was to have power ultimately to create a new force under the control of local authorities. Civil servants were to be retained at their existing salaries, though if either the Irish government wished to remove them or they wished to retire themselves, they would qualify for pensions out of Irish government funds. This part of Gladstone's bill naturally offered much scope for Tory claims that, given the extent of these exceptions and restrictions, he did not trust the Irish to govern themselves wisely or fairly. Gladstone met this criticism by pointing out that these provisions were included 'not in consequence of mistrust entertained by me, but ... of mistrust entertained by others'. Indeed, he had originally intended to give the Irish parliament extensive powers over customs and excise. He informed John Morley: 'Individually, I am perfectly ready to give to Ireland the right to impose protective tariffs on British goods. . . . But the main thing is to pass our measures. In this view we have to weigh British prejudices.' These prejudices existed not only in Tory ranks but in the government. On hearing of Gladstone's intention of giving Ireland a limited power of imposing, not protective duties, but merely tariffs purely for revenue purposes, and, additionally, power of currency regulation, Hugh Childers, the Home Secretary, stymied the proposal by threatening to resign immediately.[24] Yet the question of the powers to be invested in the new Irish assembly was far from being the most contentious part of Gladstone's Home Rule plan: the financial basis of the scheme caused serious misgiving among Nationalists and provided a legitimate ground for objections to Home Rule from Unionists.

THE PROBLEM OF HOME RULE FINANCE

It was this part of the scheme which constituted the tangible connection between the Home Rule and land schemes. Forming a separate section of the Home Rule bill, the finance provisions were included in clauses 12 to 20, while the machinery for putting these provisions into effect were to be found in part 3 of the land bill. Since there had to be an equitable division of imperial burdens, the first point to be established was the amount Ireland was to contribute to imperial taxes, and problems immediately arose on how this was to be determined. Gladstone decided that Ireland should contribute one-fifteenth of total imperial expenditure, and despite Parnell's vigorous protests that one-twentieth or one-twenty-first would be a fairer charge, and that 'without a right budget all would go wrong from the start',[25] he resolutely refused to budge. Why?

Essentially the point at issue between Gladstone and Parnell was the question of whether the basis on which Ireland was taxed was fair or not. In a letter to John Redmond, Sir J. N. McKenna, the Nationalist economist, described the problem as it presented itself to Parnell in arguing his case with Gladstone:

When Parnell and I conferred in 1886 (on the bill of that year) Gladstone had left him (C.S.P.) under the impression that he ... believed we were all along financially favoured and that England was at a loss by us. I said, be it so I shall be contented with a clause that will limit the total of our payments under the bill for imperial purposes to the scale applicable to Great Britain on the ratio of the taxable means of the two countries respectively; but both Butt and he at their respective times lacked faith in their own ability to show that we not only paid more than we cost the exchequer of the U.K. — *they in fact accepted the fact that we did so, but the question was how was it to be shown and proved* [my italics].

This was the nub of the problem, for to show that Ireland was overtaxed would have entailed an accurate knowledge of what the relative taxable capacity of the two islands was, and on this subject no information existed in any of the government departments. However, the noted British economist Robert Giffen did provide statistics to show that Ireland paid twice as much in imperial contributions than she ought to: 'Ireland, while constituting only a twentieth part of the United Kingdom in resources, nevertheless pays a tenth or eleventh of the taxes. Ireland ought to pay about £3,500,000 and it pays nearly £7,000,000.' At the same time, though, Giffen admitted the problem to be a difficult one, and while the imperial exchequer received an excessive contribution from Ireland, it did not derive any benefit from it, as all of Ireland's contribution, and much more, had to be spent in Ireland:

> Partly through excessive military expenditure, and partly through excessive civil expenditure, Great Britain spends upon Ireland a disproportionate sum.... Actually, it is beyond question, we lose as a government nearly £3,000,000 while taxing Ireland over £3,000,000 more than it ought to be taxed.[26]

Given the paucity of reliable information with which to work, it is virtually certain that Gladstone was familiar with Giffen's article, and it is likely that it provided the basis of his argument with Parnell, as described by McKenna, on the question of Ireland's imperial contribution. At any rate, it is clear that he was not prepared to investigate the relative taxable capacity of Ireland and Great Britain as a basis for determining what Ireland's contribution to imperial charges should be. Taking as his point of departure the Irish imperial contribution in 1885, which was the surplus of Irish revenue remaining after the deduction of expenditure in Ireland on Irish services, he estimated that this surplus constituted a contribution by Ireland to imperial expenses in the proportion of 1:11½, or, as Lord Welby put it in his discussion of Home Rule finance, £2 where Great Britain paid £23. Gladstone pointed out that his proposal, which was to have Ireland pay in the proportion of 1:14 or 1:15, was a generous arrangement.[27] He measured the taxable capacity of the two countries by a comparison of income tax returns, the amount of property falling under death duties, and the valuation of land. Income tax statistics showed a proportion of 1:19, which, however, Gladstone considered to be an imperfect test because it was paid on a lower valuation in Ireland than in Great Britain and because many Irishmen also held securities upon which dividends were received in London. Thus, he argued, a considerable sum ought to be added to the Irish income tax which would raise it proportionately from 1:19 to 1:17. The valuation of property, he continued, was likewise lower in Ireland in proportion to the real value than in Great Britain, though the property passing under death duties provided a better test, as the law affecting this had been recently revised, and on this basis of comparison the proportion of payments between the two countries was 1:13.

Arguing from these premises, Gladstone held that his proposed estimate of 1:15 was a generous one, justified by the necessity of starting the Irish parliament off with a balance to its credit. Moreover, he went on to add that while Ireland's existing proportionate contribution to imperial expenditure, 1:11½, was based on 'the amount of the whole gross imperial expenditure', the proportion of 1:15 that Ireland would pay when the Irish parliament was established in Dublin would be estimated on an imperial expenditure very materially cut down: it would be based on a peacetime assessment and would not incur the increased military charges of wartime. The fund out of which the imperial taxes were to be paid would be established by clauses 25-27 of the land purchase bill, which provided for the appointment of an imperial receiver to whom customs and excise and all other duties would be paid, including local taxes imposed by the Irish parliament. There were, moreover, apart from imperial taxes, other charges which were strictly Irish, such as the salaries and pensions of judges and civil servants. As decreed by the land purchase bill, the Irish parliament would be bound to impose taxes to meet these charges. The imperial receiver was to keep an Irish and an imperial account, and any surplus remaining after Ireland's imperial contribution was deducted would then be moved to the Irish account. As John Morley was later to affirm, through the imperial receiver 'all rents and Irish revenues whatever were to pass, and not a shilling was to be let out for Irish purposes until their [Irish] obligations to the imperial exchequer had been discharged'.[28] Thus the imperial receiver would constitute the security for the Irish imperial contribution. This form of guarantee, however, was far from perfect, as will be seen when examining the weaknesses of the land purchase bill and other parts of the Home Rule scheme. Not the least serious of these weaknesses was the estimated balance on the Irish budget should Home Rule be conferred.

Gladstone calculated the combined Irish revenues from imperial taxes, local taxes and the post office at £8,350,000. Irish expenditure, which included an imperial contribution of £3,602,000, £1,000,000 for the constabulary, as well as local civil charges and the cost of revenue collection, was estimated to be £7,946,000, leaving a balance between revenue and expenditure of £404,000. This sum would constitute the finances of an Irish government for all expenses other than those listed above — an aspect of the bill that critics would effectively exploit. Indeed, John Morley admitted: 'This may seem a ludicrously meagre amount, but, compared with the total revenue, it is equivalent to a surplus on our budget of that date of something like five millions.' While that may have been so, Morley's view hardly suggests a highly developed or realistic insight into the problems that would face an independent Irish government. Gladstone, though, did not accept that this arrangement was anything other than generous. Why? In fact, although Ireland was formally to contribute £3,602,000 to imperial funds, her real contribution would be considerably less. This was because Gladstone decided not to subtract from the Irish revenue the duty on goods collected in Ireland but consumed in Great Britain. The goods concerned were chiefly spirits, porter and tobacco, and the revenue, which Gladstone calculated to be £1,400,000, being paid by England and Scotland should really have been credited to Great Britain if a true financial account between the two islands was being made. However, in the interests of maintaining 'the present absolute [fiscal] freedom between the two countries',[29] Gladstone allowed this sum to form part of the fund out of which Ireland's imperial contribution was to be made.

Thus, if this sum of £1,400,000 is subtracted from the imperial contribution of £3,602,000, Ireland's real contribution would have been £2,202,000, or a proportion in relation to Great Britain of 1:26. In a reference directed to the Parnellite benches Gladstone declared: 'I hope this will be borne in the mind by those who think this charge of one-fifteenth is a heavy charge to be thrown upon Ireland.' He further emphasised the generosity of his plan by pointing out that whereas under the existing imperial arrangements Ireland's *per capita* contribution was 16s, under the new arrangements it would be reduced to 13s 5d. He also expected the Irish government to be able to make a substantial reduction in the £1,000,000 needed for the upkeep of the R.I.C., and that it would receive a 'further sum of uncertain but substantial amount', in the form of a commission paid on the collection of instalments from tenants buying their holdings under the land purchase bill. However, too much should not be made of Gladstone's generosity in crediting Ireland with revenues properly belonging to Great Britain. The fact was that he had laboured until 30 March 1886 to find a workable method whereby the Irish parliament would collect and have the use of only those customs and excise duties derived from articles consumed in Ireland. He abandoned this project, however, when he recognised that this could only be achieved by establishing customs barriers between the two islands, with the impression being created that Ireland was not really part of the United Kingdom and that Home Rule meant complete separation.[30] But more importantly, Gladstone's optimism about the additional revenue to accrue to the Irish government from handling land sales was not widely shared.

Many well-informed people — both Home Rulers and Unionists — were convinced that unless the Irish government had the benefit of this revenue it would be virtually without funds; however, they argued that because of the current agricultural crisis and the stringent terms to be imposed on tenant purchasers rents would be impossible to collect. Thus, in such a situation, an Irish government without funds would be driven to repair its finances by increasing the only taxes it would be empowered to levy — the direct taxes. Indeed, as has been noted above, an increase in the existing burden of these taxes — amounting in 1886 to £1,150,000 from stamps and income tax and representing less than one-fifth of Ireland's total tax revenue of £7,330,000[31] — was forecast by the provision in the land purchase bill binding the Irish government to raise taxes to pay pensions and the salaries of judges and civil servants. But what sum did Nationalists think an Irish government would need to function effectively?

According to Thomas Sexton, writing in 1893, £1,250,000 would be required 'at the outset'. However, if such a sum was to be realised under the terms of the Home Rule scheme of 1886, £846,000 would have to be raised from direct taxes to supplement the original surplus of £404,000 allocated by the plan; and it is highly debatable how far such an exercise would have succeeded. One means by which it might have been tried would have been to impose a tax on land values. But such a proposal would almost certainly have been opposed strongly by the Irish parliament — especially the upper chamber, which was so constituted as to give a large representation to the landed classes. It is much more likely that, rather than accept a steep increase in direct taxes, the Irish parliament — reasoning that its problems did not arise from any inherently Irish cause — would have fought to reduce Ireland's imperial contribution. Moreover, the possibility of such a situation arising would have been enhanced by the emergence of problems relating to the payment of Ireland's imperial contribution which Gladstone failed to allow for in the haste with which his Irish plan was formulated. For example, the fact that Ireland would be credited with revenues from goods consumed in Great Britain was not the guarantee for the payment of Ireland's imperial contribution that Gladstone seems to have assumed. Indeed, under the bonding system the British trader could have paid these duties in Great Britain, and, as Nationalists accepted in 1893, any change in the law intended to ensure that the Irish parliament received these duties would meet with fierce British resistance. Relatedly, equally serious problems were likely to arise from the desire to ensure the fiscal unity of Great Britain and Ireland by keeping customs and excise duties under imperial control.[32] These were pointed out by Harcourt in 1893 in a searching analysis of the financial provisions of the second Home Rule bill.

It is important to note that, unlike many critics of Gladstone's views on Irish finance, Harcourt did not accept that these views proposed an excessive imperial contribution being paid by Ireland and that a financial crisis for the Irish government would, on that account, result. He was concerned mainly with demonstrating how the imperial parliament's control of Irish customs and excise duties would impair the Irish parliament's financial autonomy and so perpetuate discord between Great Britain and Ireland. For example, Harcourt argued that a lowering of the duties on spirits, porter and tobacco would mean that the Irish government, being legally compelled to meet its imperial obligations, would have to make up the revenue lost by raising the relatively small direct taxation under her control, and this despite the fact that it was not necessitated by Irish needs. On the other hand, if, for example, the duty on spirits was raised significantly, the resultant increase of revenue would disturb the equilibrium of the Irish budget, which would be 'adjusted according to . . . [Irish] wants, on the basis of existing taxes'. Moreover, the disposal of this windfall could only be effected by reducing direct taxation, as indirect taxation would be under Westminster's control; and if direct taxation were reduced, it would benefit the wealthy classes at the expense of products consumed by the whole community. Thus the Irish would complain

> of any dealing on our part with indirect taxation, because it of necessity affects their direct taxation. . . . The taxation, which is supposed to be under their control . . . will in fact compulsorily vary inversely as the British policy in respect of indirect taxation. So far, therefore, from the bill giving to the Irish financial autonomy, they will be more at the mercy of English finance than ever. The distinction between British interests and Irish interests as regards taxation will be accentuated and exaggerated, and the British budget will be a perpetual battle-field between the two nations.[33]

Clearly, in the light of the problems that could be expected to arise over questions of taxation, it is unlikely that Gladstone's plan for Irish autonomy would have provided a final settlement of the Irish question. Moreover, the problem of taxation was bound up with the equally intractable problem of Irish representation at Westminster.

TAXATION AND IMPERIAL REPRESENTATION

Initially the idea of getting rid of the Irish from Westminster was the most attractive feature of the Home Rule scheme for nearly all members of the cabinet. Both Harcourt and Morley were enthusiastically in favour of it, as were Lords Spencer, Granville and Kimberley. Gladstone, though he had an open mind on the subject at the beginning of February, had also come down in favour of exclusion by mid-March. However, once it was decided that Ireland was to pay an imperial contribution, the question of Irish taxation without representation immediately came to the fore. The issue as it faced the cabinet was well summarised by Edward Hamilton:

> If you give the Irishmen absolute fiscal freedom, you accentuate the idea that legislative independence means separation to all intents and purposes. If on the other hand you keep the customs in the hands of the imperial parliament, you must also retain the Irish representation in the parliament. Representation must go hand-in-hand with taxation — and yet the idea of getting rid of the Irishmen commends itself to many to whom [imperial] federation pure and simple is a bug-bear.

It quickly became clear, moreover, that this was a question of great political importance. Following Gladstone's speech introducing the bill, the *Pall Mall Gazette* published a survey of press opinion for and against the bill, with particular reference to the question of Irish representation at Westminster. The survey covered all of the leading newspapers in Great Britain that had had time to react to Gladstone's bill, and its most significant finding was the number of Liberal press organs that opposed Home Rule on this issue, particularly in Scotland, where Liberal support was strongest. Of the eight most important

Scottish newspapers, only one was in favour of excluding the Irish from the imperial parliament, while two Tory and no less than five Liberal papers opposed it. In the English provinces and Wales Liberal press reaction showed a marked division of opinion on the subject.[34]

The problem was how to divide imperial from non-imperial issues. Gladstone declared that he was of the opinion that the distinction between the two could not be drawn, but that it had been made in the bill. He continued:'This house is not merely a legislative house; it is a house controlling the executive; and when you come to the control of the executive your distinction between imperial and non-imperial subjects totally breaks down.' Gladstone cited the example of Irish M.P.s coming to Westminster to take part in a discussion on foreign policy, and being thereby entitled to vote on a motion for the dismissal of a foreign minster, which, if successful, would have the effect of bringing down the entire government. Since that government would also have been charged with the affairs of England and Scotland, its removal by a vote of Irish representatives would make impossible, in practice, the distinction between imperial and non-imperial affairs. Gladstone therefore concluded: 'I arrive at the next conclusion — that Irish members and Irish peers cannot, if a domestic legislature be given to Ireland, justly retain a seat in the parliament at Westminster.'[35]

Personally he was of the opinion, supported no doubt by the fact that Parnelllites were willing to accept exclusion, that the troubled history of a country like Ireland 'must throw back the mind of a people upon itself and its own concerns', and thus the Irish would concentrate primarily on 'the management of Irish affairs'. But the necessity of finding a solution to this problem was great, and was given point when Joseph Chamberlain, who had resigned from the cabinet partly on this question, made it known that if the Irish were retained in the imperial parliament, he would vote for the second reading of the Home Rule bill. With much truth Gladstone wrote to Lord Granville that while the exclusion of the Irish was the most enthusiastic point of agreement on Home Rule in the cabinet, it was also the point most likely to ensure the 'shipwreck' of the Home Rule scheme in parliament if it was insisted on. The bill as it was printed did in fact allow for the Irish to be represented at Westminster in certain circumstances: if any alterations in the Government of Ireland Act were to be made on which there had not been previous agreements between the two legislatures. Moreover, although the Irish parliament would not have power over certain subjects that were reserved to Westminster, the addresses of the Irish parliament on such subjects might, if reasonable, 'have a great deal of influence'.[36] However, since these forms of connection between the two parliaments were deemed insufficient, more tangible relations had to be established.

Gladstone ruled out the simple retention of the existing Irish M.P.s and peers at Westminster as 'unsafe', or a reduced representation of such M.P.s and peers, as this would require new legislation to bring it into effect. Federation to include Scotland and Wales as well as Ireland was ruled out because it would mean the withdrawal of his Home Rule bill, and to this 'I do not see my way'. Any further changes that were to be made had to be such as 'would not alter the principle of the bill, nor extensively modify its framework'. Both on principle 'and as a matter of policy', Gladstone was prepared to allow the Irish the right of attendance in the imperial parliament 'on any question *altering* taxation for Ireland'; and while the possibility existed that the Irish might intrigue with others to overthrow a ministry on the budget, it was not probable: only two ministries since the Union had been overthrown on budgets, and the ministry of the day 'would have full opportunity of forecasting consequences in determining on its finance'. Apart from the question of representation with regard to taxation, there remained other subjects on which the Irish might have a right to attend at Westminster, such as matters relating to the crown and defence, foreign and colonial relations, and subjects like patents and copyrights which were reserved on practical grounds. On the crown and defence Gladstone did not see how the bill could be modified to advantage; and while it might be possible for provision to be made in the Home Rule act for 'regular communications between the British and Irish executives' on the subjects of foreign and colonial relations and patents and copyrights — similar to the way in which foreign relations were managed between Sweden and Norway — he did not see that much could be effected in that direction, especially since it would fail to satisfy the 'sentiment' for manifest symbols of imperial unity.[37]

A more hopeful idea, Gladstone thought, would be to have a standing committee or delegation, to meet periodically during the Westminster parliamentary session, composed of representatives from both orders of the Irish assembly and both houses of the imperial parliament, in the proportion of 1 to 2. Such a committee would have power to report and make recommendations upon any of the subjects reserved under the Government of Ireland Act; it would largely satisfy the craving for symbols of imperial unity and would have 'no dangerous connection under any ordinary circumstances' with the responsibility or stability of ministries. Gladstone subsequently recommended this scheme to the cabinet on 8 May and included it in his speech on the second reading of the Home Rule bill on 10 May. Given the need to eliminate Irish interference in British affairs, and the equally important necessity of having visible constitutional links between the Irish and British parliaments, it is likely that this scheme was the only one which could hope to work, though for it to have done so would have required, as a recent commentator puts it, 'a great deal of good will and mutual forbearance'.[38]

However, as a result of the misunderstanding between Gladstone and Chamberlain on the kind of representation Ireland was to have at Westminster,[39] the latter did not support the second reading of the bill and was thereby instrumental in causing its defeat. Yet the defeat of the bill was in itself an important factor in determining the nature of the Liberal contribution to Home Rule nationalism. Driven by the force of events in Ireland, Gladstone saw his Home Rule scheme as constituting the basis of a solution to the Irish question. Had it passed beyond the second reading, the process of debate and evolution in committee would, it is reasonable to assume, have produced some significant changes, particularly with reference to the financial basis of the scheme. However, the defeat of the bill in June 1886 ended the process of debate and evolution, and consequently the bill as it stood became the basis for discussion of the Home Rule question thereafter. But, as we have seen, it was in many respects far from being an adequate measure. In fact it contained enough faults to cast doubts on the extent to which the very concept of Home Rule nationalism, that is, the attempt to satisfy Irish nationalist sentiment by legislative independence within the overall sovereignty of Westminster, was viable.

THE LAND PURCHASE BILL

As Gladstone emphasised during the debate on his Irish bills in 1886, 'the aim and end of all our endeavours' was not simply for its own sake the contentment of the Irish people, but the social order of the country: 'That is the first, the greatest, the most sacred and the most necessary aim of every government that knows its duty.' It was this aim which necessitated a land purchase bill large enough to solve effectively, once and for all, the problem of agrarian violence in Ireland — a necessary condition if his Home Rule bill was to have any chance of success. This was a realisation born both of the unrest attending the fall in Irish agricultural prices in the period 1885-6 and of the urgent pleadings of both Irish Nationalists and Unionists. Consequently Gladstone, normally a champion of economy in public expenditure, wrote in the following terms to Sir William Harcourt, also a champion of economy:

> It is plain to me that if we are to cherish a rational hope of dealing effectively with the huge mass of the Irish question, we must found ourselves on an operation as to land, calculated on a scale which will exceed *any* former transaction.
>
> I am the last to desire any extension of the demands on our financial strength. But I am morally certain that it is only by exerting *to the utmost* our financial strength (not mainly by expenditure but as credit) on behalf of Ireland, that we can hope to sustain the burden of an adequate land measure — while without an adequate land measure, we cannot either establish social order, or face the question of Irish government.[40]

Gladstone's land bill was thus intended not simply as an ancillary measure to the Home Rule bill but as a vitally important and integral element of the scheme for Ireland as a whole. This was true not only in the sense most often employed by Gladstone, that agrarian peace would be essential to the proper functioning of the Irish parliament, but in an operational sense as well: if a really extensive land measure was to be enacted, it would require a local authority in Ireland actually to put the scheme into effect and carry out its day-to-day operation, and to provide security for the English money and credit lent to finance the scheme: 'The Irish revenues are the only collateral security that can be obtained for loans of English money, and Irish revenues are only available for the purpose on the establishment of an Irish parliament.' Moreover, as Lord Thring, the chief draftsman of Gladstone's Irish bills, was to point out, unlike Lord Ashbourne's land act of 1885, which had the highly undesirable effect of making the British government the actual mortgagee of Irish land by lending money directly to the tenant and exacting a debt 'which the tenant is unwilling to pay as being due to what he calls an alien government', Gladstone's bill removed this problem. The Irish government, and not the British, would become the virtual landlord:

> The substance is to interpose the Irish government between the tenant and the English mortgagee, and to make the loans general charges on the whole of the Irish government revenues as paid into the hands of the imperial receiver. . . . It would be the interest of Ireland that the annuities due from the tenants should be regularly paid, as, subject to the prior charge of the imperial exchequer, they would form part of the Irish revenues.

In effect, the Irish government would become, as Edward Hamilton described it, a 'buffer' between the Irish tenants and the British government, charged with the responsibility of ensuring that tenant annuities were paid, with all that that might imply. Gladstone could thus rightly inform the House of Commons, when introducing the land bill, that it would, 'by building upon the responsibility of the Irish state authority . . . not increase, but will greatly diminish the public risk. . . . This bill, if passed . . . will be a diminution of public responsibility.'[41]

The importance Gladstone attached to the connection between his land and Home Rule bills is important to emphasise, given the claim made by John Vincent that the land bill was a 'dummy'. Vincent argues that two such complex measures as Gladstone's Irish bills could not possibly have passed within one parliamentary session 'merely on grounds of time'; and he suggests strongly that until 12 March 1886 Gladstone was keen to implement his land bill only, 'while the bait of Home Rule tomorrow kept the Parnellites in tow'. This situation changed, he contends, when, at a cabinet meeting on 13 March 1886 which met to discuss Gladstone's land proposals, Joseph Chamberlain 'switched the business of the meeting by raising the question of Home Rule'. The result was to commit the cabinet to 'Home Rule in principle rather than as a practical and immediate legislative commitment'. In fact, Vincent argues, the land bill retained its priority until Chamberlain's resignation:

> It was Chamberlain's resignation [on 26 March] which made Home Rule the central issue and which created a situation to which Gladstone had to respond. The unfavourable parliamentary reaction to the land bill in April was its *coup de grace*, but the land bill had already fallen from first to second place by the time of the cabinet of 29 March. Gladstone began March 1886 as a discreet, possibly procrastinating Home Ruler who was anxious to legislate on Irish land while avoiding radical overtones; he ended the month as an unenthusiastic land reformer whose chief immediate commitment was to Home Rule. The details are uncertain but it is likely that 13 March 1886 was the point at which history jumped from one set of tracks to another.

Vincent's argument, however, is weak in several respects. Not only is it not supported by the foregoing description of the vital connection between the land and Home Rule bills, but Gladstone made it clear on 2 February 1886 that his land scheme would be merely part of a much larger Irish plan: 'I think it [the land issue] has a logical priority, but that practically it is one with the other great members of the trilogy, social order and autonomy.' Accordingly on 12 February he informed his son Henry: 'I have framed a plan for the land and ... finance of what must be a very large transaction. ... Unless these portions of anything we attempt are sound ... we cannot hope to succeed.'[42] In this respect it is worth noting that the imperial receiver, who was to take charge of Irish government finances and ensure that Ireland's imperial contribution was paid, was to be appointed under the land purchase bill, and that during February and early March 1886, while primacy was being given to the construction of the land purchase bill, many important elements of the Home Rule bill were also under discussion with leading cabinet members such as Morley, Harcourt and Granville.

Given Lord Welby's admission that when Gladstone took office there were no materials in government departments with which to begin the immediate construction of an 'effective' Home Rule measure, it is not surprising that he should begin work on his Irish plan by dealing with the land question — a subject which he felt most competent to deal with. But that his land bill would proceed in conjunction with a Home Rule bill there can be no doubt. Indeed, Gladstone's proposals regarding the land purchase scheme refer specifically to 'the Irish state authority' as the body that would purchase estates and put the land scheme into operation. Certainly Joseph Chamberlain, on seeing these proposals at the cabinet meeting of 13 March 1886, recognised immediately their vital connection with Gladstone's Home Rule plan: 'I contended that it was impossible to judge this scheme fairly without knowing what were to be the provisions of the Home Rule bill which was to accompany it. Upon the constitution of the new local authority would largely depend the security [for the money advanced to implement the land purchase scheme].' Thus Vincent's argument that Chamberlain 'switched the business of the meeting' to Home Rule — implying a sharp distinction between discussion of the land and Home Rule bills — is not an accurate description of what occurred. In fact, once Gladstone outlined his Home Rule proposals, debate continued on both the land and Home Rule issues.[43] The most that can be said for Chamberlain's actions at this meeting is that they forced Gladstone to elaborate on his Home Rule proposals earlier than he intended. This is not to say that Gladstone was not faced with a problem regarding the implementation of his Irish bills, but that problem was not one of alternatives — either to implement a land *or* Home Rule bill — but of procedure: how was his vast and complex Irish plan to be introduced so as to secure its enactment?

It was apparent early in March that its introduction in one piece was impractical; and Edward Hamilton noted disapprovingly on 9 March that Gladstone intended to 'expound' the policy in 'piecemeal fashion'. In the event he was to introduce the Home Rule bill first; however, what evidence exists for the reasons behind this decision does not support Vincent's claim that it was determined by Chamberlain's resignation. Indeed, the introduction 'without delay' of his Home Rule bill was urged on Gladstone by Harcourt on 7 March 1886. But the most influential communication in this respect came on 23 March from Gladstone's close adviser on Irish affairs, Henry Labouchere, who assured him that by introducing the Home Rule bill first he would succeed in enacting his Irish plan.[44] But what of Vincent's argument that the parliamentary timetable did not allow of both Gladstone's bills being passed in one session?

In fact this was not the insurmountable obstacle it might have seemed. For instance, the Ashbourne act of 1885 took but a matter of weeks to enact: introduced on 17 July, shortly after Lord Salisbury's ministry took office, it received the royal assent on 14 August. Of course, some special factors attended its enactment. Being in a minority, the Tories had only taken office on the condition that the Liberals would not obstruct the government's 'vital' work. Moreover, being a Conservative measure, the Ashbourne act had virtually automatic support from the House of Lords. Nevertheless, some special factors also attended Gladstone's land purchase bill. As Vincent admits, there was considerable support among Tories and Whigs for a comprehensive land purchase scheme. Moreover, the reaction of the Irish landlords' political organisation, the Irish Loyal and Patriotic Union, to the land purchase bill was — judged by the standard of their often hysterical anti-Home Rule propaganda — conciliatory and highly constructive. Thus, had a situation obtained where Gladstone's Home Rule bill was going to be approved by parliament,[45] it is unlikely that the passage of the land purchase bill — with its promise of saving the landlords from being 'plundered' by a Dublin parliament — would have been obstructed. At any rate, it is clear that Gladstone did not regard the parliamentary timetable as posing a serious problem to the implementation of his Irish plan.

While it is true that the land bill was withdrawn shortly after its introduction, it is, nevertheless, a popular misconception that

Gladstone had thereby abandoned it. The land bill's with-drawal was a result not only of the adverse political reaction it provoked but also of its vital connection with the Home Rule bill and its deteriorating fortunes in the period from April to June 1886. Gladstone proposed that if the Home Rule bill passed its second reading, he would not proceed further with it for the rest of that parliamentary session. Instead he would wind up the 'ordinary business' of the session and reassemble parliament 'at an early date' to deal with the Home Rule bill. In this context the land purchase bill would also be withdrawn and reintro-duced when the Home Rule bill 'is on the orders of the day with a view to immediate prosecution through its stages'[46] Clearly, then, Gladstone was prepared to proceed with his land purchase bill despite the hostility it provoked — much of which came from Liberals. But why was the bill so regarded, and what influences determined its content?

Difficult as the task of settling on an adequate land bill was, Gladstone was not without advice on the problem once it became widely known that he was taking up the Home Rule question; and as he felt personally most competent in dealing with the subjects of Irish land and finance, it was these aspects of the Irish question that he tackled first.[47] By far the most influential article on the Irish land problem was published by *The Statist* in January 1886, under the signature 'Economist', and was apparently written by Robert Giffen.

Giffen's solution to the land question involved buying out every Irish landlord by giving him government stock equivalent to twenty years' purchase of the existing judicial rents; by giving the land free to the existing occupiers subject only to a rent-charge of one-half or two-thirds of the judicial rents, payable to new local authorities in Ireland to be set up simultaneously with the implementation of the scheme; and by relieving the imperial exchequer of all payments then made out of it in connection with the local government of Ireland. In sum:

> The plan is...to throw the cost of local government in Ireland upon Irish resources exclusively, and to give the Irish people the rents of the country for the purpose of conducting it. The conflict between landlord and tenant would thus be at an end. We need no longer fear that if we give Ireland Home Rule the property of the landlords would be confiscated.

Giffen took the rent of Ireland 'settled judicially' at roughly £8,000,000, and the government stock to be given in exchange at twenty years' purchase, to be £160,000,000, involving an annual charge of £4,800,000 upon the imperial exchequer. Currently £4,000,000 was being spent on Irish local government alone, 'for law, prisons, police, education and such matters', exclusive of the outlay for the army in Ireland, the collection of revenue 'and other imperial matters which would still remain imperial'.

The position of the tenants would be that whereas they currently paid £8,000,000, they would, under the new arrangements, pay only from £4,000,000 to £5,500,000. This reduction was justified in order to allow for the variation in the prices of agricultural products which had upset the payment of judicial rents: the agricultural depression had shown the impossibility of fixing rents for fifteen years by external authority because tenants could not pay even judicial rents when prices fell. In future the rent-charge would be fixed in relation to the 'average changes in the prices of agricultural products'. If his plan was to be put into effect, Giffen argued that the new Irish local authorities would have to be their own rent-charge collectors and would thus need to have control of the police.[48]

Giffen's article was important in more respects than one: it not only recognised in a complementary way the intimate connection between the land and national questions, but provided a scheme whereby the land question could be solved with a minimum of expense to the imperial exchequer, and on the responsibility of Irish local authorities rather than Westminster. Irish reaction to the article was enthusiastic. Michael Davitt, while reserving judgment on some aspects, recommended its leading features to Gladstone as a basis on which to 'mould his legislation'. Similarly, Parnell, while not pledging himself to its details, recommended its principal tenet — the wholesale buying out of the landlords — to parliament. A similar view was taken by the *Freeman's Journal*, and by Archbishop Croke of Cashel, described by Davitt as 'next to the Irish leader the most influential man in Ireland'. Furthermore, the Catholic hierarchy as a whole endorsed the principle of the scheme in a letter to Gladstone on 17 February 1886. In England its most notable support came in the form of an article in the February issue of the *Fortnightly Review* by Joseph Chamberlain.[49]

Encouraged by the support his article received, Giffen expanded further on his ideas: while £8,000,000 was roughly correct, the exact figure of the effective rent the landlord had to sell could only be determined after an analysis of the conditions of past valuations and methods of fixing judicial rents in different localities. Similarly, the twenty years' purchase, he suggested, was only a provisional estimate, though it could be justified by the need 'to show that the scheme was practicable even if the landlords got very good terms'. More significantly, he emphasised the soundness of his proposal to finance the internal administration of Ireland by providing local authorities with the rent-charge accruing from buying out the landlords instead of contributions from the imperial exchequer. This plan, he admitted, would still leave the imperial exchequer liable for a debt of £800,000 in regard to Irish administration, but there would be no great concession involved, given that Ireland paid twice as much in income tax than she ought to. It is reasonable to assume that Gladstone, pitifully short of information on which to build his Irish scheme, and regarding Giffen as 'a very high authority on financial questions',[50] would have been influenced by his articles. Certainly one of the more important elements of Gladstone's Irish plan — the partial financing of Home Rule with commissions on rental receipts drawn from a comprehensive solution of the land question — would seem to have been inspired by the widely praised ideas sketched out by Giffen.

However, an equally important source of information would have been the communications Gladstone received from Irish landlords on the subject of Irish land reform, through the agency of Lord Hartington. Hartington's man in Ireland, William Currey, had seen several leading landlords, including T. C. Trench, W. R. Meade, Sampson French, T. Hare, J. Penrose Fitzgerald, H. H. Townsend, Sir Richard Keane, Major Robert Perceval-Maxwell, Percy Smith and Sir Robert Paul. In a letter addressed to Hartington, which was forwarded to Gladstone, Currey enclosed notes he had taken of conferences with this group and other landlords and declared that the general view was that twenty years' purchase of the judicial rental would be acceptable if land purchase became inevitable, and that purchase should be compulsory. Moreover, they all agreed that whether many landlords would remain in Ireland or not would depend mainly on whether the imperial government still maintained its hold over the country, especially over the police, magistracy and judicial administration, so as to effectively secure order and liberty. Currey himself thought that where holdings were large they would prosper, but a small holding with no manufacturing industry to supplement it would decline over the years, and unless the 'rent-charge is redeemed it would become impossible to collect'. Major Perceval-Maxwell of Downpatrick did not think that compulsory purchase was possible without attendant revolution, but that twenty to twenty-five years' purchase 'would do'. H. H. Townsend favoured twenty years' purchase of judicial rents, but thought that there should only be a partial buying out of landlords so as to 'stop them leaving the country'. Sir Robert Paul disapproved of compulsory purchase as 'unconstitutional', but if it was to come, he would require twenty-five years' purchase of Griffith's valuation, or twenty of the gross judicial rental. In so far as these views represented the most authoritative statement obtainable by Gladstone of the opinions of the class whom his land scheme was intended to benefit, their impression on him would have been strong, and would have strengthened the view he had already formed that Irish landlords as a whole would welcome his Irish bills. Early in February he informed Harcourt: 'There is before us the possibility, even the likelihood of a vast issue of consols to those now holders of land.' With the prospect, or rather Gladstone's belief that the prospect existed, of a massive sale of land by Irish landlords, the question of how much money should be advanced for this purpose became the most immediate issue facing the cabinet in discussing the land purchase bill. Gladstone had begun his exploration of the subject by taking net receipts rather than the judicial rental as the basis on which to found his land measure, a course which was felt by other cabinet members to be unrealistic, as the judicial rent was the 'ordinary basis' on which to give so many years' purchase. It was a view that Gladstone soon came to accept also.[51] But on the amount to be allocated to effect the expected massive transfer of land, considerable division of opinion began to emerge in the cabinet.

In a memorandum dated 20 March 1886 Gladstone put the view that £60,000,000, rather than the previously discussed £120,000,000, would be a better amount to begin the process of land purchase. It might be less shocking to opponents of the measure and more acceptable to Liberal opinion; and it seemed a more sensible sum, given the fact that the whole Irish scheme was still tentative and could not be certain of any operation at all: if the act worked well, parliament would still be free to enlarge it. Again, the smaller sum might have the effect of bringing round those who had doubts about the bill in general. Support for this proposed course of action came from Granville, who noted: 'Of those who are really anxious to sell, the greater number will believe that by early applications they will secure their object.' Opposition, however, came from both Lord Spencer and Harcourt. Spencer complained: 'The bill as originally intended will carry an idea of thoroughness which the new proposal would not do, and I cannot say I at all like the proposed change.' Spencer was also optimistically of the view that only 'one-fifth of the landlords would not apply for various reasons to be bought up'. John Morley's opinion was more neutral. He accepted Gladstone's view of the tactical advantages to be gained by the reduction of the sum proposed, and while he accepted Spencer's point about the need for 'finality', he believed this was secured by the fact that parliament could vote additional sums if the scheme worked well. Consequently Gladstone decided on 22 March that 'Cutting down the figure in the land bill will be a good parliamentary measure quite apart from difficulties with reluctant colleagues.' It is probable that he was influenced by the strong objections that were being voiced against the land bill even then. Subsequently it was decided that the sum of £50,000,000 in the form of imperial credit would be provided in the years 1887–90. Once the amount to be laid out on the scheme had been established, the important question of security for this extension of imperial credit immediately arose. It has been pointed out that under the financial clauses of the land bill all Irish revenues were to be collected into the hands of an imperial receiver, whose function would be to discharge all Ireland's imperial debts before Irish needs were attended to. However, it will also be seen that once the Irish administration had fulfilled its imperial charges, the amount of revenue it would have on hand to carry on the government of Ireland would be largely determined by the amount of rental receipts that would accrue from tenants buying their holdings, and that without these receipts the Irish government would practically have a deficit.[52] The clauses dealing with this part of Gladstone's Irish scheme caused serious misgivings in cabinet. The question was: would the Irish administration be able to collect rents?

Unlike Robert Giffen, Gladstone did not envisage a massive reduction in the amount of rent paid by tenants purchasing their holdings. He intended that landlords generally would receive twenty years' purchase of the *net* rental and that tenants would pay an equivalent amount. Thus, he argued, on an estate with a gross rental of £1,200 and with outgoings fixed at 20 per cent, or £240, the landlord would receive £960. However, the corresponding reduction on the gross rental involved for tenants buying their holdings would be reduced by their liability as owners for the 'half-rates' previously paid by the landlord. As for the Irish government, it would be represented by a 'state authority' that would collect rents and augment government funds by retaining 18 per cent, or £192 less £19 collection costs of the £960 received from the tenants. However, the point that raised most concern in the cabinet was the relatively small reduction on the existing gross rental that the tenants would obtain. In Gladstone's example, a saving of only £240 for all the tenants of an estate, plus their becoming liable for the total payment of poor rates, when the fall of agricultural prices had already made impossible the payment of existing rents, did not augur well for the success of the bill. When this section of the land bill was made known to the cabinet much disquiet prevailed. It was, moreover, compounded when at the same time a letter appeared in *The Times* from the economist Sir James Caird to the effect that, owing to the agricultural crisis, five-sixths of Irish land could pay no rent. Caird divided Irish land into two classes:

Of the first class there are 548,000 holdings averaging £6 each; of the second class there are 121,000 holdings averaging £58 each. The rent payable by the first class is £3,572,000 and by the second class £6,845,000. Five-sixths of the Irish tenants thus pay about one-third of the total rental, and one-sixth pay nearly two-thirds. . . . If the present prices of agricultural produce continue to decline I should fear that from the land held by the large body of poor farmers in Ireland any economical rent has for the present disappeared. A purchase of it at any price would therefore be certain loss.

As for the good land, it was held by 'strong farmers'; they were prosperous, well able to take care of themselves, and thus there was no need to buy the good land, though if it was to be bought, the current agricultural crisis meant that the risk of loss would be present here too. In an editorial based on Caird's article *The Times* declared: 'Any capital invested in buying out the landlords must be regarded as thrown away.'[53]

Taken together, the relative smallness of the rent reduction envisaged by Gladstone and the view of the Irish land question presented by Caird gave a legitimate cause for concern. Moreover, this concern would have been intensified by the process by which it was proposed to transfer the land from owners to tenants. Apart from tenancies rented at £4 and under, and land in the congested districts of the west, the tenants were to become owners if the landlord chose to sell. In other words, while the landlord had a voluntary option of whether to sell or not, if he did so, the tenants were to be compelled to buy their holdings. The reasoning behind this provision was to obviate what was considered to be the chief obstacle to all previous land schemes — securing the assent of the tenants. Moreover, compulsion was considered as acceptable for another reason: 'The tenants need not be consulted, as the purchase, if completed, will necessarily better their conditions.' As will be seen in Chapter 4, however, this view was not widely shared in Ireland. Yet it is worth pointing out that Gladstone had not originally intended that the Irish tenants should be compelled to purchase their holdings. In a cabinet memorandum written on 13 March 1886 he asked the questions:

Are we bound in honour or policy to do more than give to the landlords of Ireland fair optional terms of withdrawal from their position? Why should we not do this, and having done this, leave the land question to Ireland herself?

However, feeling was strong in the cabinet against this course of action. Lord Spencer, in particular, felt strongly that the omission to provide for the conversion of the tenantry into proprietors was a serious 'blot' on Gladstone's land proposals. Edward Hamilton, who shared the views of those who favoured compulsion, described their argument as follows:

> One of the main pleas for so revolutionary a measure as that of expropriation [given the voluntary option for landlords, this was surely an exaggerated description of the land bill] is to create a peasant proprietary which will instil into the minds of the masses a sense of property and a sense of respect for property; and I do not believe that parliament will be content to commit this task to the discretion of the Irish authority. Parliament will insist on its being ensured; and I do not think that provision to secure this will greatly enhance the complication of the measure. Moreover, the tenant cannot object to being turned into a landlord if the whole of the purchase money is found for him in return for his paying an annuity of a considerably less amount than his present rent for a certain number of years.

Gladstone, apparently, soon came to accept this view also: at a cabinet meeting on 15 March 1886 he 'agreed to provide in his [land] scheme for the re-sale of land by the Irish authority to the tenants'. Nevertheless, there were also those in the cabinet whose view of this concession, as of the land scheme as a whole, was quite the opposite of those favouring compulsion. G. O. Trevelyan, who was to resign with Joseph Chamberlain from the government on the Home Rule issue, declared the whole financial plan of the Home Rule scheme to be

> an act of lunacy. . . . The financial proposals . . . must break down. It is admitted that the Irish authority would have a deficit without the aid of rental receipts; and these will become impossible to collect. An Irish tenant will never be content with a reduction such as the commission of his rent into an annuity for a certain number of years will secure to him. Many tenants can pay nothing — an admission actually made by *The Times* today, in consequence of the great fall in agricultural products.

Even Sir Robert Hamilton, a keen Home Ruler and Under-Secretary at Dublin Castle, was convinced that Gladstone had not made out his balance-sheet on a sufficiently favourable basis: 'The Irish authority would never be able to collect rents, and if it could it would be without receipts for some time to come.' The fearful consequences of such a situation were spelled out by Joseph Chamberlain in a letter to Gladstone offering his resignation from the government:

> This scheme while contemplating only a trifling reduction in the judicial rents fixed before the recent fall in prices would commit the British taxpayer to tremendous obligations, accompanied in my opinion with serious risk of ultimate loss.
>
> The greater part of the land of Ireland would be handed over to a new Irish elective authority who would thus be at once the landlords and the delegates of the Irish tenants. I fear that these two capacities would be found inconsistent and that the tenants, unable or unwilling to pay the rents demanded, would speedily elect an authority pledged to give them relief and to seek to recoup itself by an early repudiation of what would be described as the English tribute.

Together with the heavy imperial charges imposed on Ireland, these liabilities would be far too burdensome for such a poor country, and their fulfilment by the Irish legislature could only be enforced by military intervention by the imperial parliament.[54]

It might be argued that Chamberlain's criticisms were influenced both by his personal antagonism to Gladstone and his strenuous opposition to Home Rule. Nevertheless, these considerations should not disguise the sincerity of his views, particularly on the financial basis of Gladstone's Irish scheme. It should be borne in mind that when Gladstone suggested he draw up a plan for Irish land purchase in February 1886, an important feature of this plan, considered crucial to its viability, was a provision providing for 'judicial rents to be reduced at once by ... twenty-eight per cent'. Gladstone, however, while familiar with Chamberlain's scheme — as he undoubtedly was with the work of Robert Giffen, who also argued that an extensive solution to the land question could only be based on a large reduction in existing judicial rents — was not prepared to take this course of action. His views on the subject are best expressed in his reply to the warnings of Sir James Caird in *The Times* against any plan of Irish land purchase. Gladstone rejected Caird's claims as to the extent to which Irish land was incapable of yielding rent, and while admitting that a class of estates such as Caird described did exist, he felt that such cases were 'exceptional'. He declared that, with regard to these, the Land Commission to be set up under the land purchase act would be empowered to refuse an application for purchase if it thought it inequitable that 'the state authority should be required to buy an estate at the price laid down in the act'. However, given the extent of the apprehension about the viability of the land purchase scheme, it is not surprising that Gladstone's reply to Caird failed to mobilise opinion behind the measure. Moreover, not only did fears about its workability fuel the belief that British money laid out to finance its operation would be lost, but the impression was assiduously created that this money was to be expended to support an idle clique of Irish landlords. As John Morley recorded, 'Vivid pictures were drawn of a train of railway trucks two miles long, loaded with millions of bright sovereigns, all travelling from the British son of toil to the pocket of the idle Irish landlord.'[55]

Given the weight of opinion against it from both pro- and anti-Home Rule quarters, it is not surprising that Gladstone decided to withdraw his land bill shortly after its introduction. He had, in his highly optimistic frame of mind, hoped that it would meet with immediate approval from the Irish landlords. Just a week after it had been first circulated, and before any detailed consideration could be given to it, Gladstone was complaining that it was regrettable that while sands were 'running out in the hour-glass, the Irish landlords have yet given no indication of a desire to accept a proposal framed in a spirit of the utmost allowable regard to their apprehensions and their interests'.[56] Yet while he quickly withdrew the land purchase bill, its withdrawal, as we have noted, was intended to be temporary: Gladstone planned to reintroduce it following the second reading of his Home Rule bill.

Political Opinion and the Home Rule Scheme:
The Nationalist and Unionist Reaction

NATIONALISTS AND THE HOME RULE SCHEME

WE HAVE seen in the preceding chapter that when Gladstone set about formulating his Home Rule scheme he took steps to gauge Nationalist opinion as to the general nature of an acceptable plan, and that while the bill was taking specific form he maintained contact with Nationalists chiefly through John Morley's discussions with Parnell. The plan when it emerged, however, did not meet with an enthusiastic welcome from leading Nationalists. Parnell, it has been seen, had already strongly criticised the financial scheme of the bill. The first indication he was given of the true extent of the Home Rule bill was just a few hours before its introduction in the House of Commons, and with Morley's permission he shared his knowledge with a number of leading Nationalists, including Justin McCarthy, J. J. O'Kelly, Thomas Sexton, John Dillon, E. D. Gray, T. P. O'Connor, T. M. Healy and Michael Davitt.[1]

Their reaction to the scheme was later to be a subject of some dispute during the wrangles of the party split in 1890. Nevertheless, the accounts given then provide the fullest description of leading party opinion. At a meeting of the central branch of the National League in Dublin on 4 December 1890 Parnell gave his account of what took place when he informed his colleagues of the nature of the Home Rule bill:

> Here is the bill. It is a parliamentary hit, it is nothing more. I have been told today by Mr Gladstone that it is for us to take or reject that bill, and if we undertake the responsibility of leaving it, he will make a statement in the House of Commons

tonight saying he can do no more, and that the responsibility and want of solution for the Irish question must rest upon us. . . . Here is the bill with all its defects, absence of sufficient control of the police; will you take it or will you leave it? . . . And my colleagues said to me that they would accept it *pro tanto*, reserving for committee the right of enforcing and, if necessary, reconsidering their position with regard to these important questions.

T. M. Healy, however, disputed Parnell's version of events and claimed that he had virtually curtailed discussion on the bill. According to Healy, cavilling was taking place over details, especially the lack of provision for an Irish custom house. At this Parnell rose and declared that two men — Chamberlain and Trevelyan — had already left the cabinet, and they had the opportunity of wrecking it completely. He also warned: 'It would be a fatal error if we did not close with this offer, and further . . . put it on record at once that this bill is in principle accepted by the Irish Party.'[2]

Of the two accounts, Healy's has the ring of truth. That Parnell was ready to accept a more conservative bill than his colleagues is attested by Morley, who noted his general indifference on most aspects of the Home Rule bill other than finance — even to the extent of apparently being willing to accept an upper chamber nominated by the crown, if need be. During the bill's preparation, however, leading party members were kept virtually in the dark about the form it was taking. T. P. O'Connor notes: 'He [Parnell] never consulted any of his colleagues except individually, and by questions apparently casual, during the consultations that preceded its final shape.' In such a context it was likely that Nationalist expectations would mushroom. Notwithstanding the moderate and limited autonomy that R. Barry O'Brien claimed was acceptable to Irish leaders, the widespread expectation that Gladstone was about to declare publicly his support for Home Rule provoked a meeting of the central branch of the National League in Dublin to demand nothing less than 'such a comprehensive measure as would enable them to take control of the country into their own hands, and allow Ireland to resume her proper place among the nations'.[3]

Parnell himself, moreover, contributed to such expectations.

In a letter to A. J. Kettle on 21 March 1886 he wrote: 'Things
are looking very hopeful here. I have every confidence that
Gladstone's proposals will be very large and that we shall be
able to accept them freely and build up the nation by their
means.' The reality was now very different, and Parnellites were
in the position of either provisionally accepting an inadequate
bill, and the prospect of future satisfactory amendments, or
seeing Home Rule postponed for the foreseeable future.
Ultimately there was little doubt as to their decision. The fullest
account of the factors that weighed with party leaders was provided by Michael Davitt. Parnell, he records, was severely
critical of the financial provisions of the bill, speaking strongly
against them as 'unjust and extortionate', and condemning
Gladstone's refusal to modify them, despite his most strenuous
protests:

> He led us to think that he thought the bill scarcely worth
> acceptance. He favoured, however, the dropping of the land
> settlement part of the ministerial scheme, believing that this
> would be the only way in which the Home Rule part of it
> would stand any chance of passing a second reading. . . .
> The feeling of the meeting was strongly in favour of
> accepting the bill, subject to its improvement in committee, if
> possible. Sentiment rather than the merits of the complicated
> and incongruous character of the proposed legislative body
> weighed with us. It would be something in the nature of a par-
> liament anyhow. Its many obvious defects would give
> reasonable ground for demanding amendments in the near
> future. There was in it a recognition of Ireland's right to
> nationhood, in a cribbed, cabined, and confined kind of way,
> no doubt. But it would be an end to England's rule in
> Ireland's domestic affairs. The detested Dublin Castle
> system, with its 'hacks', renegades, and informers, would dis-
> appear, and the substitute would offer our country a modest
> status of racial self-government among the nations. It would
> stand too, for a victory for the Celt, after his long and
> agonising struggle for national recognition, while the con-
> sideration also weighed that a native government of some
> kind would do more than any other change in the condition of
> the country to stem the fatal tide of emigration. For these and

other reasons it was agreed to accept Gladstone's offer, and to stand by the bargain, bad as it was, should the bill become law.

Healy's recollection supports Davitt's view: 'In those days of 1886 it seemed a mighty great thing to get control of an Irish parliament.' Immediately following Gladstone's speech introducing the Home Rule bill, a full meeting of the Parnellite party convened; general dissatisfaction was expressed by Parnell and others on four points: customs, the imperial contribution, the constabulary, and voting by orders. It was agreed that Parnell should voice these criticisms in his speech on the bill, and that if these issues were resolved in committee, the 'party and Irish people' would accept Gladstone's scheme as a final settlement.[4]

While it is true that Parnell would have settled for a more conservative Irish constitution than his colleagues would have preferred, he was nevertheless very much alive to the fact that unless the financial basis of Home Rule was right the whole experiment would fail: his speech on the bill was intended forcefully to emphasise that point. He prefaced his remarks with the observation that the limitations of the scheme were, to some extent, due to the fact that Gladstone had to 'shape his measure to meet the tremendous opposition which has been invoked against him'; but having declared his sympathetic understanding of Gladstone's difficulties, Parnell launched into an attack on the bill as forceful as that of any Unionist. By keeping control of the customs, he argued, England would retain control of three-fourths of the Irish revenues: 'It would be absolutely as much within your power as it is now, both as regards the original assessment of taxes and the receiving of the money.' With specific reference to the 'free gift' of £1,400,000 that would accrue to Ireland from duties on goods consumed in Britain, he accepted that this sum would indeed be a fair exchange for the surrendering of the customs, were it not for the fact that Ireland would still have to pay £1,000,000 'for the Irish constabulary, over whom we are not to have any sort of control whatever, at all events for the present'. In like manner he criticised Ireland's proposed contribution to imperial expenditure. Parnell emphatically denied that the basis on which Gladstone had assessed this was either just or liberal. In particular his preference for using the property passing under death duties as his chief standard for assessing the relative taxable capacity of Ireland was, Parnell argued, 'the most unfavourable standard' that could have been chosen for Ireland, which was a very poor country. Again, the small surplus on the Irish budget proposed by Gladstone would mean that

> It will be impossible for Ireland to have any credit for floating loans. Irish landlords can now borrow money at a low rate of interest for the improvement of their estates. Irish tenants can borrow money for sanitary purposes within their jurisdiction. All these are very important matters. But we shall have to surrender all of them under . . . [this] . . . scheme . . . and we shall be left with about £400,000 a year.[5]

In other words, Parnell was telling Gladstone that his scheme could not fulfil the Liberal leader's expectations of it; indeed, it would bring about a state of affairs very much worse than that which existed at present. Moreover, the budget of the scheme was based on an estimate 'which necessitates that the consumption of spirits, not only in Ireland, but also in England, should continue at its present high rate, and of course that the duty should be kept as it is now'. Indeed, Parnell continued, on the enactment of Home Rule the Irish legislature would probably wish to pass a law imposing restrictions in regard to 'the sale of strong drink on Sundays as well as on other days', and he hoped to see a reduction in the amount of revenue derived from these duties.[6]

Parnell's implication here was that not only the material, but the moral improvement of the Irish people under Gladstone's scheme would be impossible. He went further and put it that if the proposed imperial contribution was insisted on, the Irish might attempt to repudiate that debt, as had been suggested earlier by G. O. Trevelyan. Consequently it would be unfair to press so hard a bargain; and he reminded Gladstone that the provisions of his plan would have to be seen as just and 'cheerfully accepted by public opinion in Ireland'. To this end, and relying on the recently published work on Irish finance by Robert Giffen, he argued that one-twentieth rather than one-fifteenth of imperial expenditure was a fairer estimate for Ireland. Parnell also claimed that the excessive power given to the first order of the Irish assembly to obstruct measures proposed by the lower order required amendment, and concluded that if his objections were met, the bill would be regarded as a 'final settlement'.[7] Nevertheless, the inescapable fact remained that Parnell had declared Gladstone's scheme, as it stood, to be practically unworkable and had contradicted the hopes the latter had entertained of its beneficial consequences for Ireland.

It must be said, though, that this speech of Parnell's represented the height of Nationalist criticism of the Home Rule scheme. Thereafter, as the prospects of the bill's enactment diminished, so correspondingly did Parnellite criticism of its unsatisfactory clauses. Indeed, it will be seen that *United Ireland*, the most influential Nationalist paper, was already in mid-April preparing Irish opinion for acceptance of the bill without amendment if necessary; while Michael Davitt, despite his strong feelings about certain features of the measure, publicly took a similar line to Parnell's, hoping that in the future the British parliament and people would see their way to 'extend the system of self-government further'. Parnellite opinion on the land purchase bill, when it was introduced on 16 April, was unenthusiastic, with particular exception being taken to the role of the imperial receiver and the amount of purchase money to be awarded to landlords.[8] However, the quick withdrawal of this part of Gladstone's plan forestalled debate and kept their attention focused on the Home Rule bill.

When the second reading commenced on 10 May, William O'Brien, in a speech that has been described as second only to Gladstone's on the introduction of the bill, set the tone for other Parnellites. O'Brien retreated significantly from the stance taken by Parnell on 8 April — that vital amendments were necessary before the bill would be acceptable to the Irish. 'It does not pretend to be without failing or fault, or to satisfy everyone,' declared O'Brien. 'We intend to fight as strongly as we can, and to protest against some of its details'; but he added that the bill was nevertheless accepted by his party in a 'spirit of friendship, cordiality, and peace'. Once the English people saw that this was so, they would have no objection 'to give more enlarged effect to the system of local government to Ireland, and the goodwill of the two countries may determine our course'. Reading between the lines, O'Brien's speech was an admission of the inability of the Parnellite party to effect desired changes in the bill, and accordingly they would accept the bill as better than nothing. Moreover, O'Brien's alternative view, that once the English people saw that the Irish were accepting and working the Home Rule scheme in a spirit of goodwill they would extend its powers,[9] begged the question of how the envisaged equanimity in Anglo-Irish relations was to be maintained given Parnell's effective demonstration that the plan, as it stood, was more likely to aggravate than solve the Irish question.

The weakness of Nationalists in their efforts to secure a satisfactory scheme from Gladstone was graphically expressed by T. M. Healy in 1890. When it was proposed that they should secure firm guarantees from Gladstone as to the shape of the future Home Rule bill, he declared: 'The party was asked to secure the ground in advance. He would secure the ground if they gave him some millions of men and some artillery, but without them they would be in the future as they were in the past.' The tendency to forgo criticism of the details of the bill and rely instead on a vague and unstudied optimism as to its beneficial effects was taken further by John Redmond on 13 May: 'He trusted the house would accept with readiness the statement of the representatives of the Irish people that, on the whole, they were satisfied with this bill, and that, so far as their judgment went, it provided a final settlement of the question.' Later speeches by T. D. Sullivan and Justin McCarthy associated the passing of the bill with Irish loyalty to the empire and a great social and economic regeneration for Ireland. T. M. Healy informed the house that the 'blots' on the bill 'were small indeed compared with the blots you would create on the hearts of the Irish people by its rejection', while Thomas Sexton departed completely from Parnell's earlier criticisms of the powers of obstruction to be invested in the first order of the Irish assembly and cited such powers to emphasise the extent to which the minority was to be protected. T. P. O'Connor's speech on 3 June took this argument a stage further.

We are ready to accept any restrictions on the rights of democracy at the start of this grave enterprise; our work is to weld the different classes of our people into a perfectly harmonious whole, to undo the evil work of centuries of a policy, the fundamental principle of which was to divide and conquer, above all to soften and finally to extirpate the estrangement of different creeds which has been not the natural growth of kindly Irish hearts of all creeds. . . . To foster this idea of common nationhood above our strong party differences, our class hatreds, and our distinctions of creeds will be the first work of Irish statesmanship; and by way of starting that work favourably and accelerating its progress, we are quite willing not merely to submit to, but even to welcome, restraints on the rights of majorities, which in ordinary circumstances we would reject.

The very obvious Nationalist desire to get the Home Rule bill under whatever circumstances prompted Sir Henry James to declare that he had a statement by a prominent Liberal Home Ruler that Parnell was ready to accept anything. This impression might have been confirmed by Parnell's final contribution to the Home Rule debate on 7 June. Departing completely from his highly critical attitude of 8 April, he declared himself satisfied with the scheme as a final settlement, comparing it favourably with Grattan's Parliament, which was both encumbered with a House of Lords and an executive not responsible to the legislature. He still had reservations about the length of time the first order could hold up measures, but was also confident that the effect of both orders working together 'in one chamber' would lead to the resolution of disputed questions 'on a basis of compromise more or less satisfactory to both parties'.[10]

Taking an overview of Nationalist attitudes to the Home Rule bill during the debate, the line of progression from marked criticism on 8 April to equally marked acquiescence on 7 June is clearly perceivable. As was stated above, this development was paralleled by the increasingly deteriorating chances of the bill passing a second reading and the natural desire to ease Gladstone's legislative path. Moreover, Gladstone's attempts to secure the second reading by promising Unionist Liberals that they were being asked to vote only for the principle of the bill, and that its details would be recast in the autumn parliamentary session, undoubtedly influenced some Parnellites to accept the existing bill for fear than an amended scheme would be a weaker measure. Certainly Parnell became sternly committed to the bill as it stood in June. When T. P. O'Connor sought to support the Liberal leader by stating that the bill could be regarded as a 'draft' measure whose final shape was yet to be determined, Parnell impressed on him: '"This . . . is the bill we want", laying special stress on the "this".' He protested equally vigorously against Gladstone's intention, noted above, to secure support for the bill by promising to recast its details in the autumn parliamentary session.[11]

Nevertheless, this desire to hang on to a bill which he himself had so effectively demonstrated to be grievously defective appears somewhat puzzling, even when we allow for the obvious satisfaction to national sentiment that the mere existence of an Irish parliament would have given. Perhaps the most important clue to this issue is to be found by asking what leading Parnellites really expected of Home Rule; and what is surprising in this respect is how closely their views resembled Gladstone's. Of course, Gladstone's conversion to Home Rule itself necessitated an ideological readjustment on the part of Nationalist leaders: it was now important to emphasise the constitutional basis of Irish nationalism, and Gladstone's favourable references to Grattan's Parliament during the introduction of the Home Rule bill provided the common ground for the meeting of minds.[12] Thus whereas the nationalist legend propagated in Ireland was geared mainly to the inculcation of an ethnically Celtic sense of nationality, explicable chiefly through the medium of the historical record of seven hundred years of oppression of the native Irish people, the version presented in parliament was centred on the period of Grattan's Parliament. In nationalist legend it provided an example of national unity, prosperity, increasing religious tolerance, and was 'proof' that a local parliament with adequate powers would not agitate for complete separation. A peculiar feature of this aspect of nationalist thought was that the seven hundred years of English oppression that explained Ireland's woes for a domestic Irish audience now became the period in which Ireland's parliamentary 'rights' were established.

In an uncommon instance of a minor Nationalist M.P. intervening in the Home Rule debate, which was mainly monopolised by party leaders, J. C. Flynn declared that the 'claim of the Irish people to a separate parliament of their own went back very far into English and Irish history. The claim to an Irish parliament dated from the reign of King John.' John Redmond also had earlier made it the basis of Ireland's claim to a separate parliament that she had possessed 'distinct parliamentary institutions of her own for 600 years'. However, given the inseparability of the warfare and colonisation associated with the establishment of Irish parliamentary institutions, Parnellites were careful to leave the antiquity of Ireland's claim in this respect at the level of a general statement. It was rather the brief period from 1782 to 1800 that was crucial. In short, this period was presented almost as a golden age, destroyed by British rule in Ireland which subsequently resulted in eighty-five years of distress and coercion. Yet the glories of Grattan's Parliament would return once Home Rule was enacted.[13]

However, it is worth pointing out, in regard to Nationalist expectations of the benefits to accrue from Gladstone's scheme, that in accepting his bill — with its acknowledgment of Westminster's control of imperial affairs, Ireland's commitment to paying a portion of imperial expenditure, Westminster's control of Irish customs and excise, and with no Irish representation in the imperial parliament — they were accepting a scheme that, in substance, had been rejected by Grattan when offered by the Rockingham ministry in 1782. Nevertheless, this aspect of Nationalist thinking was to become the predominant ideological basis of Home Rule nationalism between 1886 and 1893, largely in consequence of Gladstone's energetic campaigning.[14] But, as will be seen more fully in Chapter 7, Gladstone's view of Ireland under Home Rule was a highly conservative one, which envisaged the return of the landlords as Irish political leaders. How far was his view of the future of Ireland compatible with that of leading Nationalists?

With the possible exception of Parnell, they certainly did not share Gladstone's view of the landlords' political prospects. But that apart, their expectations showed marked similarities in many respects. For instance, the confidence expressed by Gladstone in May that the membership of the Home Rule parliament would be socially and intellectually superior to the members of the Parnellite party, and more representative of all classes of the Irish people, was mirrored by that of Michael

Davitt. On the land question Davitt's views were far more radical than those of either Parnell or Gladstone, but this should not disguise the extent to which his view of life in the new Ireland was itself conservative. He informed Wilfrid Blunt:

> There are not many of the present parliamentary party who would be in the Home Rule parliament; the leaders would, but not the rank and file . . . perhaps a dozen or twenty, not more. . . . There are plenty of good men who in a Dublin parliament would come forward, men in professions and official life who were thorough Home Rulers, but dared not yet touch parliament. . . . The present men have been elected to get Home Rule; we shall require another sort to work it. The first years under Home Rule will be very conservative.

Indeed, notwithstanding Davitt's efforts as a labour leader — especially in promoting Irish labour representation in the Nationalist Party at Westminster in 1892 — he shared with John Dillon an essentially conservative view of the proper role of labour in Irish society. Blunt recorded a conversation with him on this subject in 1887:

> He [Davitt] had altered his views of late about education, which he was beginning to see had its dangers for Ireland as well as its advantages. Every post brought him in requests from farmers' sons for places as clerks or pressmen, and the labouring population was getting too proud to dig. If this was to be the result of education it would not be well for Ireland, and the education he was inclined to wish for was a manual one. In this Dillon cordially agreed.[15]

Thus, despite Davitt's undoubted preference for a radical settlement of the land question to dispose of the landlord garrison, as well as his democratic 'vision' of Ireland's future, it did not necessarily follow that that what social scientists describe as 'upward social mobility' on the part of Ireland's labouring masses was any part of his thinking. Indeed, given his democratic and progressive outlook it is perhaps remarkable that he should have failed to see the strong probability that the attempts of farmers' sons and labourers to 'better' themselves was a function of the nationalist agitation since 1879 that destroyed the deferential relationship of the peasantry to their landlords, raised their level of material expectations, and often produced local lay leaders to rival the predominant social position of the clergy. It is not surprising therefore that Blunt, having observed the Parnellite movement in his travels in Ireland in 1886 and 1887, should note in his diary that the Unionist view of Home Rulers as 'Jacobins' was absurd: 'There is nothing more absurd than to talk of Home Rule as Jacobinism. Ireland under her own parliament would infallibly be retrograde, at least for several years.' Michael McDonagh, a journalist well acquainted with the leaders of the movement, was to make much the same point, but in more specific terms:

> None of the very able men enlisted in its cause hardly ever attempted constructively to show how Home Rule, which was to consist of political machinery of the English type — a parliament of two houses, law courts, police, tax-gatherers — worked according to old established principles, by legislators and officials of the same social class, and fundamentally of the same types of minds and ideas, however they might differ in race, was to set to rights the economic disorders of Ireland, merely because the same kinds of strings, legislative and administrative, were to be pulled in Dublin instead of at Westminster. How were hunger and unemployment to be banished? — those grisly spectres that dogged the footsteps of the Irish wage-earner as he went out to look for work; and that sat down to table with his wife and children. If any of the leaders were asked for his opinion on this point he would be sure to reply — 'Well we could not possibly make a worse mess of Ireland than is being made by the imperial parliament; and, at any rate, the hands pulling the strings would be Irish.' Or answering in another and more decisive way, he would say, 'The Irish people want Home Rule, and that, for the present, is enough about it.' ... Vague and indefinite hopes prevailed to some extent that a good time would follow — that the worker would have more regular employment and better wages; that the farmer would get higher prices for his produce, that the shopkeeper would have quicker sales and larger profits, and so on.[16]

To McDonagh's biting critique of Nationalist thinking on the very real problems that a Dublin parliament would have faced, may be added, by way of explanation, A. J. Kettle's opinion that from the beginning of the land agitation in Ireland very few of its leaders 'knew anything about land, or about the condition of the agricultural population at all. This has been notoriously the case from the first Land League executive nominated by Mr Davitt.' There was undoubtedly some exaggeration in Kettle's claim, but its general accuracy would seem to be supported by recent research on the social composition of the Parnellite party: 'Agrarian reform had a strong urban complexion. . . . Outside the party, the most dynamic of all agrarian reformers, Michael Davitt, was from a cotton town in Lancashire.'[17] It is more than likely that in a general ignorance of agrarian realities, allied to a conservative social outlook and ill-defined ideas about the practical ends for which Home Rule was desired, is to be found the key to the readiness of leading Nationalists to accept a scheme that would, on Parnell's own estimation, greatly reduce the Irish standard of living — already considerably depressed by a severe economic crisis. It is, moreover, worth emphasising that the Nationalist view of Gladstone's scheme in parliament was presented by the elite of the party — Parnell, Dillon, Healy, Sexton, T. P. O'Connor, J. F. X. O'Brien, William O'Brien, John Redmond, Justin McCarthy, E. D. Gray and T. D. Sullivan. Apart from Parnell, who could have been expected to have a realistic idea of the effects of Gladstone's plan, none of this group had any practical experience of Irish agrarian life, while the remainder of the party took little part in the Home Rule debate. In this context it is important to see how nationalist opinion outside parliament reacted to the Home Rule scheme.

Reaction to the plan in America revealed a predictable acceptance among moderate Irish-Americans and strong condemnation from Fenians, who viewed it as wholly inadequate. However, it was reaction in Ireland that was crucial. There is a long-standing view that nationalist opinion there accepted the scheme uncritically. In 1887 Sir Charles Gavan Duffy informed J. F. X. O'Brien: 'What I said about the Irish people being ready to accept Mr Gladstone's scheme without scrutiny. . . I think . . . represents the spirit of the press and public meetings at the period.' More recently Conor Cruise O'Brien has declared: 'The national press and the people welcomed the bill; almost incredulously. . . . Irish public opinion was [not] concerned ... with the imperfections of the bill.'[18] These views, however, are not sustained by an examination of Irish opinion. As shown in Appendix 1, this has been examined by taking a sample of reactions in approximately half of the Irish local newspapers that supported Home Rule, distributed over the four provinces. But it is important, firstly, to note the views of important leaders of opinion. Davitt's opinion has already been shown, and did not vary greatly in public from Parnell's. Archbishop Walsh of Dublin, however, was more critical of the financial aspects of the scheme than Parnell. Where the latter desired that Ireland pay one-twentieth of imperial expenditure, Walsh favoured one-twenty-fifth or one-twenty-sixth. Moreover, he felt strongly that Irish representation at Westminster should be maintained in numbers proportionate to Ireland's contribution to imperial expenditure while restrictions on the Home Rule parliament lasted.

Walsh thought that representation at Westminster would not only lessen opposition to the bill, but also safeguard Irish interests in matters of taxation and other questions, as well as benefit Catholic interests in Great Britain and the empire. In this last respect his views were shared by Davitt. A more uncritical view of the scheme was taken by Archbishop Croke of Cashel. On the introduction of the scheme he and his clergy passed a formal resolution expressing their gratitude, while during the second reading Croke supported Gladstone's proposal to drop the content of the bill in return for a vote merely for its principle. Certainly he made an enormous impression on Wilfrid Blunt, who impressed on John Morley his personal importance in Ireland and influence with the clergy generally: 'He is a very powerful man personally and by position, and his word is law to all the clergy of the south, so that everything he says is of importance, especially at the present moment.' Blunt went on to describe how remarkably and entirely

the distrust of English intentions has disappeared during the past few weeks and how cordially the clergy, especially, accept everything that is being done for Ireland as the best that could be done. They quite understand the difficulties of the parliamentary position, and so long as the principle of real Home Rule is not departed from will, I am sure, do their best to urge patience on the people. To my mind the fact of the clergy being such strong nationalists is the best possible guarantee of an orderly solution.[19]

Croke, he went on, had no thoughts of separation and was probably 'at heart' as loyal to Her Majesty as 'you or I are'. But even if Blunt's opinion reflected exactly the clergy's thinking, they did not represent the totality of Irish nationalism; and it is perhaps appropriate to note the views of another important British observer — the wife of Gladstone's Irish viceroy, Lord Aberdeen — on their reception in Ireland:

> It used to be said that the new Lord Lieutenant was received with open arms because regarded as the harbinger of Home Rule. Such was by no means the case. True, it was known that a measure of Home Rule was to be prepared; but the people had no idea of giving themselves away, so to speak, before they knew what the nature of the proposed reform was to be; and so the prevalent attitude was, though by no means unfriendly, somewhat that of reserve.

It will be seen that 'reserve' provides a better key to local nationalist opinion on Home Rule than the fulsome praise for Liberal efforts that Blunt described. As for Lord Aberdeen personally, though, whatever reserve he experienced was to be quickly dissipated by his public identification with a campaign for relief of distress in the west of Ireland and his involvement in the promotion of Irish industries. The Aberdeens were to pursue this interest well into the twentieth century. Before proceeding to examine local press opinion on Home Rule, however, it is important to note the reaction to Gladstone's scheme of the two most important national organs of Home Rule opinion, the *Freeman's Journal* and *United Ireland*, especially the latter, since it was both the chief organ of the Parnellite party in Ireland, and, with an average weekly sale of 90,000,[20] easily the most influential nationalist weekly.

What is immediately striking in this paper's treatment of the Home Rule bill is its markedly moderate tone. Departing from Parnell's trenchant criticism of the scheme, it declared of Gladstone's pledge to confer Home Rule: 'This one tremendous fact eclipses all details.' The tone thus set, the limitations of the bill were largely overlooked, apart from Ireland's proposed contribution to imperial expenditure, which was described as 'monstrous'. But this imposition, it continued, would be offset by imperial expenditure in Ireland — on the military and defence and by the £1,400,000 credited to Irish customs. While admitting that £404,000 as a surplus on the Irish budget was too small, and voicing 'a strenuous protest' against the extravagant claims made upon the Irish exchequer, it stressed that 'These are not questions that need diminish one tittle of the frank and cordial satisfaction with which the bill, in its broad outlines, will be accepted by the Irish race.'[21] This encouragement to dwell on the fact of an Irish parliament being conferred, and to ignore the very details which would make or break it, seems clearly designed to prepare the Nationalist rank and file for acceptance of the bill as it stood.

Similarly, in its treatment of the land purchase scheme, every effort was made to make it attractive to Nationalists. It was denied that the average of twenty years' purchase of the gross rental suggested by Gladstone in parliament would be usual: 'oppressive landlords', on whose estates the great mass of the small tenantry were congregated, would in fact get a lot less than sixteen years' purchase of the judicial rent. Moreover, completely ignoring the vital importance of commissions on the handling of land sales to the finances of a Dublin parliament, it was strongly suggested that the Irish government would in fact rebate such commissions to the tenants to lower their repayments. Finally, in its anxiety to include all arguments for supporting the bill, *United Ireland* maintained that if Nationalists threw no impediment in the way of a land bill generous to the landlords and left the defeat of the measure to the Tories, then they would, in the next parliament, be in 'an impregnable position to demand that the landlords shall be less tenderly dealt with' in future.

By contrast, reaction to Gladstone's bills in the *Freeman's Journal*, usually more politically moderate than *United Ireland*, was far more severe. While the establishment of an executive responsible to the Irish legislature was applauded as a great advance on Grattan's Parliament, and satisfaction expressed with the safeguards for the minority, it followed Parnell's attack on the financial provisions, particularly by pointing out that 'The charges... proposed to be put upon Ireland are excessive, and such as might easily and completely break her down.' The financial existence of the country would depend upon the Irish and English people continuing to drink as much as at present, and 'the slightest reduction in the drink bill would upset the financial equilibrium' and eventually lead to the Irish exchequer being merged again with the British exchequer. Exception was also taken to the constabulary clauses, and hope was expressed that in committee the British would not drive such a hard bargain.[22]

Again, unlike the welcome given by *United Ireland* to the land purchase bill, a more critical attitude was taken by the *Freeman's Journal*. It was pointed out that in becoming owners, tenants would be liable for the payment of county cess and poor rates, and that these new impositions would largely offset the reduction in rental repayments envisaged by Gladstone. In the case of very small tenants where the landlord paid all of the county cess and poor rate, the devolution of these charges would be much heavier than in the case of larger tenancies which already shared these charges with the landlord. Indeed, in many cases it would be to the advantage of both landlord and tenant to come to an arrangement under the 1885 Ashbourne act rather than under Gladstone's plan. Under the terms of the former the landlord could obtain eighteen years' purchase of the gross rental provided he left one-fifth of the purchase money, or other security, in the hands of the Land Commissioners. Under Gladstone's plan he would receive, after deductions, the equivalent of sixteen years' purchase of the gross rental. Similarly, under the Ashbourne act, the tenant would be purchasing his holding on the basis of eighteen years' judicial rent rather than twenty.[23] In sum, then, it was significant that the two most influential nationalist papers took very different attitudes to the Home Rule scheme. This mixed reaction, however, was characteristic of Irish nationalist opinion as a whole.

Given the highly emotional content of nationalist propaganda, it was inevitable that those emotions would be reflected in Irish reaction to the Home Rule scheme, especially in the west of Ireland, which had been the centre of agrarian struggle. The *Tuam Herald* declared that if 1886 was to see the enactment of Home Rule, 'In the inspired pages of history, ages yet unborn will read of it as the brightest in the long tale of our struggles and suffering.' The *Western News* exclaimed that the enactment of the Home Rule bill would be the 'sun' of Ireland's 'freedom', that would warm and restore 'the splendour of our nationality which years of oppression and tyranny have kept smouldering'. The *Connaught Telegraph* welcomed the bill with the hope that 'never again will foreign foemen have power to forge shackles for an emancipated land': it 'religiously' ejaculated 'the fervent prayer of "God save Ireland"'.[24]

Such expressions could be multiplied many times over, and there is no doubt that among some uneducated nationalists they stimulated expectations of what self-government would entail, far in excess of what could reasonably be anticipated. The *Limerick Chronicle* carried a story it claimed was representative of working-class nationalist hopes:

> It is really amazing what mad construction the peasantry and uneducated among the working class have put upon what is known as 'Home Rule'. It was believed to be destined, the moment it came into operation, to redress every ill, and to turn the whole country into ... a lazy man's elysium. We have been informed by a large employer of labour in this city, that yesterday he was visited upon by one of his workmen, who, with a face full of seriousness, asked him, 'Now that Home Rule was given how soon would he increase their wages?' Other stories equally absurd, have been told illustrative of the omniferous belief in the regeneration of Ireland by her new leaders.

Notwithstanding the fact that this paper was virulently Unionist and would thus have had an obvious interest in descrediting Home Rule, there is no reason to doubt the accuracy of the above passage. Michael Davitt's estimate of the level of political consciousness among the same social class during the land war was not markedly different. At that time totally unjustified hopes prevailed among some that agrarian agitation would secure their holdings for nothing.[25] But while there is no reason to think that any significant sophistication in the uneducated nationalist consciousness occurred by 1886, and no reason to doubt that such extravagant expectations existed, it would be virtually impossible to know how many held them. The only means of surveying nationalist opinion generally is by consulting local newspapers, although, as shown in Appendix 1, this method is not faultless. The sample examined, covering opinion in all four provinces, reveals a mixed reaction to Gladstone's bills.

In examining local press opinion, it is first of all important to distinguish between, on the one hand, the great national rejoicing at the *fact* of Gladstone's scheme being introduced and, on the other, evaluations of the nature of the scheme as a final settlement of the Irish question. Indeed, quite often the same report combined both. The following example from the *Roscommon Herald*, one of the most radical Irish journals, is not untypical:

> The principle of Home Rule having been conceded by England's greatest statesman, and received with fervour by an applauding House of Commons, the practical questions to be considered are the extent of Mr Gladstone's offer, and ... the changes which will be necessary to render the boon one of real and permanent benefit to the country.

As Table 7 shows, in regard to the Home Rule bill as a final settlement, there was no unanimity of view. Nine papers, or just over one-third, declared it to be satisfactory as it was; nine accepted it subject to the amendments suggested by Parnell on 8 April; while eight others accepted the bill subject to various other amendments. Moreover, it is also noteworthy that the tendency to accept the bill uncritically was most pronounced in Ulster, followed by Connaught, while Leinster most uniformly adopted the attitude taken by Parnell on the first day of the debate.[26]

Reaction to the land purchase bill (demonstrated in Table 8) was more diffuse. Nine papers made no mention of it at all, which may have been due to the fact of its quick withdrawal, while other views ranged from non-commital reporting to outright rejection. However, one interesting reaction was that of the *Weekly Examiner* (1 May 1886), which endorsed the criticism of the bill made by the Ulster Land Committee. This grouping was, in fact, not primarily a political organisation, but represented the tenant-farmer interest in the north generally. Its membership included both Unionists and Home Rulers, and it was presided over by Thomas Shillington, soon to be elected president of the Irish Protestant Home Rule Association. The committee's report on the bill recommended chiefly that two-thirds of the tenants on any estate should have the same power as the landlord to compel a sale; that an average of fifteen years' purchase of the gross rental rather than twenty was a fairer figure; that a landlord should have no power to withdraw from a sale if unsatisfied with the land court's estimate of his estate's value; and that tenants should have the option of becoming state tenants 'at the lowest perpetual rents which the interest paid by the state will allow'.[27]

A survey of Irish opinion generally, then, clearly does not support the popular view of a people slavishly accepting Gladstone's plan. But equally important is the fact that whereas party leaders in parliament moved quickly to accept the bill unmodified as its chances of passing a second reading diminished, no such trend is observable in the local press. If anything, local opinion tended to harden as increasing familiarity with the scheme clarified its limitations. Thus it is hardly surprising that M. J. F. McCarthy, in noting Irish reaction to the bill's defeat, should make a sharp distinction between the attitudes of Parnellite party 'office-seekers' and the nationalist population:

In Dublin they laughed and made the best of it, taking it in the same spirit as they would have accepted the defeat of Ormonde, the famous Derby winner of that year. Wire-pullers and office-seekers who had played for large stakes felt sorely hit, but met with little sympathy from a public who, having staked nothing, rejoiced at having suffered no loss and drew a breath of relief at the end of the crisis. In the country districts there was not only no anger or indignation, but there was not even disappointment. Parnell's triumph over Gladstone had come so suddenly, the struggle for Home Rule had been so short-lived and so subordinate to the land agitation, that the people did not regard the reverse in the light of a grievance. The farmers were so keen on getting reductions of rents in the land courts or otherwise, and the labourers so preoccupied by the prospect of new cottages with

free half-acres of ground, that they did not feel as if they had
lost anything by the defeat of Home Rule. There was no dis-
turbance whatever in Dublin, and only in a few isolated
quarters in the south were there any outbreaks of ill-feeling,
and those of no serious import.[28]

McCarthy's emphasis on the disparity of view between party
leaders and their supporters on the loss of the Home Rule bill is
very much to the point. A. J. Kettle, one of the few prominent
Parnellites with an agrarian background and in close contact
with rural opinion, consoled a disheartened Parnell with the following advice:

> I think you have great reason to thank heaven that you did
> not succeed in carrying the land and Home Rule settlements
> on the lines laid down in Gladstone's scheme. You were
> giving too much for the land and three millions a year too
> much for the country. Had Gladstone's bills been passed into
> law Ireland would have fallen under the burden, and you
> might...[have left] public life, disgraced and broken-
> hearted.... You should not despond but rejoice.

Greater insight into the limitations of Parnell's ideas as to the
value of Gladstonian Home Rule to Ireland — notwithstanding
his criticisms of 8 April — is provided in the notes of a conversation on the Irish question between him and Lord Ribblesdale
in 1887, which the latter published shortly after Parnell's death.
Parnell, Ribblesdale recorded, believed strongly that self-
government would produce both an immediate and beneficial
effect on industrial development and invest the people with 'a
new sense of responsibility'. While England and Scotland, being
'highly developed and prosperous', would naturally fear great
constitutional changes, Ireland 'was in so bad a state' that the
risks involved in Home Rule were barely noticed there. There
'need be no failure', though Parnell admitted that the first years
of a Home Rule parliament 'must be years of great anxiety'.
Ribblesdale continued:

> I asked him whether Home Rule had not come to mean to the
> average Irishman the turning of sixpences into shillings, and
> what he thought would happen if the people of Ireland ever
> woke up to find that even under Home Rule the sixpences

were still only sixpences. He again said it would be a very anxious time at first, but he struck me as either shutting his eyes wilfully, or being unable to see how enormously the difficulties of the Irish question would be increased by the economic failure of . . . Home Rule.[29]

THE UNIONIST CRITIQUE

For reasons that are not surprising, the Unionist case against Home Rule has had a bad press. Given the facts of Lord Randolph Churchill's incitement to civil war in Ulster, Lord Salisbury's 'Hottentots' speech in St James's Hall on 15 May 1886 (when he declared that the Irish, like the Hottentots, were unfit for self-government) and the rabid anti-Irish and anti-nationalist prejudice of popular Unionism, it is hardly surprising that attention has been directed away from the specific criticisms Unionists made of Gladstone's scheme. Yet this was as consistently a part of their argument as was their oft-voiced prejudices.

The first Unionist speech of the debate, delivered immediately after Gladstone had introduced the Home Rule bill, was, significantly, that of G. O. Trevelyan, who had resigned from the cabinet convinced of the total unworkability of Gladstone's scheme. Trevelyan now gave vent publicly to his strongly felt views:

> I cannot but think that the right hon. gentleman in making his calculations has left out of account, not only Irish nature, but human nature itself. Here is a country intensely national, which is characterised by great intensity of political opinion, which when she has got all that this bill proposes to give, will be practically independent — for if I know anything of Ireland she will certainly regard herself as such — and which will be asked to pay to a neighbouring nation, including its contribution to the sinking fund, £3,500,000 a year. This sum she will soon begin to regard as an English tribute. . . . If you add to that . . . £1,000,000 a year for keeping up this English constabulary [R.I.C.], you have a sum of £4,500,000 which Ireland will have to pay annually over and above what it may have to pay in respect of loans . . . and the people will say that these payments are the consequence of that English con-

nection which they will affirm was forced upon them against their will.

Trevelyan, moreover, referred to the recent articles of the economist Robert Giffen, with whose findings as to Irish over-taxation Parnellites 'ominously' agreed, and highlighted the fact that Gladstone's scheme

> now proposed to make this amount of taxation permanent and eternal, and to keep it at its present figure, in order ... that the Irish may pay £4,500,000 a year to the English treasury.... How long, I should like to know, will it be before a resolution denouncing this English tribute will be brought forward in the Irish parliament? How long ... before it is passed, and how long before any English ministry which refuses to accept it will have ceased to stand?[30]

Referring to 'threats' by *United Ireland* that if the Home Rule bill was not enacted Ireland would see a violent reaction, Trevelyan argued that if the bill was passed these would still be made, to get 'everything that this bill omits to give': 'I do not say the Irish nation, but no nation that exists in the world, when it has got a separate parliament will ... pay taxes which are to be handed over to something like a foreign treasury.'[31] The importance of Trevelyan's speech lies in his direct contradiction of the reasoning Gladstone gave for the necessity of his scheme — the satisfaction of Irish national sentiment and the restoration of the 'social order' of Ireland; far from satisfying that sentiment, Gladstone's scheme would aggravate it and be the source of future Irish agitation. Trevelyan's fears were, as we have seen, shared by Chamberlain, and although Trevelyan was not the most influential of Unionists — he was, in fact, to rejoin the Gladstonian ranks in 1887 — his speech set a pattern for subsequent speakers.

Lord Randolph Churchill on 12 April elaborated on Trevelyan's views by contrasting Gladstone's professed trust in the Irish people with the extent of the restrictions in the scheme:

> Is it not an extraordinary thing that Her Majesty's government are willing to trust the Irish judges appointed by the Irish government with the lives ... liberties, and ... property of every man, woman and child in Ireland; but Her Majesty's

government will not trust the Irish judges appointed by the Irish parliament with one single penny of the British revenue?

In the context of the bill's limitations, and with reference to Gladstone's claim introducing the bill that existing English laws came to Ireland in a 'foreign garb', Churchill, with devastating pointedness, argued that Gladstone's scheme was 'no different from other English laws in this respect'.[32]

The natural development of Unionist arguments on this line was to attempt to exploit Parnellite dissatisfaction with the scheme and thereby prove its insufficiency as a final settlement of the Irish question. Ammunition was to be provided for this purpose by the injudicious speeches of T. P. O'Connor shortly before the bill's introduction. Obviously expecting a far more extensive scheme than that which emerged, O'Connor declared, in a speech at Kensington on 4 April, that the introduction of the Home Rule scheme would mean the destruction of the Union. Given Gladstone's concern to present his measure as in no way affecting the overall supremacy of the imperial parliament, such utterances could only be embarrassing, not to mention their usefulness to Unionists as proof of the real objectives of Parnellites. In the major Conservative contribution to the debate Sir Michael Hicks Beach on 13 April concentrated almost entirely on the limitations and liabilities of the Home Rule plan and 'demonstrated' its failure as a final settlement by producing the following extract from a letter on Home Rule which O'Connor had sent to *The Times* in December 1885:

> If the system of self-government given to Ireland were deemed by the Irish people insufficient, it is probable that the Irish members would act in the new imperial parliament as they do in the present. Imperial questions would be looked at by them, not from the imperial standpoint, but as affording weapons to be employed between the two English parties for purely Irish purposes. You might have then what you have now, a distracting element in your imperial councils, judging things not on their intrinsic and imperial merits, but on their bearing to Irish national aspirations.

In the light of this quotation, Hicks Beach then asked whether Gladstone's scheme would be deemed sufficient as a final settlement by Irish members. Given such contentious clauses as those relating to customs and excise, he concluded it would not be. Nationalists would never be able to revive under Gladstone's scheme the prosperity they believed to have existed in Grattan's day. His conclusion was confirmed when, in answer to a direct question on the finality of the scheme, Parnellites gave evasive replies. Consequently:

> It seems to me as absolutely certain as anything in the future can be, that if you were to institute the assembly which the right hon. gentleman proposes it would be powerless for good to Ireland, but would be powerful for mischief between Great Britain and Ireland. From the very first . . . it would be struggling to increase its authority.

Thereafter he went on to support his conclusion with reference to other aspects of the bill, such as the extent of safeguards for the minority. Interestingly, Gladstone, replying to Hicks Beach immediately afterwards, merely declared that the provisions for safeguarding the minority were inserted to meet the prejudices of the bill's critics, not his own; as to the criticism of the financial scheme, though, he was virtually silent.[33]

The Home Rule bill passed its first reading on 13 April, but when, on 16 April, Gladstone introduced his land purchase bill, it only compounded Unionist opposition to Home Rule. The nature of its financial basis provoked an outcry from Unionists and Liberals alike, while the fuller explanation of the role of the imperial receiver it contained was seen as further proof not only of the likelihood of future Irish unrest were the scheme enacted, but also of Gladstone's own distrust of the Irish. Anticipating this complaint again, Gladstone unconvincingly protested that the proposed role of the imperial receiver was not evidence of distrust: 'These provisions have nothing whatever to do with my notions; they are not intended to satisfy me, nor the British public; but these are large operations, and the provisions are intended to satisfy a somewhat peculiar and fastidious class, the class of public creditors.' Nevertheless, the charge of distrust stuck. The land purchase bill was withdrawn before any widespread Irish landlord reaction to it could be properly gauged, though when it did come it was in the form of an unusually moderate pamphlet published by the Irish Loyal and Patriotic Union.[34]

The second reading of the Home Rule bill began on 10
May, and the insufficiency of the scheme as a final settlement
was again taken up. It was again argued that, whatever
Parnellites might say, they would never be satisfied with such
'humiliating' restrictions as those in the Home Rule bill. On 13
May, moreover, Sir Henry James developed the Unionist
argument further by claiming that even if Nationalist M.P.s
accepted Gladstone's bill, they could not speak for the Irish
people. Indeed, none of the claims Gladstone had made for his
scheme — unity of the empire, supremacy of Westminster, preservation of social order and the protection of property and
minority rights — were secured by the bill:

> Given the degrading restrictions contained in the bill, I
> cannot believe the Irish will accept this as a final settle-
> ment. . . . It might meet the opportunism of the day for certain
> purposes, but it can never satisfy the wishes of a generous
> people.

Taking up the point of Parnellite acceptance of the bill, E. A.
Leatham pressed them whether they accepted it as a final settlement, and was met with a chorus of 'Yes'. But the highly lukewarm nature of their satisfaction was demonstrated on 17 May,
when Viscount Wolmer reminded the house that Parnell had
argued on 8 April that unless the bill underwent extensive modifications his party would be under no obligation to accept it. If
the bill was not modified, would it still be acceptable, he asked.
Parnell merely replied with a confirmation that he had
stipulated conditions to its acceptability on 8 April; otherwise
Parnellites were silent. Thus, even though Nationalists were
increasingly prepared to accept the bill unmodified, it was
obvious that such acceptance was notoriously devoid of
enthusiasm and, as such, provided support for the Unionist view
that it was merely transitory — that Home Rule as envisaged by
Gladstone could only be a step towards greater autonomy or
complete separation. Yet, as if to compound the obstacles in the
path of Home Rule, the Liberals inadvertently provided
support for the Unionist case when, on 20 May, John Morley
moved the second reading of an arms bill. This had been introduced on 6 May and was designed to continue the provisions of
the 1882 crimes act for restricting the sale, importation and

[handwritten margin note: Parnell did not find bill acceptable — simply being opportunistic]

carrying of firearms, prohibiting their use without government licence, and giving the police the right of searching private houses for arms in proclaimed districts. This measure was taken to indicate a fatal want of confidence in the nationalist majority, on whom the Liberals were asking parliament to bestow control of a separate Irish parliament. The bill was carried by 303 votes to 89, with the Tories and Liberals voting together against the Parnellite party and a few radicals.[35]

Of course, the views of different critics varied in the influence they had in defeating Gladstone's bill, but if any one person could be credited with having sealed the Home Rule scheme's fate, it was John Bright. Bright was known to hold strong anti-Irish prejudices, but even he was careful to maintain that his opposition was based not only on a firm belief in the maintenance of the Union as best for Great Britain and Ireland, but also on the conviction that the bill itself offered no hope of a solution to the Irish problem. He explained his views in a personal interview with R. Barry O'Brien:

> If you could persuade me that what you call Home Rule would be a good thing for Ireland, I would still object to this bill.... It would lead to friction, constant friction, between the two countries. The Irish parliament would be constantly struggling to burst the bars of the statutory cage in which it sought to confine it.... If I had trust I would trust to the full; if I had distrust I would do nothing. But this is a halting bill. If you establish an Irish parliament give it plenty of work and plenty of responsibility. Throw the Irish upon themselves... let their energies be engaged in Irish party warfare; but give no Irish party leader an opportunity of raising an anti-English cry. That is what a good Home Rule bill ought to do. This bill does not do it. Why, the... [imperial] receiver... appointed by it would alone keep alive the anti-English feeling. If you keep alive that feeling, what is the good of your Home Rule?[36]

Bright's views highlight a point that is worth emphasising about the Unionist case against Home Rule: that beneath the anti-Irish and anti-Catholic prejudice which often coloured their arguments the Unionists made a sustained and valid critique of the bill.

In the last major Unionist speech before the bill's defeat Joseph Chamberlain focused on the contradiction between Nationalist views on self-government before it was introduced and the provisions of the inadequate measure now before parliament. He asked: 'Could he [Parnell] bind the Irish people to accept his leadership if he accepts this as a final settlement of the question between Ireland and Great Britain?' Given the widespread criticism of the scheme in Ireland, and the views of A. J. Kettle already noted, this was no mere rhetorical question. There was, however, another major plank in the Unionist case against Home Rule: the problem of Ulster. Besides concern for the maintenance of the Union, this subject took up most parliamentary time during the debate. Certainly from the time of Churchill's Ulster visit in February 1886 Unionists were alive to the value of this issue: almost every critic of the Home Rule scheme expressed concern for 'prosperous and Protestant Ulster' and condemned Gladstone's readiness to deliver it into the hands of nationalists, ready to 'plunder' the province for the benefit of the less enterprising south. Joseph Chamberlain, in particular, was anxious to encourage Ulster resistance by all possible means, and saw in this issue the most effective means of thwarting Home Rule.[37] Given the importance of the Ulster problem as an obstacle to Irish autonomy, it is important to investigate in some detail the attitudes of Home Rulers towards it.

5

The Ulster Question (1):
The Parnellite and Gladstonian Views

DESPITE the strength of Ulster Unionist opposition to Home Rule in 1886 and Tory support for their case, Home Rulers insisted on the unimportance of the Ulster issue to the argument for self-government. In doing so they exhibited both their ignorance of the northern Protestant community and the seriousness of the threat it posed to the enactment of Gladstone's Home Rule scheme. This chapter will attempt to explain the causes of their misjudgment.

PARNELLITES AND ULSTER: AN INAUSPICIOUS BEGINNING

That the Ulster problem would be a formidable obstacle to Home Rule was clear well before 1886. The success which attended nationalist activities in southern Ireland during the land war, for example, was not repeated in the north. Initially successful attempts by Michael Davitt, Parnell and John Dillon to extend support for Land League activities among the many Presbyterian tenant farmers of Counties Fermanagh and Tyrone met with a serious reverse at the Tyrone by-election of September 1881. Against much informed local opinion, Parnell — incensed at the refusal of northern Liberals to support Home Rulers in parliament after the latter had 'stood aside' to let Liberals carry what seats they could in Ulster at the general election of 1880 — refused to support the Liberal candidate, T. A. Dickson, and entered a candidate of his own, the Rev. Harold Rylett. Dickson, however, was elected, and the Land League in mid-Ulster was severely damaged by the controversy.[1]

This was the first occasion on which the strength of Ulster Protestant opposition to Home Rule was really tested; previously Home Rulers, as such, did not attempt to take seats in areas of Ulster with so large a Protestant population as existed in Tyrone. Moreover, not only did Rylett fail abysmally to attract Protestant supporters, but he only took half the Catholic votes — the other half going to Dickson. Nationalist chagrin was consequently considerable. Indeed, J. J. O'Kelly, who saw the dangers in 'forcing a conflict' with the Liberal Presbyterians in Tyrone, found that for 'endeavouring to prevent this terrible misfortune I have been denounced in the most violent and unscrupulous manner by Davitt and his coterie'. As for Parnell, it was Andrew Kettle's view that the Tyrone defeat and the exultant coverage it received in the English press impelled him to favour the 'wild demonstrations' that took place during the 'invasion of Ulster' in the winter of 1883-4.[2]

After the Tyrone defeat the Parnellite cause in Ulster continued to suffer. The passage of the 1881 land act was greeted enthusiastically and utilised by Ulster tenant farmers, who had judicial rents fixed in numbers exceeding those of the other provinces. Thereafter Protestant tenant-righters who had supported the Land League, along with its Protestant membership, largely fell away. At the same time the divisions in the Land League in mid-Ulster, occasioned by the Tyrone by-election, gave the Orange Order the opportunity to take the initiative in its counter-attack against the League. Whole lodges that had supported it were expelled, while a landlord defence association, begun in Fermanagh in October 1881, drew together both Protestant landlords and tenants and began to undo the work of the League in maintaining a multidenominational organisation. This process was speeded up with the establishment of the National League in 1882 and the shift to emphasis on Home Rule rather than agrarian issues, which Orangemen could argue had always been the real objective of the agrarian agitation.[3]

NATIONALIST PROPAGANDA AND ULSTER UNIONISM:
THE ORANGE STEREOTYPE

Following the reverses of 1881-2, two events occurred which significantly influenced the Parnellite approach to the Ulster question. First there was the election of T. M. Healy for Co. Monaghan in 1883, and secondly the rejection by the House of Lords of a bill that would have facilitated greatly Nationalist registration in rural Ulster. Encouraged by the former and infuriated by the latter, Parnellites initiated the series of meetings that became known as the 'invasion of Ulster'. These were preceded by abrasive propaganda, evoking in the cause of nationalism a vision of centuries of struggle — not a method likely to win Protestant converts. The poster announcing the Rosslea demonstration is a representative example:

> Men of Fermanagh and Monaghan, prove by your presence at the meeting your unalterable devotion to the cause that your fathers fought and bled and died for — the cause of Irish nationality; prove to the hydra-headed monster of land-lordism and your English taskmasters that you will never rest contented until the land of Ireland is the property of the whole people of Ireland, to be administered by government existing for and by the will of the Irish nation,

The incident at Rosslea, in which Lord Rossmore, a magistrate, led a band of potentially violent Orangemen to 'meet' the nationalist demonstration, created a scandal, resulting in his removal from the commission of the peace, the proclamation of political demonstrations, and a series of charges and counter-charges in parliament.[4]

Speaking in the debate on the Queen's address to parliament in January 1884, Parnell denounced the government for partiality towards the Orangemen and proceeded to give his own view of why Orange meetings took place at all. They were, he argues, not spontaneous, but organised by landlords and led by criminal elements. They were also mainly Episcopalian in character, practically no Presbyterians being Orangemen; and even of Episcopalians, Orangemen formed a very small part. Most significantly, Parnell argued that they were not rural residents at all, but carpenters from the Belfast shipyards and 'the artisans of towns such as Portadown'. It was from these towns they were chiefly taken because, 'as a general rule, Orangemen, since the land movement commenced, have entirely died out amongst the agricultural population'. Parnell, of course, was not alone in having a derogatory view of Ulster Orangeism; indeed, many leading Unionists were embarrassed by its reputation for violence and religious bigotry. What was significant about Parnell's view of Orangeism, however, was how it functioned as a stereotype* which reduced the complexities of the Ulster problem to a simple moral issue in which the Unionist position was held to be the preserve of a reprehensible, unrepresentative clique whose views did not deserve to be taken into account. What were the elements that made up this stereotype? Orangemen, it was alleged, were murderous, cowardly and violent; they were unrepresentative of Ulster Protestant opinion, consisting of only a small group of Episcopalians; they were factious, having been got up and manipulated by landlords; they had no real base in the countryside, being mainly an urban phenomenon; they represented the only opposition to Home Rule, and apart from them Ulster Protestants were open to nationalist persuasion. Indeed, both before and after 1886 Parnell took the view that if Home Rule were once enacted, Ulster opposition would soon disappear. But despite the forcefulness with which he presented his analysis of Ulster Unionism, it was, to say the least, highly defective. Unionism, of course, was not merely the preserve of a narrow Orange clique, but extended to the great majority of Ulster Protestants; while the Orange Order, far from being an urban phenomenon in the early 1880s, already drew the bulk of its support from small farmers and labourers. As for Parnell's claim that the 'land movement' caused the demise of Orangeism in rural Ulster, this was hardly the case: its activities not only led to an increase in the order's membership, but this was effected mainly through an influx of Presbyterian tenant farmers[5] — the very class of Ulster Protestant that nationalists hoped to convert

---

*For the purpose of this study a stereotype is defined as a negative and simplistic belief about a community which is necessary to the interests of those who hold it — in this case Parnell's view of Ulster Unionists and his opponents' view of the Parnellite movement.

to Home Rule. How, then, could Parnell have produced so erroneous an analysis of Ulster Unionism?

Part of the answer to this question undoubtedly lies in the fact that his knowledge of Ulster was not great. Indeed, his claim that the Land League's activities had led to the demise of Orangeism in rural Ulster is clear enough evidence of that. Moreover, he had made a similar claim three years earlier in a speech at Hilltown, Co. Down, on 23 April 1881. Furthermore, speaking at Enniskillen on 9 November 1880, Parnell described Co. Fermanagh as 'Protestant and loyal' when in fact its Catholic population of 47,300 significantly outnumbered the combined Protestant population of 37,400. In addition to Parnell's inadequate knowledge of Ulster as an explanatory factor in his erroneous analysis of northern Unionism, two other factors are important to bear in mind. First, Parnell, like other nationalists, was obsessed with what might be called Ireland's 'territorial integrity' and was to firmly reject the proposal that Ulster be excluded from the jurisdiction of a Dublin parliament. Thus he was not psychologically inclined to admit that Ulster Unionism posed a serious threat to Home Rule. Secondly, and in this context, while it is true that Orangeism was but one of the forces of Ulster Unionism, it nevertheless often represented the latter in its most violent, bigoted and *visible* aspect — as indeed was the case during the Parnellite 'invasion of Ulster'. With these factors in mind, we can better understand why Parnell's analysis of Ulster Unionism seriously underestimated its importance. Yet, defective as Parnell's analysis was, his ideas were widely shared by nationalists. Nothing illustrates this point better than the extent to which the nationalist press in Ireland endorsed Parnell's view of Ulster Unionism during the Home Rule crisis of 1886. For example, reacting to Ulster Unionist threats of violent resistance to Home Rule on 29 May 1886, the *Connaught People* described such utterances as 'empty fire and brimstone talk'; Orange threats to rebel over Catholic Emancipation in 1829 and Disestablishment in 1869 had come to nothing, and it would be the same with regard to Home Rule. In the meantime the best policy was to let Orange bluster 'blow'. Other papers, to name only the *Sligo Champion*, *Limerick Reporter* and *Clare Advertiser*, produced similar reactions, identifying Unionists with Orangemen and emphasising their unrepresentativeness, violence, cowardice and bigotry.[6] Understandably, the onset of the Belfast riots, three days before the defeat of the Home Rule bill, served only to strengthen this view.

Begun in the highly charged atmosphere generated by the Home Rule struggle, these were the worst riots Belfast experienced in the nineteenth century, causing considerable loss of life and many thousands of pounds' worth of damage. They were started by an incident at Harland & Wolff's shipyard, when a Catholic allegedly told a Protestant that after Home Rule neither he nor any Protestant would get work. On the following day, 4 June, Protestant shipyard workers attacked a group of Catholic navvies, which resulted in one of them being drowned. Thereafter rioting ensued on and off until 19 September. For the greater part of that time the disturbances involved only Protestant mobs and the police; however considerable destruction of Catholic property took place and many Catholics were attacked. The reaction of nationalist Ireland to these events was a predictable and vehement condemnation of 'barbarous' Orangeism. Moreover, the blame that would be attached to certain Orange leaders by the commission of inquiry set up to investigate the riots fuelled a belief already widespread among nationalists that these disturbances were actually being organised by Orange leaders. Writing some forty years after the riots, T. M. Healy described his experiences of 'Orange rioters' in 1886 in terms which exhibited clearly the influence of this belief:

> We walked to and fro from the court without molestation, knowing that an Orange rioter never moves without orders. Unlike the nationalist mobster he is a disciplined unit. Orange leaders control the rank and file when things get out of hand by touching the 'soft pedal'.

Moreover, not only did the Belfast riots help to confirm the Nationalist view of Ulster Unionism, but, as Healy's comments suggest, this view was not likely to change over time. That this was so was due, in no small degree, to the fact that a serious lack of communication existed between the Nationalist and Unionist communities, and this state of affairs enhanced the importance of political rhetoric as a medium through which each community would understand the nature and intentions of the other. Such was the social distance maintained between them that, for the most part, they only knew each other through the public pronouncements of political leaders, whose own knowledge in this respect was usually highly deficient.[7] In fact Nationalists, in their personal relations with leading Orangemen, found support for their view of northern Unionism. This was especially the case in regard to Colonel Saunderson, a prominent Ulster Orangeman, who was leader of the Ulster Unionist group in parliament from 1886, and who for many Nationalists, personified Ulster Unionism.

When Saunderson sought to reassure southern Unionists, who feared that northern Unionists might settle for the exclusion of Ulster alone from the provisions of the Home Rule bill, by declaring that northern Unionists would stand firm with their southern brethren, Home Rulers eagerly referred to his declaration in support of their argument against both separate treatment for Ulster and its exclusion from the Home Rule scheme. But more importantly, Saunderson's carefree manner and personal friendliness towards leading Parnellites such as John Dillon, T. D. Sullivan and Justin McCarthy helped to persuade them that his frequent threats of civil war if Home Rule were enacted were bluff and could be readily dismissed. Dillon declared: 'He is in the habit of talking about civil war in Ulster, and at the same time he cracks so many jokes that . . . the impression he makes is that he does not care a half-crown whether Home Rule is granted or not.' Similarly, T. D. Sullivan described Saunderson's threatened rebellion as 'mere Saundersonian slap-dash, with about as much substance in it as a soap-bubble'. Unlike Dillon and Sullivan, Justin McCarthy accepted that Saunderson was sincere in his professions of resistance , but nevertheless admitted that just after Saunderson had dared Nationalists 'to raise the flag of rebellion in Ulster . . . he may be seen sitting in the smoking-room [of the House of Commons] with . . . these same Irish Nationalists, exchanging jokes and humorous sayings and compliments and chaff'. It is somewhat ironical that the very qualities that contributed so much to Saunderson's popularity in parliament and in Ulster were also those that helped to persuade Parnellites that Orange threats were not to be taken seriously. Indeed, this point was not lost on Liberal Unionist opinion in Ulster. In an editorial attacking Saunderson's 'self-assumed' leadership of Ulster Unionism the *Weekly Northern Whig* denounced both his Orangeism and his 'levity' on the Home Rule question precisely because they gave credibility to the Nationalists' view that only Orange extremists were opposed to them in Ulster, and, moreover, that they would not seriously oppose the implementation of Home Rule.[8]

However, important as the belief in the disreputable nature of Orangeism was in determining the Parnellite view of Ulster Unionism, of almost equal importance was the ideological context in which it had meaning. As we have seen, nationalist ideology was of a predominantly historicist nature, in which the period of Grattan's Parliament had an important place. The special relevance of Grattan's Parliament for the Ulster question lay in the predominant role taken by northern Protestants in establishing it. This action was pointed to by Parnellites as evidence of the essentially nationalist character of Ulster — a character that was being misrepresented by landlords and Orangemen. It will be seen that during the Home Rule debate the action of northern Protestants in 1782 would be the standard against which the Unionists of 1886 would be judged. But while Nationalists publicly scorned and condemned Orange extremism in Ulster, it was also important — given the need to convince British public opinion that they represented the views of the great majority of Irish people — to prevent displays of anti-nationalist sentiment there. Thus when Nationalists succeeded in defeating Orange attempts to prevent them holding a meeting in Newry in June 1884, Parnell wrote a letter to Timothy Harrington which, while it congratulated Nationalists on a magnificent victory, nevertheless urged self-restraint. Parnell declared that while 'our opinions...are the opinions of the majority of the people of Ulster', and while their right to the public expression of their opinions should be defended with energy and courage, it was also important for Ulster Nationalists to realise 'the high importance of acting with every possible regard and consideration for the susceptibilities of our Orange fellow-countrymen'. As his later correspondence shows, Parnell was most concerned in this period that county conventions in Ulster be adequately organised in anticipation of the redrawing of parliamentary constituency boundaries[9] — a

vital factor in Nationalist electoral successes in the province at
the general election of 1885.

In the light of the Liberal conversion to Home Rule and the
electoral control of nationalist Ireland achieved by Parnellites in
1885, the Unionist reaction to Parnellite activities in Ulster
came to be seen in contemporary nationalist historiography as a
desperate attempt by Ulster landlords and Orangemen, who
were on the verge of defeat, to preserve their power. This view
could draw support from the increase in National League
branches in Ulster between April 1883 and January 1886, when
their numbers rose from 70 to 287. The distribution of branches
in the province and their contributions to party funds to
January 1886 is detailed in Table 2. It was claimed that Ulster
had only five fewer branches than Connaught, while the
former's contribution to party funds exceeded that of
Connaught by £300.[10] But while it is understandable that these
considerations should serve to convince Parnellites of the
validity of their approach to the Ulster problem, what is perhaps
surprising is the extent to which the Parnellite view of the
problem was shared by leading Liberals.

Table 2.   Irish National League branches in Ulster at the beginning of
1886

	population in 1881	no. of branches	subscriptions to 5 Jan. 1886*
Antrim (including Belfast)	445,800	17	£107
Armagh	163,000	19	£196
Cavan	129,500	46	£562
Donegal	206,000	50	£450
Down	248,200	30	£177
Fermanagh	84,900	28	£198
Londonderry	165,000	21	£227
Monaghan	102,700	27	£349
Tyrone	197,700	49	£417
Totals	1,743,000	287	£2,683

*No period is specified for these subscriptions.

GLADSTONE, LIBERALS AND ULSTER

In the same way that the cabinet's role in determining the government's general Irish policy had been very much subordinate to Gladstone's, so also was this the case in regard to the Ulster problem. His conversion to Home Rule and formulation of a Home Rule scheme in 1886 aggravated this problem in two important respects: while the Home Rule bill heightened Unionist hostility to self-government by failing to provide specific safeguards for northern Protestants, Gladstone's vindication of the Nationalist case for Home Rule strengthened the belief of Nationalists that their approach to the Ulster issue was correct and needed no improvement. Moreover, of those cabinet members who were closely associated with Gladstone's Irish policy, none, with the exception of Lord Spencer, had any useful experience of Ireland; and Spencer, whose influence with Gladstone was known to be considerable, had a very unflattering opinion of Ulster Protestants. His publicly stated opinion was an endorsement of the widely held view among Liberals that they consisted mainly of intemperate bigots:

> I have some experience of Ireland. I have been there over eight years, and yet I don't know of any specific instance where there has been religious intolerance on the part of Roman Catholics against their Protestant fellow-countrymen. Bitter religious animosity has been shown, but where? In Ulster, where, I believe, the Protestants have been the chief cause of keeping up the animosity.[11]

Spencer's views of Ulster may be taken as representing an important element of cabinet opinion generally on the Ulster question, given the lack of actual experience of Ulster among its members and the reiteration of such views in much Parnellite propaganda and by other sources. For example, Wilfrid Blunt, the Tory Home Ruler, reporting on the Ulster question from Belfast for the *Pall Mall Gazette*, declared that the Home Rule cause was making great progress in Ulster: the Unionists' talk of civil war was bluff, designed merely to enable them to hold on to their monopoly of public offices, from which Catholics were excluded through discrimination. Home Rule would sweep this state of affairs away — 'hence the bitterness of the Orange side'.[12]

Blunt's assessment of the nature of Ulster Unionism corre-
sponded broadly with that of Henry Labouchere, one of
Gladstone's few, but close, informants on Irish affairs. In a letter
to *The Times* in December 1885 Labouchere argued:

> The area over which the Orangemen hold sway is growing
> smaller and smaller every year. Many of the Presbyterians of
> Ulster have already thrown in their lot with the Home
> Rulers. There is now but one single northern Irish county left
> which does not return a Parnellite — viz. Antrim. In four
> Ulster counties — Monaghan, Cavan, Donegal, and
> Fermanaugh [*sic*] — no one but Parnellites have been
> chosen.[13]

The views of Spencer, Blunt and Labouchere on the nature of
the Ulster opposition to Home Rule exhibit characteristics
which strongly influenced the Liberal approach to that
problem. Like Parnellites, they identified Unionism generally
with Protestant bigotry, but in particular with extreme
Orangemen who had no legitimate grievances against Home
Rule and who wanted merely to discriminate against Catholics;
their talk of civil war was bluff. Thus Ulster Unionism was dis-
creditable and morally reprehensible. In addition, the 1885
general election showed that Parnellites were making great
gains in Ulster — 17 Parnellites and 16 Unionists were
returned — and this was taken as a portent that Orangeism
would eventually die out. As we have noted with reference to
Nationalists, this analysis was not likely to facilitate either an
accurate estimate of the reality of the Ulster problem or effective
action to solve it.

It has been argued, however, that if Gladstone had taken
more pains to obtain Joseph Chamberlain's support for his
Home Rule plan, the Ulster problem, 'which he understood
much better than either Gladstone or Morley', would have been
examined more realistically. This proposition is highly debatable. Chamberlain's knowledge of Ulster — despite his
emphasis on the Ulster question as an obstacle to Home
Rule — was not more profound than that of his contemporaries.
For example, it was pointed out by Canon Malcolm McColl
that Chamberlain's 'central board' scheme of 1885 did not allow

for a separate council for Ulster, and as the national council proposed in the scheme was to have control of education — always a burning question between Protestants and Catholics — then 'it is clear that Mr Chamberlain...contemplated no special provision for Ulster'. Again, when he began to consider special treatment for Ulster in the form of a local assembly in December 1885, it was one to include all of Ulster; and given the fact that the province was almost equally divided between Protestants and Catholics, few Protestants would have accepted that an assembly of this nature would have safeguarded adequately their interests. Not surprisingly, Henry Labouchere, his associate at this time, remarked: 'Your Ulster fervour does not wash.'[14] Thus, even if Chamberlain had been converted to Home Rule, it is unlikely that the Liberal approach to the Ulster question would have been significantly different. Moreover, the cabinet's difficulties in dealing with Ulster were compounded by the conflicting information and suggestions supplied by the two Liberal M.P.s most closely associated with the north of Ireland, James Bryce and Sir Charles Russell, the English Attorney-General.

Bryce was alone in arguing forcefully the case for special treatment of Ulster Protestants in the Home Rule scheme. In a memorandum of considerable length entitled 'The Case of the *Ulster* Protestants' Bryce, who was born in Belfast and many of whose close relations — uncles and aunts — still lived there, set out to show that Ulster Protestant resistance to Home Rule was genuine and was not solely the preserve of a narrow bigoted Orange clique. He claimed to speak principally for Ulster Presbyterians who were unable to sit in parliament 'because the Roman Catholics, by whose help alone they could carry elections against the Orangemen, have usually played them false'. However, they deserved credit for their fidelity to Liberalism in difficult circumstances and 'are the best element in the population of the island'. Bryce argued that of the two broad religious groups in Ulster, in terms of wealth and intelligence, 'The Protestants are of course incomparably superior to the Catholics in both respects. It is the Scottish colony that has made north-east Ireland prosperous.' He then emphasised that Ulster Protestants were socially and commercially connected with Liverpool and Scotland, having little to do with the rest of

Ireland, and did not appreciate the reasons which induced Englishmen to make changes in Irish government. They feared that an Irish parliament would be priest-ridden, would 'Romanise' the whole education system and otherwise damage their Ulster industries and 'philanthropic enterprises'. Emphasising that Ulster Presbyterians were not fanatics, he argued that they nevertheless expected civil war in Ulster if they were placed under a Dublin parliament. Although they were not prepared to say what safeguards would secure their interests, believing that Home Rule could still be defeated totally, 'their resistance to some sort of Irish legislative body would be much diminished . . . and the danger (which is quite real) of a conflict between northern Protestants and Catholics removed' if safeguards to allay their anxieties were introduced into the government's Home Rule scheme. Bryce went on to suggest, vaguely, some restriction on a Dublin government's authority over Ulster, or the institution of 'a local self-governing body or bodies whose consent should be needed to give validity to any act' of a Dublin parliament. Some such safeguard was necessary both to conciliate 'the best element' in the Ulster population and to give Home Rule a chance of working peacefully.[15]

However, despite the forcefulness with which Bryce argued his case, whatever effect it may have had on the cabinet was greatly diminished by a counter-memorandum produced a few days later by Sir Charles Russell. Russell, an Ulster Catholic and an eminent lawyer, was a Liberal, not a Nationalist, and had only come to accept Home Rule at the same time as Gladstone. He was provoked to prepare his memorandum by what he took to be Bryce's erroneous analysis of the Ulster problem. He set out not only to reject Bryce's argument but to explain 'what the Ulster difficulty really means'. He refuted Bryce's claim that Catholics had always played the Ulster Presbyterians false: 'no statement could be further from the truth'. On the contrary, Liberal Presbyterians, although they relied on Catholic support, never supported Catholics for parliament: 'I speak from personal experience'. Russell condemned Bryce's reference to Catholics 'as if they were an altogether inferior race of beings' and argued that the real cause of Protestant opposition to Home Rule was the religious one. Many Ulster Protestants would regard the dominance of the Catholic majority of the people, even constitutionally and reasonably expressed, as little short of persecution; and they have been so long accustomed to look upon themselves as a favoured class, to be regarded exceptionally, that they have not yet been able to accommodate to the notion of being neither more nor less before the law than equals of their Catholic fellow-citizens. I feel strongly that once they understand that they have no right to be regarded in any exceptional way, and must cast in their lot on equal terms with their Catholic brethren, that the repugnance which they now feel would be greatly lessened, and in time altogether cease.

In effect, Russell's argument was that it would be wrong to cater to Ulster Unionist objections to Home Rule, given that the basis of these objections was morally reprehensible — a point he emphasised by citing Belfast, Derry and Lurgan as examples of Protestant bigotry in jobs and political offices. As to Bryce's suggestion that a separate legislative body might be provided for Protestant Ulster, he declared:

It seems to me impossible to suggest the conferring of any separate autonomy upon Ulster as a whole, or upon that small part of Ulster which may be called distinctly non-Catholic, and I see great peril in the future to the experiment of a national parliament should such a distinction be established. The peril would be twofold: if exceptional favour were to be extended on religious grounds to Protestants in Ulster, or in certain counties in Ulster, would that bode well for the position of Protestants in the rest of Ireland? But further, if the experiment of a native parliament is to be tried, ought it not to be tried with the aid of the intelligence and experience which every part of the country and every class of the community can supply to the common stock? I submit that no section ought to be heard to allege that they refuse to take, *pari passu* with the rest of their fellow-countrymen, their share in the government of their common country.[16]

The chief grievance in Ulster that Russell recognised was related to the land question; and if it was impressed on Protestant tenant farmers that a great land purchase scheme

was to accompany Home Rule, 'this will have an important influence on them regardless of religious division' Additionally, if
it was also impressed on them that a national authority was
necessary to implement the land purchase scheme, their
opposition to Home Rule 'will, I think, be materially abated'.
Of the two reports submitted to the cabinet by Bryce and
Russell, there is good reason for thinking that Russell's was the
more influential. Bryce was, in the main, a lone voice among
Liberals in urging the case of Ulster Protestants, and whatever
impression his argument would have had with cabinet
ministers, it would not have been helped by his obvious ethnic
prejudices in their favour. Russell's submission, on the other
hand, had the advantage of fitting well with prevailing Liberal
ideas of Orange bigotry, on the place of Ulster Protestants in the
Irish nation, and on the view that the only serious question that
concerned Ulster, apart from that of education, was the land
question. Indeed, this point was also impressed on Lord Spencer
by one of his Irish contacts, the Protestant Home Ruler, Samuel
Walker. Moreover, when Ulster Liberals declared against
Home Rule at their convention in Belfast in March 1886, any
effect it may have had on the Liberal cabinet was diminished by
Nationalist claims that the convention contained a considerable
minority in favour of Home Rule.[17] Nor, indeed, was their case
greatly furthered by the action of some members of the Ulster
Liberal deputations who petitioned Liberal ministers against
Home Rule in 1886.

Adam Duffin, a member of at least one deputation, has recorded how, when they managed to obtain interviews with
leading Liberals, one of their speakers, Finlay M'Cance, reacted
to comments with which he disagreed: 'He quite shouted down
some of the men we were interviewing when they were trying to
make an observation. Much to our horror.' Another member of
the deputation, Robert McGeogh, tried to circumvent
Gladstone's evident refusal to receive the deputation, by
enclosing his views on the Ulster problem in an extensive letter,
which could only have reinforced the already unfavourable
image of Ulster Unionists in Liberal circles. McGeogh concentrated on the fact that the linen trade was peculiar to, and
had flourished only in, Ulster, despite the ideal conditions which
existed elsewhere in Ireland. The 'fatal drawback' to its success

outside Ulster, he claimed, was the 'undue interference' of the Catholic clergy with the factory hands: deciding who should be employed, dictating how the firms should be run, and, 'lastly, but not least', enforcing the closure of businesses on saints' days, numbering some fifteen to twenty per year. Parnellites, he argued, were jealous of the prosperity of the linen industry because it was 'chiefly Protestant owned' and because Protestant employees were loyal to Britain and held in check their 'disloyal and Catholic fellow-workmen'. If placed under a Dublin parliament, the linen industry would be destroyed by nationalists. To support this contention McGeogh enclosed a leaflet containing examples of Irish Catholic newspaper articles, apparently hostile to the linen trade.[18]

McGeogh's letter exhibited a sectarian spirit which seemed to colour most Ulster Unionist arguments, and this must have militated strongly against a sympathetic treatment of the Ulster Protestant case — not just with the cabinet generally, but with Gladstone, who was in the process of formulating his Irish scheme virtually single-handed. How did he react to the emergence of Ulster Protestant opposition to Home Rule?

For Gladstone, an obvious point of contact with Ulster Protestants should have been the Liberals of the province. However, even before the rapid development of the Ulster Unionist movement in 1886, his attitude to this group — and Irish Liberals generally — was fast developing into one of contempt. R. Barry O'Brien has described his opinion of them during a meeting in November 1885:

> 'The Irish Liberals,' he said with an expression of sublime scorn which I shall never forget, 'the Irish Liberals. Are there any Liberals in Ireland? Where are they? I must confess (with a magnificent roll of the voice) that I feel a good deal of difficulty in recognising these Irish Liberals you talk about; and (in delightfully scoffing accents...) I think Ireland would have a good deal of difficulty in recognising them either.'

Gladstone clearly was in a process of estrangement from the very section of Ulster opinion, which, though it was opposed to Home Rule, was at the same time most likely to acquiesce in a Home Rule scheme if provisions to secure Ulster Protestant interests were provided. It was a process which would only have been en-

couraged by the nature of the arguments made by Ulster
Unionists and their supporters, as well as by Spencer's views on
Ulster. Certainly it is a fact that Gladstone refused to meet
Ulster Unionist deputations at any time during the 1886 Home
Rule crisis. He also, in common with his cabinet, regarded the
threat of Ulster armed resistance to Home Rule as bluff. Indeed,
the Chief Secretary for Ireland, John Morley, contemptuously
dismissed reports that Protestants were drilling in Ulster and
declared that the R.I.C. would easily deal with 'unruly
Orangemen' if violence broke out. Gladstone's view of these
reports was more restrained, but no less explicit. In the course of
introducing his Home Rule bill he declared:

> If, upon any occasion, by an individual or section, violent
> measures have been threatened in certain emergencies, I
> think the best compliment I can make to those who have
> threatened us is to take no notice whatever of the threats, but
> to treat them as momentary ebullitions, which will pass away
> with the fears from which they spring, and at the same time to
> adopt on our part every reasonable measure for disarming
> those fears.[19]

But what precisely was Gladstone's policy for dealing with
Ulster?

Gladstone's conception of the separate interests of Ulster
Protestants was, to say the least, inadequate. He apparently
believed, as late as the autumn of 1885, that these did not
extend further than concern over the education question,
which, however, did not require special consideration, as 'I
think there is no doubt Ulster would be able to take care of itself
in respect to education.' His views on this subject do not appear
to have progressed greatly following his assumption of office,
and the policy he was to follow was already settled by 14 March:
he decided to hold open 'the question as to some part of the
north', though the Ulster problem would not be allowed to
stand in the way of conferring a parliament on Ireland.[20] Essentially this position remained unchanged throughout the Home
Rule debate. That it did so was in large measure due to the
tactics of Ulster Unionists in meeting the Home Rule challenge.

Convinced that they could defeat Home Rule for Ireland in
its entirety, Ulster Unionists refused to formulate any special

arrangement for Ulster alone, even though there was a good chance that, had they done so, their wishes would have been fulfilled. James Bryce informed his uncle, in confidence, that Lord Spencer and Gladstone would, he believed, 'agree to some plan, were any proposed by the Ulstermen, but the latter, in spite of my repeated entreaties, will propose nothing'. As Bryce recorded many years later, given their complete aversion to Home Rule this was tactically the right approach for Ulster Unionists to adopt, but at the same time it also helped to sustain Gladstone's ignorance of the strength and nature of Ulster Unionism. He always took the view that if safeguards or special arrangements were to be made for Ulster Protestants, the onus was on them, and not him, to formulate them. Bryce noted:

> I tried more than once to make him understand how serious this difficulty was, how amazed the north of Ireland Liberals were at this change of front, and what obstinate opposition they would offer. He always replied, 'Let them make some suggestions as to what safeguards they want.'

This, however, Ulster Unionists consistently refused, or were unable, to do, so that when special arrangements for Ulster were proposed — ranging from the exclusion of part of Ulster from the Home Rule bill and autonomy for it, to provision for certain rights to remain with an Ulster provincial council — Gladstone felt justified in declaring:

> There is not one of them which has appeared to us to be so completely justified either upon its merits or by the weight of opinion supporting and recommending it, as to warrant our including it in the bill and proposing it to parliament upon our responsibility.

This situation remained unchanged when the Home Rule bill was defeated on 8 June. While not retreating from the attitude he had taken up on 8 April, of giving constructive consideration to suggestions from Ulstermen on their situation, Gladstone explained: 'Yet I cannot see that any certain plan for Ulster has made any serious or effective progress.' Instead he placed much importance on a recent declaration by Colonel Saunderson, the Ulster Unionist leader, emphatically disclaiming 'the severance of Ulster from the rest of Ireland'.[21] But notwithstanding the influence of Unionist tactics on Gladstone's attitude to the Ulster issue, it would be wrong to overlook other important factors.

It is highly probable that, like his cabinet colleagues and Irish informants, Gladstone was influenced by the fact that the Parnellite sweep at the 1885 general election gave them a psychologically important parliamentary majority of one in Ulster, and, as has been noted above, it appeared to some that this trend would continue. Certainly Gladstone endorsed Parnell's view that a Home Rule parliament for all Ireland would soon dissolve divisions between the people; that a separate parliament for the three most Protestant counties of Ulster would still leave 'unprotected' more than half of the Protestant population of Ireland; and that all Protestants belonged to the Irish nation. Thus, despite his apparently objective stance on the Ulster question, there is no doubt that his outlook was essentially synonymous with that of the Parnellite party. When William O'Brien informed the Commons that 'Instead of depriving them [Ulster Unionists] of any power they possess at the moment, this [Home Rule] bill proposes to confer upon them power of an enormous character,' Gladstone ejaculated: 'Hear, hear!', repeating this when O'Brien added: 'power which they have lost, and which by no earthly possibility can they hope to recover without this bill'.[22]

One other factor which considerably influenced Gladstone's view of the Ulster question was his current absorption in the history of Irish nationalism. His preoccupation with the history of Grattan's Parliament, and the part played in establishing it by Ulster Protestants, convinced him that they were essentially nationalists. Gladstone informed the Commons:

> It should be borne in mind that there was at that time [1799-1800] in existence the greatest difference in sentiment from what we now witness in Ireland. The north was more opposed to that [Act of] Union probably than the south. . . . I believe that the Irish national patriotic sentiment which I have mentioned with sympathy was more vivid in the north of Ireland than any other quarter.

The extent to which the idea that Irish Protestants were really nationalists was to take hold of his mind will be seen in his approach to the Ulster question in the period 1886-92.[23] More immediately, though, it was a view that played a significant role in the Parnellite argument on Ulster during the parliamentary debate on Home Rule.

PROTESTANT ULSTER AND THE POLITICS OF DEMOGRAPHY

Claiming that Ulster was as essentially Irish and nationalist as any other part of Ireland, Nationalists regarded the Ulster problem as consisting of the specific arguments against Home Rule put by Ulster Unionists, and the solution of that problem as lying in showing those arguments to be false. Consequently, when the case was put that Ulster was anti-nationalist and religiously distinct from the rest of Ireland, Parnellites replied by recourse to the central unifying symbol of nationalist ideology: Grattan's Parliament. The predominant role of Ulster Protestants in achieving parliamentary independence in the 1780s provided Nationalists with 'evidence' that Ulstermen were an integral part of the Irish nation.

John Dillon, in parliament and in a lecture to the Young Ireland Society, compared the actions of the Ulster Unionists' ancestors with their 'degenerate descendants...the Archdales, the Vernons, the Saundersons'. Detailing the nationalist activities of Ulstermen in 1782, Dillon declared: 'The man who says that by their past history... Protestants and Catholics are marked out apart is an unscrupulous party politician, or else ignorant of Irish history.' Ulster Protestants had been perverted by foreign influences and Dublin Castle government, but even in the darkest hour the best Protestants stood by the national cause. This argument was also made by William O'Brien;[24] however, although important, it did not constitute the whole of the Nationalist case on the Ulster question. Equally important, as will be seen, were the statistics on religious division in the province. In fact most Nationalist speeches exhibited a contradictory strain of argument. Parnellites claimed that the 'nationalist' activities of Ulster Protestants in 1782 showed that that community was essentially nationalist; but if asked to demonstrate the extent to which Ulster was nationalist, they invariably identified nationalism with the Catholic community there and argued that it was equal to, or larger than, the Protestant and Unionist community.

The religious demography of the province had long played an important part in Nationalist arguments. Writing in 1880, R. Barry O'Brien used it to counter the Unionists' 'Ulster' claims. O'Brien showed that over the whole province Catholics numbered 47.9 per cent of the population. More specifically, in the predominantly 'loyalist' counties of Antrim, Armagh, Down and Londonderry, the statistics showed that Catholics accounted for at least a third of the population, numbering 338,400, to a Protestant population of 683,800.[25] In the five predominantly nationalist counties of Donegal, Tyrone, Fermanagh, Monaghan and Cavan, an indisputable Catholic majority existed: this area comprised 459,100 Catholics and 225,700 Protestants. The facts of religious demography in Ulster were of crucial importance to the Nationalist argument: the Catholic majority in five of nine Ulster counties gave Nationalists a psychologically important overall 'majority' of one, while the substantial Catholic presence in the four most Protestant counties, together with their belief that, except for Orangemen, Protestants could be won over to Home Rule, served to validate the Nationalist strategy of 'winning' Ulster by constantly increasing their parliamentary representation there — a strategy, they believed, that had proved itself at the 1885 general election. Thus during the Home Rule debate Parnellites showed no inclination to accept special treatment for the province, in any form.

John Redmond's speech in the Commons on 13 May 1886 was typical of Nationalist arguments on the Ulster problem. Having made the usual reference to the nationalist activities of northern Protestants in Grattan's day, Redmond proceeded to cite the facts of religious division in the north to illustrate the extent to which Ulster was nationalist. Quoting a recent parliamentary return to show that Protestant Ulster did not exist, he declared that 48 per cent of the population was Catholic, and that, if Belfast was left out, the Catholics were '55 per cent of the whole population'. Moreover, even the most distinctly Protestant portion of Ulster — Antrim and parts of Down and Armagh — had a considerable Catholic population. This area comprised 542,800 Protestants and 188,200 Catholics, while in the rest of the province Protestants numbered 316,600 and Catholics 645,200.

Rejecting Joseph Chamberlain's argument that a separate parliament for Ulster was necessary, Redmond declared that it was not Ulster Protestants that might need protection but those in the three southern provinces who were in 'such a miserable minority'. But even if an Ulster parliament were constituted, the extent of Nationalist support in the province would ensure that it contained 'a majority of Catholics'. Similarly, on the question of whether Ulster would violently resist the enactment of the Home Rule scheme, Redmond declared that the Orangemen would first have to subdue the Ulster Catholics, and 'The idea of the Protestant portion of Ulster conquering the Catholic portion is as absurd as the contention that Lancashire could conquer the northern cities of England.' Redmond's argument was endorsed by T. D. Sullivan, J. F. X. O'Brien and Justin McCarthy, who also dismissed talk of Ulster resistance as bluff: such talk had been inspired by English politicians such as Lord Randolph Churchill. Citing the extent of Nationalist support in the province, McCarthy declared: 'We have shown that Ulster is...a Nationalist province of Ireland.'[26]

Of all Parnellite speakers on the Ulster question, however, it was Thomas Sexton who used the religious demography of Ulster to the best effect. He put it that Ulster was no more Protestant than the rest of Ireland: 'Leave out Belfast, and at the last census the Catholics had a majority of 100,000 over the whole province.' Sexton developed this idea further by arguing that since the last census 'the emigration of the Protestants has greatly increased, especially to British North America'.[27] Moreover, like other Parnellites, he referred both to his party's parliamentary majority in Ulster and to the likelihood of nationalist control of a provincial Ulster parliament. However, he also sought to encourage Ulster Protestant acceptance of the Home Rule scheme by emphasising their moral responsibility to the small Protestant community in southern Ireland. He declared that the Ulster Unionist leader, Colonel Saunderson, would be denounced by the world as a 'dastard' if he deserted the 300,000 southern Protestants:

Those 300,000 are in the midst of a Catholic population of

3,000,000. They would never exercise a vote, they would never have a single member in parliament, they could not form a constituency anywhere, they would be absolutely dumb in the hands of the legislature.

Turning to the question of whether a separate parliament should be created for the small Protestant part of Ulster, Sexton argued that, given the complex interrelated nature of religious affiliation in the province, such a legislature would simply create another persecuted Catholic minority there. If such a legislature were constituted and Ireland were to have two parliaments,

> You would have not one but two oppressed minorities. You would have the 200,000 Catholics and the 500,000 Protestants of the north of Ireland, and the 3,000,000 Catholics and 300,000 Protestants of the south in the other provinces, so that in order to please 500,000 people, or the men who are supposed to represent them, you will outrage the feelings of 200,000 Catholics and 300,000 Protestants. If you care to pursue the fantastic theory . . . down to the point of a parish parliament, you would not solve the question, because the Catholic population so interpenetrates every portion of Ulster that even if you have a parliament in every parish you would still have a minority in each. There is no safe standing ground except to treat Ireland as a unit, and the demand of Ireland as a demand of the people of Ireland.

The arguments used by both Redmond and Sexton as to the 'vulnerability' of southern Protestants if Ulster was excluded from the jurisdiction of the Home Rule parliament were taken up and endorsed by Parnell on the last day of the debate. The 'vulnerability' argument was thus not so unique to Parnell as Dr Lyons has assumed: 'His comment on this was . . . the voice of the quintessential southern Unionist which spoke through the mouth of the renegade landlord.'[28] It was more the case that Parnell, Redmond and Sexton were simply seeking to employ one of the Ulster Unionists' own claims — that they would not desert their fellow-Protestants in southern Ireland — in the Home Rule cause.

Certainly Parnell's attitude to Ulster Unionism during the general election of 1886 was as contemptuous as that of his party generally. Speaking in his first major election speech at Portsmouth, Parnell held up a political map of Ireland before his audience and pointed derisively to the Ulster Unionist constituencies, coloured, not very tactfully, in yellow: 'This little yellow patch covered by my forefinger represents Protestant Ulster — (*loud laughter*) — and they say now they want a separate parliament for this little yellow patch up in the north-east.'[29]

The forcefulness with which Parnellites established — to their own satisfaction — that Ulster belonged to nationalist Ireland was equally evident in their attacks on the 'economic' case against Home Rule made by northern Unionists. As it was often presented, this argument claimed that Ulster was more prosperous than the other Irish provinces, and was a Protestant and Anglo-Saxon province fighting against domination by papists and Celts who would tax the north to revive the commercially lethargic south.

THE QUESTION OF ULSTER'S PROSPERITY: A CONFLICT OF ANALYSIS

The issue of Ulster's prosperity in relation to other regions of Ireland was a deceptively simple one. It has sometimes been assumed that the fact of Ulster's greater prosperity in this respect was so obvious as hardly to require investigation.[30] However, it will be seen here that the issue was much more complicated than it outwardly seemed, especially when it came to establishing the facts of relative prosperity.

The Unionist argument of Ulster's prosperity in relation to the three southern provinces was not in fact a product of the 1886 Home Rule debate, but was already well established in 1880. R. Barry O'Brien succinctly explained how he thought the Ulster argument influenced English public opinion during the land war

> But, it is said, all these disturbances, crimes and discontent prevail only in the south. In the north all is prosperity, happiness and peace. Why? it is asked. And the answer is invariably given, because the northerners spring from a different race, and belong to a different religion. The northern is an Anglo-Saxon and a Protestant, and the

southern is a Celt and a papist. The prosperity of one district is attributable to Protestant energy, and the poverty of the other to Catholic indolence.... This explanation as it appears to me is founded upon a grave misconception of fact and is an unwarrantable reading of history.

Mabel Sharman Crawford, daughter of the famous Ulster tenant-right advocate, writing in 1887, declared this view to be prevalent also in Ulster:

> The widespread belief that Irish poverty and turbulence originate in the baleful influences of creed and race is very generally held as an unquestionable truth in north-east Ulster, where I lived.[31]

It was only to be expected that in the heat of the Home Rule debate arguments of this nature would be used.

The most prominent speech in this respect was delivered in the House of Commons by G. J. Goschen, who sought to validate statistically — albeit implicity — the stereotype of northern Anglo-Saxon Protestant prosperity and southern Celtic and Catholic poverty. Using the statistics of income tax culled from schedule D (professional and commercial incomes), he argued that if Ulster was excluded from the Home Rule scheme, a Dublin parliament would be unable to raise enough taxes to run the government of the country: excluding Dublin, the total return under schedule D was £5,584,000, of which £2,520,000, or 45 per cent, was contributed by Ulster. He continued:

> But in Ulster itself the contrast between the industrial condition of separate districts — I will call them for the moment the loyalist and the nationalist districts — is very striking. Out of nine counties of Ulster, four form one predominantly loyal — namely Antrim, Armagh, Down and Londonderry. These counties, which returned to parliament 15 loyalists and 4 Parnellites, show a return of £2,220,000 under schedule D. The remaining five counties — namely Cavan, Donegal, Monaghan, Fermanagh, and Tyrone, which are predominantly nationalist, and which returned to parliament 13 nationalists and only 1 loyalist, show a return under schedule D of only £300,000.... The proportion contributed by loyal Ulster is 88 per cent and that by nationalist Ulster is 12 per cent.

Goschen also quoted some adverse comments on the Ulster linen industry in the nationalist *Belfast Morning News* to prove the antagonism of nationalists to Ulster industries.[32]

It was, perhaps, to be expected that Goschen's claims would be answered first by this newspaper. In the issue of 24 April T. G. Rigg, in answering Goschen, amassed figures from all schedules of income tax assessment to produce a radically different picture of Ulster prosperity in relation to the rest of Ireland. The first fault he pointed to was Goschen's absence of Dublin from the return of schedule D: he continued by presenting a detailed examination of Ulster's position in Ireland, in a table giving the property and profits assessed for income tax for the year ending 1880, under schedules A, B, D and E. In round figures, the result was as presented in Table 3. Rigg also produced an impressive array of statistics to show that Belfast's income tax assessment, per head of population, was lowest when compared with the majority of Great Britain's largest cities, including

Table 3.   Irish income tax assessment, 1879-80

	population 1881	income tax assessment 1879-80	*per capita* assessment
Leinster	1,300,000	£13,300,000	207s
Munster	1,400,000	£8,000,000	120s
Ulster	1,700,000	£10,000,000	114s
Connaught	800,000	£3,000,000	73s

Liverpool, Manchester, Glasgow, Newcastle, Bradford, Bristol, Nottingham and Birmingham. Moreover, while Belfast's income tax assessment was lower than those for any of these cities, Dublin compared favourably, ranking fourth highest. To the question why, if Belfast was so prosperous, it did not rival the great British cities, Rigg concluded: 'Belfast is comparatively poor because it is the business centre of a comparatively poor district.' Dublin was comparatively rich because of its situation in one of the most fertile parts of Ireland, and in 'the really active and prosperous portion'. He also compiled a table comparing Ulster and the rest of Ireland purely on schedule D and leaving out Dublin. These comparative statistics showed that Ulster, with a population of 1,700,000, had a *per capita* assessment of 29 shillings, whereas the rest of Ireland, which had a population of 3,400,000 and a total schedule D assessment of £6,400,000, had a *per capita* assessment of 34 shillings.

Attacking as mere nonsense the implication in Goschen's claims that Ulster's loyalist counties were richer than the nationalist ones in the proportion of 88 to 12 per cent, Rigg included the schedule D assessment, which Goschen had used as the sole basis for his argument, with schedules A, B and E, to produce a different picture of the relative prosperity of the two areas (as shown in Table 4). Finally, although Goschen had made no reference to valuation statistics, Rigg emphasised Leinster's greater prosperity over Ulster with statistics showing the valuation of rateable property in the two provinces, and with Dublin left out of the Leinster assessment. In this comparison Ulster's valuation was £4,300,000, only marginally higher than that of Leinster, which stood at £3,900,000.

Table 4.   Ulster income tax assessment, 1879-80

	income tax assessment 1879-80	*per capita* assessment
Cavan Donegal Fermanagh Monaghan Tyrone	£3,000,000	87s
Antrim Armagh Down Londonderry	£7,000,000	133s

Rigg's arguments were repeated and extended on 15 and 22 May in the *Weekly Examiner*, while in parliament they were taken up by J. C. Flynn, Parnell and T. M. Healy. Thomas Sexton, in his contribution to the statistics debate, also argued that if part of Ulster was prosperous, it was not due to 'any cause of race or creed', but to the fact that while manufacturing industry was encouraged and 'Ulster custom' established, industry in the rest of Ireland was 'crushed out of existence'.

However, it was on the statistics of income tax assessment that the debate really turned, and when these were examined for all four provinces a different picture from that given to parliament by Goschen was produced. Nevertheless, they also tended to give an exaggerated view of the prosperity of nationalist areas. For example, what Rigg's demonstration of Dublin's greater prosperity over Belfast did not point out was that the assessment of income tax was disproportionately swelled in Dublin's favour by the fact that most of the major banks, railway companies, insurance offices and all government offices had their staffs of officials and headquarters there — a factor which would have complicated an assessment of the relative prosperity not merely of the two cities, but of Ulster in relation to the three southern provinces. Moreover, it was almost impossible to extricate and apportion to each province the amount of business each company conducted there. Another complicating factor was the unknown quantity of English and Scottish capital invested in Ireland through Dublin, and Irish capital invested in Great Britain, which did not show up on Irish income tax returns.[33]

But Rigg's picture of the relative prosperity of Belfast and Dublin is suspect in other ways too. For instance, it failed to show the respective development of the two cities in the period from 1871 to 1881. In this period Belfast's growing prosperity was underlined by a dramatic rise in population, from 174,400 to 208,100, while the number of electors rose from 14,400 to 22,000. In the same period Dublin's population rose much less dramatically, from 267,700 to 273,000, while the number of electors actually fell from 13,100 to 12,500. Thus not only was Belfast's rate of expansion dramatically greater than that of Dublin, but, with a significantly smaller population in 1881, Belfast had a far superior number of people qualified to vote. A comparison of the inhabited houses in each area and their rateable valuation likewise told to Belfast's advantage.[34]

Also, on the question of the relative prosperity of nationalist and loyalist regions within Ulster, Rigg's refutation of Goschen's argument rested on the fact that there was a relatively small difference in the *per capita* assessment of the two areas. What he did not show, however, was the great difference in the population balance of the two areas, with the four predominantly loyalist counties having a population some 16,500 in excess of the five predominantly nationalist ones.[35] But even taking the statistics at their face value, did they prove — as was Goschen's intention when he brought up the issue of relative prosperity — that one political faction in Ireland was intrinsically more industrious than another? This was not the case, as Nationalists, if pushed, would have had to admit that a large section of the income tax paid in the south was paid by a strenuously Unionist population.

Nevertheless, although the issue of comparative regional prosperity was clearly much more complicated than Nationalists and Unionists admitted, the fact remains that Goschen's use of income tax returns defined the terms on which the debate was largely conducted, and, as we have seen, it appeared to tell in the Nationalists' favour. But since this was so, why was it that Unionists made so much of Ulster's prosperity, and why did their case fail to register? But first, what was the case that could be made? Briefly, that north-east Ulster had little in common economically with the rest of Ireland: it was the only thriving industrialised portion of Ireland, and the region's industry, being geared to external markets, owed little to the agricultural economy of rural Ireland. Thus north-east Ulster's economic well-being necessitated the close relationship with British commercial and industrial life afforded by the Union (or by a separate parliament for Ulster should Home Rule be enacted). An adequate formulation of this case would have presented Nationalists with an argument much less easy to counter. Certainly the statistics of income tax relating to professions and trades which Goschen presented in parliament were those most relevant to the presentation of such a case, but they required a more careful and qualified presentation than they received at his hands. The fact was that Goschen raised the question of relative prosperity in terms so abstract that the issue of north-east Ulster's unique *industrially* based prosperity became submerged in a debate about regional prosperity in general — a debate in which Nationalists had the task of simply providing statistics to counter his.

As with many English politicians who knew little of Ireland, north or south, it was more attractive to Goschen to use statistics to give credibility to a general north/south dichotomy than it was to present a case that would stand close scrutiny but which necessitated a fairly close familiarity with the situation to which they referred. In fact his statistics had been supplied by Adam Duffin, a prominent Belfast Liberal Unionist who had met him the previous month as a member of a deputation to London to protest against Home Rule; and there is reason to believe that Duffin may have supplied the figures to present a more qualified case than Goschen made. Following the Nationalist refutation of his argument, Goschen wrote to Duffin thanking him for having provided the figures, but adding: 'You will have seen that I put them before the House of Commons in a rather different form from that in which you sent them to me and that they were much objected to by the Nationalist members.' He concluded by requesting verification of the figures to offset future Nationalist attacks.[36]

Certainly Goschen's mishandling of them afforded a major propaganda advantage to Nationalists. Derived as they were from the most authoritative sources available, these statistics gave a credibility to their argument on the Ulster problem that it would not otherwise have had; and given the difficulty in presenting a more favourable economic argument, Ulster Unionist M.P.s did not pursue the statistical debate further. Indeed, when an Ulster Unionist M.P. returned to it some years later he abandoned the attempt to prove Ulster's superior prosperity to nationalist Ireland in general, and argued instead, to greater effect, that the real division between Ireland's rich and poor areas was not that between north and south, but between east and west.[37] But while the Nationalist case on the Ulster question in 1886 was undoubtedly better presented than that of the Unionists, this did not bring the issue any nearer to a solution. Telling points made on the floor of the House of Commons did not solve the problem of Protestant rejection of Home Rule in northern Ireland, as can be gauged from an examination of the reaction in Ulster to the Home Rule scheme.

The Ulster Question (2):
The Problem of National Identity
and the Loyalist Reaction to Home Rule

NATIONALITY AND ULSTER UNIONISM

GIVEN Gladstone's intention to include Ulster in his Home Rule scheme, it was inevitable that the question of where the national identity of northern Unionists lay would come to the fore. That it did so, however, does not mean that the issue is easily resolved. One of the chief difficulties in coping with this problem is that the very meaning of terms like 'nation' and 'nationality' is imprecise. During the Home Rule debate both were frequently used in contexts where it is difficult to define whether or not they implied a right to statehood and independence, or, as often applied in the case of England, Scotland and Wales, were merely cultural designations referring to component parts of one political nation incorporating the whole United Kingdom. It is not surprising, therefore, that Ulster Unionist approaches to this issue should exhibit a similar ambiguity. A typical utterance on the subject claimed that the Irish were 'a divided nation' consisting of 'two irreconcilable nationalities', while T. W. Russell, soon to be Liberal Unionist M.P. for South Tyrone, confessed his ignorance as to whether Ireland was a nation or not.[1]

In approaching this subject a study (Appendix 2) has been made of a sample of thirty Unionist speeches, delivered at various venues, mainly in Ulster during the Home Rule debate. These have been examined with a view to providing some insight into the extent to which northern Unionists identified with the Irish Catholic nationalist community and the population of Great Britain, and what modifications in their political identity, community status and material welfare they believed the enactment of Home Rule would entail. Although the material in these speeches is of an essentially 'unstructured'* nature, it presents sufficient evidence to indicate a lack of any widespread, sharply defined view of the sense of national identity held by Ulster Unionists. Some speakers, particularly Orangemen, defined the Ulster loyalist community as racially superior to Irish nationalists; others defined their differences in mainly class terms. Some used the term 'nation' to include their own community and the population of Great Britain; others again used this term to refer to all the people of the British Isles. Moreover, race, class and national distinctions were often ambiguously and confusedly employed in the same speech.

At first sight these facts would seem to support the views of one of the most recent and perceptive writers on the Ulster loyalist identity, D. W. Miller. He argues that the Ulster loyalist identity cannot be explained in terms of national identity, especially British nationality. This was because loyalists did not accept what he defines as three fundamental conditions of national membership. First, they did not trust the whole people of the United Kingdom, as represented in its democratic regime, as a satisfactory guarantor of their civil rights, the most important of which, he argues, was the right to 'free expression' (including the right to march) throughout the state's territory; secondly, they did not see themselves as 'like' the other members of the United Kingdom; finally, they did not accept the United Kingdom as a 'terminal community within which there was the assumption of the peaceful settlement of disagreement based on the supreme value of national unity'. There are, however, several weaknesses in explaining the nature of the loyalist position within the United Kingdom by reference to these criteria. At a general level, they relate to the basic assumption on

*This term is used by social scientists to describe material where information has to be deduced by the investigator, rather than, as in 'structured' studies, collected in answer to questionnaires. In other words, Unionist speakers were not giving replies to specific questions on their concept of nationality and thus were not compelled to define their community's position in this respect. It was partly for this reason that an initial attempt to compile a table providing a distribution of types of identification expressed by individual speakers (including racial, national and class affinity with, or aversion to, Great Britain and the rest of Ireland) had to be abandoned in favour of the more general examination which follows.

which Miller's argument is based: the Ulster loyalist community is defined as a substantially alienated group and contrasted with the population of Great Britain, among whom a virtually total homogeneity of political views, values and practice is assumed.[2]

For example, Miller's claim that government policy — in its restriction of the marching area of Protestants to prevent riots — was a major source of their alienation from the United Kingdom state because it treated them differently from Englishmen is hardly credible. Throughout the nineteenth century in Great Britain there was a strong tradition of anti-popery and anti-Irish marches and gatherings, similar to the anti-nationalist demonstrations that occurred in Ulster, and which were subject to similar treatment by the police when violent outbreaks occurred. Thus alienation based on different or unequal treatment could hardly have existed. More importantly, though, Miller's claim that Ulster loyalists, in their readiness to enjoin conflict to enforce their 'rights', were effectively rejecting the United Kingdom as a 'terminal community within which there was the assumption of the peaceful settlement of disagreement based on the supreme value of national unity' is similarly suspect. British anti-popery protesters were as ready to enjoin conflict to enforce their 'rights' as were Ulster Protestants, and had a similar motivation. Whereas the latter ostensibly feared the threat to their spiritual and material security posed by Catholic nationalists, the former feared the threat to the security of the state emanating from the supposed 'divided allegiance' of Catholics, who, it was believed, could not be true to 'Queen and country' if they were also good Catholics and loyal to Rome. Clearly, if acceptance of a United Kingdom nationality was dependent on a rejection of violence as a means of settling disagreements, a considerable proportion of British opinion, including those Unionists who urged Ulster to rebel, would, according to Miller's criteria, have to be considered as alienated as he claims Ulster loyalists were. Moreover, as a recent study has shown, a not inconsiderable section of the Conservative Party in Britain was as suspicious of the intentions of their leaders as an Ulster Unionist could be.[3]

Similarly, Miller's view that the latter did not regard themselves as 'like' the population in Great Britain, but rather took the more calculated view that 'Ulster chooses to remain British' because that was the best way of protecting their interests, is also questionable. Rather what is noticeable in the speeches listed in Appendix 2 is the high degree of ideological and emotional commitment to Britain and what they saw as British values and traditions. This attitude of mind was forcefully and succinctly expressed by a deputation of four Presbyterians and one Baptist, who, in the course of petitioning British political leaders against Home Rule in 1886, gave an interview to the *Pall Mall Gazette*:

> We are against the loss of our birthright as British citizens. We are against being cut off from the country to which we are proud to belong, and being disinherited of the empire which we and our fathers have helped to build up.

Speaking at a slightly later date, one Ulster Presbyterian clergyman, in describing his own brethren's attitudes to the empire, could justly have included the Protestant population of the north generally:

> It is something to be an Englishman in the widest sense of the word, a citizen of the great empire on which the sun never sets, and whose flag wherever it waves, brings justice, liberty and peace. Whatever quarrels with British policy...[we] may have had from time to time...the sentiment of loyalty towards, and pride in the British inheritance and commonwealth of peoples, has been common to all.

The extent to which these sentiments prevailed was also noted by a reporter analysing the causes of the Belfast riots in 1886. He spoke of 'the indignation aroused in northern Protestants by the prospect of being cut off from the empire in whose greatness they exult and in whose justice they trust'. Moreover, such devotion to 'the British inheritance' was allied, as will be seen, to Anglo-Saxonist arguments which stressed that Ulster Protestants were not merely 'like' Britons, but belonged to the same race, the same 'flesh and blood'. Miller, it is true, recognises that Ulster Protestants did identify strongly with the empire, but closely associates this with a belief he claims they subscribed to which 'denied being "merely" British'. Miller also points up the instrumental aspect of imperial identification for Ulster Protestants; by identifying primarily with the empire they could avoid the awkward question of one's political obligation if one dissented from the 'national' will[4] — a question which arose in relation to the Westminster parliament. Yet while it would be rash to deny that this last was a part of loyalist thinking, it would nevertheless appear that pride in their imperial identity was for northern Protestants a logical extension of their pride in their attachment to the British race and nation rather than an alternative to it.

Such an interpretation, however, also informs the central thesis of Miller's work, which is that the essence of the Ulster loyalists' relationship to the British people was 'contractarian': they came to Ireland in plantation times to perform a great colonising service on England's behalf, and, for the latter's part, it was bound, in return for this service, not to hand them over to their enemies — as they believed Home Rule would do. And if this situation were to occur, the loyalists would consider themselves absolved from the obligation to obey England's laws and empowered with the right to 'try to coerce [the Westminster parliament] into keeping the bargain'[5] or 'contract'. That such a notion was a part of the northern loyalist world-view is certainly true, but as to whether it occupied the central role in their political outlook that Miller ascribes to it, at this time, is debatable. In none of the thirty speeches studied in Table 9 did any speaker specifically refer to such a 'contract', while only nine speakers implied a contractual relationship by describing the enactment of Home Rule in terms such as 'betrayal'. Here again, it seems, pride in their British nationality and membership of that great 'progressive' entity — the empire — far outweighed notions of a merely contractual relationship with Britain; though, of course, for Unionists the key to their continued inclusion in the empire was the maintenance of the Act of Union between Britain and Ireland.

In other words, the maintenance of their imperial heritage was to be achieved through continued membership of the political nation comprising the whole United Kingdom. That a widespread confusion in the meaning they attached to terms like 'nation', 'nationality' and 'race' existed among loyalists is not necessarily evidence to the contrary. Joseph Chamberlain, for example, could on one occasion deny nationality to Ireland, and on another claim that Ireland was one of four nationalities comprising the United Kingdom. Indeed, Ulster Unionist notions of nationality and patriotism, far from being different from mainstream Conservative thought on such matters in this period of great imperial fervour, were apparently highly representative. R. A. Hufford has shown that, in terms of the time devoted to them, the subjects of Ulster and the maintenance of the integrity of the empire through the preservation of the 'supreme sovereignty of the parliament at Westminster' were the two foremost issues in the parliamentary debate on Home Rule.[6]

Thus to argue, on the basis of the three criteria employed by Miller, that Ulster loyalists did not fully subscribe to a sense of United Kingdom nationality is to ignore some highly important aspects of their relationship with the British population. By not examining the population of the state as a whole he ignores the extent to which the actions of northern Unionists were paralleled by those of groups in Britain and overemphasises the homogeneity of political values and practices in the latter. Indeed, it could be argued that Scotland, by retaining its own legal, administrative and educational systems, and in having its own established church, retained many of the trappings of separate nationality and subscribed in a far more limited degree to a 'complete' sense of United Kingdom nationality and sovereignty than Ulster loyalists did. The national distinctiveness of Scotland was emphasised during the Home Rule debate by Sir Lyon Playfair:

> Scotland preserved by the Union all the institutions which were peculiarly national. Her own system of laws and courts of justice were maintained. Her much-cherished Presbyterian form of worship was made the state form of faith. Her parochial schools and her four democratic universities, so unlike those of England, were included in the articles of the Union. And . . . Scotland is as much a nation now as when the Union Act was passed. Every attempt to weaken her distinct nationality has been indignantly repelled. I am old enough to recollect how profoundly Scotland was agitated when the royal arms were altered, and when the lion of Scotland was removed from the dexter to the sinister side of the shield.[7]

The case of Scotland indicates an important characteristic of United Kingdom nationality and the concept of sovereignty associated with it: both were based on compromise and were subject to qualification. In this context the insistence of some Ulster Unionists that there was a limit to their loyalty to the Westminster parliament could hardly be described as aberrant behaviour.

A related issue to that of how far northern Unionists saw their national identity as British at this time is the extent to which an Ulster 'nationalism' began to emerge. This argument has been put forward most recently by Dr Peter Gibbon. Referring, albeit, to the slightly later period of 1892, he claims that 'insofar as northern Unionists laid claim to an identity which was territorially based' they 'were creating a form of nationalism'. Moreover, their claim to 'self-determination' involved the creation of a new being: 'the Ulsterman . . . with the provision for him, by an array of publicists, of a unique "character", "heritage" and destiny'. Additionally, the ideology which accompanied their claim to self-determination was 'filled out' with a species of social-imperialist arguments. Unlike 1886, he argues, when Unionist apprehensions about Home Rule were expressed in terms of a direct threat to the very lives of Ulster Protestants, the emphasis in their arguments in 1892 was on the threat to Ulster's economic life and the extension of social reforms to the working class that Home Rule posed.[8] There is, however, reason to doubt seriously the validity of Gibbon's argument.

First, as has been seen, the territorially based identity to which the loyalist community laid claim extended far beyond the confines of Ulster and included the rest of the United Kingdom and the empire. Secondly, the development which Gibbon perceives in Unionist ideology in the period 1886-92, from a literal fear for their physical well-being to more sophisticated social-imperialist arguments concerning the Home Rule threat to Ulster's economic life and the prospects for social reform, does not reflect the reality of the Unionist world-view. Certainly, as Table 9 shows, they did literally fear at this time for their physical security; of thirty speakers, twenty-seven expressed this apprehension. Simultaneously, though, it also shows that the social-imperialist dimension to their ideology, which Gibbon asserts did not appear until 1892, was already being developed in 1886. Thirdly, and most importantly, the development of an 'Ulsterman' type, on which his theory of Ulster nationalism is largely dependent, did not appear in 1892, but began as early as mid-century, and must be seen in quite a different context.

The crucial event in this development was the meeting in Belfast in 1852 of the British Association, which promoted an intense interest in the heritage and history of the Ulster Protestant community; and this must be seen as a local dimension of the general Victorian preoccupation with British history and racial identity that was widespread at this time. The most immediate result of the Ulster phase of this phenomenon was the founding of the *Ulster Journal of Archaeology*, whose first series of universally popular articles was collectively entitled 'Origin and Characteristics of the Population in the Counties of Down and Antrim'. These articles subscribed to prevailing race theories about the supremacy of the Anglo-Saxon race — among which they included Ulster Protestants — over the Irish Celts. More specifically, the characteristics of the 'Ulsterman' that Gibbon identifies as developing in the post-1892 period — respect for law and order, thrift, hard work — were, in fact, first widely developed in this series of articles.[9] Thereafter the notion of a separate Ulster ethnic identity with attendant virtues developed throughout the late nineteenth century in much the same way as such ideas did in Great Britain.

Moreover, the racial sense of Ulster loyalists was apt to be heightened by the injudicious utterances of prominent Nationalists. When Michael Davitt claimed that Ulster Unionists were only alien settlers in Ulster, neither Celtic by race or habit, the *Belfast News-Letter* retorted: 'We have every reason to be thankful . . . that Ulstermen are not Celts and not being so, why should they be subject to a government of the worst class of Celts.' But with reference to how far this aspect of Unionist thinking might be seen as supporting the view of an emergent Ulster nationalism, it must be remembered that what was being affirmed in these race theories was not just the sharp ethnic division of communities in Ireland, but also the close blood relationship of Ulster Protestants with the population of

Great Britain. As Colonel Waring put it in a speech at Maralin during the Home Rule crisis, he did not think the English and Scots would desert 'their own flesh and blood'.[10]

HOME RULE: THE LOYALIST REACTION

Although the Ulster Unionist campaign against Home Rule only became fully organised in 1886, the intensity of emotion associated with it had been steadily building up in previous years. For northern loyalists the salient fact of the nationalist land and Home Rule campaigns had been the surrender of British Liberalism to revolutionary acts and outrages: the Phoenix Park murders, dynamite explosions in London and the continuous stream of revolutionary propaganda by nationalist orators provided for Unionists the immediate background to the 'invasion of Ulster' in the winter of 1883-4. Additionally, the events associated with the 'invasion', the adverse publicity attaching to the Orange Order and the dismissal of Lord Rossmore from the bench intensified the feeling, especially among Orangemen, that they were being abandoned by the country to which they wished to remain united.[11]

Their unease, moreover, was intensified by the changes brought about by the franchise and redistribution acts of 1884-5, which enabled Nationalists to increase their parliamentary representation in the province from three to seventeen at the general election of 1885. Explaining the state of confusion in Ulster on political affairs in January 1886, Thomas McKnight, editor of the *Northern Whig*, declared:

> An utterly unexpected state of things had appeared. The attitudes of parties, the intentions of public men, the questions at issue, seemed to have changed since the new parliament had been chosen, and before it had actually met.

Indeed, Ulster Unionists felt doubly threatened, since Gladstone at this time was not only being associated with Home Rule, but the Conservative Party was involved in an informal alliance with Parnellites. Ironically, given Lord Randolph Churchill's close identification with Ulster Unionists shortly afterwards, it was the belief that he was about to 'betray' Ulster Protestants over Home Rule that moved Colonel Saunderson to re-enter politics in 1885. Thereafter Ulster Unionists began to organise as a separate group in parliament, and at a meeting in Dublin on 18 December 1885 Saunderson obtained support for such a move from the Irish Loyal and Patriotic Union and soon afterwards emerged as the leader of the group. With this development the forces of Ulster Unionism quickly united to oppose Home Rule.[12]

As was seen in the preceeding chapter, in order to forestall the enactment of Home Rule for any part of Ireland, northern Unionists not only rejected the policy but also refused to formulate a plan that would secure either special treatment for Ulster or exclusion from the jurisdiction of a Dublin parliament. The intensity of their reaction to the Home Rule scheme, however, can only be appreciated properly through a wider understanding of how the Nationalist campaign for Home Rule functioned within their total world-view. There were various elements to Ulster Protestant ideology, and one of the most prominent was, as Appendix 2 illustrates, their deep-rooted and historically based view of Catholic nationalism. Before the rapid development of Victorian historical research from 1860 the Ulster loyalist view that Irish Catholic nationalism was a movement representing an ethnically and religiously backward people, historically intent on persecuting Protestants, was one shared by most sections of British political opinion; as we have seen, it found its two most popular exponents in Macaulay and Froude. Regretting his inability to comply with an invitation to speak in the province in 1886, Froude, in an open letter to Ulster Unionists, declared:

> The present state of things is the inevitable consequence of all that has gone before. It will end as the 1641 business ended, or the 1690, or the 1798. The anarchy will grow until it becomes intolerable. John Bull will then pull on his boots and will do as he did before. What will happen in the interval I do not pretend to guess. You in Ulster I hope to see holding your own ground. Stand steady, whatever comes.

Froude's identification of the contemporary Home Rule campaign with previous Irish rebellions naturally struck a highly responsive chord in the Ulster Protestant community, mixing both assurance as to the ultimate failure of Home Rule with apprehension as to 'what will happen in the interval'. Moreover, this apprehension fed on the idea of Catholic aggression would not be open and direct, but cowardly and treacherous. In late 1885 one correspondent, writing to congratulate Colonel Saunderson on his election to parliament, expressed confidence in him as a leader of the Protestant cause and concluded: 'When a Protestant thinks of their cunning deeds such as the 5 November [the Gunpowder Plot] how could they [*sic*] give them their support.' More specifically, Lynn Doyle (Leslie A. Montgomery) has left a revealing record of how such anxieties and impressions could be inculcated from early childhood:

> Home Rulers to my childish mind were a dark, subtle, and dangerous race, outwardly genial and friendly, but inwardly meditating fearful things...and one could never tell the moment they were ready to rise, murder my uncle, possess themselves of his farm, and drive out my aunt and myself to perish on the mountains...in my aunt's stories it was on the mountains we always died....

Well before the introduction of Gladstone's Home Rule bill, rumours were circulating in Ulster that Nationalists and Catholic priests were already raffling Protestant-owned farms and properties, to be confiscated on the enactment of a scheme for Irish autonomy; their intention was 'to drive the successors of the planters and the colonists out of the country, and then to take possession of the lands they occupy in Ulster'. Despite reports in the *Freeman's Journal* and *Derry Standard* ridiculing such views, the *Londonderry Sentinel* refused to be convinced: 'Not a bit of proof has been shown to show that it has not been taking place.' There is, however, no reason at all to disbelieve the denials of the Nationalist press. Such rumours were simply a part of the folklore of Ulster Protestantism that was likely to be widely publicised in a period of political crisis. In 1798, for instance, it was rumoured in Ulster that Presbyterians among the United Irishmen would take the farms of those Protestants who stayed loyal. Nevertheless, the belief that the success of the Home Rule campaign would entail an effective reversal of the plantation remained a major theme in Ulster Unionist propaganda in the period up to the introduction of the Home Rule bill. Indeed, two of the most important Unionist newspapers in Ulster carried articles on Ulster history whose only purpose seems to have been to intensify Protestant hatred and fear of Catholics and Home Rule. The *Belfast News-Letter* ran a series detailing the atrocities it claimed were perpetrated on Protestants down the centuries by the Catholic church, while the *Londonderry Sentinel* carried one entitled 'The Irish St Bartholomew' — an account in gory detail of the atrocities supposedly inflicted on the northern Protestant community during the 1641 rebellion.[13]

Similarly, a leaflet entitled *Read What Was Done to the Protestants When the Rebels Had Home Rule* also detailed the 1641 'atrocities', emphasised the role of the priests in these activities — 'From the start it was a Romish rebellion' — and concluded: 'It is no wonder that the Protestants have a dread amounting almost to terror of being ever again placed in the power of Home Rule.' This theme was also prominent in the speeches of Colonel Saunderson, whose popularity as a Protestant leader grew rapidly throughout the Home Rule crisis. The credibility of such arguments among Ulster Protestants, moreover, would have been heightened by the sheer lack of social contact generally maintained by the two communities in the north. Of course, social intercourse did occur to some extent, and to the extent that it did it could invalidate the stereotype of Roman Catholics in Protestant culture. Lynn Doyle remarked that despite their fear of Home Rulers in the mass,

> It seems strange to me that both my aunt and myself should have totally exempted from our ban those Roman Catholics — for in my youth Roman Catholics and Home Rulers were synonymous terms — with whom we came in contact. To me Paddy Hegarty, our second ploughman, was simply Paddy Hegarty.... As for my aunt, I know that in matters demanding honesty and fidelity she would have trusted Tom Brogan, her thirty years' retainer, sooner than the worshipful master of an Orange lodge. Nevertheless, the unknown Home Ruler remained to me an object of fear and suspicion.

Indeed, even the most determined Unionists could have congenial personal relations with Catholic Home Rulers, but a

frequently expressed opinion among Unionists that overcame
the contradiction between their knowledge of Catholics as
individuals and their stereotype of them in general took the form
of accepting that while Catholics individually might be fine
people, they were yet, as a group, in thrall to the political
machinations and secular ambitions of their church. Further,
such apprehensions were supported by perceived contradictions
in Nationalist propaganda. Well before 1886 Colonel
Saunderson produced a pamphlet emphasising this characteristic of Nationalist speeches. His *Two Irelands; or Loyalty
versus Treason*, published in 1884, consisted mainly of extensive
quotations from the speeches of leading Parnellites. These
extracts showed how, in their addresses to their militant
supporters in America, the real revolutionary and separatist
aims of the movement were propagated; how they posed in
parliament merely 'as a much ill-used class, deprived of their
constitutional liberties and thwarted in their lawful designs'; but
most importantly, that in their appeals to Ulster Protestants not
a word was said about 'the Protestant garrison' that was to be
'driven into the sea' — a prominent theme in their southern
Irish propaganda. Emphasis was placed instead on how the
agrarian struggle could procure farmers the ownership of their
land and relieve them of the hated yoke of the landlord. Similar
contradictions were also apparent in Nationalist writings during
the Home Rule debate. For example, the Nationalist M.P. for
Newry, J. Huntley McCarthy, writing in February 1886,
argued that what self-government meant was simply a position
for Ireland in relation to England similar to that which existed
between a state of the union and the federal government of the
United States of America. Such an arrangement could secure
the empire and ensure equality and fair treatment for all
religions and classes in Ireland. Having proceeded in this vein,
however, McCarthy concluded his article with a vision of the
future Ireland couched in terms which gave expression to the
historically based Catholic world-view. A new day was dawning
for the Irish people, and the church 'that has for so long guided
the nation through darkness and the shadow of the valley of
death [*sic*] will exercise its loftiest duty as the guardian of a
regenerated race'.[14]

The duality of reasoning in McCarthy's argument was

fastened on by Ulster Unionists, already intensely suspicious of Nationalists. Reaction to McCarthy's article in the *Belfast News-Letter* was predictably hostile. In outlining the future role of the Catholic church in Ireland he had unintentionally described the Parnellites' real objectives:

> The aim of the Home Rulers is not merely an Irish parliament, but a universal religion. The Protestants of the country must be forced to submit to 'The Church'. Mr McCarthy has been incautious enough to reveal the truth, and we trust that his paper may be widely read by the English Protestants.

That Nationalists had any such intention is, needless to say, unlikely in the extreme, but the case presented by McCarthy was influential and lost none of its menace for Ulster loyalists when the Home Rule bill was published. It was assumed by Nationalists and Liberals that the propertied first order of the Home Rule assembly would naturally defend minority interests, but the higher property qualification necessary for election to this order reflected more a concern for the voice of property in national affairs than for minority cultural and religious matters. Naturally this 'safeguard' was looked on as illusory, and declarations by *United Ireland*, shortly after the introduction of the bill, to the effect that Home Rule would merely be 'regulating' a system of government which already was under the sway of the National League from Donegal to Cork, only reinforced Unionist fears. Distrust was heightened when it was made clear during the Home Rule debate in parliament that no attempt would be made to cater specifically for Ulster Unionist interests.[15]

The broad spectrum of Ulster Unionist anxieties was exhibited in the speeches of Ulster Unionist M.P.s. These focused especially on the disparity between Nationalist claims and the limited autonomy offered by Gladstone's Home Rule scheme, and the likelihood of the persecution of Protestants under nationalist rule. Outside parliament, the economic argument against Home Rule, made much of by many Unionist speakers around the province, was specifically highlighted by a special meeting of the Belfast Chamber of Commerce on 22 April 1886. Fears were expressed about the businesses of the north, the lack of finality in Gladstone's scheme, the future of

Ulster's commercial links with Great Britain and the empire under Home Rule,[16] as well as the business acumen of nationalists.

Colour was given to Ulster Unionists' fears, moreover, when Protestants in Sligo were attacked early in June 1886 by a nationalist mob who believed them responsible for attempting to endanger the life of Laurence Gillooly, Bishop of Elphin, by dangerously unhinging the gates of his residence. The discovery that this action was in fact the work of the leader of the nationalist mob, apparently in order to justify attacking local Protestants, was greeted by the Ulster Unionist press as further evidence of the real intentions of nationalists towards the Protestant minority. Many Ulster Protestants were already convinced that the police trying to contain the Belfast riots had been sent from southern Ireland by John Morley, the Chief Secretary, with the intention of shooting Protestants.[17]

WILL ULSTER FIGHT?

As the political atmosphere surrounding the Home Rule crisis intensified in May 1886, the Ulster question and the preparations for rebellion then believed to be under way in northern Ireland came increasingly to dominate the issue. As one Liberal political journal put it,

> The question of whether or not we are going to pass the Home Rule bill is becoming more and more a question as to whether we are prepared as a last resort to bombard Belfast.[18]

The belief that Ulster Unionists were preparing for rebellion at this time was to become part of the tradition that they would act on in 1914; but to what extent was it accurate?

Certainly it would appear that preparations by the Orange Order for resistance going beyond mere public meetings began as early as January 1886. Colonel Waring informed a meeting of Lurgan Orangemen that in the Orange Institution they had the nucleus of a good loyal army: 'They had appointed emergency secretaries all over Down, and were now in a position to set the entire Orange machinery of that county in motion in twenty-four hours.' However, it was not until the end of April that an attempt was made to organise resistance on a province-wide basis following offers of support for such a move from groups of sympathisers in Canada and Great Britain. On 28 April William Johnston, the Orange M.P. for South Belfast, recorded that the Grand Orange Lodge had formed a 'provisional committee', chaired by Lord Erne, to resist the repeal of the Union. But that preparations to resist Home Rule by violence in Ulster were so quickly and widely publicised in Great Britain was due not so much to Orange actions in the province as to the reaction to these threats by the *Pall Mall Gazette* — widely acknowledged as the most influential London political journal at this time. For example, it reacted dramatically to William Johnston's claim, on 7 May 1886, that a Unionist revolt in Ulster would have the support of Lord Wolseley and Lord Charles Beresford: Ulster resistance was inevitable, it claimed, when such was supported openly by Lord Randolph Churchill and tacitly by Wolseley and Beresford — 'the leaders of the fighting services of the empire' — who allowed it to be 'openly proclaimed without contradiction that they will join the revolt'. Johnston described this reaction as 'hysterical', but it undoubtedly gave great publicity to his cause, which received further declarations of support on 15 May from both Lord Salisbury[19] and Joseph Chamberlain.

The effect of these developments in Ulster was to increase widely the enthusiasm for resistance. According to Thomas McKnight,

> The word 'Resist! Resist!' was on the lips, not merely of Orangemen, but of Liberals, of those who by their profession were men of peace, merchants, manufacturers, bankers, medical men, and even clergymen.

That Lord Wolseley was a descendant of one who had commanded the Enniskilleners and defeated Mountcashel at Newtownbutler and had distinguished himself at the Boyne was well known in Ulster and gave credibility to the belief that at the moment of supreme crisis he would act a similar part. As to how far this was a realistic expectation, however, is debatable. When pressed on this question, Wolseley gave an equivocal answer, simply denying knowledge of the existence of such reports; while during the second Home Rule crisis in 1893 he could assure his commander-in-chief, the Duke of Cambridge, that Ulster

Protestants 'will fight *à outrance*' if they were placed under a Dublin parliament, yet also advise 'a swift descent on, and coercion of, Ulster' when riots appeared to be starting again in Belfast. Nevertheless, the credibility of Ulster resistance was further enhanced when the *Pall Mall Gazette* returned to the story at the end of May. In a leading article entitled 'Is Civil War in Sight?' it provided a 'muster roll', with statistics of the 'Orange army', consisting of a reported total membership of 73,561 men, plus a map of Ulster indicating prospective areas of operations. It was urged on the government that they immediately tackle this problem with a view either to calling the Orangemen's bluff or meeting a challenge to lawful government that if allowed to develop would assume enormous proportions. On the following day the paper's Ulster reporter affirmed his belief that an Orange military organisation did exist in Ulster, though whether they really meant to fight could not be properly assessed. His belief was that many hoped they would not be called on to fight, and that 'when the moment of coercion comes the people of England and Scotland would not permit the Queen's troops to be sent against them'. This issue also noted that until the publication of the muster roll of the Orange army the British public had a very hazy idea as to the existence of any organisation capable of effective resistance in the north of Ireland: 'Its publication brought home to the English mind more clearly than had before been possible the existence and the power of the organisation which loyalists have established in the Protestant province of Ulster.' Moreover, it published a list of fifty-one Orange M.P.s, landowners and gentry allegedly involved in the organisation of this army. Yet it also reported that Dublin Castle dismissed the threat of armed resistance in Ulster — the view there being that the whole enterprise existed only 'on paper' and that 'there was really nothing of which the government could take hold'.[20]

There is much evidence to support the official view. R.I.C. investigations into advertisements in the *Belfast News-Letter* for arms and drill instructors in May 1886, for example, discovered little of substance. It was found that the advertisements were inserted by an unnamed 'country gentleman' — quite likely Colonel Saunderson, among whose papers estimates for arms shipments exist — but strong doubts were cast as to 'how far he is bona-fide in his intentions'. And although support for military action came from Orangemen in Great Britain, Australia, Canada and New York, only one actual instance of drilling was reported — at Richhill, Co. Armagh, with 300 unarmed men. Significantly, the strongly Orange paper, the *Portadown and Lurgan News*, while admitting that drilling was taking place, ridiculed the idea that such an army would take the field on the passage of a Home Rule bill; such a force would only go into action 'in the event of a direct attack on Ulster Protestants'. This remark provides an important clue to Unionist policy on opposition to Home Rule: violent resistance would be contingent on the nature of the threat posed by Home Rule to Ulster Protestants. E. S. W. de Cobain explained their policy once Home Rule was enacted: they would send no members to the Dublin parliament and would refuse to pay its taxes, and they would insist upon the maintenance of the status quo:

> We shall not march against anybody, nor shall we shoot anybody; we shall simply refuse to recognise in any shape or form the authority of the parliament at Dublin. Then if an attempt is made to compel us to submit, our passive resistance will become active, and you will see that the one hundred and twenty thousand who are already enrolled will be but the advance guard of the force which will rally round the standard of the empire.

De Cobain's views were endorsed by Colonel Saunderson, and in this context it is understandable that preparations for armed rebellion would be in a provisional stage. Home Rulers, however, refused to believe in the possibility of an Ulster rebellion under any circumstances, while John Morley argued that people who wished to arm the Ulster Protestants would hardly advertise for 20,000 Snyder rifles.[21]

In its final article on the subject, entitled 'Will Ulster Fight?', the *Pall Mall Gazette* gave probably the best analysis of how far Ulster Unionists could resist Home Rule. It noted that the non-payment of taxes imposed by a Dublin parliament was the method of resistance most favoured in the north, and that many Unionists believed the army to be so 'honeycombed' with Orangemen that it would not march on Ulster. While conceding that the Orange Order could muster many men, this report also declared that it lacked arms. Moreover, Liberal Unionists were most unlikely to rebel, while Orangemen themselves were divided on the question, with the great majority, certainly in Belfast, contenting themselves 'with a strong verbal protest, at any rate until their property, their liberty, or their lives were directly imperilled'.[22]

7

Gladstone's Concept of Irish Nationality and the Moral Crusade for Home Rule, 1886-92

Mr Gladstone sees everything as in a mirage. The promised land flowing with milk and honey is always just a little ahead. With siren eloquence he allures his hearers to press onward, ever upward, in the path of justice and right. It is true, that the fascinating oasis which nerved them to such exertions vanished as they approached: but nothing daunts the Old Man's faith, or damps the fire of his enthusiasm. His speech [referring to one made the day before at Liverpool] recalls memories of the old alchemists who were always just on the point of discovering the philosopher's stone, until death came and dissolved their dreams. He is a poet, an idealist, and a prophet. The people sit at his feet as at those of one who sees visions, and discourses to them of things invisible. He keeps the great controversy on the heights, and defends every shift and wile in the political game with all the moral fervour of a Moses descending from a new Sinai. Herein lies his superiority as an electioneering force to all his competitors. He is always going to inaugurate the millennium.

Pall Mall Gazette, 29 June 1886

'I had no other motive than that of promoting, what I think dangerously deficient in many places, an historical and therefore a comprehensive view of the Irish question': so wrote Gladstone to Lord Hartington explaining his intention in encouraging a greater public awareness of the nature of the Irish problem, following his trip to Norway in the autumn of 1885.[1] As will be seen, his emphasis on the importance of an historical approach to the question provides an important key to understanding Gladstone's perception of Irish affairs and how they should be dealt with. This chapter attempts to analyse the Gladstonian concept of Irish nationality, the sources on which it was based, its relationship to what he hoped Home Rule would achieve, and how it influenced his view of Irish Unionism.

GLADSTONE, NATIONALISM AND THE
IMPORTANCE OF IRISH HISTORY

Given Gladstone's preoccupation with the historical basis of the Irish question and his acceptance of the validity of the nationalist demand for Home Rule, it was natural he should concentrate on the historical claims put by Irish nationalists. But Gladstone also perceived that British acceptance of nationalist claims was largely dependent on removing the historically well-established prejudice that coloured British opinion on Irish questions. Anti-Irish animus, heightened in the early 1880s by the obstructionist tactics of the Parnellite M.P.s in parliament and dynamite attacks in London, fed, as we have seen, on a long-established tradition of anti-Catholic prejudice. In the heated atmosphere surrounding the Home Rule crisis of 1886 this prejudice found frequent expression in Unionist propaganda, especially in material intended for a working-class readership.

In the course of a speech in Dublin on 29 November 1886 John Redmond detailed for his audience the contents of a pamphlet circulated by T. H. Sidebottom, the successful Conservative candidate for Hyde at the general election of that year:

> Q. Have the Irish ever had Home Rule, and how did they behave?
> A. They murdered every Englishman and Protestant they could lay their hands on in 1641. They were set on by the priests, who said that the killing of them was a meritorious act. Altogether they killed in that year 150,000 Protestants — men, women and children.

And while not all Unionists resorted to propaganda such as this, even among the more discriminating critics of the first Home Rule bill the view was widespread that Ireland's troubled past provided a reliable guide to the future under Home Rule:

> We are bound to allow that its wisdom or unwisdom, its justice or injustice, the probability or improbability of its success, depended to a very large extent upon the accurate reading of the history of the past.[2]

Given the extent to which ethnocentric notions regarding the

Irish prevailed in British society, it is obvious that any attempt to dislodge such ideas from the public mind was likely to be difficult; and notwithstanding the progress being made in academic circles in demolishing the view of Irish affairs propagated by Macaulay and Froude, the general public was still largely ignorant of Ireland. Not surprisingly, therefore, there was little demand for books dealing with Irish historical and political subjects. The problem was exacerbated, moreover, by the fact that anyone wishing to be impartially informed on the contemporary Irish situation would have had extreme difficulty in finding sources of information. James Bryce, professor of civil law at Oxford and a prominent Home Ruler, noted that part of the trouble British politicians had in dealing with the Irish question was due to their sheer ignorance of the subject and the lack of means to rectify it:

> Irish history... is a blank subject to the English. In January 1886, one found scarce any politicians who had ever heard of the Irish parliament of 1782. And in that year, 1886, an Englishman anxious to discover the real state of the country did not know where to go for information. What appeared in the English newspapers, or, rather, in the one English newspaper which keeps a standing 'own correspondent' in Dublin [*The Times*] was (as it still is) a grossly and almost avowedly partisan report, in which opinions are skilfully mixed with so-called facts, selected, consciously or unconsciously, to support the writer's view. The nationalist press is, of course, no less strongly partisan on its own side, so that not merely an average Englishman, but even the editor of an English newspaper, who desires to ascertain the true state of matters and place it before his English readers, has had, until within the last few months, when events in Ireland began to be fully reported in Great Britain, no better means at his disposal for understanding Ireland than for understanding Bulgaria.

Publishers in the metropolis were reluctant to touch works dealing with these subjects, as 'there was a very small market' for such studies. Even G. J. Shaw Lefevre, later Lord Eversley, who was a politician of cabinet rank, had difficulty in finding a publisher for his study of parliament's attempts to deal with the Irish question in the first half of the nineteenth century.

Apologising to Gladstone for asking him to give the book a public recommendation so as to encourage sales, he remarked:

> My publishers tell me that for books on Ireland there is, in the present state of opinion of the 'classes', very little demand, and that mine could not be expected to sell well. . . . . The book has been given very favourable notices by the provincial press, but it has been ignored by the London papers, with the exception of the *Saturday Review*, which, to my surprise, spoke well of it though differing from its conclusion.

Such was Gladstone's concern with the history of the Irish question, however, that he was unlikely to be put off by such discouraging information. Indeed, despite the arguments of both Sir Charles Gavan Duffy and R. Barry O'Brien in 1885 — that articles on Irish autonomy would be more relevant if they dealt with contemporary Irish politics rather than the historical background to the problem — Gladstone's view remained unchanged. His preoccupation with Irish history requires some further explanation. It is true, as has been pointed out, that such an approach to the question of Irish nationalism was in keeping with the practice of the times, but there were other reasons. For instance, Gladstone's historical sense, in general, was profound, especially as historical developments could be seen, as he believed, to exhibit the working out of Christian influence in world affairs. It will be seen that this outlook strongly influenced his perception of Irish nationalism. Moreover, as Edward Hamilton emphasised, Gladstone was much given to finding precedents for courses of political action he wished to take[3] — a penchant clearly exhibited in his emphasis of Grattan's Parliament as a model for Home Rule. Furthermore, recent political history provided an appropriate model for the operation of the Home Rule campaign itself, in the Bulgarian agitation of the 1870s.

Here was a moral cause not dissimilar to the Irish problem, with the Disraeli government committed to the support of the corrupt Turkish empire that had perpetrated atrocities on Christian minorities. Gladstone's increasing involvement with the Bulgarian question led to his seeing the solution to the problem in terms of national self-determination, which he earlier had espoused for Italy, and was now doing for Ireland;

and it is in regard to promoting Irish self-determination that one of Gladstone's strongest reasons for adopting an historical approach to the problem lies — his own confessed lack of knowledge of the inner nature of nationalism in Ireland. Historians have generally credited Gladstone with a greater breadth of vision on subject nationalities than most of his contemporaries, especially in regard to Ireland. This view is well expressed by Nicholas Mansergh: 'It was because Gladstone possessed, or rather acquired through European channels, this insight into the Irish mind, that he was the one English statesman of his epoch to make a positive contribution, so ambitious in character as to hold out hope of a final settlement of the Irish question.' There was, however, a limit to which insights drawn from the experience of European nationalism could be applied to Ireland. What this experience provided Gladstone with was a penetrating insight into the dynamics of national consciousness in subject nationalities as a general phenomenon, as he demonstrated in his account of Jewish ethnic solidarity:

> The Jew remains a Jew, and carries a peculiar stamp. . . . Is it not probable that the stamp is monumental? That it is the surviving record of persistent mediaeval persecution, which went far below the surface and cut deep lines in character? Such experiences sharpen self-consciousness, and give fresh tension to whatever in the human being is distinctive. . . . If an influence has been at work, drawing closer and closer the ties that bind one Jew to another, and thus making one Jew become more to another, giving to each Jew a larger share in the being of every other Jew, has it not recorded a significant though silent protest against cruel and inveterate injury. For thus it is that the being of one human creature can be imparted to his brothers and theirs to him.

What is instructive here is Gladstone's recognition of the role of persecution and grievance as agencies in the formation of national consciousness and cohesion. He went on to argue that what was true of the Jews, was true of other European subject nationalities, and of the Irish: 'It is no wonder if after seven sad centuries the Irishman says of Ireland, in the words of a beautiful . . . Scotch song . . . "And she's a' the world to me"'.[4]

Penetrating as this insight was, however, it was so at a rather abstract level; while it emphasised the crucial nexus between struggle and national consciousness in general, it provided no explanation of the unique historical experience central to the growth of a specific nationality. Gladstone was aware that the circumstances in each case were different, and that for Ireland, an understanding of her nationality had to be sought in a study of the special historical processes which gave rise to the contemporary situation. Thus, while his insight into the dynamics of national consciousness might well have enabled him to perceive — as did J. S. Mill — the existence of Ireland in terms of an alienated nationality much earlier than the 1880s, it would have provided no specific record of how that state of national consciousness came about. Indeed, in 1888, after three years of studying the historical growth of nationalism in Ireland, Gladstone admitted that its development 'has been singular and not quite easy to trace'.[5] In 1885, when he came to consider the Irish question ripe for settlement, his conception of Irish nationalism had not progressed beyond the general level of understanding indicated above. That this was so is not surprising. As we have seen, he had hoped, until that time, that Irish national sentiment could be satisfied with something short of a national parliament, and only proceeded to shape a Home Rule scheme when he saw no alternative. Moreover, despite his considerable experience of Irish legislation since 1869, Gladstone, as will be seen, regarded that experience as highly qualified in its relevance to the question of how to satisfy Irish national sentiment.

What needs to be emphasised about Gladstone's analysis of the Irish question is the sharp distinction he made between the land question and the question of nationalism. That he made extensive researches into the nature of landholding in ancient Ireland as a basis for understanding the concept of tenant right has been well established. However, he did not identify these researches with the historical development of nationalist sentiment: unlike many of his contemporaries, he refused to accept that agrarian grievances or the land problem in general was central to the question of national consciousness. This distinction between the land and national questions is apparent in his correspondence during the early stages of the Home Rule debate of 1886, when he informed Harcourt that the elements of the Irish question he felt most competent to deal with were 'land and finance'.[6] His considered judgment on the relationship between the land question and Irish nationalism was recorded in 1888.

Briefly, Gladstone, tracing its beginnings in the period of Henry II down to the era of Grattan's Parliament and beyond, conceived nationalism as a spiritual essence imbued with the power of making converts, which testified to its moral worth. More exactly, in Gladstone's mind it took on the character of a religion whose history was a great moral tale of survival and regeneration through persecution and adversity; and like a religious faith it was vulnerable to debasement and corruption. There was no essential place in this conception of nationalism for anything so materialistic as the struggle for land. Gladstone declared: 'The land question so far from being its basis is an incidental, unhappy, and hampering accompaniment' — a conclusion no doubt reinforced by the illegalities associated with the Plan of Campaign, then in full swing. Gladstone fully recognised that a settlement of the land question was essential if a Home Rule scheme was to have any chance of success, but its settlement, in itself, was quite a distinct matter from that of satisfying nationalist sentiment, the source of which was to be found in Irish history.[7]

Gladstone's belief that Irish history held the solution to the problem of nationalist sentiment, however, raises an important question. Given, as was noted above, the scarcity of materials for a thorough and impartial study of this subject, how reliable was his understanding of Irish nationalism likely to be? Despite the enthusiasm with which Gladstone threw himself into the subject, he was always uneasy, at least in the period 1886-7, about the extent to which he had mastered the facts of Irish history. In answer to A. V. Dicey's caution that the use of Irish history for propaganda purposes would be likely to revive old feuds best forgotten, Gladstone replied that he was aware of the danger, and while the prospect of an early settlement of the Home Rule question was possible he did not make a central issue of it, but such was its importance to the case for Home Rule that it could not be dispensed with. However, he continued: '. . . as to the knowledge of the historical facts. I have worked on them to the best of my ability; and harder I think than any other

politician; but I am far from having mastered them.' That this
should be so is not surprising. Irish government records for the
post-1769 period were not then available to scholars, and, as one
correspondent wrote to Gladstone, 'A study of Irish history is
impossible for the period since that date without them. Without
the[m]... one has to search for enlightenment in the pages of
Froude and Lecky.'[8] Lecky's historical works were the most
important texts dealing with Ireland to have appeared in recent
years, and it will be seen that Gladstone's knowledge of Irish
history and consequent beliefs as to the true character of Irish
nationalism drew heavily on them, especially with regard to the
history of Grattan's Parliament.

Apart from Lecky, the works that apparently most influenced
Gladstone in the early period of his study of Irish nationalism
dealt either indirectly with Irish history or abstractly with
politics in general. The most important of these sources were
Edmund Burke's *Works* and A. V. Dicey's *Law of the Constitution.*
Of these, Burke's influence was clearly the greater, as
Gladstone's diary shows:

> *December 18* [1885]. — Read Burke; what a magazine of
> wisdom on Ireland and America.
> *January 9* [1886]. — Made many extracts from Burke — *some-
> times almost divine.*

Indeed, Burke's view of nationality, centring on an organic
theory of society, belief in the aristocracy as a governing class
and in the state as a great spiritual entity uniting the living and
the dead,[9] was virtually identical to his own. The temptation to
invoke Burke's sanction on Home Rule was therefore great.

For the several centuries of Irish history before the eighteenth
century, however, Gladstone exhibited little interest and
seemed content to rely on nationalist propaganda. For example,
in criticising Dicey's lack of Irish historical knowledge,
Gladstone recommended O'Connell's highly propagandist
history of Ireland, 'which ought I think to be regarded as among
the first elements of necessary knowledge on this subject'. But
O'Connell's book was as far from an impartial history of Ireland
as it was possible to get. Composed mainly of citations from
other authorities, it was a product of the Repeal campaign of the
1840s and was intended as an historical indictment of the wrong

done to Ireland by England. Its spirit was aptly expressed in its motto: 'On our side is virtue and Erin, On theirs is the Saxon and guilt.' Lecky criticised it thus:

> It is a choice specimen of a kind of history that is still abundantly written in Ireland — a 'history' consisting of the crimes and oppressions perpetrated by English government in Ireland, aggravated to the highest point, and a complete omission of all circumstances of provocation and palliation. It is a picture of an innocent and long-suffering people persistently crushed by almost demoniacal tyranny.... In history... half truths are the worst of falsehoods.

However, the very trait which Lecky condemned — the use of history to present a political and moral argument — was that which most recommended the work to Gladstone. it sustained that sense of moral righteousness which was the driving force behind his campaign for Irish Home Rule. Indeed, the lesson of England's injustice to Ireland, which it was the purpose of O'Connell's book to impart, had been forcefully impressed on Gladstone in 1883 by Harcourt, who described the effects of an extension of the franchise in Ireland:

> When full expression is given to Irish opinion there will be declared to the world in larger print what we all know to be the case, that we hold Ireland by *force and by force alone* as much today as in the days of Cromwell, only that we are obliged to hold it by a force ten times larger than he found necessary.... We never have governed and we never shall govern Ireland by the good will of its people.[10]

The value of O'Connell's book was that it seemed to offer proof of the truth of this assertion. Again, the fact that O'Connell had dedicated his book to the Queen was evidence of that 'nationality with loyalty' which Gladstone was inclined to define as the 'real' national sentiment of Ireland and which he believed had found its fullest expression in Grattan's Parliament.

NATIONALITY WITH LOYALTY:
THE IMPORTANCE OF GRATTAN'S PARLIAMENT

Gladstone's general conception of the historical development of Irish nationalist sentiment can be divided into three sections: the beginning of the growth of national consciousness in the reign of Henry II, coming to maturity with the establishment of Grattan's Parliament in 1782; from 1782 to 1795, the golden age of Irish nationalism, marked by social cohesion and the demise of religious strife; from 1795 to the passing of the Act of Union and beyond, when the gains of the previous period were undermined by English-inspired sectarianism and rebellion and the failure of Westminster to govern Ireland efficiently and fairly.

Gladstone's assessment of what was historically significant in the development of Irish nationalism was largely determined by the importance he attached to Lecky's work. Comparing the Irish historian with Carlyle and Macaulay, he declared:

> Lecky has real insight into the motives of statesmen. . . . Carlyle . . . mighty as he is in flash and penetration, has no eye for motives. Macaulay, too, is so caught by a picture, by colour, by surface, that he is seldom to be counted on for just account of motive.

Indeed, such importance did Gladstone attach to Lecky's *Leaders of Public Opinion in Ireland* that in a later edition of this work the author credited Gladstone with having lifted the book from obscurity to 'sudden and most unexpected popularity. Mr Gladstone in several of his speeches and writings appealed to it as a justification of his policy, and his example was followed by three or four other conspicuous members of his government.'[11] Moreover, Lecky's Irish history was heavily balanced in favour of the latter half of the eighteenth century, and this was in accord with Gladstone's desire to concentrate on the development of constitutional nationalism in Ireland rather than the earlier and more violent forms of nationalism associated with the many rebellions against English rule.

Reviewing Lecky's *History of England in the Eighteenth Century* in June 1887, Gladstone declared that Irish history before the eighteenth century had

> a dismal simplicity about it. Murder, persecution, confiscation too truly describe its general strain; and policy is on the whole subordinated to violence as the standing instrument of government.

It was a view which he had expressed more forcefully some

months earlier in an article entitled 'Notes and Queries on the Irish Demands':

> In those centuries of cruelty and neglect Mr O'Connell has demonstrated, not by assertion but by citations from authority, that the policy, so far as there was a policy, was in the main a policy by no means of mere subjugation, but actually of extirpation, for the Irish race inhabiting the island.... All these decency forbids us to defend; and we consign them to condemnation and wash our hands of such proceedings.

In so far as this period had any political value for Gladstone, it lay in the fact that it provided the parliamentary seedbed from which would eventually spring the fully developed plant of Irish nationality: Grattan's Parliament. For Gladstone as for Lecky, the growth of Irish national consciousness was inseparable from the development of parliamentary institutions. In the course of his speech introducing the first Home Rule bill Gladstone, led by such reasoning, declared that the ancient Irish parliament was always 'as nearly as possible on a par' with the parliament of Great Britain:

> ... for the parliament of Ireland had subsisted for 500 years. It had asserted its exclusive right to make laws for the people of Ireland. The right was never denied, for gentlemen ought to recollect, but all do not, perhaps, remember, that Poynings' Law was an Irish law imposed by Ireland on herself.

This theme recurred in his public addresses and publications in the period 1886-7. Speaking at Liverpool during the general election of 1886, he described the Irish parliament: 'The parliament of Ireland when it was extinguished was over 500 years old. It was not a gift to Ireland: *it had sprung from the soil* [my italics].' It was within this conceptual framework that Gladstone could admit that although that parliament represented only a small section of the people, it contained the 'repressed principle of national life'; while it was 'corrupt, servile, selfish, cruel' and deserving of 'almost every imaginable epithet of censure', there was more to tell: 'It was alive, and it was national.' But why, declared Gladstone, posing a rhetorical question, did the spirit of nationality exist in an institution of which the constitution and the environment were alike intolerable? The answer, he declared, exhibiting his insight into the nexus between struggle and national consciousness, lay in the fact that 'that parliament found itself faced by a British influence which was entirely anti-national, and was thus constrained to seek for strength in the principle of nationality'.[12]

The principle of nationality, according to Gladstone, once having taken root, was fundamentally irrepressible, and when English violence in Ireland passed over 'into legal forms and doctrines, the Irish reaction against it followed the example. And the legal idea of Irish nationality took its rise in very humble surroundings.' Thereafter it proceeded to develop by a zigzag process, amid great difficulties and restraints, corruption and adversity: 'By a national law... there came into existence, and by degrees into steady operation, a sentiment native to Ireland and having Ireland for its vital basis.' The logic of this process was towards full autonomy and national feeling, which, Gladstone argued, was in its final stage of being worked out with the establishment of Grattan's Parliament in 1782.[13]

A highly significant feature of Gladstone's theory of the development of national consciousness in Ireland before 1782 is his concern to locate its origin and growth within a strictly parliamentary framework.[14] In this respect his outlook shows a marked difference from that of his political allies, the Parnellites. As we have seen, the historical vision in the Parnellite concept of nationality was both longer and wider. They argued that an Irish nationality had existed long before the coming of the Normans, and in the history of that nationality they were more concerned to identify its harbingers with the leaders of the many insurrections against English rule in Ireland rather than with a corrupt parliament; indeed, it was usual for them to treat the latter with the utmost contempt (though it is true that when it was politically expedient during the parliamentary debate on Home Rule an occasional Parnellite could be found to endorse the interpretation presented by Gladstone). But whatever their difference of analysis on the history of Irish nationalism, both found common ground on the period of Grattan's Parliament.

Certainly this period lent itself more easily to the political purposes of Home Rulers. It had been a prominent feature of

Parnellite propaganda in recent years; it afforded a thoroughly constitutional precedent for Gladstone's proposed local parliament in Ireland; and it was, moreover, not obscured by the mists of time, but had been a central feature of the most influential Irish historical work of recent years. It is in his understanding of this period and the lessons he believed it held for the future of Irish self-government that Lecky's influence on Gladstone was most apparent. Indeed, the extent to which Gladstone based his hopes for Irish Home Rule on the precedent of Grattan's Parliament has already been demonstrated in Chapter 3, and the extent to which his reading on this period was based on Lecky's writings was clearly explained during a reception given to some Irish delegations in October 1886. Gladstone 'appealed very happily' to the historical works of Lecky and Goldwin Smith and 'dwelt on the curious circumstances that two of the strongest opponents of Home Rule had, as historians, said the very things which formed the foundation of the Home Rule bill'. More specifically, the appeal of Lecky's work for Gladstone lay, to a considerable extent, in his belief in the importance of the landed gentry as a governing class. Indeed, Lecky's concept of Irish nationality, as many commentators have pointed out, did not extend to the whole Irish people, but was restricted to the Protestant and Catholic landowning gentry, who alone were endowed with governing capabilities. The qualities of this class he described in the first volume of his Irish history:

> In every community there exists a small minority of men whose abilities, high purpose, energy of will, mark them out as in some degree leaders of men. They take the first step in every public enterprise, counteract by their example the vicious elements of the population, set the current and form the standard of public opinion.

It was in the period of Grattan's Parliament that Lecky saw these qualities expressed and being worked out most fully. Gladstone's views on the natural order of society were almost identical. In an article assessing the ties of the British people with the American he also described their differences:

> The English people are not believers in equality; they do not,

with the famous declaration of July 4th 1776, think it to be a self-evident truth that all men are born equal. They hold rather the reverse of the proposition . . . in practice, they are what I may call determined inequalitarians. . . . Their natural tendency from the very base of British society, and through all its strongly built gradations, is to look upward; they are not apt to 'untune' degree.

Thus, despite their differences on Irish Home Rule, Lecky and Gladstone agreed in their hierarchical notions of the proper ordering of society. It is not surprising, therefore, that Lecky, writing of Grattan's hopes for the Irish gentry in the late eighteenth century, was, in effect, describing Gladstone's hopes for the same class in the late nineteenth:

It was the dream of Grattan that a loyal Irish gentry of both denominations could form a governing body who would complete the work [of finally obliterating internal Irish divisions and making the Irish one people], and that, although a Protestant ascendancy would continue, it would be the modified and mitigated ascendancy which naturally belongs to the most educated section of the community and to the chief owners of property, and not an ascendancy defined by creeds, and based on disqualifying laws.[15]

But if Lecky's views on the natural order of society in general were almost identical to Gladstone's, his concept of nationality was far too rationalist and too well grounded in an awareness of the realities of political power to believe, as we shall see Gladstone did, that once removed from its politically and economically dominant position in Irish society the political power of the landed gentry could ever be restored. Why did Gladstone believe that it could? The answer to this question is to be found in the properties he believed the nationalist idea to possess and the meaning he attached to the period of Grattan's Parliament in terms of its lessons for political life in a future independent Ireland. In his 'Lessons of Irish History in the Eighteenth Century' (his review of Lecky's history) Gladstone described the influence of the nationalist idea in Grattan's Parliament:

If there be such things as contradictions in the world of

politics, they are to be found in nationality on the one side, and bigotry of all kinds on the other. . . . Whatever is given to the first of these two is lost to the second. I speak of a reasonable and reasoning, not of a blind and headstrong nationality; of a nationality which has regard to circumstances and to traditions, and which only requires that all relations, of incorporation or of independence, shall be adjusted to them according to the laws of nature's own enactment. Such a nationality was the growth of the last century in Ireland. As each Irishman began to feel that he had a country, to which he belonged and which belonged to him, he was, by a true process of nature, drawn more and more into brotherhood, and into the sense of brotherhood, with those who shared the allegiance and the property, the obligations and the heritage. And this idea of country, once well conceived presents itself as a very large idea and as a framework for most other ideas, so as to supply the basis of a common life.

This was a large claim to make for the power of an idea; but why would it necessarily entail the restitution of the landed classes to positions of political authority? The answer to this question Gladstone provided in his 'Notes and Queries on the Irish Demands'. Governing power would devolve on the aristocracy because 'The natural condition of a healthy society is, that governing functions should be discharged by the leisured class. . . . For the general business of government it has peculiar capacities'; and however good a political system may be, 'when the leisured class is deposed as it is to a very large extent deposed in Ireland, that fact indicates that a rot has found its way into the structure of society'. He continued:

Formerly the upper class of Irishmen, whatever their faults, were Irishmen as much as the mass, and fought and won many battles for nationalism both before and after 1782. It was a nationalism combined with loyalty, as nationalism has always been combined with loyalty until driven to desperation.

The separation of gentry and people, Gladstone argued, had been an effect of the Union, which had promoted absenteeism and shifted the centre of all Ireland's special interests and placed it out of Ireland. However, once a parliament was established in Dublin,

> the position held by the leisured and landed classes of Ireland as towards the people, will be entirely changed. As one at least of their number to his great honour has said since this controversy began, 'We shall reside, and shall form friendly relations with all other classes, and shall become the natural leaders of the people.'[16]

It is highly likely that Gladstone's informant here was Parnell, who, it has recently been pointed out, saw eye-to-eye with Gladstone in his highly conservative vision of Ireland under Home Rule, and who was described by one of his close colleagues as 'no democrat'. Indeed, there is a substantial similarity in the views of both men in this respect. Like Gladstone, Parnell both believed in the virtue of the landowning classes as social leaders and was also affectionately drawn to the working classes. Gladstone saw no reason why this preferred state of affairs should not come to pass. What kept the Parnellite party united, he argued, was their demand for Home Rule, and the attainment of this objective would remove the reason for their unity. Moreover, the Irish were a highly conservative people: 'The religion, the character, and the old traditions of the Irish are all in favour of them leaning upon the leisured classes, and desiring to be represented by them.' They had never shown a disposition to be represented by men of low social origins. Parnell, he claimed, owed his leadership of the Catholic Irish as much to his social position as to his 'remarkable powers'. John Morley has remarked that Gladstone's conception of the Irish problem was best expressed by Lord Salisbury, who declared that while Gladstone's land and ballot reforms may have been necessary, they nevertheless destroyed the Irish gentry's governing role while failing to supply 'any institutions' by which Ireland could be governed.[17] Gladstone's Home Rule scheme was to be a comprehensive experiment aimed at restoring the landed gentry to their governing position.

The beneficent influence with which Gladstone endowed the nationalist idea was twofold: in an autonomous Ireland it would be, 'according to the laws of nature's own enactment', both a mechanism for restoring the hierarchical structure of society and an agent of social cohesion by dissolving religious bigotry. The evidence that these things would come to pass rested, according to Gladstone, in the history of Grattan's Parliament. But how far was there a real correspondence between the Ireland of 1782 and of 1886? Despite the obvious historicism of Gladstone's approach to the Irish question, it was at the same time grossly unhistorical in its treatment of the relationship between Ireland's past and present. His assumption that the nationalism of the 1780s could be essentially re-created in the 1880s revealed a fundamental weakness of historical perception: it failed to take account of the very different political realities and ideas in the two periods, especially the very influential imperial consciousness of the 1880s; it failed to take account of the unique social and industrial progress of north-east Ulster since the Union, which marked it off from the rest of Ireland; but perhaps most importantly it failed to recognise the important difference in the social and economic determinants of nationalism in the two periods. Concerned chiefly with the moral and political lessons of Irish history, Gladstone overlooked these conditions. Such, however, was not the case with James Bryce.

Bryce, an historian of repute, fully realised the limitations of historical precedents for political policies, and in his introduction to a book published in 1888 and compiled by several authors to publicise the background of the Irish question, he outlined, in effect, the defects of Gladstone's use of history:

> The worth of history for the purposes of practical politics is... gravely overrated. History furnishes no precepts or recipes which can be directly applied to a political problem.... Situations and conjunctions of phenomena arise which seem similar to those which have gone before them, but the circumstances are always so far different that it is never possible confidently to predict similar results, or to feel sure that it is necessary either to avoid a remedy which failed, or to resort to that which succeeded on a previous occasion.

This point was more directly made by Lecky, who argued that 'for good or ill' Grattan's Parliament was 'utterly unlike any body that could now be constituted in Ireland'.[18]

The most important weakness in Gladstone's application of

the nationalist model of 1782 to the contemporary Irish situation was his failure to see that the agrarian struggle, while unconnected with the flowering of nationalism in Grattan's day, was the engine which pulled the train of nationalist agitation in the 1880s. It was essential to the internal consistency of Gladstone's concept of Irish nationality that the landlords be defined as essentially nationalists. To have accepted that agrarian struggle was a central feature of contemporary Irish nationalism would have logically entailed the admission that those who were carrying on the struggle were nationalists, while those against whom it was being waged were not. Gladstone based his belief that the Irish peasantry would support the political restoration of the Irish gentry on a view of the peasant as naturally conservative and socially deferential, and emphasised his community of interest with the landlord. This certainly was an unrealistic view, and indeed was obviously so to Liberal Home Rulers with any experience of Ireland. For example, Lord Spencer, in his preface to a book promoting Home Rule in 1887, defined the reasons for the radical political consciousness of the Irish peasant:

> The Irish peasantry still live in poor hovels, often in the same room with animals; they have few modern comforts; and yet they are in close communication with those who live at ease in the cities and farms of the United States. They are also imbued with the advanced political notions of the American republic and are sufficiently educated to read the latest political doctrines in the press which circulates among them. *Their social condition at home is a hundred years behind their state of mental and political culture* [my italics].

Michael Davitt, in his analysis of this question, also put great emphasis on the role of Irish experience in America and how it reacted on nationalist political thought and practice in Ireland. Moreover, at the very time that Gladstone was expounding his theory of the deferential Irish peasant the Plan of Campaign was at its height and William O'Brien was declaring the social and racial excommunication of landlords from the Irish nation.[19]

How could Gladstone's view of Irish nationalism be so at odds with the facts? There were several reasons, but probably the most important was his power of self-deception — something to which he had long been prone and which became more dominant towards the end of his life. Committed to a belief in the 'proper' hierarchical ordering of society, Gladstone simply refused to believe that the Irish gentry would not occupy a leading role in Irish politics when Home Rule was established. There were influential factors supporting this attitude. For example, his concept of nationality, as we have seen, was highly spiritual; it did not allow that agrarian struggle had a central place in nationalist sentiment. Thus it contained no analytical tool with which to explain the interconnections between the two. In addition, there was his simple ignorance of nationalist opinion. Apart from Parnell, who shared his outlook, 'most of the other Irish Nationalist members were strangers to him'.[20] He had little practical experience of Ireland, and his knowledge of Irish opinion — apart from occasional reports — was accordingly highly restricted. This was true of Unionist as well as nationalist opinion.

Gladstone's approach to Ulster Unionism in this period will be considered in detail in Chapter 9, but generally his attitude to all Unionist arguments was determined by his identification of the evolution of Irish nationalism as the central process of Irish history. This constituted an 'objective' standard, or 'natural law', against which opposing developments and ideas were judged. Thus, while he could recognise the validity of nationalist sentiments, the logic of his thinking denied the legitimacy of Unionists' ideas and beliefs. To Gladstone's mind these constituted, to use a Marxian term, 'false consciousness'. He was encouraged in this view, moreover, by his contacts with the Irish Protestant Home Rule Association, a small group consisting mainly of Gladstonians, who were engaged in propagating the Home Rule cause among Irish Protestants, and who, by their activities and propaganda, encouraged Gladstone to believe that the Irish Protestant community would be converted to Home Rule. A communication which well reflects his thinking in this respect was his letter to C. H. Oldham, secretary to the Dublin executive of the Protestant Home Rule Association, on the occasion of a meeting to be held in Dublin in April 1887. Gladstone wrote: 'I trust your meeting in Dublin will do much to dispel the absurd idea that the Protestants throughout Ireland are, as a body, apprehensive of the consequences of Home Rule to themselves, or are anything like unanimous in opposing it.'[21] It was, moreover, with this attitude of mind — allied to his dismissive approach to Unionist arguments in general — that Gladstone embarked on his propaganda campaign to publicise the Home Rule cause.

HISTORY AS PROPAGANDA AND THE HOME RULE CRUSADE

In his forceful presentation of the historical case for Home Rule, Gladstone, convinced that history was on his side, took to provoking his Unionist opponents. Speaking at Glasgow on 22 June 1886, he declared that Unionists never 'had any regard for history at all', and at Manchester two days later he asserted: 'Our opponents will not refer to history.... I think they are very wise in not touching history; at every point it condemns them.' What Gladstone meant specifically by this remark was how the destruction of Irish independence at the end of the eighteenth century — effected mainly through English intrigue — brought a series of disasters on Ireland whose effects were felt to the present day. He gave succinct expression to this view in his article 'Notes and Queries on the Irish Demands':

> When the critical year of 1795 opened, religious animosities were at their nadir, because the spirit of nationality was at its zenith. The Protestant and landlord parliament of Ireland spoke out boldly and nobly for the Roman Catholics... on the dark day when Lord Fitzwilliam was recalled. After that fatal act it became necessary for the executive, in its headlong career, to dissolve the holy alliance, for such it was, formed between Irishmen of different churches. It was something like the ruin of the Table Round after the sin of Guinevere.... For then came in Ireland the deplorable foundation of the Orange lodges; the gradual conversion of the United Irishmen into a society of separatists; the disarmament of the people with all its cruelties; the reign of lawlessness under the reign of law; the rebellion of 1798 with some examples of bloody retaliation; and the nameless horrors recorded by the manly shame of Lord Cornwallis. Thus was laid the train of causes which, followed up by the

Act of Union, has made Ireland for ninety years a sharply divided country.[22]

It was to get this view across to the public that Gladstone encouraged prominent Liberal figures such as G. J. Shaw Lefevre, Lord Thring and James Bryce to produce historical works on the Irish question. He also wrote to the Parnellite propagandist J. G. Swift McNeill with the same advice. By coincidence, McNeill had just completed a book on exactly the lines Gladstone had suggested. His letter in reply to Gladstone offers a good impression of the effect such literature was supposed to have on the public mind:

> A book... detailing the leading iniquities of the Union — I mean the method of its enactment — should be distributed far and wide. The transition from hatred of the means by which the Union was carried to active desire to atone for the past will be an easy one for the people of England.

The widespread confidence amongst Home Rulers that history supported their case has been shared also by one recent commentator of this aspect of the Home Rule crusade, R. A. Cosgrove: 'The denial of Irish history lulled Unionist opinion into a fundamental misapprehension of the forces in Ireland symbolised by the Home Rule movement.'[23]

However, while it is certainly true that the sophisticated historiography of the period offered much material which could be used to support nationalist arguments, there was, nevertheless, a limit to how useful it could be; and while Dicey's influential *England's Case against Home Rule* represented the most sophisticated statement of the Unionist case, taking a professedly constitutional and unhistorical approach to the Home Rule question, there were other Unionist arguments which attempted to meet Gladstone's historical challenge. In terms of propaganda, the weakness of Gladstone's historical argument was that while it may have been based on the highest standard of available scholarship, the contemporary political conclusions to be drawn from the scholarship need not necessarily be sympathetic to Home Rule. For example, the recognition that the passing of the Act of Union was associated with corruption did not necessarily lead to the conclusion that

Home Rule should be established in Ireland in 1886. A. V. Dicey could inform Lecky that although his books had long ago convinced him that the Act of Union was a blunder, 'reflection seems to me to show that its repeal would now be a blunder of much the same kind'. This point is more clearly illustrated with reference to the controversy surrounding the publication in 1887 of J. D. Ingram's history of the passing of the Act of Union.[24]

Given the scarcity of competent historians willing to undertake propaganda work for the Unionist cause, Ingram's history was enthusiastically welcomed. Edward Marjoribanks, later Lord Tweedmouth, sent Gladstone a copy of the book with the information that Lord Randolph Churchill was 'exceedingly anxious that it should be brought to your notice'. In a letter to 'an Irish country gentleman' John Bright praised it as 'a complete answer to the extravagant assertions of Mr Gladstone' and urged that a cheap edition of the book be quickly produced. Ingram's book set out to make three substantial claims about the events associated with the enacting of the Union: that if Irish Protestants were opposed to the Union, it was because it would have endangered their political supremacy; that no bribery attended the passing of the Union; and that the people of Ireland, Protestant and Catholic, were in favour of it. However, Gladstone, reviewing the book in the *Nineteenth Century*, effectively demolished the substance of Ingram's argument, exposing inconsistencies, lack of proper references, misuse of sources, and unsupported generalisations. So effective was the demolition that Ingram, in reply, could only fault him for one minor mistake, and the book played no important part in Unionist propaganda thereafter. Marjoribanks wrote to Gladstone marvelling at the effectiveness with which he had routed Ingram: 'The article seems to me to utterly paralyse Dr Ingram.' Even Lord Randolph Churchill admitted that 'great loss and damage' had been inflicted on Dr Ingram,'which he would find it difficult to repair'. Yet the Unionist position was far from lost. Taking up the argument for the Unionists, Lord Brabourne replied to Gladstone with 'A Review of a Review'.[25] Brabourne's article was an effective exposure of the weaknesses in Gladstone's use of history for propaganda purposes. Writing in defence of Ingram, he wisely avoided those aspects of the argument of which Gladstone had displayed a mastery, and exposed some specific errors in his review; but most importantly he showed how Gladstone had 'misread' the history of Grattan's Parliament in general.

Brabourne declared that the essential point about Grattan's Parliament was that it was 'in truth the parliament of a weak country joined to a strong one . . . subservient to the government and parliament of Great Britain' and that Gladstone's view that it was free and working out the regeneration of Ireland was incorrect. Moreover, as the British government pressure on their behalf in 1793 — for franchise extension — showed, Catholics had more to gain from a British government than from the Protestant ascendancy's parliament. On the question of the Union, unlike Ingram, Brabourne admitted that corruption did attend its enactment, but he went on to make an important criticism of Gladstone's method of judging the historical past by the moral standards of the present:

> It is impossible to judge the morals of 1800 by the standard of 1887, and it is unjust to condemn the statesmen of the earlier period without a full consideration of the circumstances in which they were placed.

He continued with an attack on Gladstone's approach to history in general:

> It was an indefensible course to adopt a policy which condemned that of all British ministers who had preceded him, upon the ground that they had misread history and misunderstood Ireland, and to adopt it with a knowledge of that history so confessedly 'imperfect'.

In a following letter to *Blackwood's Magazine* that, however, was apparently not sent, Gladstone did not effectively meet these criticisms, but merely repeated his belief that 'the parliament of the Pale grew into the parliament of the nation and would have obtained ninety years ago a worthy constitution' had it not been for the British government. He also recommended that Brabourne read O'Connell's history of Ireland for proof of the 'cruelty and fraud' which had characterised English treatment of Ireland down the centuries.[26]

However, the weaknesses Brabourne exposed in Gladstone's approach to the general history of the period had earlier been exposed in more restricted form in a published correspondence on Edmund Burke conducted between Gladstone and the prominent Ulster Liberal Unionist H. de F. Montgomery. The point at issue here was the unanswerable question of whether or not Burke would have approved of Gladstone's Home Rule scheme of 1886. Gladstone, as we have seen, was strongly influenced by Burke's writings on Ireland. He argued that given Burke's support for Grattan and the parliament of 1782, and his occasional hostile references to a union between Britain and Ireland, it was also logical that he would have approved of Home Rule. Montgomery, with greater historical sensitivity, put it that Burke's views had to be considered in their historical context, and that it was unlikely, given his aristocratic political beliefs, that he would have approved of a parliament controlled by Parnellite 'Jacobins'.[27] On the basis of these positions there followed a correspondence in which, given the nature of the argument, neither side could expect to gain a decisive advantage. Yet it was not necessary for Unionists to gain a decisive advantage to thwart Gladstone's purposes.

Gladstone had hoped to use the history of Grattan's Parliament to establish an indictment against the existing political arrangements between Britain and Ireland. However, given the contentiousness of this period and the fact that government records for the post-1769 period were not available, it was logical that speculation and conjecture would figure largely in political assessments. It was also impossible to determine whether historical figures would, or would not, have approved of Home Rule in 1886. To be convincing Gladstone's arguments would have had to be conclusive, and given the nature of his case this was not likely; Unionist as well as Home Rule conclusions could be drawn from substantially the same facts. Irish history was not a subject which lent itself easily as a tool of political propaganda. To the general public, unschooled in Irish history, the effect of the controversy must have been at best confusing. Nevertheless, until 1890 Gladstone pursued his moral crusade, greatly buoyed up by the report of the Special Commission in that year. It was inevitable, however, that the Parnell split, especially in view of its source and the moral issues associated with it, would have a detrimental effect on the Home Rule campaign. Certainly after 1890 there was a significant falling off in Gladstone's output of the historically based material which formed the groundwork of the moral crusade between 1886 and 1890. Moreover, his relations with the Nationalists were not improved by the wrangles over Home Rule finance that took place in 1893; and it is indicative of his attitude to Home Rule at this time that he was prepared to retire from politics over a dispute in cabinet about an increase in naval estimates.[28]

CONCLUSION

This chapter has sought to explain the nature of Gladstone's concept of Irish nationality as an ideological basis for understanding both what he hoped to achieve by his Home Rule schemes of 1886 and 1893 and how he thought Home Rule could be best promoted.

It has attempted to show that his insight into the nature of the Irish problem was, ironically, most penetrating at its most abstract; that while his insight into the relationship between struggle and national consciousness was generally incisive, his conception of Irish nationalism was based on an understanding of Irish history that was not extensive, and which depended for its validity on an historical precedent of little practical relevance. Moreover, his conceptualisation of Irish national sentiment in spiritual terms, divorced from the agrarian question and reliant on the precedent of Grattan's Parliament, left him ideologically ill-equipped to take a constructive and realistic approach to the problem of Irish Unionism, sustained his unrealistic hopes of the re-emergence of the Irish gentry as Ireland's political leaders, and led him to believe that all that was needed to make British converts to the Home Rule cause was to publicise the horrors and iniquities associated with the history of Anglo-Irish relations in general and with the enacting of the Union in particular.

The Home Rule Debate, 1886-92:
The Search for an Irish Constitution

DEFINING THE TERMS OF DEBATE, 1886-7

On the rejection of Home Rule, Gladstone immediately called a general election and began his campaign in the country. In major election speeches at Edinburgh, Manchester and Liverpool, on 18, 25 and 28 June respectively, he set out the general lines of his approach to propagating the Home Rule cause in the period 1886-92: the rejected bill was now dead, and only its principle — 'to establish a legislative body in Ireland to manage exclusively Irish affairs' — remained. It would be for the acceptance of this principle, rather than specific clauses or details, that he would campaign — a course of action he presumed his followers preferred. Essentially, and despite 'ill-defined' alternatives to Home Rule offered by Lord Hartington and Joseph Chamberlain, the only real options available were either Home Rule or coercion. Gladstone publicly renounced the inseparability between his extremely unpopular land purchase scheme and Home Rule and put it that until Home Rule was conferred British reforms could not be achieved.[1]

There were two reasons for Gladstone's adoption of this rather simplistic approach to propagating the Home Rule cause. First, he was influenced by his reading of Daniel O'Connell, who during the Repeal campaign of the 1840s had urged the simple repetition of a 'new proposition' to establish it in the public mind; and undoubtedly the reduction of a complex issue like Home Rule to a simple, easily assimilated formula for public consumption made sense. Secondly, and more importantly, such a policy made easier the cohesion of the Liberal

Party on a subject to which few were emotionally committed; a wide-ranging and detailed debate might have endangered the party's unity of purpose, with differing factions supporting different and probably inadequate plans for Irish autonomy — a possibility that both Wilfrid Blunt and Parnell were very much aware of. Thus it is understandable why Gladstone wanted to maintain debate on Home Rule at the level of a relatively few simplified propositions.

Ironically, his energetic pursuit of the Home Rule campaign invited precisely the kind of multifarious discussion that he sought to forestall. Indeed, within days of the rejection of his Home Rule bill, Arthur Kavanagh, the severely deformed but active Irish landlord, communicated to Gladstone a paper entitled 'A Few Suggestions for Consideration as to the Future Policy of Government for Ireland'. He proposed to establish a large and yearly increasing class of yeoman proprietors, with the state providing credit for the purchase of land, and to replace the 'Castle system' with a 'permanent' government, independent of party changes at Westminster, to be based on the Irish Privy Council with a 'representative' element introduced into it. Nothing, however, came of Kavanagh's suggestions.[2] Gladstone's bill of 1886 was — as he was later to describe it — too near the 'irreducible minimum' to admit of further amendment in the direction of limiting self-government.

A few days after this offering, Lord Powerscourt, in a letter to the *Freeman's Journal,* declared that many Conservatives and Unionists would support Home Rule provided imperial integrity, Westminster's supremacy and the 'administration of justice' were secured, in addition to adequate protection for property and religion. Unionists did not consider that the Home Rule bill of 1886 secured these objects, but since Gladstone had declared that bill to be dead, there was now room for common ground. In a new scheme, Powerscourt continued, Irishmen should be allowed to fill the posts of Lord Lieutenant and Chief Secretary, and an extensive land reform enacted, since Gladstone's land purchase bill was defeated by the British taxpayer and not the Irish landlords, who had had little opportunity for expressing their opinions on it. However, as with Kavanagh's suggestions, Powerscourt's letter was to elicit no considerable response.

By far the most significant contribution to the Home Rule debate at this time was that of Dr R. W. Dale, an influential Liberal Unionist from Birmingham. In an article in the June issue of the *Contemporary Review* Dale sketched out a Home Rule plan that sought both to unite the Liberal Party and diminish Unionist fears of nationalist government by proposing an Irish parliament with the extent of its powers strictly fixed — as opposed to Gladstone's defeated bill, which merely defined certain subjects as outside its competence. The problem of securing the supremacy of Westminster without offering scope for Irish interference in internal British affairs would be solved by having either a statutory parliament for Great Britain or separate assemblies for England, Scotland and Wales. The imperial parliament, with the Irish represented in it, would continue to deal with imperial affairs. In the working out of this scheme, Gladstone's bill, suitably amended, would form the Irish and first element to be implemented.[3]

Dale's ideas attracted the attention of William Walsh, Archbishop of Dublin, who incorporated them, along with ideas for extensive land purchase on the basis of land *value* rather than rent, in two interviews given to the *Freeman's Journal* in August 1886 and also appearing simultaneously 'in a leading newspaper in every great city of the United States'. The purpose of these interviews was to assist the Parnellite delegation to the Chicago convention of 1886 in pledging that body to a moderate constitutional policy. Gladstone, however, immediately rejected Dale's proposal, considering it a 'contraction' of Home Rule, though he declared that he was now willing to examine, 'on a wider historical basis' than in early 1886, the financial basis of a future bill with the possibility of a favourable result for Ireland. Warning against Unionist attempts to 'shuffle off' Home Rule in favour of land purchase, Gladstone also declared that Irish measures 'which could not be accepted as final but which might be tolerated as intermediate, if they contained substantial... good' would, depending on Irish opinion, 'weigh much with... the Liberal Party'. Gladstone's letter contains a brief outline of his general Irish policy in the period 1886-92: reluctant to consider an extensive revision of his own Home Rule ideas, apart from the financial question, he would seek to pursue 'intermediate' measures of reform. Nevertheless, Walsh was to remain enthusiastically in favour of Dale's ideas, and further — and rather testy — correspondence with Gladstone ensued in 1887, in which the latter again rejected Dale's proposals. He also urged Walsh and other Irish leaders to meet and settle definitely on the kind of Home Rule measure they desired, so that they would 'have then a solid point of departure and can proceed to deal with England'. Dr Dale personally may have been concerned to contribute to a solution to the Irish question, but he represented more of actual distrust than of 'contingent support'.[4]

Gladstone's dislike of Dale's ideas would have been greatly reinforced by information he received from John Morley in December 1886, to the effect that the prospect of Scottish Home Rule was 'greatly alarming' their supporters. Nor is it likely that he would have been particularly impressed by Walsh, whom Lord Aberdeen believed to be both lacking in political judgment and not in Parnell's confidence.[5] In noting Gladstone's view of Dale's plan, though, it is also worth pointing out that he was in touch with another source of Irish opinion at this time, which suggested that Nationalists were happy with his approach to Home Rule and ready to follow his leadership. An extensive memorandum submitted by C. S. Roundell to Gladstone in August 1886 consisted of an interview he had had with Alfred Webb, a leading Dublin Protestant Home Ruler, on the Irish question: it confirmed everything Gladstone would have wanted to believe about existing Irish attitudes to Home Rule.

Webb argued that the scheme of 1886 was basically satisfactory: Home Rule was not wanted as an instalment of separation but as an end in itself; present Irish leaders were now older and more conservative, and 'they will lead the sympathies of the people into conservatism'. On the important question of Home Rule finance, Webb declared that the Irish members felt themselves weak on this subject, and, recognising Gladstone as a master of finance, they were prepared to 'leave themselves in his hands'. He was also reassuring on the willingness of tenants to pay 'fair' rents, and on the disinclination of Catholics to persecute Protestants. Being a Gladstonian himself, it is hardly surprising that his own opinions should reflect those of his leader, and his view as to the best method of advancing the Home Rule cause was virtually synonymous with Gladstone's: 'Patience and quiet firmness, the moderation of the demand and conduct of Ireland, the general extension of historical information, and the progress of reflection on the subject will in no long time, we may rest assured, bring about the triumph of right.'[6] But given that Home Rule could not be implemented until the defeat of the Unionist government, Gladstone was, as we have seen, prepared to pursue 'intermediate' measures of Irish reform, and a letter to *The Times* by Lord Monck provided the stimulus in this direction.

Monck noted that although Unionist and Gladstonian Liberals were divided on the Home Rule issue, they were at least agreed on conferring an extensive measure of local government on Ireland, and that Parnell was committed to the acceptance of a scheme that specifically subordinated Ireland to Great Britain by limiting autonomy to internal Irish affairs. He believed that herein lay the basis for agreement between Parnell, Chamberlain and Hartington on large powers of local government being conferred on Ireland, provided these were delegated from Westminster. Indeed, the precedent for such action had already been established by the practice of conferring on municipal bodies and public companies the power to make by-laws. Monck, however, recognised that problems would arise in defining what powers an Irish assembly should have. Nevertheless, Gladstone regarded Monck's suggestions as significant, though not in the way that their author would have wished — as a basis on which to settle the Home Rule problem — but rather as a basis for the implementation of useful short-term measures which might ease the transition to Irish self-government when it was possible to enact a Home Rule bill.[7]

Parnell's attitude to this policy, however, was initially hostile: he feared it would provoke a revolt 'in his own army'. However, on being pressed a second time by John Morley, he declared his willingness to accept 'for what it was worth' any measure expressly limited to local government reform, provided it could not be mistaken for even a partial settlement of the Home Rule question. In this respect he explicitly rejected a 'central council' scheme because it would be 'an attempted substitute for a parliament'. The discussions and agreement with Parnell on short-term measures were important, as they cleared the ground for

Liberal participation in the Round Table talks held in January and February 1887. These discussions have been comprehensively treated by Michael Hurst, and the object here will be mainly to illustrate how they clarified the different meanings Gladstonian and Unionist Liberals attached to terms like 'local government' and 'Home Rule'. The talks were instigated by Joseph Chamberlain, under pressure from Liberal Unionist colleagues anxious that he should pursue a progressive Irish policy. On 23 December 1886 he made a conciliatory speech appealing to Gladstonian leaders to meet the dissentients for discussions on the enactment of extensive Irish land and local government reforms. This elicited a favourable response from John Morley, who saw 'some chance of daylight' if Chamberlain could be 'got to advance' and Parnell took a 'moderate' view.[8] But how close were the positions of the two sides?

Chamberlain hoped to enact an extensive land measure that Nationalist M.P.s would have to accept: 'Their constituents would stand no nonsense on this point and would not allow the question to be postponed for Home Rule or anything else.' This measure could easily be followed by local government reform, with a possible basis found for approaching the difficult autonomy issue: 'Time and full discussion may work miracles.' So far such a policy has advantages for Gladstonians: in solving the land question it would remove 'the great object of discord' between Irishmen and enhance the prospects for the success of Home Rule, a prime object of which was to eliminate gradually the 'social alienation which is the curse of Ireland'. Parnell, however, felt that any conference with Chamberlain would mean a compromise on Home Rule and ridiculed the idea mooted by Morley that local authorities be set up as 'buffers' between the tenants and the British government to effect land purchase: 'If you give the local authorities the option of buying, they will never exercise it except at inadequately low prices. If you compel them to buy, then they won't pay the instalments.' Gladstone understood Parnell's fears but thought them unnecessary: the 'national question for Ireland' was too big 'to play pitch and pass' with. It was another thing, though, 'to recognise the facts around us and adopt present action to them', which Parnell seemed inclined to do.[9]

However, Gladstone's insistence on any policy of Liberal

reunion involving no compromise on 'the national question for Ireland' highlights the basic incompatibility between what Chamberlain would offer and what Gladstonians would accept. At about the same time as Gladstone was writing to Morley, Chamberlain was outlining to Harcourt his fundamental argument on the Home Rule question:

> I did not believe in the possibility of granting an Irish parliament without endangering the Union. I did not think that Ireland could be recognised as a nation without conceding separation. Ireland was a province — as Nova Scotia was a province in Canada and the cardinal difference between Mr Gladstone and myself was that he had treated the question from the point of view of the separate nationality of Ireland, while I had regarded it from the point of view of a state or a province.

Chamberlain hoped that, given the impossibility of enacting Home Rule immediately, agreement on subsidiary issues such as land and local government might lead to the discussion of 'any alternative plan for self-government which might be brought forward as a substitute for Mr Gladstone's bill'.[10]

The first two meetings took place at Harcourt's house on 13 and 14 January 1887, with Morley, Harcourt and Lord Herschell for the Gladstonians, and Chamberlain and George Trevelyan for the Liberal Unionists. According to Chamberlain's account of these talks, his own proposals for a land scheme based on a new separate and individual valuation of estates, with 'county boards' established to deal with the tenants, found substantial support. Again, he recorded that his suggestion that the imperial parliament should have the same degree of control over the future Home Rule legislature as the Canadian dominion parliament had over the provincial legislatures — which had specifically enumerated powers — was also widely acceptable. General agreement also existed, he claimed, on the questions of local government, public works and education. Chamberlain concluded that, apart from the 'fundamental' question of Ulster, 'all the other questions raised were dealt with as matters of detail to be determined by further discussion and...did not raise question[s] of fundamental principle'.[11]

Chamberlain's sanguine view of the progress made at these talks, however, was far from reflecting the reality of the case. Writing to Gladstone on 15 January, Morley described Chamberlain's land proposals as 'ingenious but resting on air' and his intention of conferring on an Irish parliament the functions of a Canadian provincial legislature as being 'launched in mid-ocean'. There was, finally, the Ulster question, on which no agreement was likely. Writing in reply a few days later, Gladstone was already expressing grave doubts about the outcome of the conference: the Home Rule bill of 1886 was too near 'the irreducible minimum' for a plan such as Chamberlain envisaged to be successful. Of Chamberlain's land proposals, Gladstone declared: 'No land bill as good as ours on the financial side [the bill of 1886] can properly be framed without keeping a hand on all Irish public receipts and making [the] Irish authority dependent on the surplus.'[12] From this point on, the hopes for an agreement between Gladstonian and Liberal Unionists on land and Irish autonomy fast disappeared.

Criticism of the talks from Liberal radicals was severe, while Parnellites declared that they would wait twenty years for a 'national' measure of Home Rule rather than accept Chamberlain's provincial legislature. Moreover, public declarations by John Morley to the effect that no concessions were being made to Chamberlain except on points of insignificant detail fuelled Tory fears that too much was being conceded. Chamberlain himself did not improve the prospects for a successful outcome of the talks when, in an an open latter to an American correspondent published in *The Times* on 18 January 1887, he declared that while Gladstone was prepared to give 'national Home Rule', which was essentially 'separatist', he was not prepared to go further than provincial Home Rule:

> Once grant that Ireland is a nation, and not ... a part of a nation, and you must follow this out to its logical conclusion and give them all the rights of a nation, including separate taxation, foreign relations and military forces.[13]

A subsequent letter by Chamberlain in *The Baptist* on 25 January, claiming that the Gladstonians were preventing the enactment of British reforms by concentrating only on Home Rule, angered Gladstone, who refused to reveal a memorandum he had prepared on the talks. In this atmosphere it was inevitable that the last scheduled meeting on 14 February 1887, which concentrated on the insuperable problem of Ulster, would fail. Subsequently Gladstone declared that the conference could only proceed if Lord Hartington was made a party to it. However, Hartington believed that Home Rule based on the Canadian constitution could only work well in the case of a people who desired 'union', not in the 'opposite case of a people who have been taught to desire the largest possible measure of separation'. Thus the Round Table conference floundered and was finally buried when the Tories planned to introduce the crimes act of 1887. Thereafter the public development of Unionist and Home Rule arguments intensified, fuelled on the Unionist side by leading public and professional figures — such as A. V. Dicey — concerned to provide a more intellectual basis for arguments often lacking in coherence and characterised by coarse prejudice.[14]

RESPONSES TO COERCION, 1887

With the introduction of the crimes act of 1887, the publication of the 'Parnellism and Crime' letters, and the progress of the Plan of Campaign, conditions were hardly favourable for a constructive or dispassionate debate on Home Rule. Gladstone, in a major speech at Swansea on 4 June 1887, cited these factors as having crowded Home Rule out of the public mind. But there was also his own reluctance publicly to discuss any plan for Irish autonomy in detail. He declared his 'great horror of premature decisions'. On this occasion, however, he did reveal something of his current thinking on the Home Rule and land questions. As the land purchase bill of 1886 was rejected because of a feared massive outlay of imperial funds, he would now be prepared to consider a scheme which did not involve imperial credit. Moreover, he now publicly declared that the financial scheme of his Home Rule bill would require 'further consideration': Anglo-Irish financial relations since the Union had been of 'extreme complexity' and the time available for consideration of the subject in 1886 was inadequate. Referring to the vexed question of Irish representation at Westminster, Gladstone refused to commit himself to a 'specific plan', declaring that it was 'a choice of difficulties'.[15]

Apparently he wished to retain public attention on the principle of Home Rule rather than its possibly divisive content at a time when he believed the effect of coercion in Ireland would create converts to Home Rule in England. Accordingly, when Joseph Chamberlain declared his willingness to consider another plan for Irish autonomy which might entail Liberal reunion, Gladstone preferred instead to 'wait and see', believing negotiations would only be worthwhile if they included Hartington. For Chamberlain's part, he was informed by Lord Hartington, supported by Lord Randolph Churchill, that even a modified scheme of Home Rule based on the Canadian constitution would probably mean the break-up of the Unionist alliance.[16] Thereafter the chances of an agreed Liberal scheme of Irish self-government disappeared completely.

But events in Ireland did not all work to the Liberals' advantage. Parnell certainly had not brought his views on the linkage between the land and Home Rule questions into line with those of Morley and Gladstone. Believing that the land purchase scheme of 1886 had been the cause of the Home Rule bill's rejection, Parnell had subsequently thought it best for the prospects of self-government to forgo any large-scale solution to the land question and to rely instead on amendments to the land acts of 1881 and 1885. However, he now accepted Gladstone's and Morley's view that this problem had to be solved concurrently with Home Rule. Parnell also stressed the 'sovereign importance of a favourable financial arrangement' and was reassured on this point by Morley.[17]

What worried Morley and Gladstone, however, was the impetus given to extreme nationalism by the effects of coercion in Ireland. In particular they noted that at the annual convention of the Gaelic Athletic Association in Thurles on 9 November 1887 the Fenian or 'extreme' element 'carried the day against the priests and constitutional party'. Morley declared that unless Liberals showed in a marked way that '*we* are not daunted and not holding back', extremists would take the lead in nationalist politics. Consequently a great Home Rule demonstration in Dublin, attended by Liberals, took place at the beginning of 1888. However, the tendency of the agrarian struggle in Ireland to produce hardline expressions of opinion by nationalists had reverberations in Great Britain that could hardly have helped the Liberals' 'union of hearts' policy and the argument that Home Rule did not mean separation.[18] Moreover, it also — and to a greater extent — would affect detrimentally any attempt to find agreement among different sections of Irishmen on the Home Rule issue; and just such an attempt was made in 1887.

A FAIR CONSTITUTION FOR IRELAND

While political conditions in Ireland in 1887 were hardly propitious for the discussion of any Home Rule scheme, it is nevertheless true that if an Irish contribution to the debate was to be made, few Irishmen would have been as well qualified to undertake it as Sir Charles Gavan Duffy. A leading member of the Young Ireland movement of the 1840s and founder of the Irish Tenant League of the 1850s — which sought to unite the Protestants and Catholics in political action — he had emigrated to Australia, become Prime Minister of Victoria, and was subsequently knighted by the Queen. Thus both his nationalist activities and his involvement in the political life of the empire gave him credentials for impartiality that few other contemporary Irishmen possessed. Duffy saw clearly the need to rethink the whole question of Home Rule in the post-1886 period: unless Irish agreement on Irish autonomy could be obtained, any plan would ultimately fail. In 1887 he declared that a new constitution was needed, and must be based on a recognition of the fact

> that the Irish nation is not homogeneous; that it is composed of various races, creeds, and interests each of which has an absolutely equal claim to the protection of the law and the enjoyment of all the rights and privileges of citizens; that we must constantly acknowledge and act upon the principle that in all public affairs, from the parish to the parliament, it is the highest interest of the country that the majority and minority should be fully representative and neither of them suppressed nor overborne.

The conceptual distinction between Duffy's view of the Irish people and Gladstone's was that whereas the latter viewed Irish internal religious and class alienation as merely temporary manifestations of an unnatural social state that would disappear once Home Rule was established and Protestants accepted their true role in the Irish nation, Duffy recognised the depth of these divisions and the need to cater properly for the fears arising from them. Thus whereas Gladstone's scheme of 1886 merely implied the protection of Protestant interests in the constitution of the proposed propertied first order of the Irish assembly, Duffy insisted that a new Irish constitution must involve the minority in its making and must provide explicit safeguards for their interests. A gathering such as the Round Table conference, however well intentioned, could never completely achieve what was properly a task for Irishmen themselves:

> If Irishmen cannot frame a constitution for their native country, what security is there that they can administer effectively a constitution framed by other hands? They must prove their fitness for self-government in the same manner that all committees of civilised men have done before them. In the history of constitutional liberty there is not, so far as I know, a single case where the fundamental statute was not the work of the people whose right it was designed to establish.[19]

Duffy criticised the manner in which Gladstonian Home Rule had been sprung on the country and argued that a necessary prelude for the formation of a Home Rule constitution should have been a royal commission, sitting alternately in Belfast and Dublin, 'to ascertain the will of the people with certainty'. For the future he envisaged a commission composed equally of Irish Conservatives and Nationalists with an impartial English chairman. In the meantime he proposed a thorough discussion in the Irish press on what a proper Home Rule scheme should consist of.[20]

The first priority of the new Irish constitution would be 'to make the substitution of Celtic or Catholic ascendancy for the Protestant ascendancy... impossible'. Appeals to the past conduct of Catholics as security for Protestant interests were inadequate, as were Gladstone's provisions in the 1886 scheme to limit the functions of the Irish legislature and executive: 'to make them powerless to do much good in order that they may be able to do no wrong'. This policy had satisfied no one, and in a new Home Rule scheme the 'fundamental security for sober, ordered liberty must lie in the character of the legislature'. Duffy, who was to edit Thomas Davis's history of the 1689 parliament — in which the actions of a generally just and impartial Catholic administration were marred by an insufficient regard for Protestant interests — argued for 'solid and adequate' guarantees. He advocated a two-chamber assembly, with minority representation guaranteed by proportional representation at constituency level, with provision for it to elect about one-third of M.P.s in parliament. It was also necessary to ensure that an opposition in parliament existed that would have a real possibility of forming an alternative government, and that procedures were established to prevent the enacting of oppressive legislation. He proposed also a nominated senate with ecclesiastical representation and retention of the crown veto. Duffy continued with an attack on one of the most important symbols in nationalist ideology — Grattan's Parliament:

> The minority would detest the parliament, which, instead of being national in the true sense, would be monopolised by one section of the nation; and who can wonder or blame them? Wolfe Tone, Lord Edward, John Keogh, and the nationalists of their day detested Grattan's Parliament for the same reason. And in the end Grattan himself detested it, so natural is it to revolt against foul play.

Moreover, in providing an outline of the unfair taxation imposed on Ireland since the Union, Duffy drew on the recent work of Robert Giffen to demonstrate the unfair imperial burden paid by Ireland and urged an immediate inquiry by a royal commission of competent men into the financial relations between the two countries. As for the land question, he thought Gladstone's scheme of 1886 'substantially just' except for the 'humiliating' provision for putting in an imperial receiver on behalf of the imperial government; this provision would bring the credit of the country at the outset into undeserved contempt: 'The record of Irish farmers did not justify it.'[21]

Duffy's intention, on the publication of his article, was to instigate 'a searching and public discussion' on the Home Rule question as might gradually make its elements familiar to the entire people. E. D. Gray copied the article into the *Freeman's Journal* unabridged, and offered to open the columns of the paper to controversy on all questions requiring further elucidation. At first it seemed that the time was right fc. such an initiative. One Irish Unionist peer wrote privately to Duffy in terms which appeared to reflect widespread Unionist opinion: 'We do not think we are going to be beaten, or that there will be any need for an Irish constitution, but, if there were need, your plan is a fair and satisfactory one.' The Dublin *Daily Express*, the most 'authentic' voice of southern landlord opinion, went further, and having specified some conditions for the settlement of the land question, stated that when this issue was settled, Duffy

> will find the Conservative Party, English and Irish we believe, ready to join with him and them [Nationalists] in striking out some *modus vivendi*, as regards the international question, and the degree of self-government which may be awarded to the country consistent . . . with the preservation of imperial and internal unity.

The *Dublin Evening Mail* expressed itself in similar terms, while the *Northern Whig* admitted that Duffy's plan was 'substantially just and adequate'. However, Unionists predicted that though the plan was a good one, it would be unacceptable to the Nationalist Party, and if such was the case, it would be purely academic. To obviate just this difficulty Duffy took the trouble, before his article was published, to submit his ideas on an Irish constitution to leading Nationalists, including Parnell, Archbishops Croke and Walsh, and the Protestant Home Rulers Alfred Webb and the Rev. J. A. Galbraith. It met with general approval: 'Principles were applauded, and details reserved for further consideration.'[22]

Of leading Liberals, Gladstone, significantly, declined to express any opinion, though some of his colleagues gave the plan a frank and cordial acceptance. Four of these considered Duffy's proposals and gave it 'as large an assent as a minister usually obtains from his colleagues for the heads of a new reform bill when it is first submitted to them'. Subsequently Duffy published the scheme as an appeal to public opinion, and more than eight English and Scottish journals criticised it, 'generally with keen insight, and generous appreciation'. Nevertheless, the existing political climate made the possibility of agreement by all parties on his Home Rule ideas very unlikely. Most disappointingly, conditions in Ireland, and a poor Nationalist response generally, rendered the kind of discussion Duffy sought impossible, just as these factors had killed a proposal earlier in the year by Archbishop Walsh for Irish landlords and tenants to meet in an Irish Round Table conference to solve the land question.[23]

DIVERGENT STRATEGIES, 1888-92

The year 1888 marks a watershed in the Home Rule debate: the attempts to find a united Liberal solution to the Irish problem had completely failed, and the emphasis in both Home Rule and Unionist camps was for existing political alignments to become more firmly established, and for separate solutions to the Irish problem to be more actively pursued.

Certainly on the Home Rule side the propaganda effort in Great Britain was to be pursued with greater organisation and depth than had been the case hitherto. Despite Parnell's initial misgivings that Irishmen would be unable to influence English opinion on Home Rule, the party expended £13,000 on propaganda in Great Britain in the period 1886-90. At the same time Liberal activists engaged in an extensive propaganda campaign in the constituencies, while the Liberal Party was to gain twelve by-election successes in the same period. Nevertheless, it is by no means clear that these successes indicated increased popular support for Home Rule. In a revealing article published in 1888 a Liberal constituency worker contrasted the political zeal of middle-class activists with the apathy of working-class voters on issues that did not materially affect them: 'The things they grumble about are connected chiefly with house rents, local rates, the price and quality of food, and the demands of labour. All these are studied within the limits of the court [immediate neighbourhood]. ... The broad truths of political economy are not known, whilst the narrower local interests are all-powerful.' Liberal by-election successes probably had more to do with the usual unpopularity of the party in office than with any great concern for Ireland. However, the 'union of hearts' between

Liberals and Nationalists received a boost in 1888 when the report of a number of Liberal deputations to Ireland in 1887 was published. Predictably, their findings endorsed party propaganda on Home Rule: Irish demands for land reform and autonomy were 'extraordinarily' moderate; only aggressive action by the authorities endangered the peace, while the National League was the chief agency for the maintenance of law and order; Ulster would ultimately support Home Rule; when Home Rule was enacted many people of 'special culture and qualifications' who had formerly held aloof would become involved in politics; the present system of Irish government was 'the most heavy and unnecessary burden' on British taxpayers. Such findings, of course, would have delighted Gladstone, as they both confirmed informal reports such as C. S. Roundell's[24] and endorsed his own publicly expressed views.

Gladstone made his first important contribution to the Home Rule campaign in 1888 with an article in the *Contemporary Review* in which he unambiguously endorsed the Nationalist argument that the share of the national debt levied on Ireland under the Act of Union had led to her being 'fleeced' by England. Gladstone's admission on this score was taken up immediately by Nationalists. W. J. O'Neill Daunt wrote pressing the point that Ireland had been deliberately overtaxed by the Act of Union, and, as an aid to establishing fair fiscal provisions in a future Home Rule bill and a test of Ireland's taxable capacity, added information showing that over the period 1860-63 Irish wealth was 'only the 25th part of British wealth'. Gladstone replied immediately, stating that since October 1886 he was increasingly convinced that the question of finance between England and Ireland would require to be made the subject of 'a careful and impartial examination'. Thus encouraged, Daunt supplemented his original letter to Gladstone with a detailed statistical argument bearing on the subject. Indeed, Daunt's argument as to relative wealth did prove to be a good guide: the royal commission which studied this question in 1894 estimated that, as regards wealth, Ireland stood in relation to Great Britain in the proportion of 1 to 21.[25]

Gladstone also met Parnell at this time to discuss Home Rule and future political tactics. Their conversation was based on five points drawn up by the Liberal leader: to keep the administration of the crimes act of 1887 before the country and parliament by speeches and statistics; to remain detached and in a condition to accept a settlement from the Tories if such was forthcoming; to accept without prejudice measures, good in themselves, but insufficient as a final settlement of the Home Rule question; to promote non-Irish legislation; to inquire whether or not 'the idea' of the American union offered a practical point of departure in the formulation of a Home Rule scheme. Parnell, apparently, was prepared to follow Gladstone's lead on all points and agreed that non-Irish legislation should also be promoted. Indeed, he not only accepted Gladstone's suggestion that the American political system provided 'a possible basis of a plan of Home Rule', but 'did not wholly repel even the idea of parliamentary intervention to stop extreme and violent proceedings in Dublin. . . . Undoubtedly as a whole his tone was very conservative.'[26] Thereafter, and until the split of 1890, Parnell's views on Home Rule were virtually synonymous with Gladstone's. His increasing moderation was notably exhibited in his talks with Cecil Rhodes in July 1888.

The main outlines of this episode are well known, and, briefly put, the discussion terminated with a donation by Rhodes of £10,000 to Irish Party funds in return for a pledge by Parnell that a future Home Rule scheme would contain a clause retaining Irish members in the imperial parliament. As Dr Lyons remarks, this move suited Parnell at this time for two reasons: first, it could serve to demonstrate that the Irish demand for Home Rule *per se* was genuine and not the thin end of the wedge of separation; and secondly, if certain important subjects, such as land, police and the judiciary, were to be held over by the imperial parliament after a Dublin assembly was established, it would be necessary to have the Irish represented there. After the meeting with Rhodes, Parnell, publicly at least, took an interest in imperial federation, and in particular conveyed a message through J. G. Swift McNeill to the Indian National Congress in 1888, arguing that it should use whatever limited powers of self-government it possessed as a means of education for a more extended system of Home Rule, as well as attempting to elect Indians to the House of Commons to air their grievances. But while both the increasing compatibility between Parnell's and Gladstone's ideas on Irish autonomy and the possibility of adverse public reaction to the crimes act seemed to augur well for the Home Rule case, Tories — particularly Balfour — also thought their own policies were succeeding. Balfour, in fact, was greatly encouraged by the 'comparative' failure of Liberals to prevent the 'vigorous' working of the crimes act in Ireland by 'raising a storm in England' and also believed that the success of the crimes act enabled many Catholics who had hitherto sat 'on the fence' to come down on the government's side: 'The result is satisfactory.'[27] Nevertheless, as Joseph Chamberlain recognised, it was also important for Unionists to offer a constructive alternative to Home Rule.

Accordingly, when Parnell introduced a bill for the reduction of rent arrears in Ireland, Chamberlain objected to it as being too large and proposed instead a bill that would really aid tenants by reducing not only their rent arrears but also other debts to usurers and shopkeepers. The Parnellites, however, vetoed this suggestion. Again, when Gladstone sought to link Irish local government with the English and Scottish measure then under consideration, Chamberlain objected that two bills on such complex issues could not be dealt with in one session of parliament, though he also objected to undue delay in Ireland's case. In 1888 Chamberlain also made proposals for Irish reform based on his Round Table ideas of 1887: land purchase, provincial councils, and public works for congested districts. These he sought to have made official government policy, but they received no backing from Lord Hartington, who even persuaded him to publish them anonymously: they appeared under the title *A Unionist Policy for Ireland*. Nevertheless, Chamberlain's ideas had considerable influence on subsequent government policies, especially those regarding land purchase and congested districts, and as such they were warmly commended by Gladstone. At a more propagandist level, Chamberlain cleverly employed nationalist terminology to argue that Ireland was only part of a wider British nationality; her association with past British glories, geographical position, common interests with Britain and the security of both countries necessitated one parliament to 'bear supreme and unquestioned authority in the United Kingdom'.[28]

The most significant legislative enactment for Ireland in 1888 was an act to amend the 1885 Ashbourne act, providing the sum of £5,000,000 to the original figure of the same amount to facilitate further land purchases. Gladstone's reaction to this measure was to repeat his criticism of the original 1885 act: that as compared with his proposed land bill of 1886 it left no 'intermediate party' to ensure the payment of instalments to the government; the British exchequer would be 'the direct uncovered creditor of an indefinite number of men paying £4, £5, £10, £20 a year in Ireland, and has to take its chance of the recovery of these sums'. He was apparently oblivious to the impression this argument created — that he was exhibiting the kind of distrust of the Irish with regard to land purchase that he accused the Unionists of with regard to Home Rule. Some elements in the Liberal Party, though, particularly R. B. Haldane, took the view that it was wise to support additions to the Ashbourne act 'on the ground that the more landlords are bought out, the less will be the difficulty when the time comes [for Home Rule]'.[29]

In 1889 the nature of a future Home Rule bill began to be more concretely debated in the Liberal Party. Lord Rosebery argued unsuccessfully in mid-January that a future Home Rule bill should be constructed by a commission of jurists and civil servants. Later in the year Gladstone and Parnell met again, and the former's notes for this meeting provide a useful indication of his thinking on Home Rule at this time. On the land question there were now three options: an 'Irish guarantee', as in 1886; or compulsory purchase, as advocated by T. W. Russell, Liberal Unionist M.P. for South Tyrone; or to leave this question for settlement by a Dublin parliament. Other questions listed included: the issue of contracts, and whether or not the Irish parliament should be prevented from voting laws against them in the same manner as American states were restrained; whether a future Home Rule bill should include a clause explicitly stating the imperial parliament's supremacy over the Irish body in common with the rest of the empire; whether or not imperial questions should be enumerated; and whether delegated powers should be fixed by enumeration.[30]

On the question of Irish representation at Westminster, Gladstone explained that it would be retained in *some* form if public opinion at the 'proper time' required it; he would prefer that initial legislation in this respect be tentative, as experience might dictate changes. The most important question for the viability of a Home Rule parliament, though, was that dealing with finance. In compliance with his recent statements on the question, Gladstone noted that the relative amount of financial burden in respect of imperial charges would be considered by a commission and estimated with reference to 'capacity and history' for the decision of government and parliament. Also, as in 1886, the imperial charge would be 'a first charge on all Irish receipts'. Gladstone also attached the utmost value to retaining the imperial receiver, 'into whose hands all Irish receipts would be paid'. The reason was 'for British opinion now and the Irish *credit* hereafter'. The problem of what 'items of charge' were imperial would be settled by the commission, which would also deal with the issue, present in 1886, of items charged in one country though consumed in the other. Furthermore, it would deal with the question of whether Ireland had any financial claim in respect of 'bygone transactions'. Finally, the imperial parliament would tax ireland only on customs and excise, leaving 'direct and mixed taxation' to the Irish legislature. The meeting with Parnell was all Gladstone could have hoped for, and while no concrete decisions were taken on the specific details for a Home Rule bill, he was left with the clear impression that his ideas would prevail. He was also, undoubtedly, greatly encouraged by subsequent speeches of the Irish leader emphasising faith in himself and the strength accruing to the empire by the conferring of Home Rule.[31]

In 1890 the prospects for Home Rule could not have been better, following the exposure of the Pigott forgeries and the consequent vindication of Parnell by the Special Commission. Moreover, Balfour's proposed Irish land bill of this year, which provided £33,000,000 to extend land purchases, was seen by certain Liberals, Nationalists and Unionists as providing the impetus for the conferring of elected local government on Ireland, empowered to handle land sales. Joseph Chamberlain in particular was strongly of this opinion. In a letter to Lord Hartington he argued: 'It is not decent to mortgage the rates and the contributions from the exchequer without giving the local authorities some voice in the matter. I feel that the question is urgent and this is the psychological moment for dealing with it.' He also declared, however, that if the government was against his advice, he would regard his duty to it as discharged, apart from doing nothing to bring about its downfall.[32]

The belief that local government and land purchase should be interconnected, moreover, was supported by Parnell, though for very different reasons. Like Spencer and Morley, he believed that the land question had to be settled concurrently with Home Rule. To this end he desired that the £33,000,000 to be made available under Balfour's land bill should be used 'as wisely as possible'. By this he meant that it should not be used for purchasing large holdings — those which gave no trouble to governments — but only those which could be a source of trouble to a future Home Rule administration. Thus he sought to limit the size of holdings to be purchased, and most importantly — given his rejection of this proposal in early 1887 — recommended the establishment of local authorities to conduct land purchases; they could exercise a veto on the purchase of holdings and thus ensure 'that the money went in the right way'. As to local government in general, he had moved considerably from his first position in late 1886 and now thought that it was a step nearer Home Rule, and that it should be accepted, if offered, as it could be changed as desired when Home Rule was established.[33]

There was never any chance, however, that Balfour would agree to do as Parnell desired. His thinking on the relationship between land purchase and Irish local government was clearly expressed earlier in the year in correspondence with A. V. Dicey, who advised strongly against Chamberlain's suggestions on making the working of the land purchase act dependent upon local authorities. Balfour agreed with Dicey's views: 'no improvement in local administration' could be expected from Chamberlain's ideas. Nevertheless, their party had been committed to the establishment of Irish local government since 1886, and undoubtedly that policy could not now be repudiated without splitting the Unionist Party. However, he continued:

> The answer to this question turns on whether or not it be the fact that county councils in Ireland would be used as an effective means for the oppression of the minority, or as an important instrument for effecting the dissolution of the United Kingdom. I myself am disposed to think that a bill framed upon the proper lines would steer clear of both these dangers, and that such a measure if not effective for good, would, at all events, be powerless for evil. But under no cir-

cumstances would I consent (until Ireland is in a very changed condition) to giving any control over the machinery of land purchase to locally elected bodies.

This letter in fact provides a very accurate indication of the nature of the Irish local government bill Balfour was to introduce in 1892; this measure was so hampered by petty restrictions, including special minority representation, that it was laughed at by Irish M.P.s. Indeed, Balfour's defence in introducing it was: 'There are very great advantages in doing a stupid thing which has been done before, instead of doing a wise thing that has never been done before.' The bill never got beyond its second reading. Before this eventuality, however, the prospects of Home Rulers had diminished dismally with the divorce court revelations. The general effects of the crisis on the Home Rule cause were succinctly detailed by John Morley:

(1) ... We have no longer an authoritative spokesman to deal with;
(2) faction in Ireland has revived old English misgivings as to Irish fitness for self-government;
(3) England will be more adverse than ever to a wide measure of Home Rule, and the Irish less ready to accept a narrow measure;
(4) ... dependency ... of ... Nationalists on the Catholic clergy will worsen our case in Great Britain, to say nothing of Ulster.[34]

The details of this crisis have been covered extensively elsewhere, and its importance here is only in its implications for Home Rule. As is known, Parnell's consent to relinquish the leadership of the parliamentary party could only be obtained if the party could persuade Gladstone to give definite assurances as to the settlement of the land question and Irish control of the constabulary in a future Home Rule scheme.

Gladstone, however, refused to become involved in the dispute and merely declared that the only guarantee that mattered was that which all Liberals accepted: that no scheme worth having could be carried without 'the support of the Irish nation as declared by their representatives in parliament'. Nevertheless, as Conor Cruise O'Brien points out, a Nationalist Party no longer led by Parnell and which would overthrow him at Gladstone's bidding 'would stand in a new and humbler relation to the Liberal Party'. Gladstone, though, was to relent and did give assurances that in a future Home Rule bill provision would be made for the conversion of the R.I.C. from an armed military-style force into a civil body, and that the imperial parliament would deal with the land question within three years of enacting Home Rule, or, alternatively, let the Irish legislature deal with it.[35] However, the breakdown of the Boulogne negotiations with which these assurances were linked, the subsequent break-up of the Parnellite party into opposing factions, and a public dispute about the extent to which they had accepted the 1886 Home Rule bill as a final settlement — all provided Unionists with damaging propaganda material in the period up to Gladstone's final accession to office.

The Liberal/Nationalist Alliance and the Ulster Question, 1886-92

PARNELLITES AND ULSTER, 1886-90

Although the 1886 general election saw the overwhelming defeat of the Liberal Party in Britain, it produced virtually no change in the political representation of Ireland. In Ulster, it is true, the electoral successes of Timothy Healy and William O'Brien in South Tyrone and South Londonderry, which seemed in 1885 to herald a trend of continued Nationalist successes in the north, were not repeated. These, however, were compensated for by the winning of West Belfast by Thomas Sexton and Londonderry City by Justin McCarthy, the latter following a successful election petition.[1] Thus the Parnellites retained the political advantage they acquired in 1885 of winning a majority of the parliamentary seats in Ulster. But the strength of Ulster Protestant opposition to Home Rule required a more forceful reply than a simple reference to the relative parliamentary strength of political parties in the province, and Parnellites answered the Ulster Unionist challenge stridently, both on a practical and ideological level.

As has been shown in Table 2, by 1886 the National League had established 287 branches in Ulster, though the membership these branches represented was not given. However, an R.I.C. Special Branch assessment of the strength of nationalist associations in 1889 gave estimates for Ulster as shown in Table 5. It would seem that the organisation's Ulster membership was higher than that of both Connaught and Munster, though lower than Leinster; the figures for these provinces were 26,466, 35,103 and 47,091 respectively. Northern Ireland, then, was well represented in the Parnellite movement; however, the significant role in the nationalist struggle it consequently might have been expected to play never materialised. Despite the fact that the agricultural crisis of 1886-7 affected Ulster as much as southern Ireland, and that a majority of Ulster farmers were Catholics, the enthusiasm which greeted the Plan of Campaign in the south was noticeably absent in the north. As a rule, it would appear that Catholic as well as Protestant tenant farmers sought to keep the agitation for lower rents on a non-political level. Lord O'Neill's Catholic and Protestant tenants held a meeting in Toomebridge in December 1886 — arranged by the local Catholic priest and Presbyterian minister — to discuss a demand for a 25 per cent rent abatement, but there was no question of adopting the Plan of Campaign, and this was true also of the Ards tenantry of John Mulholland, the Cahore tenants of B. H. Lane, and of tenant meetings generally in connection with the rent reductions in many parts of the north at this time, particularly in Counties Down, Tyrone and Londonderry.[2]

Table 5. Estimated membership of the Irish National League in Ulster in 1889

Antrim	925
Belfast	3,960
Armagh	4,923
Donegal	5,486
Down	2,810
Fermanagh	5,231
Londonderry	4,630
Monaghan	8,744
Tyrone	8,169
Total	44,878

Catholics, it seems, were concerned to conduct a strictly legal agitation for lower rents. The president of one meeting at Draperstown, in calling for the formation of a tenants' defence association, emphasised that 'they were simply there to protect themselves by some legal means'. For Protestant tenant farmers, any action in pursuit of agrarian objectives similar to that employed in the Plan of Campaign was hindered by an intense distaste for the inevitable association with nationalism such action would have entailed. Thus the union of Protestants and

Catholics on agrarian questions in Ulster was only really feasible on a non-political basis; and while *United Ireland* could describe the joint action of Protestant and Catholics demanding a rent reduction on the Earl of Charlemont's Castlecaulfield estate as 'the spirit of the north aroused', the 'spirit' aroused was not a nationalist one. It would seem that attempts to extend the Plan of Campaign into Ulster were kept to the predominantly Catholic counties of Donegal and Monaghan. William O'Brien declared that he and John Dillon had 'persistently refused' the most pressing invitations to come to Ulster to instigate the Plan of Campaign because they understood the tenants' difficulties in the north, where the divisions between them were a source of strength to the landlords.[3]

Hereafter Nationalist attempts to attract support among Ulster Protestants generally took the form of cautioning against acceptance of what they argued was the inadequate remedial legislation of the Unionist government, and, relatedly, of holding out the prospect of extensive social and land reforms to be enacted once Ireland had Home Rule. In a speech in Belfast in April 1887 Michael Davitt held out the prospect of a prosperous Ireland when Home Rule was established: 'landlordism' would be abolished, rents reduced by half, new industries established, and other benefits obtained. Later that month John Dillon addressed a meeting at Ballymoney, composed mainly of Presbyterian tenant farmers, and urged them not to purchase their holdings under the land bill then before parliament, as the crimes bill which accompanied it was intended to break all combinations of tenants. Existing rents were too high, and if they were accepted as the basis of land purchases, the government would use the crimes act to ensure that no combinations to effect reductions would succeed. Similar advice was given by Davitt later in the year at Sheepbridge, Co. Down. Davitt described tenants buying their holdings from the Duke of Abercorn as 'fools', as the terms were too high; they should have awaited the enactment of Home Rule: 'An Irish state could easily find the money out of which to give to the landlords such compensation as would be reward or justice for the transfer of their rights to the Irish nation.'[4]

However, Davitt's vision of Ireland's future was inconsistent with the glaring financial inadequacies of Gladstone's Home

Rule bill. The *Weekly Northern Whig* pointed out that what Davitt envisaged a Home Rule government doing 'in two or three years' would be frankly impossible. Indeed, it was inescapably the case that a state without credit or money would have to 'lay hands' on the wealth of its subjects: 'We see that the Irish farmers might soon be the victims after the landlords, especially the Ulster tenant farmers, who as loyal citizens of the crown might easily be put into the same category as the landlords.' The unattractiveness of Nationalist policies for Ulster farmers is perhaps best illustrated by the extensive selling off of landed property in Ulster in the 1880s, particularly that of Lords Charlemont, Gosford and Lurgan and property belonging to the London Companies. Of 16,788 tenants who bought their holdings during the six years from 1885 to 1891 that the Ashbourne act was in operation, about half were in Ulster. Indeed, even among committed Protestant Gladstonians· in northern Ireland the shift in emphasis in Liberal policy away from land legislation to the Home Rule issue in the late 1880s had a very disappointing effect: the enthusiasm of some for Tory land legislation was to become much more pronounced than their support for Home Rule.[5] Moreover, as if to compound the inadequacies of Nationalist policies on land and Home Rule in Ulster, these were accompanied at a more ideological level by a propaganda campaign that, given its nature, could not hope to appeal to the northern Protestant community.

Parnellite chagrin at the role played by Ulster Unionists in the defeat of Home Rule in 1886 was exhibited in more ways than one. At one level, it manifested itself in a demand by a southern branch of the National League for a boycott of ships belonging to the White Star Line, because they were built in Harland & Wolff's shipyard where the Belfast riots had started. That this call did not find support among southern Nationalists, and was in fact condemned, did not alter its effect in the north, where it was taken as evidence of future Nationalist intentions towards Ulster industries. These, many Protestants believed, were already being boycotted by their Nationalist customers in rural Ulster. Support for this belief was provided by a call supposedly made by E. D. Gray's newspapers for Nationalists to boycott 'Unionist and Protestant journals' as advertising mediums. At another level, the nature of Nationalists' reaction to northern Unionism was demonstrated by their evident need to emphasise Ulster's place in nationalist ideology — a need dramatically displayed in *United Ireland*'s description of Justin McCarthy's victory in taking Londonderry City from the Unionists. Given the importance of Derry's place in Ulster Protestant politics and culture, Parnellites put great significance on winning the seat for the Home Rule cause. *United Ireland*, in describing McCarthy's victory, employed enthusiastically the historically infused rhetoric of nationalist propaganda:

> Derry is ours. 'No surrender' has got a new meaning. It is a national watchword now. The nation holds the inviolate city and means to keep it for all time. . . . The difference between the situation in Ireland when Derry was beseiged two hundred years ago and the present situation, is in the main the difference between the seventeenth century and the nineteenth. The Irish nationalists then held every part of the country but Derry and Enniskillen. . . . The English garrison had been driven out of every corner of the south and west and the greater portion of the north. They had fled from Kenmare to Enniskillen, from Cavan to the city of the London Companies. The parliament [James II's Irish parliament] was giving the 'aboriginal Irish' (as Macaulay calls us) their own again. . . . At Lough Foyle and Lough Erne the Englishry who refused to coalesce with the aborigines alone held out. Today the territory occupied by the West Britons who won't become Irishmen is growing narrower and narrower.

This article went on to deny that the besieged in Derry in 1689 were members of the 'imperial Anglo-Saxon race', and thus racially separate and superior to the native Irish, as argued by Froude and Macaulay.[6]

To Ulster Protestants, already imbued with their own historically infused apprehensions of Irish nationalism, this attempt at what might be termed 'cultural sabotage' could not be expected to allay those fears. Nevertheless, this aspect of their propaganda remained important to Parnellites. John Redmond contributed to the campaign stressing Ulster's place in nationalist ideology with a lecture on Hugh O'Neill in 1887 that was to be repeated many times over. He argued that the struggle of O'Neill and Red Hugh O'Donnell against the English and

Ireland's 'hereditary enemies' was the same as that being waged by the Parnellites, and that it would soon be successfully completed. In Redmond's synthesis of sixteenth-century and nineteenth-century struggles, the position occupied by the Ulster Protestant community was necessarily among 'Ireland's hereditary enemies'; and it is indicative of the Ulster Protestant reaction to such propaganda that Ronald McNeill, writing nearly forty years later, could single out Redmond's lecture for comment. Ulstermen, he declared, were aware of those earlier Irish rebellions and were under no illusion as to the design for which arms had been taken up: 'The names of Hugh O'Neill, of Owen Roe, of Emmet, or of Wolfe Tone . . . carry very definite meaning to the ears of Irishmen, whether Nationalist or Unionist.' Thus the use of arguments emphasising the historical strife associated with the Irish question made no contribution at all to the solution of the Ulster problem, but merely reinforced existing political positions and inspired future acrimony — a tendency that was already well promoted by the Belfast riots of 1886 and their aftermath. These were to provide much material for Nationalist propaganda on Ulster in this period. The riots did not end until September 1886 and though they involved, for the greater part, Protestants and the police, it was the Catholic community in Belfast that suffered most. Of £2,600 awarded as compensation for malicious injuries, £2,500 was awarded to Catholics; of thirty public houses destroyed, twenty-eight were owned by Catholics; and some 3,000 people evicted from their employment were dependent for their survival on collections made by a 'committee of Catholic gentlemen, headed by a bishop'.[7]

Material for controversy in parliament arose in the debate on the appointment of the commission to inquire into the riots. Nationalists argued that the composition of the inquiry, consisting of three Protestant commissioners and only one Catholic, whose position would be merely that of secretary, was unfair. Objection was also taken to the presence on the commission of one Commander M'Hardy, whom they accused of being an Orange partisan. M'Hardy kept his position, though the Catholic representation was increased by the inclusion, as president, of the eminent English judge, Justice Day. The Ulster Unionist contribution to the debate was strong if not constructive. Colonel Saunderson, for example, concentrated mainly on provoking Parnellites, while his position as an Orange leader gave colour to the Nationalist view that the riots were all the work of Orangemen. As the *Weekly Northern Whig* put it, for Saunderson to speak on the riots as the Orange leader 'will only confirm the statements of the Nationalist press that the rioters were all Orangemen, and that the attacks were, in effect, the work of the Orange lodges'. Certainly this view was widely accepted by Parnellites; but how far was it accurate? Although the inquiry into the riots did not implicate the Orange Order, as such, the Orange M.P. for East Belfast, E. S. W. de Cobain, and other Protestant leaders were named for heightening tension during the disturbances by encouraging the rioters and spreading the false idea that Catholic policemen were being drafted into Belfast from the nationalist south to shoot Protestants. It was also on the basis of such evidence that the Parnellite analysis of the riots rested, and plausibility was given to that analysis by the less than wholesome activities of some prominent Orangemen. In June 1886, for example, Viscount Cole publicly called on Protestants not to employ Roman Catholics. This plea was made the subject of a nationalist leaflet and widely distributed in Great Britain to show that Ulster Unionists were only interested in religious ascendancy. Moreover, in the aftermath of the riots, several Protestants, charged with offences arising out of them, were tried at Omagh, with some scandalous results. In more than one case juries refused to convict defendants despite explicit directions from the bench to do so. The worst example was the case of Joseph Walker, who was charged with the murder of a soldier and a head constable. Although he was tried twice and the juries instructed to find a verdict of wilful murder, they refused, with the result that Walker went unpunished for about six months until convicted of manslaughter in April 1887 — the jury again refusing to bring in a verdict of wilful murder. In a case of riotous behaviour the jury not only refused to convict the defendant, but local magistrates persistently frustrated the attempts of the Attorney-General to have the case retried.[8]

The publicity Nationalists gave to such incidents ran in tandem with more traditional themes in their propaganda on Ulster Unionism, stressing the disreputable history of

Orangeism, its encouragement by English politicians anxious to keep the Irish people divided, and self-government as the only remedy for the religious bigotry promoted by Orangeism: 'He [the Orangeman] will soon learn to bless you for it. He will forget his factious fanaticism and remember that he is an Irishman.' Indeed, some very slight evidence appeared to support such a view when W. G. Flood, Grand Master of Dungannon Orange lodge, acted as a sponsor for William O'Brien at the general election of 1886. Flood, however, was swiftly removed from his post shortly afterwards by his outraged brethren

Nationalist propaganda had a major fillip when the report of the commission of inquiry into the Belfast riots was published early in 1887. Blame was firmly placed on Protestant mobs, while Catholic restraint was praised. Most important, though, were the appendices attached to the report detailing the exclusion of Roman Catholics from positions of employment under Belfast Corporation. Of its eighty-nine employees, only two were Roman Catholics, both in lowly paid positions. This evidence of discrimination was to figure prominently in Parnellite and Liberal propaganda in subsequent years.[9]

But what were the implications of the Belfast riots in general for the northern Ireland question? For Ulster Unionists, even those who most deplored them, the riots could be used as a demonstration of what would inevitably occur if Home Rule were enacted: 'Their lesson . . . is that the attempt to rule the north by Parnellite police will create a rising of a most serious character.' For Nationalists, though, a different lesson was to be drawn, especially with reference to the proposal that part of Ulster might be given its own parliament:

> If Ulster is split up and a separate parliament given to the Protestant counties what guarantee will there be for the safety of the Catholic community? The Orange riots in Belfast supply the answer. *The Protestant majority is too strong to be coerced, and too bigoted to be trusted with power* [my italics].[10]

Thus for Nationalists the riots could serve a twofold purpose: they could be used to show that Ulster Protestants were strong enough to deal with any supposed coercion emanating from a Dublin parliament, and, at the same time, that separate treatment for Ulster was undesirable because of the threat to the northern Catholic community.

Apart from their propaganda on the Ulster question and attempts to instigate agrarian agitation in the north of Ireland, Parnellites sought also, by action in the House of Commons, to demonstrate that they could exercise a decisive influence on how the Westminster parliament dealt with Ulster issues. When T. W. Russell introduced a bill in 1887 with the intention of enabling 35,000 leaseholders to enjoy the benefits of the 1881 land act, it was blocked by Nationalists even though it would have effected for this class of landholder what Parnell's rejected tenants' relief bill of 1886 intended. The *Weekly Northern Whig* noted: 'They do not like any member to have the credit of carrying a bill in favour of the tenants unless he is a member of their own party.' More significantly, Parnellites succeeded in preventing for over a year the passing of a bill to provide a main drainage system for Belfast, costing over £500,000, on the grounds that the municipal franchise in Belfast was too high and, at £10, far higher than any city in Great Britain. Eventually a compact between Ulster Unionist and Nationalist M.P.s was agreed, whereby the drainage scheme bill passed at the same time as a franchise bill lowering the municipal franchise from £10 to £4. Nationalist obstruction of Unionist measures continued, in varying degrees, into the 1890s. When William Johnston introduced an 'Asylum Superannuation Bill' stiff opposition came from Joseph Biggar, though Timothy Healy informed Johnston that he 'had prevented that ruffian [Dr] Tanner blocking it'.[11] At the same time Parnellites were keen to detach, if possible, any able member from the Unionist group.

T. W. Russell, widely accepted as the most able of the Ulster Unionist M.P.s, was personally approached by Parnell in this period to join the Nationalist Party:

Mr Parnell pleaded with me to stop what he called my war against Ireland — to come over and help the Nationalist Party. I told him what I thought of the [National] League, of the Plan [of Campaign], and all the rest of it, and I succeeded in eliciting the great man's views, which did not differ materially from my own. I was vehement. Mr Parnell was calm. The interview resulted in nothing save a great memory for me, and as we parted the Irish leader said: 'Well, think it over, and remember there will always be an open door for *you.*'

In general, though, the Parnellite attitude on Ulster appears to have hardened in the late 1880s. Nationalists resented particularly the practice of southern landlords in 'importing' bailiffs and 'emergency men' from Ulster to do their 'dirty work', and their attempts to encourage Ulster Protestants to occupy vacant farms in the south. By 1890 it would seem, according at least to one important source, that Parnellites were becoming less inclined to claim that Ulster Protestants were really nationalists than to describe them instead as a foreign element in Ireland. In his compilation of the historical and political case for Home Rule, *The Home-Ruler's Manual*, R. Barry O'Brien declared:

> The Ulster colony...represents...a comparatively weak force in Irish politics. The nation has upon the whole conquered. But the question still is, 'shall the Ulster colony dominate all Ireland?' So far the tide of events has flowed in favour of the nation. Is the tide to be turned back? Is the 'whisper of a faction' to prevail against 'the voice of a nation'?[12]

THE ULSTER DEBATE IN BRITISH POLITICS: THE GLADSTONIAN POLICY, 1886-90

Notwithstanding the fact that Liberals and Parnellites were in alliance from 1886, their positions on the Ulster question were not entirely synonymous. Parnellites argued forcefully for the inclusion of Ulster in any Home Rule scheme. Gladstone, as befitted his position as Prime Minister and potential Prime Minister, was concerned, publicly at least, to display a more objective attitude to the problem by indicating his willingness to listen to proposals for separate treatment for Ulster, or part of it, if such were made. Indeed, in being prepared to give Ulster this option, he argued, 'we are giving more . . . in that shape than we are giving to any other part [of Ireland]'.[13] This was how the position stood when the Liberal Party found itself in opposition after the 1886 general election, and, as such, it at least offered the possibility of a resolution of the issue. However, such was not to be, and the close of this period was to see the Ulster problem as far from resolution as ever. Unionists, for the most part, had little interest in seeing the most formidable obstacle to Home Rule removed, and thus were not going to take the initiative in that direction. This left the onus on Gladstone. What determined his approach to the northern Ireland problem in this period? This question will be approached through an examination of Gladstone's political strategy, his temperament, and the ideological framework within which he viewed the problem.

This last is of crucial importance in understanding the Gladstonian view of the Ulster question. It has been shown in Chapter 7 that Gladstone's campaign for Home Rule was heavily influenced by his views on Irish history. His attitude to the Ulster question was similarly influenced, but in a more marked degree. Indeed, there is evidence to suggest that he had become so emotionally involved with the history of the problem at this time that he was incapable of taking a detached view of the subject; and nothing invoked Gladstone's prodigious moral and emotional senses more than the atrocities which made up so much of Irish history. Lord Rosebery has left a revealing record of his impressions of Gladstone's state of mind on this subject, during a visit to Hawarden Castle:

> I sent for the boys [Rosebery's sons]. . . . They went to a performance at the Hawarden gymnasium, sitting on each side of Mr G. He later came back chilled and tired, and lost control of himself (for the third time in my experience) in speaking of the Irish rebellion of 1798. In vain did I try to keep him off and turn the subject.[14]

Given that Gladstone shared the Parnellite view that strong opposition to Home Rule in Ulster came only from bigoted Orangemen, it is important to relate his increasing preoccupation with their role in the 1798 rebellion to his attitude towards their political actions in the late 1880s if his approach to the Ulster question is to be properly understood.

Gladstone's views of their action in 1798 were explicitly and vehemently expressed in 1889, when, in the course of explaining the atrocities perpetrated by government forces, he referred to the 'ferocious proceedings such as those by which Orange bigotry desolated the County Armagh; the disarming of the Roman Catholic population with circumstances of extreme violence'. He was, as his son Herbert records, 'always aroused by injustice, by anything that was cowardly and bad, and particularly by any defence of what was bad'; and the moral outrage conveyed in his reference to the activities of Orangemen in 1798 had a direct carry-over to the actions of their descendants in the 1880s. In particular the policies of the Ulster Orangemen in parliament, especially Colonel Saunderson, were greatly to increase Gladstone's distaste for them. In general their arguments, as we have seen, were infused with a virulent anti-Catholicism. As the professedly partisan biographer of Saunderson put it, 'It must be admitted that he persistently spoke of Roman Catholics with pointed harshness. It was a fixed principle in his philosophy.' Saunderson in fact made it a part of his policy to bait Gladstone whenever possible. In one speech he denounced Gladstone for associating with those he had once accused of murder and treason — a charge Gladstone described as 'deliberate misrepresentation' by one whose threats to use violence to resist Home Rule in 1886 placed him closer to crime than Parnell had ever been. Following some evictions on Gladstone's Hawarden estate in 1889, Saunderson, employing 'a violent use of personal illustration', sought to make capital out of them with reference to English Liberals who came to Ireland to support the Plan of Campaign. But much the worst aspect of his campaign against Gladstone was his repeated jibes that the Liberal leader would soon be destined for a 'higher and more peaceful place'. To protests against this kind of remark, Saunderson replied that he meant the House of Lords, but the implications of such utterances were unavoidable. Saunderson was fond of boasting that 'There is no one Gladstone fears as he fears me.' This was certainly untrue, but that he could provoke Gladstone is clear enough. Whereas most Parnellites generally dismissed — indeed, often enjoyed — Saunderson's taunts, such was not Gladstone's way: 'Intensely earnest about everything, big or little, he had no time for toying with topics.' Thus there is no reason to doubt the accuracy of Saunderson's estimate of his effect on Gladstone following one of his thrusts: 'The G.O.M. was terribly angry. . . . He looked quite mad.' A similar reaction was noted by William Johnston and by John Ross, who declared: 'I found to my great delight that it was easy for me to "draw" Gladstone. . . . I was astonished that he would allow himself to be moved by the attack of an obscure young Tory.' Following an interview with Gladstone on the Ulster question, Thomas McKnight, editor of the *Northern Whig* newspapers, affirmed that he 'greatly' distrusted the Ulster Orange M.P.s, 'whom he looks upon as fanatics' and who seemed incapable of 'influencing in any satisfactory manner intelligent Liberal opinion in Great Britain'.[15] His evident distrust of Ulster Orangemen was, it will be seen, an important influence on Gladstone's Ulster policy in this period.

The first opportunity for seriously discussing the Ulster question was occasioned by the Round Table conference of 1887. At first sight the prospect of agreement on this issue seemed reasonable. Gladstone was maintaining his willingness to consider favourably a workable plan of separate treatment for Ulster if such were forthcoming, and this was not inconsistent with Joseph Chamberlain's demand that Ulster be given its own assembly in any Home Rule plan. Moreover, Liberal Unionist opinion in Ulster, as expressed in the *Northern Whig* newspapers — the most important organs of Liberal Unionism in the province — strongly favoured a separate assembly for northern Ireland. Chamberlain made the establishment of a 'provincial' assembly for Ulster an essential part of his argument, his idea being that two such assemblies would be set up in Ireland, one for Ulster and one for the rest of Ireland, 'entirely subordinate to the Unionist principle', and in the same relationship to Westminster as that enjoyed by Quebec or Ontario to the federal Canadian parliament. The problem was raised as a 'fundamental' issue in the second set of Round Table talks on 14 January 1887. It was suggested that some power be given to Ulster, or part of it, to join the southern legislature if desired. Interestingly, it was suggested that the jurisdiction of the two local assemblies should be decided by means of a plebiscite of counties to be taken either immediately or 'at the expiry of a fixed time'. At this point discussion of the question ended, as John Morley, Gladstone's intermediary with the Parnellites, 'desired to consult with others'. However, Morley, whose role in these talks was most important, was intensely suspicious of Chamberlain and informed Gladstone to the effect that the former was not sincere in wanting to settle the Ulster issue: the discussion of provincial assemblies had been 'launched in mid-ocean', and Chamberlain, if an excuse was wanted to break off the talks, would use the Ulster question to do it. Nevertheless, Morley resolved 'to see whether Mr P[arnell] has any ideas about Ulster during the next few days'. Apparently Parnell, while wary of the fact that the conference in itself implied a readiness to compromise, was also 'awake' to the satisfactory significance of 'the Chamberlain overtures', though the Irish Party generally were very uneasy about any compromise 'at the expense of the nation's rights'. Shortly afterwards Morley informed Gladstone:

> As to Ulster, I am firmly persuaded that there can be no sort of severance; severance would rob the Dublin body of a valuable element; it would damage the whole financial scheme; and it would be a standing affront to the rest of the nation. Parnell, I am certain, will have nothing to do with such a plan.

As to whether Morley's information was the result of a personal interview with Parnell — not the most accessible of men at this time — or merely his own conclusions based on past experience is not absolutely clear. Gladstone was later to inform Chamberlain that he did not believe Parnell had been informed in any detail of the result of the Round Table discussions.[16]

Parnell himself, in a speech four years later in Belfast — though in a very different political climate — was to claim that Gladstone had kept him in complete ignorance of what was occurring at the talks. In any event, the January meetings effectively ended the discussions, as relations between the two sides deteriorated so much between then and the meeting of 14 February that the latter was reduced to little more than a formality; the Ulster question, moreover, was the most important topic discussed. Chamberlain insisted that separate treatment for Ulster was essential. Harcourt and Morley declared that it was a 'great difficulty', as Parnell objected that it would both destroy the chance of giving full satisfaction to the idea of nationality and seriously interfere with the financial position of the Irish legislature.[17] There the conference ended.

But surprisingly, despite Parnell's undoubted refusal to

consider a separate settlement for Ulster, Gladstone continued to maintain that such a solution was possible if Ulster Unionists proposed a workable plan. When Thomas McKnight visited him in 1887 Gladstone repeated the offer and added: 'There will be some difficulty, I know, in inducing certain parties to consent to such a proposal, but I have no doubt that we can carry it. Let the Ulster Unionists think over a plan.' Perhaps Gladstone's view of the Nationalist attitude to Ulster was similar to that of his son Herbert, who speculated that while Parnell was against separate treatment, if it had been acceptable to northern Unionists he would not have wrecked Home Rule on that account. In any event, when McKnight tried to persuade Ulster Unionists to formulate such a plan he was met with a blank refusal: the 'universal response' was that it was not part of their job to make Home Rule easier to carry and that 'complete separation' would be preferable to any Home Rule scheme. The debate on the Ulster question, however, continued in 1887. When Gladstone repeated the offer of separate treatment in a speech at Swansea on 4 June, during a tour of south Wales, John Bright entered the fray and in an open letter pointed out the nub of the Ulster problem: 'You must know that any plan for dealing only with the Protestants of Ulster by themselves' and not associated with the Catholics of the province 'is an impossible plan and not worth a moment's consideration.' Gladstone replied that he was aware of no final or general pronouncement about Ulster, or a part of Ulster: 'The only Tory declaration as yet known to me in particular is that of Colonel Saunderson strongly against the severance [of Ulster from the rest of Ireland]. Our position is exactly what it was on 8 April 1886.'[18] Gladstone's reply to Bright is important and could explain why he publicly adhered to his offer of separate Ulster treatment even though such was against the frequently expressed wishes of Parnell. Such a 'conciliatory' proposal could be safely made if it was certain, as Unionist rejection of it indicated, that it would never be accepted, or, indeed, if accepted in principle, would be found unacceptable and unworkable in practice. As Bright explained, given the extent to which the differing religious communities were intermixed, any separate treatment for Ulster Protestants alone would be virtually impossible to devise; and contrary to his insistence on constructing his own Home

Rule bill in 1886, Gladstone always insisted that the onus to devise a *workable* scheme of separate treatment was on the Unionists of the province. Moreover, he did not, as he could have done, assist in the construction of such a scheme by suggesting — as was discussed at the Round Table conference — the use of a plebiscite to settle the political identity of religiously mixed areas. Additionally, the prospects of a compromise between Home Rulers and Unionists on Ulster were impaired by the enmity between Gladstone and Orangemen.

When he made it know later in the year that he was prepared in a future Home Rule bill to keep Irish M.P.s at Westminster, the Grand Master of the Orange Order in Belfast, Dr R. R. Kane, requested an elaboration of his views, claiming that these could affect the Ulster Unionist attitude to Home Rule. Gladstone's reaction, however, was intemperate and negative. His son Herbert, who was acting as his secretary at this time, records that Gladstone's letter answering Dr Kane was 'formidable', and it was only after three attempts that he could be persuaded to reply 'in a more conciliatory spirit'. Even then it could hardly be described as a straightforward expression of opinion, being studiously vague and non-commital. Of the correspondence, when published, the *Weekly Northern Whig* declared that it was 'not uninteresting as an example of skill in controversial fencing but it adds absolutely nothing to our knowledge of Mr Gladstone's attitude'.[19] The Ulster question, however, was to be more intensely debated in the last few months of 1887 than at any other time in this period.

Shortly after the Gladstone/Kane correspondence an English deputation arrived in Ulster on what would now be called a 'fact-finding' mission, with the object of assessing support for Home Rule in northern Ireland. Their appraisal of the situation, however, exhibited a strong desire to minimise the strength of Ulster Unionism. They concluded:

> In Ulster the great majority of the people who are opposed to Home Rule will, when Home Rule is granted, forget past differences. . . . Considerations of common interests will make them join with their fellow-countrymen in carrying on the government of Ireland. . . . They themselves even now are well aware that this will be the case.[20]

Such a conclusion was, no doubt, highly satisfying to Parnellites, and would also have been to Gladstone, as his expressed views at this time illustrated. Uncongenial as he found contacts with Ulster Orangemen, Gladstone was to urge them repeatedly to return to what he described as the nationalist sentiments of their forefathers in the 1780s, from which they had 'degenerated' by their adherence to the Union. The frequency with which Gladstone was to make such appeals indicates the strength of their hold on his mind and the extent to which his hopes for a resolution of the Ulster problem was dependent on a view of Ulster Protestants derived from the history of Grattan's Parliament.

At a meeting in Derby on 20 October 1887 Gladstone, having presented his audience with an account of the Ulster Protestant role in establishing Grattan's Parliament, declared:

> Gentlemen, depend upon it, when you see now the utter falsity of the supposition that there is a radical and ingrained hostility among Irish Protestants to Irish local government, depend upon it that there is a misunderstanding, and a complete misunderstanding on the part of our opponents of what it is that the Protestants of Ulster want. What the Protestants of Ulster want, because, after all, they are intelligent and reasonable men . . . is full assurance that the connection of Ireland to this country is to be maintained.

This, Gladstone suggested, could be effected by Irish representation at Westminster. His tendency to draw contemporary political conclusions from the 'evidence' of history indicates, to say the least, an inadequate analysis of the problem, but it was an element in Gladstone's thinking that seemed to intensify rather than diminish in succeeding years. More immediately, the Ulster issue was kept to the forefront of politics by Joseph Chamberlain's visit to the province in October 1887. His motives in coming to northern Ireland were inspired less by a concern for the intrinsic welfare of Ulster Protestants than by a desire to exacerbate what he considered to be Gladstone's greatest problem in regard to Home Rule. As he cautioned Hartington before leaving for America at the end of October, 'Do not forget Ulster — it is a terrible nut for the G.O.M. to crack.'[21]

Consequently in his Ulster campaign he emphasised the northern Protestants' racial, economic and religious separation from, and superiority to, the rest of Ireland. At meetings in Coleraine and Belfast he endorsed a radical programme of reforms, including extensive land purchases and elected local government, and made a point of addressing business and professional men as well as tenant farmers. In particular he stressed that while Parnellites may have had a majority of M.P.s in the province, they did not have a majority of the votes, as in county constituencies the Nationalist vote averaged 30,000 and the Unionist 50,000. But most importantly, it was known that Gladstone was to speak at Nottingham on 18 October, and Chamberlain put several questions for him to answer. For example, would he coerce Ulster to accept Home Rule or would he give a separate government to all, or a part of, the province? He went on:

> We all know that though Mr Gladstone has hinted something about being willing to concede a separate government here, he has proposed no plan to effect that object, and he will not propose one. He dares not do it. Mr Parnell has unmistakably intimated that he will have no Home Rule for Ireland without Ulster being included in it, and Mr Gladstone must do what Mr Parnell wishes.

This was indeed an accurate description of Gladstone's position, but while it is true that his scope for manoeuvre on this question was certainly limited, it could hardly be said that Chamberlain's utterances were couched in terms likely to inspire a constructive approach from Liberals. The cynicism of his motives, as much as what he had to say, provoked John Morley to exclaim: 'Chamberlain's performance in Ulster is surely one of the most dishonest that was ever seen. It is really quite desperate.' Gladstone shared this view, and in his speech at Nottingham on 18 October 1887 declared his refusal to be drawn into a trap:

> When I am asked at this juncture, without knowing the sentiments of my friends, without knowing the sentiments of the English people, the Scotch people, or the Welsh people, without knowing the sentiments of Ulster ... to bind myself to

the proposition that Ulster, or part of Ulster shall be absolutely excluded from any Irish arrangements ... gentlemen, I
tell you that is rather too large a demand upon the credibility
or even the folly of man.

What is significant about this part of Gladstone's speech,
however, is its emphasis on *not* accepting the proposition of
separate treatment for Ulster: Chamberlain, it would seem, had
effectively called Gladstone's bluff. The latter's argument, that
he could not commit himself to separate treatment for Ulster
because he did not know the views of all interested parties, was,
given the many occasions on which these views had been
pressed on him — especially those of Irish Unionists and
Nationalists — hardly a convincing argument. In particular it
was at odds with his previously confident assertions that if
Unionists formulated a plan, he was sure he could have it
carried. He was, in fact, not to mention separate treatment for
Ulster again, except to point out that such an option had been
rejected by Ulster Unionists. In his Nottingham speech he set
the pattern of his future and more vague approach to the Ulster
difficulty by declaring his intention 'to act as might seem fair for
the protection of minorities'. He also specifically ruled out any
debate with Chamberlain on the Ulster issue, on the grounds
that such would 'exasperate the dispute, and render more difficult and distant the solution'.[22]

Gladstone's unwillingness to meet Chamberlain on this issue,
however, was felt by some Liberals to reflect badly on their Irish
policy. At the end of November 1887 John Morley was pressing
on him the necessity of a 'counter-demonstration' in Dublin to
offset the effect of Chamberlain's Ulster visit; though in
Morley's proposed counter-demonstration it would seem that
the Ulster issue would be played down — representatives were
to be invited from all over Ireland except Belfast. Chamberlain's
northern Ireland campaign, however, did elicit one thoughtful
contribution to the Ulster debate, from R. T. Reid, a Liberal
lawyer who was to represent Parnellites at the Special
Commission proceedings of the following year. Reid's article
endorsed many of the standard elements in the
Liberal/Nationalist view of the problem, with regard to Orange
extremism, the small area in which Unionists had an over-

whelming majority, the 'nationalist' sympathies of Protestants in Grattan's time as proof of their political identity, the relative prosperity argument, and the groundless fears of Unionists about Parnellite persecution. Nevertheless, he concluded that if northern Protestants were to maintain their opposition to Home Rule after a Dublin parliament was established, it would be useless to force them to accept union with the rest of Ireland. In that event the only sensible course open for Nationalists in the independent part of Ireland would be to persuade Unionists 'by sensible government' to accept Home Rule.[23] In making this admission Reid's was the only Home Rule contribution to the Ulster debate that attempted to face up to and accept the reality of continued Protestant opposition to self-government. Gladstone's policy on Ulster, however, increasingly relied on his reading of Irish history in the late eighteenth century, and in particular on arguing that current Unionist policy was the same as that of English governments in the past that had brought so much suffering to Ireland.

When Lord Hartington visited Belfast in October 1888 Gladstone professed himself 'astonished' that Ulster Protestants should gather 'to applaud everything that their grandfathers condemned, and to condemn everything that their grandfathers applauded'. Similarly, when 864 out of a total of 999 Irish Nonconformist ministers signed a petition against Home Rule that was shortly to be presented to Lord Salisbury, Gladstone dismissed them as 'a handful of men in the north' whose appeal to religious prejudice was no better than that employed in Irish government in the sixteenth and seventeenth centuries. But how did Ulster Protestants answer Gladstone's charge of political 'degeneracy'? Briefly, their reply was twofold. Orangemen and Conservatives denied that any real union of the religious groups occurred in the 1780s, but, faced with Gladstone's condemnation of Orange atrocities during the 1798 rebellion, were mostly concerned to defend the reputation of their ancestors. Presbyterian Liberal Unionists, though, to whom Gladstone's complaint was believed more to apply, argued that they felt utterly bereft of the 'incentives to disaffection and disloyalty' that goaded their ancestors to insurrection:

The commercial and manufacturing restrictions that

oppressed our grandfathers have long since been abolished, and our trade and industries are now unfettered and free; the civil and religious disabilities they groaned under have all been swept away; the tithe system that galled them is a thing of the ... past; no state church now lords it, and extorts reluctant tribute; complete religious equality exists, and religious animosities are fast dying away; and educational privileges are unsurpassed, and within reach of the poorest classes; our parliamentary representation exceeds proportionately that of any other part of the United Kingdom, and we have the protection of the ballot; and, above all, the occupiers of the soil hold their homesteads and farms — not as their fathers did, at the pleasure or caprice of a despotic landlord, under cruel arbitrary exactions and degrading serfdom, but — as joint owners in the land they till, with a fixed and secure tenure, subject only to a rent which is equitably determinable. ... Yes, Ulster has gained all our fathers fought and bled for, and has thriven and prospered under the united parliament.

This reply to Gladstone's charge of political degeneracy was, in substance, repeated many times in the late 1880s, but did not affect his perception of the Ulster question. Indeed, given Gladstone's view that the Act of Union and the 'corrupt' methods by which it was carried were morally reprehensible, constituting an evil which had to be atoned for, the fact that Ulster Unionists could claim to have benefited by it might well have seemed a compounding of the error. In 1889 he replied to resolutions passed at a meeting of the Belfast branch of the Young Ireland Society by congratulating them on their efforts to bring Ulster Protestants back to the patriotism of their forefathers:

Here is the sacred fire that should again be lighted. It alone can guide those who have been misled by sinister influences back to the love of country which ... affords the only solid basis for true loyalty to the empire and the throne.[24]

A record of how far Ulster had materially benefited by the Union was irrelevant if, as it appears Gladstone's view was, the issue at stake was essentially a moral one: of a people led astray by 'sinister influences' and requiring redemption by a 'sacred fire'. Indeed, in such a conception of the Ulster question, northern Unionist emphasis on the material gain that had attended the Union might well have seemed analogous to the Israelite worship of the golden calf.

Just how far apart the views of both sides were on the Ulster issue was further demonstrated in Gladstone's article, 'Home Rule for Ireland', published in 1890. He exhibited his ignorance of the province by declaring that since Protestants in Ulster were 'possibly near half a million in number', and thus in a similar number to Ulster Catholics, they could 'hold their own'. Commending their refusal to accept separate treatment for Ulster, he also emphasised that this only made their opposition to Home Rule all the more unreasonable: 'to meet the views held in a corner of the country' the majority of the Irish people were being asked to sacrifice their national traditions and long-held desire for self-government, now within 'one stage of its accomplishment'. Declaring that the desire for self-government was strongest among northern Protestants one hundred years before, Gladstone could not understand their present opposition to Home Rule: 'The result of our endeavours to find an answer to the great and troublesome Why? has not thus far been encouraging.' Nor would the frequent Liberal contacts with Protestant Home Rulers in Ulster have enabled Gladstone to acquire a more perceptive understanding of the views of the province's Unionist population. Liberals were always ready to take heart from their assurances that their cause would ultimately succeed in the north. Just before the Parnell divorce crisis erupted John Morley was gleefully informing Gladstone of a conversation he had had with the Protestant Liberal M.P., T. A. Dickson, who informed him that by advocating compulsory purchase and putting forward Protestant candidates 'we should win seats in Ulster, and not lose any except West Belfast'.[25]

FROM THE PARNELLITE SPLIT TO THE GENERAL ELECTION OF 1892

As John Morley confided to Gladstone, the realignment of Nationalist politics occasioned by the Parnellite split, with the Catholic clergy becoming vigorously identified and involved with the larger anti-Parnellite faction, would inevitably damage the Home Rule cause in Ulster. The salient issue in the crisis for northern Protestants rapidly became that of the political power of the priests, and, as will be seen, the defeat of the Parnellite faction for political control of southern Ireland would be viewed in the province as validating age-old fears as to the secular ambitions of the Catholic church. Moreover, the plausibility of these fears was already accentuated by the fact that clerical control of Nationalist politics in Ulster was much more complete than in other parts of Ireland. Indeed, from the occasion of the alliance between the Catholic church and the Parnellite party in 1885, the clergy virtually took control of Ulster Nationalist politics. In Belfast they provided 29 members out of a local executive of 80, in Armagh 32 out of 98, and in Antrim 25 out of 66. Thus the conflicts between the two Nationalist factions in Ulster following the Parnellite split inevitably produced a higher degree of political involvement by the priests than elsewhere. This was especially the case in the campaign led by Bishop McAllister of Down and Connor against the *Belfast Morning News*, which continued to support Parnell after the Nationalist Party split. Almost immediately the clergy moved both to establish a rival, the *Irish News*, and to instigate a boycott of the *Belfast Morning News*. So effective were their efforts that the latter was taken over by the *Irish News* eighteen months later.[26]

But while the anti-Parnellite faction was undoubtedly supreme in Ulster, the Nationalist split did produce a rather modified view of the northern problem from Parnell. In a speech in the Ulster Hall on 29 May 1891 he dealt with the question in a manner different from his previous bellicose utterances on the subject. Among other things, he praised Ulster for its industry and commerce and for the settled agricultural aspect of the province compared with other parts of Ireland. In particular his remarks on the problem of Ulster Protestant opposition to Home Rule were highly conciliatory. Parnell declared that it was the duty of Nationalists to

> leave no stone unturned, no means unused to conciliate the reasonable or unreasonable prejudices of the minority.* I

*The misprint 'majority' which occurs in the newspaper report of the speech has here been corrected.

think the majority have always been inclined to go a long way in that direction; but it has been undoubtedly true that every Irish patriot has always recognised . . . from the time of Wolfe Tone until now that until the religious prejudices of the minority, whether reasonable or unreasonable, are conciliated . . . Ireland can never enjoy perfect freedom, Ireland can never be united.

Parnell went on to say that so long as the minority felt that Ireland's 'legitimate freedom' threatened their spiritual and temporal interests, 'the work of building up an independent Ireland will have upon it a fatal clog and a fatal drag'. Much has recently been made of these remarks: it has been suggested that, freed from the constraints of an alliance with the Catholic hierarchy, Parnell could give expression to his real views on the place of Protestants in Irish politics: 'The truth is that it is inconceivable that any of his major lieutenants of the 1880s could have produced so substantive an analysis of the obstacles to Irish unity. . . . The doctrine that there could be no legitimate freedom for Ireland until the minority was conciliated fell on unreceptive ears.'[27] But just how 'substantive' was Parnell's analysis of Ulster Unionism, and how far did it really differ from that of Catholic Nationalist?

Parnell's remarks, in fact, were innovative only superficially. His call for the conciliation of the 'reasonable or unreasonable prejudices of the minority', and what was perhaps the major theme of this speech — that it was only he who was pressing for thoroughgoing self-government — are only compatible at the most general level. On closer examination the mutual incompatibility of these demands becomes clear. The crucial question here is: what was the constitutional framework within which Parnell thought it appropriate for minority prejudices to be conciliated? The best way to approach this issue is to examine, in the context of this speech, how Parnell defined the nature of Ulster Unionism. Before addressing himself directly to the Ulster question he argued that if his Nationalist rivals persisted in their alliance with Gladstone, they would be presented with a measure that was not Home Rule; a measure such as Lord Salisbury would 'be willing to give at any time'; one that 'our Orange friends in Belfast would be willing to accept (*laughter*)'; a bill in which all powers over land, the magistracy, law and order and the police would be retained at Westminster. Clearly, as his references to the Orangemen indicate, the Home Rule scheme he would accept would inevitably go far beyond one that might be acceptable to them; their prejudices were not to be conciliated. But more importantly, what these remarks suggest is how far Parnell's 'new' attitude to Ulster Unionism retained the essential features of the orthodox Nationalist view. As has been shown elsewhere, the basis of that analysis was to identify the Ulster Orangemen as the only element in the northern Protestant community that was irreversibly opposed to Home Rule, and that while the Protestant community generally was fearful of self-government, they were open to persuasion on the question. This is also the context within which Parnell's conciliatory overtures to the Ulster Protestants have to be seen: militant Orangeism could not be conciliated, but Protestants generally would accept self-government for the whole of Ireland. Thus it was clearly within the framework of an all-Ireland parliament that their prejudices would be conciliated. Parnell's adherence to the orthodox Nationalist analysis of the Ulster problem is clearly demonstrated in his remarks on the consequences of a failure to conciliate the Protestant community. The outcome of such an eventuality he describes in the following terms: 'Ireland can never enjoy perfect freedom, Ireland can never be united ... practically united. ... The work of building up an independent Ireland will have upon it a fatal clog and a fatal drag.'[28]

What is essential to note here is that Parnell, like other Nationalists, did not envisage continued Protestant alienation from their Catholic fellow-countrymen as a fatal obstacle to the *achievement* of self-government. The disunity he refers to is defined, not in political, but implicity and vaguely in social, economic and religious terms, as a factor that would hinder the general progress of a self-governing Ireland. This was the central weakness of his 'new' approach to the problem; for in failing to point out the implications of Protestant alienation for the achievement of Home Rule his remarks were deprived of the necessary incisive element that might have stimulated a meaningful debate on the most important problem facing the

Home Rule cause. Instead Parnell assured Ulster Unionists that the majority of Nationalists 'have always been inclined to go a long way to conciliate Protestant fears'. But, as this study has shown, Nationalists made no special efforts in this direction; they rather tended to rely on Protestants simply accepting the situation once Home Rule was established. Moreover, for all his concern to conciliate Ulster Protestants, Parnell made no practical suggestions towards that end, while his successor as leader of the Parnellite faction, John Redmond, was to reject absolutely any concessions whatever to northern Unionists. To accept Parnell's call for Nationalists to conciliate Protestant prejudices at face value is to miss what was really novel in this part of his speech, namely how he managed to restate the orthodox Nationalist view of the Ulster problem in language which appeared to reject that position and offer a radically new approach. In fact his remarks on the Ulster issue are of the same order as his 'republican' appeals to the 'hillside men', also made at this stage in his career — superficially striking but in reality meaning very little. Certainly they were to find no responsive chord among Ulster Unionists, who saw the dissolving of Parnellite support in Nationalist Ireland as a demonstration of the power of the priests. Not surprisingly, therefore, Parnell's death was seen to mark the supremacy of the Catholic church in Nationalist politics. As the *Belfast News-Letter* put it, 'The rule of Mr Parnell is now the rule of the priest.'[29] And, as will be seen, Ulster Protestants were to find evidence of that clerical power in the Meath election petitions of 1892. But how accurate was this view of the Parnellite crisis?

Patrick O'Farrell's researches have shown that there is indeed much truth in it: the split did realign Nationalist politics in a way that brought the Catholic hierarchy into a dominant position, and, just as importantly, it produced a conviction among the bishops that it was necessary to re-establish and enhance a Catholic world-view in Irish politics. Both these developments were highly inimical to a rapprochement with Ulster Protestants, which, if possible at all, could only have been established on a definitely secular basis. A survey of nationalist associations in Ireland compiled by the R.I.C. in December 1892 demonstrated the predominant role now taken by the Catholic clergy in Nationalist politics in northern Ireland. This survey was of a more sophisticated nature than previous efforts: it sought not just to show the number of branches and membership of each association, but to make a distinction between those who were merely nominal members and those in 'good standing' or active membership. Moreover, in contrast to previous attempts to estimate the strength of nationalist movements, much greater confidence was expressed as to the accuracy of the statistics involved, especially those for Ulster.[30]

A memorandum attached to the statistics for the R.I.C. Northern Division, which consisted of Ulster plus Co. Louth, provides a revealing insight into the strength of the clergy in the north. Of 153 branches of the anti-Parnellite Irish National Federation in this division, it was noted that no less than 129 were controlled by the clergy. The Parnellite National League was dismissed as having no influence, their supporters having been won over to the National Federation 'by the R.C. clergy who completely control the Nationalist electorate in Ulster'. The relative strength of the two movements is demonstrated in Table 6. The most obvious feature of these statistics is, of course, the demise of the Parnellite faction, reduced to ten branches from 287 in 1886, and to less than 1,000 members, only two-

Table 6.   Estimated membership of the Irish National League and Irish National Federation in Ulster in 1892[31]

	National League			National Federation		
	branches	members	approx. number in 'good' standing	branches	members	approx. number in 'good' standing
Antrim	—	—	—	5	605	80
Armagh	—	—	—	13	1,907	1,907
Belfast	1	350	350	1	2,000	2,000
Cavan	1	180	100	39	6,759	6,000
Donegal	1	6	—	28	4,443	2,392
Down	2	126	20	17	1,721	1,327
Fermanagh	1	45	20	25	4,006	2,273
Londonderry	—	—	—	6	1,623	748
Monaghan	1	50	—	20	3,672	1,996
Tyrone	3	176	176	28	4,501	3,163
Totals	10	933	666	182	31,237	21,886

thirds of whom were active. Interestingly, though, the Irish National Federation, while outnumbering the National League by more than 30 to 1, had a similar proportion of active to nominal members.

Also included in the information supplied from Ulster were figures showing the growth of the Ancient Order of Hibernians: although divided into two factions, this organisation had a total of 118 branches and a membership of 5,877 across the province, and was most numerous in areas where both Catholics and Protestants were highly represented — Armagh, Fermanagh, Tyrone, Londonderry and Belfast. The only non-sectarian development was the emergence of trade and labour societies, with a membership of 32,823, though it was reckoned that three-quarters of these were Unionists. Moreover, the Divisional Commissioner for northern Ireland added: 'All the same ... the old lines of severance on political questions — especially that of Home Rule — remain clearly marked.' Evidence for this assertion was easily obtained, and had indeed already been dramatically demonstrated earlier in the year at the great convention of Unionists in Belfast. Deliberately timed just before the general election of 1892, it was to demonstrate to the world, in a more striking way than heretofore, the strength of Ulster Protestant opposition to Irish autonomy. The effectiveness of this gathering, as a great propaganda act, lay in its almost faultless organisation: 12,000 delegates from all over the province assembled under the presidency of the Duke of Abercorn in a specially erected pavilion, and in sober, well-constructed speeches affirmed their determination not to accept Home Rule and to follow a policy of passive non-cooperation with a Dublin parliament if such was established.[32]

Impressive as the convention was, it produced no change in opinion on the part of either Liberals or Nationalists. Justin McCarthy, leader of the anti-Parnellites, dismissed the convention as a gathering mainly of those who feared the downfall of the Protestant ascendancy; and while admitting that Ulster did contain 'a considerable minority sincerely against Home Rule', he declared that the province had a majority of M.P.s and population in favour of autonomy. Nor did he believe that 'respectable and reasonable' ratepayers would stage a rebellion to oblige the Duke of Abercorn. Other reactions from

Home Rule sources were equally dismissive. The *Freeman's Journal* described the convention as a skilfully manipulated political demonstration organised for a purely party purpose. Lord Rosebery took the view that Ulster's interests were ultimately guaranteed by the House of Commons, and that the convention was a device to save the Conservative government. John Morley declared that the real lesson of the demonstration was that Ulster Unionists were strong enough to take care of themselves in a Home Rule parliament, and that no speaker at the convention had argued that Irishmen could not live in peace together. Sir William Harcourt, having no strong liking for either northern or southern Irishmen, dismissed threats of resistance by Colonel Saunderson in a sarcastic letter which pre-dated the convention: 'I assure you that I shall watch your strategy with interest, and try to alarm myself as much as I can manage.'

The most important reaction, however, was that of Gladstone, and his reply was delivered the day after the convention in a major speech at Clapham, London. He pointed to the unreasonableness of the Ulster Unionist claim to overrule the wishes of the majority of Irishmen, and to Irish history for proof that Catholics would not persecute Protestants. Indeed, with the proceedings of a recent parliamentary investigation into the local government of Belfast in mind, Gladstone highlighted the continued discrimination against Catholics in public offices there. Furthermore, he referred to the Nationalist rejection of the papal rescript of 1888 and the fact that Parnellites represented one-third of the Irish electorate as evidence that they were not dominated by the clergy. Gladstone dismissed threats of resistance to Home Rule made at the convention by noting that despite the incitement to rebellion recently made by Lord Salisbury and A. J. Balfour, the sobriety of the speeches was creditable. In particular:

> They have spoken about not electing members to the Home Rule parliament, using every legitimate method of resisting, *not every method of resistance* [my italics], and repudiating this parliament.... I think that the limitation which they have put upon their own prophecies ... of what is to come, does them no inconsiderable credit.[33]

On the question of a separate assembly for 'the small proportion of Ulster in which the Protestants are so concentrated', he again congratulated Colonel Saunderson and Dr R. R. Kane for having rejected such an idea, and was confident that there was 'no reasonable and... fairly presentable proposition' for the protection of minorities to which Home Rulers would not agree. As to the future of Protestants in a Home Rule Ireland, Gladstone returned yet again to the precedent of Grattan's Parliament and recommended Ulster Protestants to consult 'the deeds of their ancestors' which would tell them that 'Irish freedom' would 'unite Protestants and Catholics into one indissoluble mass' and restore social peace and stability to Ireland. Thus, if a major objective of the Ulster convention was to force a reconsideration of his Irish policy on Gladstone by a means of a massive demonstration, it was a signal failure.

Nevertheless, Unionists could take some heart from the general election which followed shortly afterwards, for although the Liberals would win, the Nationalist parliamentary majority in Ulster would be lost. This reversal of Nationalist fortunes has recently been attributed to the work of Unionist electoral agents. However, there were other factors. For example, as police reports reveal, there was the failure of Nationalist agents to take care properly of constituency registration work, especially in the important marginal constituency of South Tyrone, which Nationalists failed to regain, and North Fermanagh, which Unionists won.[34] The highly important West Belfast seat was also lost in 1892, and this was attributed by Belfast Nationalists to the fact that Protestant Home Rulers who had voted for Home Rule in 1886 failed to do so in 1892. However, a more plausible account of the Unionist victory is provided by Mary Arnold-Forster, wife of the successful candidate, H. O. Arnold-Forster. She credited his success to the efforts of earnest working-class Protestants in the period 1886-92:

> working men... who quietly took the matter into their own hands, and, at any cost to themselves, moved into each house that fell vacant in our debatable land, and at last by their determination converted the minority of 1886 into the solid Unionist majority of 1892.

Probably the most serious loss to Nationalists in the north, though, was that of Londonderry City. It is true that their hold on the seat was tenuous, having been secured in 1886 only after an election petition unseated the sitting Unionist M.P., but in view of its place in Protestant ideology it was of great importance, and A. J. Balfour was determined that it should be retaken for the Unionist cause. To this end he persuaded John Ross, who was committed to stand elsewhere, that it was of vital importance that he contest the Londonderry seat. Ross's chances were undoubtedly enhanced by the fact that he was a local man and his family were popular in the city. The result gave the Unionists victory by a small but clear majority, with Ross polling 1,986 votes and Justin McCarthy 1,960.[35] With these gains Unionists succeeded in decisively eliminating the Nationalist parliamentary majority in the province: they now had 18 seats and the latter 15.

Interestingly, it has been pointed out that of the votes cast in the area that was eventually to be encompassed in Northern Ireland, the combined vote of Nationalists and Liberals, at 41,300, was not quite 4,000 votes less than the Unionist figure for the same area, which was 45,100.[36] Nevertheless, the Ulster Unionist position was greatly strengthened by the reversal of the Nationalist majority. Moreover, the election was to provide evidence — in the form of Bishop Nulty's pastoral letter to the electors of Meath not to vote for the Parnellite candidates — to support the Ulster Protestant view of Nationalists as being priest-dominated. As a result of this letter, the anti-Parnellite victors in Meath, Michael Davitt and Patrick Fulham, were unseated on petition.

Colonel Saunderson cited the Meath petitions especially to emphasise the strength of the Ulster Unionist case, and the political activities of the priests generally to account for the fact that John Redmond's party was able to elect only nine M.P.s. William Redmond in reply pointed out that 70,000 votes had been cast against the influence of the priests. Nevertheless, the effectiveness of the clerical intervention at the general election was unmistakable, and Ulster Unionists were anxious to exploit its less acceptable aspects.[37]

10

Liberals, Nationalists and the Struggle for Home Rule, 1892-3

THE NEW ADMINISTRATION AND THE HOME RULE SCHEME

Conditions in 1892 were unfavourable for the preparation of Gladstone's second Home Rule bill. Following the Parnell scandal, it was only his personal influence that kept Home Rule at the forefront of Liberal Party policy. Moreover, the Liberal Party majority at the 1892 election, which Gladstone had expected to be substantial, was low: 273 Liberals, 81 Nationalists and 1 Labour member provided a majority of 40 over 269 Conservatives and 46 Liberal Unionists. His own personal majority fell from the 4,000 of 1886 to 690. Gladstone, mortified, blamed this situation on the Parnell scandal and the adverse effect of the Nationalist Party split on the English people, who 'cannot comprehend how a quarrel utterly unintelligible...should be allowed to divide the host in the face of the enemy; and their unity and zeal have been deadened in proportion'.[1]

Nevertheless, he proceeded to construct his Home Rule scheme. Now that the Irish had thrown over Parnell in their support for the Liberal leader, there was, as Morley pointed out, little else he could do. As to its prospects of success, Gladstone informed Lady Aberdeen: 'We can sum up the whole position in one word, "Oremus" (let us pray).' A significant change had occurred, however, since 1886. John Morley was now taking a far more prominent role in prosecuting the Home Rule cause and, being a vain man, excluded both Lord Aberdeen and Sir Robert Hamilton from his Irish administration on the grounds that his leading role would be jeopardised by their presence: 'He . . . wished to carve out his own way and felt that any of "the old gang" in his immediate entourage would be an impediment, both to himself and the cause.' But surprisingly, for one so committed to Home Rule, Morley believed the Irish had great character defects: he thought the 'despotic' rule of the landlords had made the peasantry prone to laziness and untruthfulness. Sir Herbert Jekyll, Lord Houghton's secretary, held similar views. He informed Sir Algernon West: 'There would seem to be some racial instinct in the pure Celt too strong to be overcome, otherwise it is impossible to account for the deliberate squalor in which he elects to live.' As we have seen, a not dissimilar opinion was expressed by James Bryce, comparing the merits of Catholics and Protestants in Ulster in 1886, while in 1907 he was to consider the Irish unfit for Home Rule. In addition to critical attitudes towards the Irish, moreover, the cabinet was unenthusiastic about Home Rule. Morley described it thus:

> The temperature of feeling for the Irish task was not by any means uniform or equable. Some took that task prosaically as coming in the day's work and they contributed with sober loyalty to the common cause. Others proved disappointing to themselves and their colleagues alike.

The preparation of the Home Rule bill was entrusted to a committee of the cabinet, including Gladstone, Morley, Bryce, Campbell-Bannerman, Lord Herschell and Lord Spencer. Formed on 21 November 1892, it set to work immediately, assisted, initially at least, by a more agreeable attitude on Gladstone's part as to what Home Rule should consist of. In contrast to 1886, when he had practically constructed the scheme himself, he was now 'eager to do justice to all the points and arguments of other people. . . . He went into counsel for the sake of counsel, and not to cajole, or bully, or insist on his own way because it was his own way.'[2]

Essential to the effective construction of a Home Rule bill, of course, was consultation with Nationalists. Indeed, as regards the Parnellites, this was necessary even before the general election of 1892 to ensure that despite their internal divisions, all the Nationalists would join with Gladstone in presenting a united front on the essentials of a satisfactory scheme. To this end John Redmond and J. L. Carew met with William Mather and Sir Charles Hall, Q.C., on 30 March 1892 in the Devonshire Club. This meeting and subsequent correspondence between Redmond and Mather produced agreement on Redmond's ideas for a future Home Rule bill. He suggested a bill similar to that of 1886, conferring an Irish legislature which would have complete control over internal Irish affairs, with the maintenance of imperial 'prerogatives', but with two 'houses' instead of 'orders'. He was indifferent as to whether the Irish were represented in the imperial parliament or not, though if the latter retained control of the police and judges, he wanted full Irish representation until such control was relinquished. Redmond theoretically accepted the idea of a tribunal or court to oversee the Irish parliament, but in practice saw no need for it and thought the Irish legislature should not be subject to a judicial tribunal in the management of any Irish business. As to religious safeguards, Redmond thought the bill of 1886 perfectly adequate and expected the royal veto to be regarded as effectively extinct, as in Great Britain. Finally, he thought the land question incapable of a final settlement and that it should be left to the Irish parliament. Following Gladstone's return to office, John Morley met with Redmond and assured him that the new Home Rule scheme would be one Parnellites could freely accept despite the fact that some in the cabinet preferred a 'county council' type of administration for Ireland.[3]

The initial process of consultation with the anti-Parnellites was naturally more even-flowing, and — as the correspondence of both Michael Davitt and Justin McCarthy reveals — they were confident of obtaining a satisfactory scheme, given Gladstone's repeated admissions of the need for improving on the 1886 bill. Preliminary meetings between Gladstone and leading anti-Parnellites to discuss the general shape of a future Home Rule bill took place on 7 March and 21 June 1892 and were broadly satisfactory to the Nationalists: Gladstone reiterated his commitment to producing a better financial scheme than that proposed in the bill of 1886 and declared his intention to instigate an inquiry by royal commission into the financial question. He also appeared to accept their objections to any kind of 'tribunal' or external body empowered to judge the legitimacy of any act passed by the Irish parliament. Shortly

before he took office on 15 August 1892 Gladstone, in company
with John Morley, had another meeting with John Dillon,
Justin McCarthy and Thomas Sexton. According to McCarthy,
Nationalists were highly satisfied with its outcome. Even the fact
that the Liberal majority of forty depended upon Nationalist
support was not a cause of consternation. It was accepted that,
given so small a majority, Home Rule would be rejected by the
House of Lords in the next session of parliament. Nevertheless, it
would be submitted a second time, rejected again, and then
'Gladstone would ask the Queen's permission to create new
peers, and they would give in'.[4] The only cause for worry,
apparently, was whether or not Gladstone would live to see this
process through to a successful conclusion.

John Dillon's record of this meeting, however, differed considerably from McCarthy's. He noted that Gladstone was des-
pondent at the prospect of the strenuous Unionist opposition
that would be provoked by the small parliamentary majority for
Home Rule: 'He looked very much worse than when I last saw
him.' But most significantly, in contrast to McCarthy's explicit
projection of the course to be followed should the House of Lords
reject the Home Rule bill, Dillon recorded that 'during the
whole conversation' the issue was not debated: 'The matter was
not raised.' Judged against Dillon's account of this meeting, the
expectations held by McCarthy appear to have consisted largely
of wishful thinking. When the Lords did reject his bill,
Gladstone apparently did not consider the idea of creating
Liberal peers — at least as a first step — but preferred an appeal
to the country. Nevertheless, in the short term, further discussions between anti-Parnellites and Liberals took place, conducted chiefly by Dillon, Sexton and Morley. These were so successful in the period up to mid-December 1892 that both sides
were confident of a trouble-free settlement of the Home Rule
question. McCarthy wrote: 'Nothing could be more satisfactory
than the way things have gone, and I think we shall be in perfect
understanding.' Morley, for his part, conveyed a similar
message to Gladstone. In a memorandum referring to the
meetings the latter announced that on the 25 November Sir
Henry Jenkyns was given material for drawing up a bill, and
Morley, having had several meetings with Nationalists, hoped
'by the middle of next week to bring his conferences in Ireland to

a close'. Consequently Gladstone hoped to have the bill discussed in cabinet before Christmas and to deal with it in January
1893: 'The impression as to the temper of the Irish members is
favourable, but there are some points of importance raised by
them or inherent in the case which only the cabinet can determine.'[5]

That the early discussions with nationalists on the general
nature of an acceptable scheme went so well must have been
due, to a considerable extent, to Edward Blake. Of Irish
ancestry, Blake, a respected Canadian lawyer and politician,
had agreed to come over to Ireland to play a part in the prosecution of the Home Rule cause. But even before Blake left for
Ireland, James Bryce wrote asking about the working of local
legislatures in Canada, especially the working of single- and
dual-chamber assemblies. Blake replied stating that the
experience of Canada — especially that of his native province
of Ontario — was so 'moderate', peaceful, and unlike Irish
experience over the past fifty years that it could not provide a
'safe guide' for Ireland. In effect, he argued that the events of
1886 determined generally what course should be taken. For
instance, since Parnell had endorsed a two-chamber type of
legislature in 1886, it would 'certainly be used against you' if it
were rejected now. But as to the upper chamber in the Home
Rule legislature, Blake suggested that it should be of a smaller
number than in 1886, so as to dissuade it from assuming the
position of a 'co-ordinate power'. Blake also placed the utmost
importance on the distinction being made between 'permanent'
and 'transitory' provisions in a future Home Rule bill: 'Ireland
could not accept to work under defective stipulations unless they
were to be clearly seen to be liable of elimination.' The composition and powers of the upper chamber should be changeable
— a departure from the bill of 1886, which allowed for no such
alteration. Bryce replied agreeing with virtually every word of
Blake's recommendations,[6] and the general influence of his ideas
is clearly perceivable in the memorandum on foreign and
colonial legislatures drawn up by Bryce at Gladstone's request.

Bryce's memorandum began by surveying the several types of
such legislatures, but cautioned against using any one as a model
for Ireland, since their 'political conditions differed too widely
from those of Ireland to make conclusions drawn from them

applicable to her'. The question was: was Ireland to have a single- or dual-chamber assembly? In answering this question Bryce quoted directly from Sir Charles Gavan Duffy's 'A Fair Constitution for Ireland' to the effect that the only 'true' way of allaying minority apprehensions and those of the British without at the same time alienating nationalists was not, as in 1886, to rely on restrictions imposed on the actions of a Home Rule parliament, but to provide, in framing the scheme, ample safeguards against 'haste' and full protection for minorities. To this end Bryce suggested a two-chamber assembly with special minority representation in the upper house — as Duffy had recommended in 1887. The Irish knew that Parnell had accepted Duffy's scheme, and it had thus been accepted provisionally by them. In recommending a two-chamber assembly Bryce repeated Blake's view that since a two-tier system had been accepted in 1886, it could not easily be rejected now without both hostile English criticism and a lack of corresponding satisfaction in Ireland. Comparing the 'two orders' system with the 'two houses' type, Bryce favoured the latter: two orders emphasised in too sharp a way the check of the wealthier classes and 'loses the benefit of fresh and healthy discussion'. Regarded as a 'check', the bicameral system would probably be more efficient 'and would certainly seem so'.

As to the character of the upper chamber, Bryce made some suggestions, based on an examination of foreign and colonial systems. First, it should be a small assembly, given the paucity of suitable men in Ireland to stock it. The numbers in the 1886 scheme were too large: 100 for the larger house and 30-40 for the smaller body was now suggested instead of 204 and 103 — a conclusion supported by the 'experience of foreign bodies and of the British colonies'. Secondly, as in 1886, the majority of the upper house should be elected, otherwise it would lose touch with the people, have little weight with them, and be out of touch with the lower house. Thirdly, the franchise of such a chamber should not be too high, otherwise the numbers qualified to enter it would be too small: 'Ireland is so poor a country that a franchise not high for England would be very high there.' Bryce doubted whether a property qualification would improve the composition of the upper house, and only in the legislature of Victoria did such a system prevail.[7] Fourthly, a small number of places in the upper house should be left to be filled by Irish peers 'by election or otherwise'. The peers should also be eligible for election to the lower house, so that the more 'public-spirited' among them could identify with the public life of the country. Fifthly, foreign examples suggested a larger term of office for the upper house. It was, moreover, important that effective means for the lower house to oppose the dictates of the upper should exist, either by a proportional majority, or by a joint majority of both houses (as in 1886), or for the vote of the lower house to prevail after a certain period when a disputed bill had been submitted two or three times to the upper house.

This memorandum was, as will be seen, the basis on which the second Home Rule bill was constructed. Also, two days after it was printed, it was agreed in cabinet that the constitution of any Irish assembly succeeding the first 'may be altered by Irish act', thus following the advice urged strongly by Blake. However, from the middle of December 1892 until the Home Rule bill was introduced in the Commons on 13 February 1893 discussions between the government and anti-Parnellites were strained. On 19 December Justin McCarthy wrote to Mrs Campbell Praed of divisions in the cabinet, of ministers reluctant to follow Gladstone, and of the inability of the Nationalists to go any further 'in the way of compromise'. Yet on 22 December he received a telegram from the deputation negotiating with Morley in Dublin, stating that all was satisfactory. One point of discussion at this time was the question of a royal veto and how it should be used,[8] but of much more importance was the question of Home Rule finance. Gladstone's repeated admissions in the period 1886-92 that Ireland had suffered financially under the Act of Union fuelled Nationalist hopes that the fiscal clauses of the new bill would be based on an extensive examination of the taxable capacity of Great Britain and Ireland, and that, as such, they would be much more favourable to Ireland than those proposed in 1886. This expectation, however, was not to be fulfilled.

LIBERALS, NATIONALISTS AND HOME RULE FINANCE

Gladstone's views on Home Rule finance in late 1892 were expressed in a cabinet memorandum of 24 November, which illustrated the extent to which his thinking was still influenced by the scheme of 1886. For example, he apparently held to the principle adopted then that Ireland's imperial contribution should be a fixed quota of imperial expenses, though he now proposed a contribution of one-twentieth rather than the one-fifteenth proposed in 1886. Again, as in 1886, the imperial contribution, in conjunction with £950,000 for the constabulary, would be a first claim on Irish revenues, while customs and excise would again remain under imperial control. Moreover, a court of exchequer was to be established, as in the bill of 1886, whose decrees would be supported by civil and, if need be, military force. The financial provisions, though, could be altered after twenty years by the imperial parliament in compliance with an address from the Irish legislature. The Irish body would also have control of Irish post and telegraphs in respect of revenue and charges, but would be forbidden from raising postal rates.[9]

Some of these recommendations, especially those regarding the allocation of constabulary expenses and the control to be exercised by the imperial exchequer over Irish finances, were, with minor changes, to be included in the financial clauses of the bill. However, Gladstone's views on how Ireland's imperial contribution should be determined were to undergo fundamental changes as a result of a memorandum on Irish finance which was drawn up by Lord Welby, Edward Hamilton and Alfred Milner on 14 December 1892 and which made an important contribution to cabinet discussions on the subject.

First, they uncovered sources of revenue overlooked in the haste with which the Home Rule bill of 1886 was constructed. These derived from small branches of hereditary revenues, payments made to the Bank of England, profits on silver coinage, patents, etc., and, a large sum realised by the Commissioners of Woods from 'the sale of quit-rents forming part of the crown revenues in Ireland'; this sum was invested in England, and the resulting interest, amounting to £14,000 or £15,000 per year, was credited to crown estates in England rather than Ireland. Allowing for reparation in respect of past Irish losses, the authors estimated that a total of £683,000 was due to Ireland from both sources of revenue. Secondly, they made a strong argument against using the financial scheme of the bill of 1886 as a model for a future bill. In 1886 it was intended that Ireland would be credited with taxes on spirits consumed in Great Britain though paid in Ireland. That sum now amounted to £1,800,000 and — as in 1886 — if Ireland was credited with it, her contribution to imperial charges would appear larger than it was. But more importantly, it was now recognised that this sum could actually disappear, because the law allowed for spirits to be moved from warehouse to warehouse within the United Kingdom with duty not being paid until they were actually sold. Enormous problems for both British and Irish exchequers would occur were this to happen. Again, if the financial scheme of 1886 was adopted, difficulties would arise if customs duty had to be increased, or if stamp and income taxes under Irish control were levied at a different rate from that of Great Britain. Thirdly, they made proposals for a new financial scheme. Despite Gladstone's repeated assurances since 1886 that future fiscal provisions would take better account of Ireland's taxable capacity than was the case in 1886, the compilers confessed that their attempts to assess the taxable capacity of both countries involved such complicated calculations that they were unable to complete that part of their task. However, they declared that a 'more recent and complete examination of Irish finance' led to the conclusion that it constituted not more than one-twentieth of United Kingdom resources, and that the Irish proportion of imperial expenditure could be calculated on the basis. But it was also important that Ireland's imperial contribution under Home Rule did not exceed the present contribution, so that the Irish could not plead that they paid more under Home Rule than under the existing system — something that could not be guaranteed if the Irish contribution was to be a proportion of an imperial expenditure, which, in a period of imperial expansion, was likely to rise steadily. Alternatively, it was proposed that the imperial government retain the collection and management of Irish revenue equivalent to the sum of Ireland's existing imperial contribution, leaving the rest for local expenditure. Two plans were proposed to effect this, both of which envisaged imperial retention of Irish customs duties, and this proposal was eventually accepted by Gladstone and the cabinet on 21 January 1893.[10]

Two factors in particular commended it. First, John Morley

informed Gladstone of his belief that the retention of Irish customs duties was preferred by the Irish as 'payment in full of their liabilities'. Secondly, and more important, was the discovery that by 'a curious coincidence' the total of Irish civil expenses and charges connected with the collection of inland revenue and post office revenue amounted, for 1892-3, to £5,660,000 — exactly equivalent to Irish combined revenues from excise duties on beer and spirits paid by the consuming classes in Ireland, stamp duties, income tax, excise licences and the postal service, in addition to miscellaneous revenues and revenue from crown lands. Accordingly the account of Ireland when credited with this sum would have exactly balanced. But it was necessary for Ireland to have a working balance, and to this end she would be rebated £500,000 — one-third the cost of maintaining the R.I.C.; this was justified on the grounds that the R.I.C. was a quasi-imperial force and that it would be wrong to expect Ireland to pay the full cost. Moreover, the R.I.C. would gradually be replaced by local Irish forces, and the charge would thus be temporary. Apart from this rebate, Ireland would contribute to imperial charges after Home Rule what she now contributed: 'This is the underlying principle of the financial scheme of the bill and is the simplest that can be devised.'[11] But how did Nationalists react to the cabinet's deliberations on Home Rule finance?

It seems that they were informed by Morley of cabinet thinking on this subject some time in late December 1892, when Gladstone's favoured proposal that Ireland contribute one-twentieth of imperial expenditure was still under consideration and before the scheme outlined above was finally settled on. Their reaction was one of dismay, though they realised that any public expression of disagreement would be 'distinctly injurious'. Instead John Dillon urged on Morley that the cabinet should reach no final decision until they had conferred with him again, when a memorandum on Home Rule finance, prepared by Thomas Sexton, would be submitted for the cabinet's consideration.[12] Delivered by Justin McCarthy to Morley on 13 January 1893, Sexton's memorandum presented an argument greatly at odds with cabinet thinking on the subject.

Nationalists complained of the departure from the policy of

1886 which credited Ireland with all taxes collected there, and argued that, had time allowed in 1886, they would have pressed Gladstone to reduce his nominal estimate of Ireland's imperial contribution from one-fifteenth to one-twentieth. Taking into account the £1,400,000 derived from British taxes on spirits that were collected in Ireland, this amendment would have meant an effective reduction in contributions from one-twenty-sixth to one-forty-seventh, and should again be considered. However, they also accepted the cabinet's view, outlined above, of the problems that could arise through the transfer of spirits before duties on them were paid, and also that any law designed to credit the Irish exchequer with duties on spirits consumed in Britain would be fiercely resisted. As an alternative, they proposed that Ireland's imperial contribution be fixed 'at a stated proportion of her annual income'. To fix Ireland's contribution as a quota of imperial expenses was, they maintained, unfair, because the empire was wealthy, was expanding, and her expenses were likely to increase, whereas Ireland was a poor country, with her revenue mainly derived from consumer goods; given that her population was diminishing, it was reasonable to expect that her revenue would diminish also. However, a quota of Irish revenue would be free from this danger:

> Such a quota would be measured by the only genuine test — how much could Ireland spare? And this could be determined by the answers to two simple questions: what balance of Irish revenues was left after local charges were met, and what part of this balance does Ireland need to establish and maintain her credit . . . without laying new burdens on the people?

Taking into account both local charges and an allowance made for various other expenses incurred by the imperial parliament, Sexton estimated that balance to be £1,679,000. But what amount would the Irish government need for its own purposes? The memorandum argued as follows:

> It must be borne in mind that the Irish government, unless their credit is established by the possession of a substantial surplus, cannot hope to take up and continue the loan services

of the Board of Public Works — amounting last year to £348,000 — advanced to town councils and commissioners, grand juries, Poor Law Guardians, harbour and drainage boards, and other public bodies for necessary public purposes, as well as to landlords, tenants, and occupying purchasers for main and through drainage, planting for shelter, farm buildings, and dwellings for agricultural labourers — a class of services certain to make more extensive demands as the system of land purchase is developed.

To meet these commitments the Irish government would need £1,250,000 at the outset. Gladstone's argument that a surplus should be obtained by retrenchment in public expenditure did not hold up. This could only be a work of small beginnings, with a lapse of years before any substantial surplus was acquired, while an Irish government would need extensive sums to begin its work. For example, it would be impossible for the Irish government substantially to cut down the civil service, since these were the only class of people qualified and trained to carry on the Irish administration; the Home Rule government would have no such experience. Moreover, Ireland could not cut down charges returned by the imperial parliament, and there was again the question of the police. Sexton argued that since they were imperial forces they should be financed by the imperial exchequer while they existed, especially since the cost of establishing an Irish local force to replace them was likely to be £800,000. The report ended by declaring that if the Irish claims were reasonably met on the terms set out, they would not press the case for a 'special abatement' or restitution for Ireland in respect of her financial exploitation since the Union.[13]

Gladstone's reaction to this communication — with its intention, effectively, to reduce Ireland's imperial contribution to a sum smaller than the surplus he would propose for an Irish budget — was explosive. Under great pressure of work and suffering from deteriorating eyesight and hearing, he was in no mood to question dearly held principles of public economy, even in regard to Home Rule. He declared that if the Irish did not like his scheme, they must 'lump' it. The question for them was whether they would accept 'Home Rule with my finance or no Home Rule'. His view of the Nationalist argument on finance, throughout this period, was that it consisted of 'large pecuniary claims'.[14]

The dispute between Gladstone and Nationalists on Home Rule finance reflected their widely differing perceptions of the responsibilities of an Irish government. Nationalists expected that it should at least be able to maintain the existing levels of public expenditure — something for which the proposed small budget surplus would be wholly inadequate. Gladstone — as he put it to a deputation from the Belfast Chamber of Commerce — thought that the Irish should be concerned primarily with removing what he believed to be a great evil — fiscal extravagance. Moreover, he would not have been disposed to take a conciliatory attitude towards Nationalist claims, given that his request for nationalists to sit on the government side of the house — something Gladstone considered would be of immense importance for purposes of consultation during the debates on the bill — was refused by Justin McCarthy, who argued that Irish opinion would not tolerate their being pledged to any English party. However, Gladstone's financial scheme for Home Rule also came under attack from Sir William Harcourt, the Chancellor of the Exchequer. Harcourt had no enthusiasm for Home Rule and was excluded from the cabinet committee preparing the bill, but his memorandum on Home Rule finance on 16 January was one of the best contributions on the subject. This document, which has been cited already in assessing the scheme of 1886, concentrated on the problems that would be created for the Irish and British exchequers were any change in the levy of duty on goods such as spirits, porter and tobacco to occur. If the duty was lowered, it would diminish the fund out of which Ireland was to pay the imperial contribution; if raised, it would provide Ireland with a great surplus that would not have been budgeted for by the Irish Chancellor. Harcourt concluded: 'The result of all this will be that the financial policy of Great Britain, which represents twenty-five parts out of twenty-six, will practically, if a conflict is to be avoided, have to be regulated by considerations belonging to the twenty-sixth part.'[15]

Harcourt would have preferred the Irish to have 'no finance', merely a 'fixed sum' from imperial funds to cover civil expenses and provide a 'respectable balance'; but this was rejected on the grounds that if it was adequate for all Irish wants, 'they may reflect that it is not necessary to pay taxes at all. . . . What it proves is that the best plan which is possible is impossible — an observation which applies to a good deal else in the same connection.'[16] The financial scheme of the bill was the cause of much discord between Morley and Harcourt; nor, indeed, were discussions with the Nationalists concluded when the Home Rule bill was introduced on 13 February 1893.

THE HOME RULE BILL AND THE STRUGGLE IN PARLIAMENT

The second Home Rule bill began with a preamble clearly designed to allay Unionist fears: it declared that the bill did not impair or restrict 'the supreme authority of parliament'. Subsequently clauses 1 and 2 set out the basic structure of the legislature, consisting of the crown and two houses — a legislative council and assembly. Clauses 3 and 4 set out the exceptions and restrictions to their powers and followed generally the bill of 1886, apart from inland trade and navigation, which now came under Irish jurisdiction. As in 1886, executive authority would rest in the Lord Lieutenant, representing the Queen; and, as in 1886, it was left to the discretion of the crown to decide what his powers should be, while these were again to be vested in the Lord Lieutenant alone and not the Lord Lieutenant in Council. Unlike 1886, though, when an indefinite period of office was proposed for the Lord Lieutenant, it would now be for a period of six years.[17]

The clauses defining the membership of the Irish legislature exhibited the influence of Duffy's and Blake's thinking, though there was to be no special minority representation. The proposed upper house, or legislative council, would consist of 48 members, elected by owners and occupiers of land or tenements of a rateable value of £20 or over. They would be elected for eight years, with one-half of their number retiring every fourth year, and their seats filled by a new election. This was a significant change from the bill of 1886, which proposed a first order of 75 elected and 28 peerage members. The lower house, or legislative assembly, would consist of 103 members, instead of the 204 proposed in 1886, to be elected under the existing franchise for a five-year term. Moreover, after six years the Irish legislature would have the power of altering the qualifications of electors, constituencies, and the distribution of members within them, provided that in such distribution due regard was had to their populations.[18]

Settlement of disagreements between the two houses would be by a joint majority vote if a bill was introduced after a dissolution, or lapse of two years, as opposed to three in 1886. Irish representation at Westminster would consist of eighty members on an 'in-out' basis, voting only on imperial matters or in debates discussing whether particular bills should be extended to Ireland. As to the powers reserved to the imperial parliament, whereas in 1886 these consisted of the power to erect forts and dockyards, this power was now applied to land laws, which would remain under imperial control for three years. As to finance, particularly Ireland's imperial contribution, the scheme outlined above was adopted. Additionally, customs and excise duties were to be regulated and collected by the imperial authority, which was also to fix postal rates, but all other taxes were to be imposed by the Irish legislature. Moreover, in an attempt to prevent the difficulties for the British and Irish budgets that could arise from the increase or decrease in excise duty outlined by Harcourt, it was proposed in clause 10 that if excise duty was increased above the rate in force on 1 March 1893, the net proceeds in excess of the above rate in Ireland would be paid into the imperial exchequer. On the other hand, were the excise duty lowered, 'a sum equal to the deficiency' would be paid from the imperial exchequer to the Irish exchequer. However, it was also proposed that the financial scheme could be revised after a period of fifteen years. Finally, the interests of judges and civil servants would be secured as in 1886; and while existing police forces would be under imperial control as long as they existed, a locally controlled police would gradually be established to replace them.[19]

Nationalist reaction to the scheme was mixed. The anti-Parnellites decided not to criticise the Home Rule bill too sharply, as it was a better bill than that of 1886, though the fiscal clauses would need amendment. They also issued an address 'to the friends of Ireland abroad', declaring their acceptance 'without hesitation' of the constitution proposed in the bill; its enactment would be 'a final and triumphant close of the long, bloody and sorrowful Irish struggle'. A rather more critical attitude was taken by Parnellites. John Redmond, while praising the two-chamber legislature, criticised the royal veto and argued that as long as the police and land were to remain under Westminster's control the Irish should have full representation in the imperial parliament. The reaction in the press and country generally was 'lukewarm in both commendation and recommendation'. For nearly everyone except Mr Gladstone 'the subject was threadbare'. However, the campaign of opposition in parliament was to be ferocious. It was observed that the general campaign was threefold, with the Conservatives concentrating on the unfairness of the bill's provision in regard to England and the English taxpayer, Liberal Unionists on the danger to the empire and prestige of the United Kingdom, while Ulster Unionists emphasised the danger to Irish loyalists.[20]

The intensity of Unionist opposition can be gauged by the amount of time spent on the bill, which occupied parliament for eighty-two days, and by the number and length of speeches devoted to it by both opposition and government. Apart from the last three days of the debate, the government delivered 459 speeches on Home Rule, lasting $57\frac{1}{4}$ hours. Unionists, however, delivered 938 speeches, occupying $152\frac{3}{4}$ hours, giving a proportion of 2 to 1 in number and 3 to 1 in time. Moreover, the nature of their opposition was simply to obstruct the passage of the bill by any possible means. The bill was debated clause by clause, and on each of these, destructive, contradictory or impractical amendments were proposed. For example, on 12 May an amendment to clause 2, which defined the powers of the Irish legislature, sought to specify the powers the latter would have rather than those to be restricted. This was followed on 15 May by an amendment that proposed cutting out all restrictions from the bill. Again, in the debate on clause 3, which explained those restrictions, it was proposed on 7 June to include the power to restrict and control trade, and on 8 June to forbid the Irish legislature from giving bounties or enacting protectionist measures. Additionally, the debate on the executive power in Ireland, defined in clause 5, included an attempt to destroy the bill by making the cabinet system unworkable: an amendment on 3 July proposing to give the Lord Lieutenant sole executive power was followed two days later by another investing the imperial parliament with the power to appoint the Irish cabinet. Yet another amendment, on 23 August, proposed giving the imperial parliament the power to dissolve the Irish parliament. The Unionist approach to the bill on all clauses followed this pattern; nor was this policy without some success. Owing to obstruction and diminishing majorities, Gladstone was compelled to postpone the second reading of the bill until after Easter 1893. Indeed, Gladstone's method of conducting the debate facilitated Unionist aims. Morley has described it thus: 'His discursive treatment exposed an enormous surface. His abundance of illustration multiplied points for debate. His fertility in improvised arguments encouraged improvisation in disputants without the gift.'[21]

Unionists succeeded, moreover, in obtaining a number of amendments. On 16 May Gladstone agreed to accept an amendment attached to clause 1 making imperial supremacy much more explicit — a move which antagonised both Nationalist factions, who viewed it as an insult, without encouraging Unionists to take a more constructive approach to the bill. On 1 June Unionists succeeded with another amendment preventing the Irish parliament from constituting a centralised force to replace the R.I.C., a concession which provoked vigorous protests from Nationalists. They were annoyed as much by the manner in which these concessions were made as by the concessions themselves. Gladstone tended to make them on the spur of the moment without consultation with Nationalists, nor would he consider such consultation. When Morley pointed out the 'obvious drawback of setting delicate questions as we went along', and urged discussion, Gladstone declared this impossible owing to lack of time.[22] Moreover, he would hardly have been disposed to conciliate Nationalists in this matter given their refusal of his request to sit on the government benches to facilitate consultation.

The anti-Parnellite faction, though, was concerned not just with the Home Rule bill, but with intense personal jealousies and disputes over what was to be done about the Paris funds of the old National League. The effect of these disputes on Michael Davitt was well expressed in a letter to Dillon: 'I feel almost ashamed to go before an educated English audience while we are showing ourselves so unworthy of Home Rule.' So dismayed was Edward Blake with these internal divisions — which more than once threatened to break out into open conflict — and with the apparent disinclination of Nationalists to prepare any organised method of argument during the Home Rule debate, that he eventually resigned from the committee charged with prosecuting the anti-Parnellite approach to the Home Rule bill. In addition, the internal dissensions almost provoked Thomas Sexton, the best financial mind in the party, to resign from public life — a possibility Justin McCarthy took so seriously that he intended to have Gladstone dissuade him. In some despair McCarthy declared:

> It is all a conflict of jealousies and hates, and the national cause is forgotten. And we are fighting this difficult battle with a narrow majority and with Gladstone's declining years — and we are frankly telling our opponents that we are not able, even at such a crisis, to govern ourselves and our rancours and our tempers! I am well nigh sick of it all. . . . I am sorry from my heart for Blake . . . who gave up his home and his well-earned ease to come and fight this hopeless battle — which is to be lost by our fault! He says he feels broken-hearted — and his conviction is that the present bill is lost. I am not quite so unhopeful — but I feel terribly depressed.

Moreover, in addition to the effect of Nationalist divisions on the Home Rule cause it was soon evident that two important parts of Gladstone's bill would require amendment: the proposals for Irish representation at Westminster, and the financial provisions. The former was an object of special attack. In fact, as shown in discussing the bill of 1886, it was difficult to establish any mode of Irish representation at Westminster that did not permit Irish interference in domestic British politics. Nor did the change Gladstone made in 1893 solve the problem. Intending initially to have eighty Irish M.P.s attend at Westminster for imperial affairs, the strength of parliamentary opposition to this proposal moved him to adopt the only other proposal which had not yet been taken up — the inclusion of eighty Irish members with power of voting on all questions. Gladstone frankly admitted that the decision was based not on principle but on 'expediency', and such was the Liberal radical reaction to this decision that for a time it appeared that the government would be defeated on this clause.[23]

Amendments to the financial scheme, however, had an even greater basis in necessity. Seven weeks after the bill's introduction it became apparent that the basis on which the financial clauses were constructed was false. The 'curious coincidence' noted above — that apart from customs duties Ireland's revenue and government expenses balanced exactly, and so provided a simple method of arranging Irish finance — did not in fact exist. Erroneous statistics had been supplied by inland revenue officers, which resulted in Irish revenue from spirit duty being considerably overestimated. When corrected it would have left Ireland with a greatly reduced surplus on the Irish budget to begin the work of self-government. More specifically, the error, attributed mainly to one unnamed individual, would have reduced the proposed £500,000 surplus by £353,000. This sum, of course, could have been restored by a relatively small grant from the imperial exchequer, but Gladstone, describing the mistake as a 'heinous crime' without precedent in his huge experience, decided to recast extensively the financial clauses in committee. This course of action, moreover, was favoured by Harcourt, who, as we have seen, had opposed the original financial scheme.[24] The real difficulty would lie in getting Nationalists to accept the new scheme. As we have noted, the chief thrust of their criticism of the Home Rule bill was directed to the fiscal clauses, and shortly after the bill's introduction the views of both Nationalist factions on this aspect of the measure were aired in various political journals.

Writing in the *Nineteenth Century*, Justin McCarthy praised the bill generally, but declared that the financial proposals threatened 'at the very outset something like national bankruptcy'. His detailed criticism of this issue, though, consisted of an extensive statement compiled by Thomas Sexton and included verbatim in the article. Sexton argued against the proposal to take Irish customs revenue as an imperial contribution, as it was an expanding revenue, involving a significantly larger sum than existed in 1886. He pointed out that Nationalists had objected to the amount of their imperial contribution then, and Liberals since had admitted that it was excessive. Thereafter

Sexton concentrated on the inadequacy of the surplus allowed to Ireland, compared with the excessive expenses she would be committed to, and concluded that the surplus would easily be swallowed up: 'We demand a real surplus.' In the April issue of the same journal John Redmond argued that Ireland should not have to pay more than one-third the cost of the R.I.C., nor more than one-half of the pensions and gratuities of the civil service, which on Gladstone's own estimation was twice as large as it should have been. The proposal to take control of Ireland's customs duties as an imperial contribution 'could not be accepted'. Like Sexton, Redmond complained that the imperial contribution was larger than in 1886, and that the £500,000 surplus could easily be swallowed up by the Irish government's expenses. But perhaps most importantly, Redmond argued that in view of the complexity of the financial question and the impossibility of it being adequately dealt with by a committee of the House of Commons, a 'small representative commission to ... inquire into and report on the subject' should be established before the financial clauses reached the committee stage. At any rate, he concluded, no one now talked of 'finality' in regard to Home Rule, though a suitably amended bill could provide the basis of a settlement. A virtually identical argument was made in the same month by Redmond's fellow-Parnellite, J. J. Clancy, in the *Fortnightly Review*.[25] To conciliate Nationalist opinion Morley promised conferences with treasury officials with a view to satisfactory amendments being made. But with the decision to recast the financial clauses, the plans changed, and the cabinet, faced with strenuous Unionist obstruction, sought for ways to mitigate it.

One such proposal was for the imperial parliament to retain control not just of customs and excise, but of Irish income tax as well. Personally Morley approved of this plan but anticipated Nationalist objections. Indeed, both Nationalist factions strenuously opposed the adoption of such a plan. Consequently Morley, fearing the advantage that 'the turbulent element in Irish society' would reap from a quarrel between Liberals and Nationalists 'on a critical part of the bill', proposed that the safest course to take would be to retain the original financial plan, with the imperial parliament paying a larger proportion of the upkeep of the police, or to adopt 'the [old?] quota plan'.

However, on 20 June Gladstone decided on a plan that entailed letting Irish customs duties fall into the common stock of Irish revenue and taking out of the total one-third of the *true* Irish revenue as an imperial contribution. Under the amended financial scheme Ireland would retain £4,660,000 of her total true revenue of £6,922,000 for domestic government expenses. But the latter were equal to that sum, so to provide a surplus on the Irish budget Ireland's imperial contribution would be reduced by one-third the cost of maintaining the police — £512,000. In addition, true revenue derived from customs and excise was to be ascertained by a joint committee of the treasury and Irish government, while the imperial government would retain control of Irish customs, excise and income tax for six years, and then revert to the original proposal of securing the Irish customs duties as an imperial contribution.[26]

This scheme, however, had no greater degree of approval from Nationalists than had the others. Conscious of the admitted error in establishing the original scheme, Edward Blake informed Morley: 'Having...no material in our possession to enable us to analyse the figures on either side of this...it is impossible for us to treat it as a basis upon which the financial relations of the two countries for future years should be fixed.' They did accept the amended financial scheme, but only 'under protest' and in view of the provision which limited the imperial parliament's control of Irish finance to six years — a provision that had, in fact, been insisted on by Thomas Sexton. Michael Davitt wrote of the bill in terms which could well have reflected the general Nationalist attitude:

> I cannot and will not help to destroy this bill, so long as the admitted deadly enemies of *any* form of Home Rule oppose and denounce it as dangerous to their principles and to the ascendancy and anti-Irish party in Ireland.
>
> When Balfour, Salisbury, Chamberlain and co., *espouse* this bill — laud it as a new Act of Union, and help Gladstone to pass it into law: then but not till then will you find me willing to help wreck this measure.
>
> ...I look at the whole of what this constitution will enable the *Irish people* — the Celtic people — to do, and I am satisfied that it would be unwise and unpatriotic on the part of the

Irish Party to reject a constitution which will take the government of Ireland out of the hands of the anti-Irish classes and
place it in those of the elected representatives of that race
which England has failed to exterminate.

If Davitt's view was representative of Nationalist opinion, it
appears that the Nationalists' acceptance of Gladstone's bill was
determined less by considerations of any good it might achieve
for Ireland than by the emotionally satisfying prospect of
inflicting a defeat on their enemies. Of course, there was the
commitment to estimate Ireland's true revenue from customs
and excise by a joint committee of the treasury and the Irish
government, which could eventuate in some financial benefit for
Ireland. The necessity of conciliating the recalcitrant Parnellites, however, was to result in a more substantial concession
still — a commission of inquiry into the financial relations of
Great Britain and Ireland since the Union. This subject came up
at a dinner attended by Lord Welby, Sir Algernon West, Sir T.
Wemyss Reid and R. Barry O'Brien. Welby and West put the
case for the retention of the collection of Irish revenue for six
years, which O'Brien seemed to agree with. The latter also
accepted that the government could not guarantee the £512,000
surplus on the Irish budget without leaving themselves open to
damaging criticism from Unionists. On the other hand, Welby
and West reacted favourably when O'Brien suggested a commission of inquiry into Anglo-Irish financial relations since the
Union — all agreeing that it should be set up in the following
year. The meeting ended with O'Brien declaring that 'if this
commission were granted, he believed Mr Gladstone would
have no further trouble with the Parnellites'. For his part,
Gladstone — who, indeed, had proposed such an inquiry to
Parnell in 1889 — thought it was the best arrangement that
could be made.[27] Shortly afterwards Redmond formally asked
for the commission in parliament, and Gladstone agreed; it was
chaired by Hugh Childers in 1894.

The Home Rule bill was thrown out by the Lords on 9 September 1893 by 419 votes to 41. Given the smallness of the
Liberal majority in the Commons, it was easy for the Lords 'to
assume that they had a "mission" from the country to destroy
any measure passed through the Commons which harmed

vested interests, or prejudiced the prospects of their party'. Moreover, few Liberal peers actually favoured Home Rule, despite the fact that thirty-eight held offices in the government or had been made peers in recent years. Henry Ponsonby has described how all those he knew

> express delight at being saved from speaking on Home Rule, and do not show any enthusiasm at the prospect of voting. . . . I am anxious to find a hearty Home Ruler but, except Mr Gladstone, he is not easy to find.

Perhaps the best comment on the debate in the Lords was made by Harold Spender, describing the defeat of the bill:

> There was a slight cheer, and then a great laugh as the whole body rapidly melted out of the house. Both sides joined in the laugh. It was impossible to keep up the big farce any longer.

Angered both by the rejection of his Home Rule scheme and the 'mutilation' of other Liberal measures by the upper house, Gladstone sought to call an election on the issue of 'Peers *versus* People'. His cabinet colleagues, however, were never enthusiastic for Home Rule and refused the call. Consequently Gladstone let the matter drop, though with the optimistic belief that when the upper house mutilated further Liberal measures the cabinet would take his advice. But as R. C. K. Ensor argues, despite its defeat, the second Home Rule bill was not without importance:

> Had it [the 1886 bill] lacked a sequel for nineteen years there might not have been one. But the bill of 1893 went through all stages in the elected house. It emerged a complete measure which, but for the veto of the House of Lords, would have come into force. It was almost bound to be revived if and when a majority of the nation took the view that the Lords used their veto unfairly.[28]

There was, however, one very important question that the defeat of the Home Rule bill would — in the long term — aggravate: the Ulster problem. It will be suggested here that had the second Home Rule bill been enacted, a real possibility would have existed of a peaceful settlement of this issue.

HOME RULE AND THE ULSTER QUESTION, 1892-3

The reintroduction of the Home Rule question in 1892 naturally brought to the fore again many of the controversies associated with the Ulster problem. However, as we have seen, Gladstone's position had changed somewhat since 1886, and while he had abandoned his willingness to accept a separate assembly for Ulster, he was prepared to go to some lengths to conciliate Ulster Protestant fears of being 'plundered' in a Home Rule parliament.

In the approaches he made to John Redmond through William Mather and Sir Charles Hall, Q.C., in March 1892 Gladstone sought to provide some safeguards for 'the prejudiced and feeble-minded' in Ulster, with particular reference to allaying their fears of being overtaxed by a Dublin parliament. Redmond, however, replied indignantly: 'I only remind you of this fact. The Ulster people cannot object to the same *principle* of taxation as that which prevails in Great Britain.' Shortly afterwards he declared that, as to the Ulster question generally, 'I don't consider any special safeguards necessary at all.' His disposition on this subject was to become increasingly negative as the Home Rule debate progressed. At one stage he argued that there was 'no Ulster question', only a question of a 'small corner of Ulster': the agitation against Home Rule was waged by a 'small minority' of Protestants, while the rest were only fearful for their position and of the 'dictation' of the Catholic clergy. As to the latter, the election of his own party against the wishes of the priests had shown that Protestant fears were largely ill-founded.[29] Redmond's intransigence on Ulster, moreover, was mirrored among anti-Parnellites.

During his meeting with Dillon, McCarthy and Sexton on 21 June 1892 Gladstone asked 'how they would view a provision [in the Home Rule bill] giving power to any public body in Ireland to raise a question of *ultra vires* in relation to any part of an ... act' passed by the Irish parliament, with such questions to be settled by the judicial committee of the Privy Council, as was the case with colonial legislation. The Nationalists objected strongly to this proposal, pointing out that it would enable 'the Belfast Corporation ... to bring forward in a most offensive way the subordinate position of the Irish parliament'. Despite

Gladstone's argument that their acceptance of this provision would have a 'very powerful conciliatory effect', they remained adamant, adding that their acceptance would 'give a powerful argument to Parnellites'. Nevertheless, during the preparation of the Home Rule bill the issue of safeguards for Ulster was again considered. In a memorandum discussing what changes were to be made in the Home Rule bill of 1886 it was set out as a question for discussion whether, in the clauses containing the restrictions on the Irish legislature, the following additions should be included in an effort 'to meet the Ulstermen':

(1) a limit on the amount of borrowing by the Irish executive so long as the debt due to the British exchequer under the Irish land act of 1891 remains undischarged: a limit on local debt;
(2) a restriction to secure equality of taxation, and to prevent (say) a common poor rate for the whole country, so as to relieve Ulster from the fear of being unduly taxed for the benefit of the poorer parts of Ireland;
(3) a prohibition on the alteration for a term of years of the Irish land act, 1891;
(4) a prohibition on controlling or hampering the exercise of authority under the imperial government.

Given the Nationalist opposition to any concessions for Ulster, however, and, equally, the refusal of Ulster Unionists to aid in any way the enactment of the Home Rule bill, it is not surprising that these were not major issues of debate. But that some such provisions were essential to allay the fears of northern Unionists was clear from the latter's opinion of the financial scheme of the bill. They agreed with the Nationalists' view that the proposed small surplus on the Irish budget would leave the Irish government virtually without funds and concluded that if the Home Rule scheme were enacted, a Dublin parliament would inevitably 'waste taxes raised in Belfast and Ulster' in an attempt to create and foster trade in other places on an 'unnatural foundation'. Similarly, it would establish a system of 'extravagant bounties' to bring trade to other parts of Ireland, to Ulster's detriment. Nor did they believe that Ulster M.P.s in the Home Rule parliament would be of sufficient number to protect the province's interests. They expected that the upper house of the parliament — which, as we have seen, was to have 48 members elected on a £20 rating qualification — would have only eight or ten members elected from Ulster.[30] Ulster Unionists, however, were to be given the opportunity, denied to them in 1886, of putting their objections directly to Gladstone; this they did in an interview which took place on 28 March 1893 and which is worth following in some detail.

The deputation consisted of ten members, representing the Belfast Chamber of Commerce, the Harbour Commissioners and the Linen Merchants' Association. The spirit in which Gladstone approached the meeting can be gauged from the fact that, despite his subsequent claims of having listened to 'interminable speeches', he allowed only twenty minutes to the representatives of the Chamber of Commerce, practically none at all to the representatives of the other two bodies, and during that time interjected fourteen times. Indeed, one member of the deputation recorded: 'The old man was jumping with impatience and we have had it clearly brought out that he closured us.' The influence that recent disclosures on the employment practices of Belfast Corporation had on Gladstone's thinking was immediately apparent, when, on the representatives of the Belfast Chamber of Commerce having introduced themselves, he declared that the latter was 'almost entirely Protestant I think. . . . I have understood that there were eight out of 260 who were not Protestant.' The deputation, having instanced the facts of religious division in Ulster and Ireland, emphasised the spectacular growth in the population and prosperity of Belfast and the fact that since the introduction of the Home Rule bill on 13 February 1893 £938,000 was wiped off the stock of the seven banks in Ireland and £1,000,000 off that of Irish railways. The union between Britain and Ireland, they argued, had been the cause of great prosperity, while an impoverished Home Rule parliament would attempt to effect an extravagant system of bounties to establish trade that would be harmful to Ulster industries and place them in a position where they could not compete with their English competitors.[31]

Gladstone answered these points by stating that since the propertied classes opposed Home Rule, he only expected that their securities would momentarily 'undergo an unfavourable influence', while the argument that most of the Irish people had no interest in Ulster's prosperity was unacceptable: it was tantamount to saying that they had no interest in Irish prosperity. On the issue of religious antagonism, he referred yet again to the harmony between the various creeds at the time of Grattan's Parliament and declared that the presence of the deputation suggested that it was certainly not the Catholics who entertained such antagonism. More importantly, though, on the question of Irish resources, Gladstone argued that Ireland's case was comparable to that of Canada, in terms of revenue and population, and that Home Rule had worked well there despite religious antagonism between French and British settlers. His argument on this point, however, turned out to be very superficial. In a supplementary letter answering these points the Chamber of Commerce could show that in terms of size, mineral resources, value of imports, railway systems and land availability, Canada was extremely rich and Ireland pitifully poor. The issue of Ireland's relative lack of natural resources had obvious implications for the finances of a Home Rule parliament, and this subject was heatedly debated. When the deputation pointed out that a surplus of £500,000 was a contemptible figure for the purposes of running a government, Gladstone disagreed, saying it was 'a very large amount indeed' and that Irish government was conducted on terms of 'enormous extravagances', with civil expenditure at £1 per head of population when it was only 10s in Great Britain. He continued: 'Ireland is a poor country. Ought Ireland to require more expenditure on civil government than England and Scotland which are richer countries . . . ?' Gladstone expected the advent of Home Rule to result in a gradual decline in the expense of running the country, to a level proportionate to that of Great Britain: it would then be possible, 'with prudence', for a saving of more than £2,500,000 to be made.[32]

In a written reply to his financial argument, however, the deputation was able to show that his contention that Ireland's civil expenditure was twice that of Great Britain was wrong. An estimate based on the most recent parliamentary returns showed a *per capita* estimate for Great Britain of 19s, and for Ireland £1 4s. Moreover, the Irish charge included the police, special expenses under the 1891 land act and charges for education, whereas in Britain similar charges were supplemented by local rates. A true comparison could only be made by eliminating these items from both accounts, with results for Great Britain and Ireland of 15s and 13s per head respectively. On these figures it was impossible for Ireland to make the economies envisaged by Gladstone. But accepting that a saving of £2,500,000 was to be made, from what items was it to come? The total amount of Gladstone's expenditure budget was £5,160,000, and if £2,500,000 were deducted, it would leave a balance of £2,660,000. However, there were combined charges for education, the post office and the collection of revenue, amounting to about £2,000,000, and this sum could not be reduced. Thus about £600,000 remained to meet government expenses for the police, land act charges, grants in aid of local charges, salaries for judges and other officials, and for all other purposes whatever. These expenses were estimated to be about £2,500,000, and given these facts, Ulster Unionists argued, Gladstone's expectation of great economies to be made in Irish government was 'a mere dream'.[33] The case made here was substantially the same as that made by Nationalists, but made to much greater effect. But whereas Nationalists sought for necessary amendments, Unionists were simply reinforced in their opposition to Home Rule.

Ulster Unionists did not profess to favour a separate parliament for Ulster, or separate treatment if Home Rule was enacted, being content to argue instead that, if given time, Ireland's problems could be solved within the Union. But there is some evidence to show that if Gladstone had made a proposal for separate treatment for Ulster, it might have been taken up. For example, while Unionists argued against Home Rule for all Ireland, the substance of that case more clearly applied to Ulster. But although the Liberal Unionist M.P.s T. W. Russell, Thomas Lea and H. O. Arnold-Forster opposed an amendment to the Home Rule bill by Jesse Collings which sought to exclude Ulster from its scope — on the ground that they were opposed to any kind of separate treatment — they did accept that if a Home Rule bill was enacted, they would press for Ulster's exclusion from it.[34]

Here was an opportunity, had Gladstone been willing to grasp it, of at least seriously debating the issue of separate treatment. Moreover, conscious of the antagonism to himself in

Ulster in 1886, John Morley was now making a special effort to appear to be acting fairly towards the northern Protestant community. His policy of maintaining an impartial attitude when rioting appeared to be beginning in Belfast was noted favourably in the north. Indeed, one source put it that his action, in not appearing to be the dupe of the Nationalist Party, helped considerably to defuse a potentially explosive situation. There would, of course, be opposition from Nationalists to any policy that would exclude Protestant Ulster from the scope of a Home Rule scheme, but it was at least debatable whether they would have rejected the chance of gaining Home Rule for the greater part of the island because of a provision to exclude part of Ulster from its jurisdiction. However, Gladstone's feeling towards Ulster Protestants merely became increasingly intolerant. At one stage during his meeting with the Ulster Unionist deputation on 28 March 1893 he accused them of creating the disunion of parties and creeds in Ireland:

> It is the disunion of Ireland which constitutes the real obstacle [to social and economic progress] now . . . disunion, for which you, I think, are largely — frankly let me say so ('No, no') — I beg your pardon, allow me, I wish to put it without any offence whatever — your opinions constitute the disunion.

The failure to compromise on Ulster appeared to leave only one solution: that if Home Rule was enacted, Ulster Protestants would resist its application to the province, by force if necessary. And certainly — as in 1886 — there was plenty of encouragement for Ulster Protestants to fight against Home Rule. During their visits to Ulster in 1892 and 1893 such a policy was urged by Lord Salisbury and A. J. Balfour. Again, Joseph Chamberlain repeatedly called on northern Protestants to rebel and was convinced that they would: 'His own agents sent to Ulster reported that the deeper you went down among the Protestant masses the starker was the spirit [of rebellion].'[35] That this should be so, however, is not surprising: the willingness of the Protestant working class for this kind of activity was amply demonstrated in Belfast in 1886. The question is: to what extent and in what circumstances were their political leaders prepared to lead a revolt?

Certainly warlike preparations were being made by some at

this time. The Irish correspondent of the virulently Unionist *Birmingham Daily Gazette* claimed to have seen 'proof positive' of such plans in the form of documents offering massive quantities of arms and ammunition with offers from England to assist the Ulster rebellion. The 'guarantee fund' for the first campaign, he was told, was nearly £1,500,000, while on Lord Ranfurly's authority he was informed that 'ten thousand and five' offers to fight in Ulster had come from Great Britain. Again, it is known that Colonel Saunderson was in correspondence with potential volunteers in England and Scotland at this time, who were assured of Ulster's will to resist the authority of a Dublin parliament by force. Moreover, another group entitled 'Young Ulster', under the leadership of F. H. Crawford, was also making warlike preparations. Nevertheless, the policy that appears to have had most support among Ulster Unionists — as an immediate reaction to Home Rule — was in fact 'passive resistance', such as that proposed by William Johnston in 1886. It was explained by the province's leading Liberal Unionist, Thomas Sinclair, at the Ulster convention of 1892:

> We shall have nothing to do with a Dublin parliament. If ever it be set up we shall simply ignore its existence. Its acts will be but as waste paper; . . . [its] police will find our barracks pre-occupied with our own constabulary; its judges will sit in empty courthouses. The early efforts of its executive will be spent in devising means to deal with a passive resistance to its taxation co-extensive with loyalist Ulster.

It was with this speech in mind that Gladstone congratulated the Ulster Unionists on being prepared not to go beyond the law in their opposition to Home Rule. A plausible scenario in which passive resistance would be enacted as a policy for northern Protestants was sketched by St Loe Strachey, an Englishman in close contact with Ulster Unionists:

> What would happen supposing Mr Gladstone were to pass his bill would be something like this. The Home Rule act would probably direct that writs should be immediately issued for the return of the Irish parliament. In the north, the returning officers would throw writs aside, risking the actions that would be brought against them, and no election would take

place. This, however, would not prevent the Dublin parliament meeting and falling to business. Presumably that parliament's earliest duty would be to fill its coffers, and taxation would be at once imposed. Here, then, would come the first point of friction. The Ulstermen would, of course, refuse to pay a tax levied in Dublin, and then the Dublin parliament would be face to face with a strike against taxes in which every merchant of wealth and position in Belfast and Derry and every landlord in the north would be engaged.[36]

The result of this action would be a 'Quaker rebellion', an extensive passive resistance, in which attempts by the Dublin parliament to punish the Ulstermen by seizing their goods would be met by a boycott of all the institutions of the Home Rule state and their supplanting by a 'voluntary government' based on the grand jury framework and the municipalities. This policy would be successful, Strachey argued, because a 'penniless' Dublin parliament could ill afford the enormous expense involved in raising a few pounds of taxation. This certainly seemed to be an effective course of action: it would not only secure Ulster Unionists exclusion from the Home Rule scheme, but would do so without recourse to a rebellion that could bring them into conflict with the British army. Indeed, it was argued by J. A. Rentoul — who first thought of holding the Ulster convention — that passive resistance was the farthest any Ulster Unionist leader was prepared to go:

'We will not have Home Rule' became a watchword among Unionists, but I never met anyone who regarded that statement as committing us to civil war or war against Great Britain in any contingency whatever. These words were simply taken to mean 'We will oppose Home Rule by every constitutional means. . . . ' Lord Randolph Churchill's statement, 'Ulster will fight and Ulster will be right', though quoted with great frequency was, so far as I know, *never regarded seriously even by the keenest Unionists* [my italics]. It was merely used as a political catchword.

This passage clearly supports the view that rebellious utterances made in the emotional atmosphere of the Home Rule crisis gave a very unreliable indication of Ulster Unionists' intentions. In this respect it is worth noting that in 1892 Thomas McKnight assured Joseph Chamberlain that Lord Dufferin had told him that if the Home Rule scheme was enacted, he would come home and place himself at the head of the Protestants. But in his reminiscences, published a few years later, he described Dufferin's plan as 'a rumour'. An interesting incident took place when the question of an Ulster rebellion was raised in the House of Commons. Thomas Sexton, with William Johnston's agreement, informed the house: '"My hon. friend, if I may so call him" — and Mr Johnston nodded — "will never fight."' Moreover, Adam Duffin, a leading organiser of the Convention League which followed the great demonstration of 1892, was anxious to ensure that there was no fear of it 'getting left without proper control in dangerous hands'.[37]

Of course, it could be argued that, in contrast to its position in 1914, the House of Lords in 1893 was still a powerful impediment to Home Rule, and that there was thus less need for a militant stance by Ulster Unionists. But although they were certainly mindful of the importance of the House of Lords to their cause, it was not regarded as the absolute guarantee against Home Rule it might have seemed. A. J. Balfour confided to John Ross his view — correct as far as Gladstone's intentions were concerned — that when the House of Lords threw out Gladstone's Home Rule bill he would call a general election on the issue and return with a massive majority to enact it. Again, the heightening tension in Belfast as the Home Rule debate progressed did not suggest the existence of a widespread confidence that the House of Lords could be safely left to dispose of the issue. Thus it is highly unlikely that 'passive resistance' was adopted as a policy which Unionists believed would never have to be put into effect. Nor indeed — as in 1886 — was it entirely the case that this policy had no place for armed revolt. What information there is on those who were preparing military resistance to Home Rule indicates quite clearly that this was to take place, not on the implementation of Home Rule, but when, and if, a Dublin parliament sought to deal with passive resistance by force: 'at that point the Ulster rebellion would occur'. However, Thomas Sexton declared in parliament: 'There will be no fighting in Ulster, unless there is something to fight about, and the Irish parliament will never give them a reason.' Sexton's remark indicates a policy on Ulster that a Dublin parliament might well be driven to by sheer force of economic circumstances: 'sensible government' such as that suggested by R. T. Reid in 1887.[38] Such a policy would have had — as one of its chief purposes — to demonstrate that Irish autonomy was not inconsistent with the promotion and safeguarding of specific Ulster interests.

Conclusion

IN THE course of this study many long-established views associated with the Home Rule struggle have been questioned: views about Gladstone's conversion to Home Rule, his insight into Irish nationalism, his Home Rule schemes, the Irish demand for Home Rule and the reaction in Ireland to Gladstone's plans, and the importance of the Ulster question in this period. That misconceptions about many of these subjects have existed for so long can, to a significant extent, be seen as a demonstration of the influence of contemporary political arguments in defining the terms within which historians would deal with the Home Rule question.

For example, the claims of Nationalists in 1886 — that they represented a people earnestly desiring Home Rule and whole-heartedly in favour of Gladstone's proposals — have been accepted by historians, convinced, in the words of Robert Kee, that 'experienced politicians like Parnell, O'Brien, and Healy' would never have accepted Gladstone's scheme had there been any danger of a great wave of 'national disappointment' with it. This study, however, has shown that the Irish attitude, both to Home Rule in general and to Gladstone's proposals, was distinctly less enthusiastic. It is too simple an equation to read Irish support for the Parnellite party as an index of Irish commitment to Home Rule — as Timothy Harrington's assessment of the reasons behind the great upsurge in party support in 1885 shows. Harrington's view — that the motive force here was the desire in each county to have its interests represented at Westminster — suggests, ironically, that the party's great electoral triumph in 1885 — usually seen as evidence of an intense Irish desire for Home Rule — was based more on an appreciation of the imperial connection and a desire to exploit it rather than a wish to see it broken. In this context it is worth remembering that Parnellites in the parliament of 1880-85 were known generally not just as strong nationalists but as good constituency M.P.s. In fact their electoral successes in 1885 served to mask the difficulties of Home Rulers since 1882 in increasing the membership of the National League and the worries of the party leadership that the Home Rule agitation could collapse. Certainly there is little to support Patrick O'Farrell's view that the 'illusion' of Home Rule 'dazzled the Irish'.[1]

Of course, it was only to be expected that following the 1885 general election Gladstone would take Nationalist claims at face value. Nevertheless, neither the election result nor the influential parliamentary position it gave the Parnellites accounts adequately for Gladstone's decision to introduce a Home Rule bill in 1886. A mere commitment to Home Rule in general would have aligned the Parnellites with the Liberal Party; and, as was intimated by both Davitt and Healy, Nationalists realised the need to educate British opinion on the Home Rule question if there was to be any hope of a successful outcome. Gladstone's rejection of this course of action was determined by his belief — certainly exaggerated — that Ireland was on the verge of revolution and that there was no time to pursue a gradual approach; and this belief in turn derived from the fact that he had virtually no personal knowledge of Ireland and that his sources on Irish affairs were limited. Thus that Gladstone was not well informed about Ireland was of greater importance in determining his actions as 1886 than any special insight he had into the Irish problem. Indeed, both Morley and Gladstone seem to have been convinced throughout the period 1886-93 that only their commitment to Home Rule prevented a revolutionary situation from developing in Ireland. When a violent reaction failed to follow the rejection of the second Home Rule bill, Morley declared: 'The tranquillity is profound for the time.'[2]

However, the view given here of Gladstone's reasons for producing a Home Rule bill in 1886 differs not only from the traditional interpretations, but also from the recently more influential case made by Cooke and Vincent. Arguing that

Gladstone was motivated mainly by reasons of intra-party advantage rather than by either morality or political necessity, they claim that his Home Rule plans were nothing more than 'useful contingency exercises' produced purely 'for his own benefit', and that their importance or otherwise would be determined by

> the political situation as it developed. . . . [Home Rule] might be tailed to a land bill . . . or . . . linked to coercion and a land bill. Context would be everything, and it would be impossible to see Home Rule emerging as front runner to an Irish programme until the last moment. It is impossible to say when Gladstone decided to make Home Rule the centre of his policy for 1886, but it could have been very late in the spring. The land bill . . . looked during February as though it would smother Home Rule, and yet within weeks it had been quietly pigeon-holed.

This argument, however, is open to the same objections as that made by John Vincent in *Gladstone and Ireland* and dealt with in Chapter 3. For example, it was shown that the relationship between the land and Home Rule bills was not haphazard, with the latter coming to the fore as a result of political chance: on the contrary, Gladstone conceived both bills as vitally related parts of one comprehensive scheme aimed at solving the Irish problem. His decision to construct the land purchase bill first was determined by the fact that no materials were available with which to construct an effective Home Rule bill when he took office, while he felt more qualified to deal with the land issue.[3]

Certainly it is true that the land bill was 'pigeon-holed' shortly after its introduction, but surely this is less significant than the fact that its shelving was designed primarily to facilitate the passage of the Home Rule bill, and that Gladstone planned to reintroduce it when the former was at a later stage of its progress through parliament. Indeed, Gladstone had been convinced in 1882 that a comprehensive solution to the land question necessitated some kind of local government authority to actually put it into effect; such an authority would constitute bodies charged with the 'working of the clauses' of a land act. The vital importance he attached to the linkage between the land and Home Rule elements of his Irish plan in 1886 can best be appreciated through an understanding of what the scheme as a whole was intended to achieve. Its first purpose, of course, was to establish Irish autonomy; but this study has argued that there were two other objectives he considered highly important: first, the removal of the land issue as a source of social strife, so paving the way for the reintroduction of the landlords into the political life of Ireland and thus restoring what he considered was the 'natural' order of society; secondly, that the Irish would meet their commitments to the imperial exchequer when Home Rule was established — an object to be effected by the provisions for appointing an 'imperial receiver' to ensure that Ireland's imperial contributions were made, and for making the finances of a Dublin government partially dependent on commissions drawn from the collection of tenants' repayments for land purchases.[4]

Historians generally have failed to appreciate the close interconnection between the land and autonomy elements of Gladstone's scheme — an omission, no doubt, largely due to the fact that the enormous scope of the project meant that its introduction in one piece was highly impractical, and that the land scheme was quickly withdrawn. Consequently they have also failed to deal adequately with the question of how far the financial clauses of the scheme contributed to its rejection. The proposal to appoint an 'imperial receiver' to enforce Ireland's imperial commitments, the stringent financial basis of the Home Rule scheme, and the unfavourable economic circumstances in which it was to be implemented — all provided abundant evidence to contradict Gladstone's claim that his scheme would be a final settlement of the Irish question. And, as we have seen, these factors were at the centre of the Unionist case against Home Rule — a case sometimes unjustly dismissed as one simply of anti-Irish prejudice. The cost of the scheme's failure, moreover, could be measured in terms of the sums being committed to its operation. For instance, Gladstone planned to commit £50,000,000 to the operation of his land measure at a time when the yearly cost of the navy — the mainstay of the empire — was only £12,000,000.[5]

One of the most criticised aspects of Gladstone's financial proposals was the small surplus of £404,000 on the Irish budget he envisaged, yet he remained impervious to criticism. Why? There was, of course, his passion for economy, but while this would explain why he proposed such a small surplus, it fails to account adequately for his refusal to heed the warnings of both Nationalists and Unionists during the Home Rule debate as to the difficulties it would create for an Irish government. The answer to this problem would appear to lie more in a peculiarity of his moral outlook.

Lionel Tollemache recorded that what Gladstone found most offensive about slavery was not the actual physical suffering involved, but the moral debasement: slavery 'degrades God's creatures below the human level'. J. L. Hammond has written that on a visit to Birmingham in 1877 Gladstone was unimpressed by the immense reforms that had swept away the slums and made Birmingham 'the pioneer city' in respect of public amenities and the general level of its social life:

> Gladstone's warm praise of Birmingham — had little to do with its municipal achievements or with the use it made of its best men; it was concerned with its active life of discussion and government and its power of attracting its best citizens to its service. These were to him of sovereign value.

Both these observations on Gladstone demonstrate a pre-occupation with the probity of social and political actions and a remarkable tendency to undervalue their human or material effects, whether bad or good. A similar attitude was evident in his approach to Home Rule. Concerned to satisfy the Irish desire for self-government, restore social peace and bring Ireland's 'best citizens' — the landlords — once more into the centre of political life, Gladstone failed to perceive that the practical effects of his financial provisions would very likely have rendered impossible the realisation of these hopes. Indeed, they could very well have encouraged the revival of the revolutionary nationalism that the conferring of Home Rule was intended to forestall. That this could happen does not seem to have occurred to Gladstone, who, moreover, was not inclined to allow for difference of opinion once having convinced himself of some view. In this respect it is worth remembering that despite his admissions in the period 1886-92, that Ireland had been over-taxed since the Union and that it was therefore necessary to deal generously with her in a future Home Rule bill, the scheme of 1892 proposed a surplus similar to that of 1886, while, unlike its predecessor, it was to be unaccompanied by a land measure that could have provided a much-needed additional source of revenue. That the second Home Rule bill was not linked with a land bill can be seen as an effect of Tory land legislation since 1886; by 1893 the land problem was regarded as much less acute.[6]

Of course, the defeat of Gladstone's measures meant that their defects never produced the problems expected of them, and in this context there was surely much point to A. J. Kettle's claim that the defects in the scheme of 1886 were so enormous that Parnell's reputation and position as an Irish political leader had been saved by its demise. It could be equally well argued that the defeat of his Home Rule plans also ensured Gladstone's reputation as one of the few British politicians who possessed a correct understanding of Irish nationalism and who proposed enlightened legislation to deal with it. This aspect of the Home Rule struggle presents another significant example of how contemporary political argument has influenced subsequent historiography, for despite the claims of both contemporaries and historians commending Gladstone's insight into Irish nationalism, this study shows that his perception of it was highly flawed. In emphasising the supposedly 'constitutional' character of its historical development and ignoring the bloody struggles that more truly characterised it, Gladstone exhibited a striking failure of historical perception — most evident in his inability to understand the strength of Ulster Unionist fears about Home Rule. Thus his arguments were easily faulted by his Unionist critics: indeed, not only did his historical arguments present a distorted view of the development of Irish nationalism, but they were notoriously weak as propaganda in Britain, where the public's acquaintance with Irish history consisted mainly of tales of 'Romish' persecution during the 1641 rebellion.[7] In ignoring these aspects of Irish history Gladstone failed to deal with the only subject on which he was likely to have a point of contact with the public, and which had been the source of much anti-Irish prejudice. The factors that conditioned his view of Irish nationalism and history — especially his power of self-deception — have been dealt with in Chapter 7; however, our understanding of Gladstone's thinking on these subjects is enhanced when we remember the political background to the Home Rule crusade. Gladstone's study of Irish nationalism was hurried and concurrent with his belief as to the necessity of producing a Home Rule scheme to stave off a revolutionary situation in Ireland. Since this was the purpose of Home Rule, it was necessary to prove that Irish nationalist sentiment was constitutional in character and would thus be satisfied with it. Obsessed with his Home Rule crusade, Gladstone thereafter looked to Irish history with a fixed idea of what he wanted to discover, oblivious to the glaring inadequacies of his arguments and the scope for criticism they provided for Unionists.

Probably the least convincing of Gladstone's arguments, and most indicative of his ignorance of Irish political realities, was his claim — made during the Plan of Campaign — that when Home Rule was established the landlords would once more come to the fore as Irish political leaders. Gladstone was not contradicted by Nationalists, almost certainly because of his importance to the Home Rule campaign. Moreover, given that Liberal and Nationalist propaganda efforts were designed for different audiences — in Ireland and Great Britain — and that the energies of both parties were mainly given over to fighting the Tory government's Irish policies, it was easy to let Gladstone's claims in this respect pass unchallenged. Nevertheless, the disparity of view between Gladstone and Nationalists on the place of the landlords in the Irish nation was certainly real. Nor, moreover, were their ideas entirely in accord regarding the Ulster Unionists, notwithstanding their agreement on the preferred solution to the problem of the north. For instance, at the level of political debate, it was seen that Gladstone, as befitted his position as Prime Minister and potential Prime Minister, had to appear to be dealing impartially with the problem, and so professed a willingness to accept separate treatment for Ulster despite the Nationalist rejection of this option. At a more ideological level, whereas Gladstone emphasised the unifying influence of nationalism by reference to the political activities of northern Protestants in Grattan's time, Nationalist propaganda, while making similar references, invoked also the divisive struggles of plantation times, with the implication that the success of the Home Rule campaign in Ulster would mean the victory of Catholics over Protestants.[8]

Relatedly, although both shared the view that Ulster Unionism was largely created by English intrigue, Nationalists' attitudes — because they were more closely involved with the Ulster problem — tended to be more sharply defined than Gladstone's.

Although repelled by the violent reputation of Orangeism and the antics of Orange M.P.s in parliament, Gladstone relied generally on the precedent of Protestant involvement in Grattan's Parliament as an assurance of the eventual acceptability of Home Rule in the north. Nationalists, however, concentrated more on their Orange stereotype, which defined the only real Ulster Unionists as bigoted Orangemen, unrepresentative of northern Protestants who were open to persuasion on Home Rule — a viewpoint, ironically, which exhibited a similar kind of stereotypy to that of Unionists who argued that nationalist agitators were unrepresentative of Irish opinion, which was naturally law-abiding and loyal to the Union. In both cases the source of the stereotypy lay in their refusal to accept an unpalatable reality. However, 'evidence' of sorts could be found to support the views of Home Rulers. For instance, both Gladstone and Nationalists placed much importance on the activities of Colonel Saunderson, the Ulster Unionist leader, to 'prove' that Ulster Unionists would not only decline to resist Home Rule but would eventually accept it. Additionally, there were the activities of the small but vociferous Protestant Home Rule movement, which could be read as portending increasing Protestant support for Irish autonomy; the Nationalist majority of one seat in the province; the fact that the relative prosperity argument was not well handled on the Unionist side and appeared to tell in the Nationalists' favour; the difficulty of defining a specifically Protestant 'homeland' to be excluded from Nationalist rule, and, relatedly, the fact that the Unionist tendency to apply the term 'Ulster' to the Protestant and Unionist parts of the province favoured Nationalists, who could then 'prove' the falsity of Unionist arguments by pointing to the large Catholic population in the province as a whole.[9]

At best, however, these were debating points and did not change the fact that a large proportion of Ulster was Protestant, Unionist, economically distinct from the rest of Ireland, and denying the legitimacy of Nationalist claims to obtain Home Rule for the whole island. But while Ulster Protestant opposition to Home Rule was certainly intense, there is nevertheless little evidence to support the view — still widespread — that they were prepared to resist violently the implementation of Home Rule in this period. For instance, A. T. Q. Stewart — reading the open rebellion planned by Ulster Unionists in the period 1912-14 back into 1880s — has written: 'It is sometimes assumed that the Protestant plans to resist by force of arms appeared first in the crisis of 1912-14, but when we look more closely we find that this is not true. . . . It was in 1886 that the first co-ordinated proposals were made by Ulster Unionists, led by Colonel Saunderson, for resisting Home Rule by force.' The similarity between 1886 and 1912, however, is more apparent than real. Unlike the period 1911-14, when open rebellion was planned in conjunction with a specific project for taking over the government of Ulster on the enactment of the Home Rule bill, no such plans existed either in 1886 or 1892-3. As John Morley wrote, in regard to the Ulster Unionist reaction to the introduction of the second Home Rule bill, there was 'no fear of an organised rising'.[10] Instead a rather vaguely conceptualised programme of passive resistance was envisaged, which, it was hoped, would be successful enough to secure for Protestant north-east Ulster either its own administration or some kind of special treatment. The possibility that violence might be resorted to was not overlooked, but that eventuality would be clearly dependent on how a Dublin parliament reacted to events in the north.

Thus, in contrast to the situation in 1914, resistance to the point of violence was not a policy to be pursued, but rather a contingency of a political situation the outcome of which was yet very unclear. It was this more circumspect policy of Ulster Unionists in 1892-3 that gave Gladstone grounds for hope that some kind of peaceful settlement of the problem was possible without at the same time invalidating Home Rule.[11] As for Nationalists, given the financial constraints within which a Dublin parliament would have operated, it is unlikely that they could have afforded to pursue any other policy towards Ulster Protestants than that of conciliation.

Appendices

APPENDIX 1

Nationalist Opinion and the Home Rule Scheme of 1886

This attempt to assess nationalist opinion on Gladstone's first Home Rule plan is based on a study of predominant themes in local press reactions to the Home Rule scheme. A sample of 26 local newspapers out of approximately 55 that supported Home Rule were examined; about half of these circulated mainly in areas of the west of Ireland that had seen much agrarian agitation. In each case the unit of study has been the leading article, as this item invariably expressed the political views of newspapers, and for many of the smallest local papers was the only political column. The particular leading articles used in the study were those providing the fullest discussion of the Home Rule and land bills in the period from April to June 1886.[1] The choice of newspaper studied was determined partly by availability, but also by the desire to use the most popular papers.

There is, of course, a debate about the extent to which newspapers reflect public opinion rather than mould it. But however this may be, for this period local newspapers provide the only sources on which to base a study of public opinion. Moreover, it is a reasonable assumption that they reflect the political concerns of their readers, though, as D. G. Boyce rightly puts it, 'we also have to remember that we are seeing it [public opinion] through the eyes of some intermediary'.[2]

The following newspapers were used in this study:

ULSTER
Anglo-Celt, 17, 24 Apr.
Derry Journal, 9 Apr.
Newry Reporter, 13, 24 Apr.
Weekly Examiner, 10 Apr., 29 May

LEINSTER
Dundalk Democrat, 10 Apr.

Kilkenny Journal, 10 Apr.
Leinster Leader, 10 Apr.
Midland Tribune, 15 Apr.
Nationalist and Leinster Times, 10, 24 Apr.
The Nation, 24 Apr.
The People, 14, 21 Apr.
Wexford Express, 17 Apr.

MUNSTER

Clare Examiner, 10, 17 Apr.	*Connaught People*, 17 Apr.
Cork Daily Herald, 9, 23 Apr.	*Connaught Telegraph*, 10, 24 Apr.
Limerick Reporter, 9, 21 Apr.	*Mayo Examiner*, 10 Apr.
Munster News, 9, 21 Apr.	*Roscommon Herald*, 10, 24 Apr.
Waterford Dail Mail, 17 Apr., 10 May	*Sligo Champion*, 17, 24 Apr.
	Tuam Herald, 10, 17, 24 Apr.
CONNAUGHT	*Tuam News*, 16, 30 Apr.
Ballina Journal, 14 June	*Western News*, 10, 24 Apr., 8 May

Table 7. Predominant themes in nationalist press reactions to the Home Rule bill of 1886

		No. of times recorded
1	uncritical praise	9
2	acceptance subject to unspecified changes	4
3	approval with objections to the extent of minority safeguards	1
4	acceptance subject to modifications suggested by Parnell in parliament on 8 April	9
5	approval with objections to the financial scheme	3

Table 8. Predominant themes in nationalist press reactions to the land purchase bill of 1886

		No. of times recorded
1	spectrum of general reactions to the land bill:	
	(a) no mention	9
	(b) non-commital	2
	(c) uncritical praise	1
	(d) accepted as moderate and generous to landlords	1
	(e) accepted as a necessary evil despite its being over-generous to landlords[1]	5
	(f) rejected as over-generous to landlords and unfair to tenants[2]	3
	(g) accepted but feared its expense and complexity would render the bill unworkable by the Irish parliament	1
2	endorsed the bill but objected to lack of provision for evicted tenants to repossess their holdings	2
3	acceptance subject to amendment granting tenants lower rental repayments	1
4	approval subject to amendments published by the Ulster Land Committee[3]	1

[1]'Over-generous' usually referred to the average number of years' purchase to be awarded to the landlord.
[2]'Unfair' usually meant the failure to make provision for tenants to compel landlords to sell, and to the expected small reduction in existing rental repayments.
[3]See pp 113-14 above.

APPENDIX 2

Ulster Unionists' Expectations of how they would be affected by Home Rule in 1886

The purpose of this study is to provide some insight into how the Ulster loyalist community defined their national identity, and how they believed Home Rule would affect both it and their material welfare. To this end an examination of thirty speeches, delivered by Unionist orators at various venues, mainly in Ulster, during the Home Rule debate, has been made. As with Appendix 1, the technique found most appropriate to this study has been 'thematic'; however, there are some differences of treatment. First, whereas the study in Appendix 1 seeks to identify predominant themes in the material examined, this study is restricted to the identification of themes specifically relevant to the purpose stated above. Secondly, whereas the analysis of reactions to specific pieces of legislation is relatively straightforward, the task of assessing the variety of apprehensions raised among Ulster Unionists by the prospect of Home Rule in general is much more complex.

An essential basis for such a study is an extensive familiarity with the dimensions of Unionist ideology in 1886, and an awareness of the meaning invoked by key symbols and phrases, given that in material such as political speeches the same theme is likely to find more than one form of expression on different occasions. For example, while the warning, 'Under Home Rule the Catholic priesthood will attempt to exterminate Protestants as in centuries past', is self-explanatory, the meaning of the phrase 'the historical ambitions of the Catholic priesthood' is only apparent if its ideological context is fully understood, even though it expresses the same theme. Consequently the thematic categories established for this study have generally been more complex than those in Appendix 1, and have been based on inference as well as explicit expressions of opinion.

The speeches used in this study, which is a revision of a study of Unionist speeches prepared for my doctoral thesis, were taken from issues of the *Belfast News-Letter* and are listed as follows with dates of publication:

Rev. R. J. Lynd, Belfast, 6 Jan.
Sir John Leslie, Glaslough, 6 Jan.
Col. Saunderson, Lurgan, 8 Jan.
R. W. B. Ker, M.P., Ballynahinch, 9 Jan.
Rev. Hugh Hanna, ibid.
A. H. Gordon, ibid.
Rev. Mr McCreedy, ibid.
Rev. Mr Alexander, ibid.
Earl of Erne, Florencecourt, 15 Jan.
Frank Brooke, ibid.
Dr R. R. Kane, Dungannon, 30 Jan.
Rev. Alex Dobbin, Lisburn, 3 Feb.
Rev. W. Browne, ibid.

Rev. Canon Fitzgerald, Antrim, 11 Feb.
Dr Byrne, Dean of Clonfert, Omagh, 15 Feb.
Rev. James Dill, ibid.
Rev. Michael Beattie, Lurgan, 4 Mar.
Rev. Dr Morrell, Belfast, 10 Mar.
W. Q. Ewart, Belfast, 20 Mar.
Viscount Mandeville, Tandragee, 28 Mar.
Rev. Mr M'Endoo, ibid.
Rev. J. A. Crozier, ibid.
Mr Ledlie, ibid.
Col. Waring, Battle, Sussex, 8 Apr.
E. S. W. de Cobain, Belfast, 1 May
Rev. Dr Gray, ibid.
Thomas Sinclair, Ulster Hall, 1 May
Lord Ernest Hamilton, Fintona, 8 May
Thomas Porter, ibid.
T. W. Russell, Dungannon, 18 June

Table 9.　Selected themes in speeches by Ulster Unionists in 1886
reflecting their views of how Home Rule would affect them

		No. of times recorded
1	Home Rule would mean the betrayal of Ulster loyalists.	9
2	Under Home Rule nationalists and the Roman Catholic priests who largely control them would persecute the Protestant and loyal community.[1]	27
3	Nationalists had no respect for law and order, and their policies (e.g. protectionism) would mean social and economic ruin for Ireland.	17
4	Under Home Rule Ulster would have to pay the expenses of the rest of Ireland.	4
5	Unlike an impoverished Irish assembly, the imperial parliament had the resources to finance the social and economic regeneration of Ireland.	5
6	Home Rule was inconsistent with imperial integrity, and by relegating Ulster loyalists to representation by a subordinate parliament it would deprive them of their imperial heritage and reduce their status in the world.	25

[1]Included in this category were fears expressed for the civil and religious rights of Protestants, as well as historically based fears for their actual physical welfare.

Notes

The following abbreviations are used in the references.

B.L.	British Library
B.N.L.	*Belfast News-Letter*
C.R.	*Contemporary Review*
C.S.O., R.P.	Chief Secretary's Office, Registered Papers (in S.P.O.)
F.J.	*Freeman's Journal*
F.R.	*Fortnightly Review*
G.P.	Gladstone papers (in B.L., Add. MSS)
H.P.	Hamilton papers (in B.L., Add. MSS)
I.L.P.U.	Irish Loyal and Patriotic Union
J.H.R.U.	*Journal of the Home Rule Union*
L.S.	*Londonderry Sentinel*
L.U.A.	Liberal Unionist Association
N.C.	*Nineteenth Century*
N.L.I.	National Library of Ireland
P.M.G.	*Pall Mall Gazette*
P.R.O.	Public Record Office of England
P.R.O.N.I.	Public Record Office of Northern Ireland
R.I.C.	Royal Irish Constabulary
S.P.O.	State Paper Office, Dublin Castle
T.C.D.	Trinity College, Dublin
U.I.	*United Ireland*
W.N.W.	*Weekly Northern Whig*

Other bibliographical abbreviations are in accordance with T. W. Moody, *Rules for Contributors to Irish Historical Studies*, revised ed. (Dublin 1968).

Chapter 1: Nationalism and the Home Rule Movement, 1882-6 (pp 5-34)
1. J. E. Redmond, *Historical and Political Addresses* (London 1898), 181-2; *Northern Whig*, 16 Aug. 1883; R. B. O'Brien, *Parnell*, 2nd ed. (London [1910]), 285. However, Davitt, who was not a member of Parnell's party, had in 1882 declared himself in favour of a constitution for Ireland 'similar to that in Canada'. As for Parnell, F. S. L. Lyons has argued that he gave no 'precise explanation' of Home Rule partly because he was an 'improviser, not a theorist', and partly because he was a 'pragmatist' who

believed vagueness was best when it was impossible to tell how the British political situation would develop. At this time he was attempting to have a Grand Committee of Irish M.P.s established to examine proposed Irish legislation. See D. B. Cashman, *Life of Michael Davitt* (Glasgow [1882]), 253; F. S. L. Lyons, *Charles Stewart Parnell*, 2nd ed. (London 1978), 259; Alan O'Day, *The English Face of Irish Nationalism* (Dublin 1977), 173.

2. R. B. O'Brien, *The Home-Ruler's Manual* (London 1890), 70; H. M. Stephens, 'Modern Historians and their Influence on Small Nationalities', *C.R.*, lii (July 1887), 108-20; Hans Kohn, 'Nationalism' in Anthony De Crespigny and Jeremy Cronin (ed.), *Ideologies of Politics* (London 1975), 152-3; Kenneth Minogue, *Nationalism* (London 1967), 54-8.

3. G. P. Gooch, *History and Historians in the Nineteenth Century* (London 1959), 276; Stephens, 'Modern Historians', 107-8; E. H. Carr, *What Is History?* (Harmondsworth 1973), 9; J. W. Burrow, *The Uses of Philology in Victorian Britain* (London 1970), 181, 187-8; W. R. W. Stephens, *The Life and Letters of E. A. Freeman* (London 1895), 108. Historical inquiry was established as a university discipline shortly after mid-century. See J. R. Hale, *The Evolution of British Historiography from Bacon to Namier* (London 1967), 35.

4. C. J. Dewey, 'Celtic Agrarian Legislation and the Celtic Revival: Historicist Implications of Gladstone's Irish and Scottish Land Acts, 1870-86', *Past and Present*, 64 (Aug. 1974), 30-70 (Probably the most influential writer expounding historicist views on Irish land problems was J. S. Mill (see Mill, *England and Ireland* (London 1868), 11-12)); E. R. Norman, *Anti-Catholic Prejudice in Victorian England* (London 1968), passim, and G. F. A. Best, 'Popular Protestantism in Victorian Britain' in Robert Robson (ed.), *Ideas and Institutions of Victorian Britain* (London 1967), 116; George Salmon, *The Infallibility of the Church: A Course of Lectures delivered in the Divinity School of the University of Dublin*, 2nd ed. (Dublin 1890), 3; W. J. O'Neill Daunt made much the same point. See Daunt, *A Life Spent for Ireland*, ed. by his daughter (London 1896), 366.

5. A. S. G. Canning, *Revolted Ireland, 1798 and 1803* (London 1886), 10. Macaulay's *Eng.* (5 vols, London 1848-61) was an influential text in the dissemination of ethnocentric views about the Irish. For Acton's view of the Celts as an essentially 'retrogressive' race, made in the course of criticising Goldwin Smith's *Irish History and Irish Character* (London 1861) for its ambivalence on the role of race in Irish history, see Lord Acton, *The History of Freedom and other essays*, intro. J. R. Figgis and R. J. Lawrence (London 1907), 240.

6. See J. P. Prendergast, *The Cromwellian Settlement of Ireland*, 2nd ed. (London 1875), 10-14. Prendergast wrote his book to refute the assessment of the Cromwellian period in Goldwin Smith's *Irish History and Irish Character*. Froude's *Ire.* was published in 3 vols (London 1872-4). He described his attitude to historical inquiry thus: 'I do not pretend to impartiality. I believe the Reformation to have been...the root and source of the expansive force which has spread the Anglo-Saxon race over the globe' (quoted in Hale, *Evolut. of Brit. Hist.*, 54). Lecky's *Ire.*, originally produced as part of his *Eng.* (8 vols, London 1878-90), received separate publication in 5 vols (London 1892).

7. Lecky, *Ire.*, new impression (London 1919), i, 396-7.

8. Lecky, *Leaders*, new ed. (London 1912), i, pp vi, xiv-xv. See also Helen Mulvey, 'The Historian Lecky: Opponent of Irish Home Rule', *Victorian Studies*, i, no. 4 (June 1958), 337-51.

9. Fox to Lecky, 4 Feb. 1890, T.C.D., Lecky correspondence, no. 574. Quotations from source material in the text have been silently edited to book style, e.g. in use of capitals and lower case, spelling variations, etc.

10. Davitt (*Fall of Feudalism*, 715) and T. P. O'Connor (*The Parnell Movement* (London 1886), 347-51) on Sullivan's influence with the peasantry; T. D. Sullivan, *Green Leaves: A Volume of Irish Verses*, 12th ed. (Dublin 1888), 76.

11. Donal McCartney, 'James Anthony Froude and Ireland: An Irish Historiographical Battle of the Nineteenth Century' in T. D. Williams (ed.), *Hist. Studies VIII* (Dublin 1971), 184; Prendergast to Lecky, 10 July 1892, T.C.D., Lecky correspondence, no. 719; A. G. Richey, *A Short History of Ireland down to the Plantation of Ulster*, ed. R. R. Kane (London 1887), 1; Donal McCartney, 'Lecky's *Leaders of Public Opinion in Ireland*', *I.H.S.*, xiv, no. 54 (Sept. 1964), 133-5; Huxley to Lecky, 26 July 1890, T.C.D., Lecky correspondence, no. 606; L. M. Cullen, 'Irish Economic History: Fact and Myth' in Cullen (ed.), *The Formation of the Irish Economy*, 2nd ed. (Cork· 1976), 119-20.

12. McCartney, 'Froude', 176-7.

13. See Burke's lecture on the 1641 rebellion, in T. N. Burke, *Ireland's Vindication: Refutation of Froude and other lectures* (Glasgow n.d.), 197-201; W. P. Joyce, *Editors and Ethnicity: A History of the Irish-American Press, 1848-83* (New York 1976), 150-87; Sir C. G. Duffy, *A Short Life of Thomas Davis* (London 1895), 112-13.

14. T. W. Rolleston (ed.), *Prose Writings of Thomas Davis* (London [1889]), xii; R. B. O'Brien, *A Hundred Years of Irish History* (London [1902]), 108-9: Sir C. G. Duffy, *My Life in Two Hemispheres* (London 1898), i, 89; Jeanne Sheehy, *The Rediscovery of Ireland's Past: The Celtic Revival, 1830-1930* (London 1980), 28.

15. See list of nationalist publications in A. M. Sullivan, *New Ireland*, 10th ed. (Glasgow n.d.); William O'Brien, *Irish Ideas* (London 1893), 52-3; *Irishman*, 4 Jan. 1868.

16. John Denvir, *The Life Story of an Old Rebel* (Dublin 1910), reprinted with intro. by Leon Ó Broin (Shannon 1972), pp vii, 137; Eugene O'Curry, *MS Materials*; John O'Donovan, *Ancient Laws of Ireland*, 6 vols (Dublin 1865-1901); Brown, *Ir.-Amer. Nationalism*, 31-2; F. S. L. Lyons, *Ireland since the Famine*, 2nd ed. (London 1973), 87-8.

17. O'Brien, *Hundred Years of Ir. History*, 83; Sinn Féin, *The Irish Year Book, 1909* (Dublin 1909), 214; M. J. F. McCarthy, *The Irish Revolution* (London 1912), 24-6; S.O.G., 'Imperial Government and the Irish National Schools', *Graphic*, 20 Aug. 1887. 'S.O.G.' was quite possibly Standish O'Grady.

18. Sir Isaiah Berlin, *Against the Current: Essays in the History of Ideas*, ed. Henry Hardy (London 1979), 349. Sam Clark has shown that it was the urban group to which these leading Parnellites generally belonged that provided the organisational leadership of the Land League. See Clark, 'The

Political Mobilisation of Irish Farmers', *Canadian Review of Sociology and Anthropology*, xii, 4, pt 2 (1975), 496; Clark, *Social Origins of the Land War* (Princeton 1979), 263.

19. Justin McCarthy, *The Story of an Irishman* (London 1904), chs 1 and 5; *Special Comm. 1888 Proc.* (London 1890), ix, 352; T. W. Moody, *Davitt and Irish Revolution, 1846-82* (Oxford 1981), 8-9; Hamilton Fyfe, *T. P. O'Connor* (London 1934), 39-40; William O'Brien, *Recollections* (London 1905), 1-13, 28-9.

20. Maev Sullivan, *No Man's Man* [T. M. Healy] (Dublin 1943), 1-4; Duffy, *My Life*, i, 80; T. P. O'Connor and Robert McWade, *Gladstone–Parnell, and the Great Irish Struggle* (Philadelphia 1886), 406; Lyons, *Parnell*, 32; Ged Martin, 'Parnell at Cambridge: The Education of an Irish Nationalist', *I.H.S.*, xix, no. 73 (Mar. 1974), 72-82; F. S. L. Lyons, 'The Political Ideas of Parnell', *Hist. Jn.*, xvi, 4 (1973), 749-50. E. R. Norman has detected a similar combination of personal alienation and 'advanced' political theories as motivating agents in the leading Young Irelanders. See Norman, *A History of Modern Ireland* (London 1971), 120.

21. *U.I.*, 13 Aug. 1881.

22. Ibid., 16 Jan. 1886.

23. O'Brien, *Parnell and his Party*, 2nd ed. (Oxford 1974), 5-6; List of Nationalist M.P.s with details of their political views, S.P.O., Police and Crime Records, Crime Branch Special files, 1890-1920; C. J. Woods, 'The Catholic Church and Irish Politics, 1879-92' (Ph.D. thesis, University of Nottingham, 1968), 139 n. 2, 434-5.

24. Timothy Harrington was to inform the Special Commission in 1889 that as to agrarian issues, the National League sought to relieve evicted tenants left over from the land war and to judge every other case on the tenants' 'ability or inability to pay their rent'. See *Special Comm. 1888 Proc.*, ix, 202-3, 234.

25. O'Brien, *Parnell*, 238; Harris and Dillon, quoted in *Special Comm. 1888 Proc.*, i, 254; O'Day, *Eng. Face of Ir. Nationalism*, 29-30; O'Brien, quoted in *Special Comm. 1888 Proc.*, ii, 265. For nationalist attitudes to physical force see extracts from *U.I.*, 19 Sept. 1885, ibid., viii, 194; evidence of T. D. Sullivan, ibid., 217.

26. *Nation*, 2 Jan. 1886. For more examples of politically motivated historical series see *Midland Tribune*, 24 Apr. 1886; *Leinster Leader*, 1 May 1886; *Kilkenny Journal*, 5 May 1886; *Western News*, 29 May 1886; *Waterford Daily Mail*, 7 June 1886; *Cork Daily Herald*, 17 June 1886.

27. F. H. O'Donnell, *A History of the Irish Parliamentary Party* (London 1910), ii, 191-2.

28. For example, see O'Connor and McWade, *Gladstone–Parnell*, 121; T. M. Healy, 'Jubilee Time in Ireland', *C.R.*, li (Jan. 1887), 30; Sullivan, *Green Leaves*, 217.

29. *Special Comm. 1888 Proc.*, ix, 73; ibid., i, 408, 434; ibid., 182-3.

30. Ibid., ii, 17-18.

31. Ibid., i, 409, 625; ibid., ix, 547.

32. Brown, *Ir.-Amer. Nationalism*, 107; Joseph Lee, *The Modernisation of Irish Society, 1848-1918* (Dublin 1973), 96; E. D. Steele, *Irish Land and British*

Politics: Tenant Right and Nationality (Cambridge 1974), 3, 19-20 (On these
views see also Paul Bew, *Land and the National Question in Ireland* (Dublin
1979), 21-2): Davitt, *Fall of Feudalism*, 164.

33. Bew, *Land*, 20; Sullivan, *Green Leaves*, 222; O'Donnell, *Ir. Parl. Party*, ii,
194.

34. Michael McDonagh, *The Home Rule Movement* (Dublin 1920), 13.
McDonagh is here speaking of the Home Rule movement of the 1870s, but
his remarks apply equally to the 1880s.

35. Parnell's political appeal in Bew, *Land*, 227-8; J. S. Donnelly, *The Land and
People of Nineteenth-Century Cork* (London/Boston 1975), 6, on 'rising expectations'; McCarthy, *Ir. Revolution*, 288. Lyons, however (*Parnell*, 610),
argues that Parnell never believed that 'such progress as could be won on
the way to that final goal [Home Rule] would corrode the people's will to
liberty'.

36. *Special Comm. 1888 Proc.*, x, 179; W. S. Blunt, *The Land War in Ireland*
(London 1912), 47, 93; John Morley, *Recollections* (London 1917), i, 210.

37. William O'Brien, *Recollections* (London 1905), 326-7; Entry from Tuke's
diary for 1886, quoted in Sir Edward Fry, *James Hack Tuke: A Memoir*
(London 1899), 248.

38. O'Brien, *Parnell and his Party*, 85-6; O'Brien, *Recollections*, 360, 497-503.

39. McCarthy, *Ir. Revolution*, 384-8. O'Brien argued before the Special Commission that the party just let *The Irishman* die quietly (*Special Comm. 1888
Proc.*, viii, 89); however, the truth was that active efforts were made to stimulate its fortunes. When the Fenian James Stephens published his
memoirs, they were serialised in *The Irishman* and advertised in *U.I.* (28
Aug. 1882).

40. Based on information in *Newspaper Press Directory* (London 1887), 143-52;
Registry of Newspapers (undated) [1891?] in Irish Crime Records, 1886-
92, S.P.O., viiiB, window press 3/9.

41. McCarthy, *Ir. Revolution*, 169, 335; *Special Comm. 1888 Proc.*, viii, 129-30;
see evidence of Captain Owen Slack (ibid., ii, 197), and report on National
League by Inspector-General, R.I.C., 17 Jan. 1886, S.P.O., C.S.O., R.P.,
1886/17972.

42. *Special Comm. 1888 Proc.*, ix, 202-3; ibid., x, 94; Clark, *Social Origins*, 329,
quoting W. L. Ferngold, 'The Irish Poor Law Guardians, 1872-86: A
Revolution in Local Government' (Ph.D. thesis, University of Chicago,
1974), 143; McCarthy, *Ir. Revolution*, 141, 328-9; *Northern Whig*, 28 Aug.
1883; Lyons, *Parnell*, 616.

43. Evidence of Head Constable Bernard O'Malley on Nationalist meetings,
in *Special Comm. 1888 Proc.*, i, 434; Lyons, *Parnell*, 178-9; *Special Comm. 1888
Proc.*, ix, 203, 235. Harrington's estimate of 1,700 branches existing in 1886
is supported by Jeremiah Jordan (*Hansard 3*, cccv, 651 (10 May 1886)) and
contradicts the estimate of 1,286 given in Tom Garvin, *The Evolution of
Irish Nationalist Politics* (Dublin 1981), 80.

44. *Special Comm. 1888 Proc.*, viii, 136; ibid., 200.

45. Notes of conversation between Sullivan and Parnell, 16 July 1881, N.L.I.,
Sullivan papers, MS 8237(14); Sullivan to Patrick Egan, 14 July 1881,
ibid., MS 8237(15); O'Donnell, *Ir. Parl. Party*, ii, 194.

46. Circular dated 19 May 1883, N.L.I., Webb papers, MS 1745; Diary entry dated 31 Dec. 1882, in Daunt, *Life*, 380; Daunt to Lecky,? June 1882, T.C.D., Lecky correspondence, no. 262.
47. Andrew Dunlop, *Fifty Years of Irish Journalism* (Dublin 1911), 135-6, 269, 277; I.L.P.U., *The Real Dangers of Home Rule*, 3rd ed. (Dublin/London 1887), 11-12; William O'Brien, *'The Party': Who They Are and What They Did* (Dublin 1917), 5-6.
48. Karl Deutsch, *Nationalism and Social Communication: An Enquiry into the Foundations of Nationality*, 2nd ed. (Cambridge, Mass. 1966), 100; Earl of Courtown, 'The Celts and Teutons in Ireland', *National Review*, lx (1887), 91.
49. Report on National League by Inspector-General, R.I.C., 17 Jan. 1886; Parnell at Cork, 21 Jan. 1885, in *F.J.*, 22 Jan. 1885.

Chapter 2: Gladstone and the Liberal Conversion to Home Rule (pp 35-52)

1. The most famous statement of this interpretation of Gladstone's motives for adopting Home Rule is, of course, J. L. Hammond, *Gladstone and the Irish Nation* (London 1938). It has received influential endorsement by Philip Magnus, *Gladstone: A Biography*, 2nd ed. (London 1963). It is a view supported also by T. J. Dunne, 'The Political Ideology of Home Rule' (M.A. thesis, N.U.I. (U.C.C.), 1972), 153-9.
2. A. B. Cooke and John Vincent, *The Governing Passion: Cabinet Government and Party Politics in Britain, 1885-6* (Brighton 1974). See also John Vincent's Raleigh lecture, *Gladstone and Ireland* (Oxford 1978).
3. Gladstone in Midlothian, 9 Nov. 1885, in John Morley, *The Life of William Ewart Gladstone*, 2nd ed. (London 1911), iii, 179.
4. Hammond, *Gladstone*, 401; Cooke and Vincent, *Governing Passion*, 52; Herbert Gladstone, *After Thirty Years* (London 1928), 282; Letter of Lee Warner to *The Times*, 10 Oct. 1913, quoted in Michael McDonagh, *The Life of William O'Brien* (London 1928), 81.
5. See F. W. Hirst, 'Mr Gladstone and Home Rule, 1885-92' in Sir Wemyss Reid (ed.), *The Life of William Ewart Gladstone* (London 1899), 699. Similarly, Justin McCarthy, who was as close to Gladstone as it was possible for a member of the Parnellite party to be, dismissed the idea that Gladstone had made a sudden conversion to Home Rule. See McCarthy, *Reminiscences* (London 1899), ii, 456-7.
6. W. E. Gladstone, 'History of an Idea — Why I Became a Home Ruler' in O'Connor and McWade, *Gladstone–Parnell*, 824-5.
7. Morley, *Gladstone*, iii, 220.
8. Lord Selborne, *Memorials: Part 2, Personal and Political, 1865-95* (London 1898), ii, 194-5.
9. Gladstone to Rosebery, 13 Nov. 1885, in Morley, *Gladstone*, iii, 181; H. Gladstone, *After Thirty Years*, 287; Morley, *Gladstone*, iii, 175.
10. Bryce, 'Irish Opinions on the Irish Problem', 11 Dec. 1885, G.P. 44700.
11. Gladstone to Grosvenor, 7 Jan. 1886, G.P. 56447.
12. Hammond, *Gladstone*, 521; Cooke and Vincent, *Governing Passion*, 317 (Vincent in *Gladstone and Ire.*, 220, accords more importance to this fear but regards it as unduly alarmist); O'Brien, *Parnell and his Party*, 162.
13. Hamilton to Herbert and W. E. Gladstone, 14 Jan. 1886, G.P. 56447

(Hamilton also informed the leading Conservative, W. H. Smith, that Ireland was 'in a state of revolution' (L. P. Curtis, jr, *Coercion and Conciliation in Ireland, 1880-92: A Study in Conservative Unionism* (Princeton/London 1963), 96)); Labouchere to Chamberlain, 24 Dec. 1885, in Algar Thorold, *The Life of Henry Labouchere* (London 1913), 261; Healy to Labouchere, 'Xmas' 1885, ibid., 263-4.

14. *Earl Cowper, K.G.: Memoir by his Wife* (London 1913), 622; Cooke and Vincent, *Governing Passion*, 53.

15. For the development of the movement see files of *Tuam News* for Jan. 1886; Police report from Tralee, marked 'Confidential', 20 Jan. 1886, S.P.O., C.S.O., R.P., 1886/1699.

16. *Times*, 13 Mar. 1886 (When questioned in the Commons in March 1886 (*Hansard 3*, ccciii, 979 (16 Mar. 1886)) as to what action the government was taking to deal with the House League, Gladstone said that 'at present' it was not causing 'great or general alarm'); Balfour to the press, 5 July 1886, quoted in A. J. Balfour, *Chapters of Autobiography*, ed. Blanche Dugdale (London 1930), 211-12, Gladstone also expressed similar fears to Lord Hartington. See Morley, *Gladstone*, iii, 199-200.

17. Gladstone to Balfour, 23 Dec. 1885, B.L., Balfour papers, Add. MS 49682; H. Gladstone, *After Thirty Years*, 397-8; Gladstone to Harcourt, 12 Feb. 1886, G.P. 44200. See also Morley, *Gladstone*, iii, 225: 'Social order in Ireland was in a profoundly unsatisfactory state. *That fact was the starting-point of the reversal of policy which the government had come into existence to carry out* [my italics].'

18. Healy to Labouchere, 23 Dec. 1885, in Thorold, *Labouchere*, 258-9; Letter marked 'Private', from Davitt to Labouchere, 29 Jan. 1886, G.P. 44494.

19. Gladstone, 'History of an Idea', 842; *Hansard 3*, ccciii, 979 (16 Mar. 1886).

20. See Arthur Ponsonby, *Henry Ponsonby: Queen Victoria's Private Secretary: His Life from his Letters* (London 1942), 199.

21. Hammond, *Gladstone*, 405; K. O'Shea to Gladstone, 30 Jan. 1886, G.P. 44269.

22. Stuart to Gladstone, 30 Jan. 1886, G.P. 44494; Midleton to Gladstone, 17 Feb. 1886, ibid.; Webber to Gladstone, 18 Feb. 1886, ibid.; Powerscourt to Gladstone, 19 Feb. 1886, ibid.; Parnell to K. O'Shea, 6 Jan. 1886, G.P. 44269.

23. Hartington to Gladstone, enclosing Currey's reports of meetings with Irish landlords, 11 Mar. 1886, G.P. 56447.

24. Peter Marshall, 'The Imperial Factor in Liberal Decline, 1880-85' in J. E. Flint and Glyndwr Williams (ed.), *Perspectives of Empire* (London 1972), 135.

25. R. C. K. Ensor, 'Some Political and Economic Interactions in Late Victorian England', *R. Hist. Soc. Trans.*, 4th series, xxxi (1949), 27 (However, for a revisionist work which argues that the positions Liberals took on the Home Rule question were unrelated to their social status see W. C. Lubenow, 'Irish Home Rule and the Social Basis of the Great Separation in the Liberal Party in 1886', *Hist. Jn.*, 28, no. 1 (1985), 125-42); Morley, *Gladstone*, iii, 198; Morley, *Recollections*, i, 219; H. A. L. Fisher, *James Bryce* (London 1927), i, 210; A. G. Gardiner, *The Life of Sir William*

Harcourt (London 1925), i, 580. For an excellent recent discussion of the effect of Gladstone's Home Rule policy on those intellectuals who deserted the Liberal Party in 1886 see Tom Dunne, '*La trahison des clercs*: British Intellectuals and the First Home Rule Crisis', *I.H.S.*, xxiii, no. 90 (Nov. 1982), 134-73.

26. Morley at Chelmsford, in *Times*, 8 Jan. 1886 (For a fuller description of Morley's Home Rule views see D. A. Hamer, *John Morley: Liberal Intellectual in Politics* (Oxford 1968), ch. 12); Childers's objections regarding powers of the Irish parliament (p. 69 below): Fisher, *Bryce*, i, 221; Christopher Harvie, 'Ideology and Home Rule: James Bryce, A. V. Dicey and Ireland, 1880-87', *E.H.R.*, xci, no. 359 (Apr. 1976), 313; James Bryce, 'How We Became Home Rulers' in Bryce (ed.), *Handbook of Home Rule* (London 1887), 50; Ponsonby, *Henry Ponsonby*, 209.

27. Morley, *Gladstone*, iii, 215; R. A. Hufford, 'An Analysis and Criticism of the Rhetoric of the Debates on the Irish Home Rule Bill of 1886' (M.A. thesis, University of Durham, 1958), 293, 295, 299; Undated newspaper cutting entitled 'The Essential Basis of the Irish Question' in vol. 2 of letter cuttings and speeches, N.L.I., Webb papers, MS 1746.

28. *P.M.G.*, 28 Apr., 1, 5, 7 May 1886. Editorially committed to imperial federation, this newspaper gave qualified support to the Home Rule cause provided Ireland continued to be represented at Westminster.

29. Ibid., 3 May 1886.

Chapter 3: The Home Rule Scheme of 1886 (pp 53-94)
1. Labouchere to Chamberlain, 18 Oct. 1885, describing the contents of a letter he had received from T. M. Healy regarding the kind of Home Rule scheme that could satisfy the Parnellite party, in Thorold, *Labouchere*, 237.
2. Lyons, *Parnell*, 294-7; A. J. Kettle, *Material for Victory*, ed. L. J. Kettle (Dublin 1958), 63-4; K. O'Shea to Gladstone, 14 Dec. 1885, G.P. 44260; Davitt to Labouchere, 9 Oct. 1885, in Thorold, *Labouchere*, 234; Davitt, *Leaves from a Prison Diary* (London 1885), 349-50.
3. Parnell to E. D. Gray, 24 Dec. 1885, in Alan O'Day, *Parnell and the First Home Rule Episode, 1884-7* (Dublin 1986), 130-1; O'Brien, *Parnell*, 374; R. B. O'Brien, 'Federal Union with Ireland', *N.C.*, xix (Jan. 1886), 35-8 (O'Brien's scheme shared many similarities with the federal plan devised by Isaac Butt in the 1870s; for the latter see David Thornley, *Isaac Butt and Home Rule* (London 1964), 98-102).
4. Gladstone to K. O'Shea, 29 Jan. 1886, in Lyons, *Parnell*, 342; Morley, *Gladstone*, iii, 229. Parnell, in fact, was to inform Gladstone at the only meeting he was to have with him during the 1886 Home Rule crisis that the bill might eventually be rejected by Nationalists on the finance question. See ibid., 231.
5. Harcourt to Gladstone, 31 Jan. 1886, G.P. 44200; Hamilton diary, 9 Mar. 1886, G.P. 48643. For more on Harcourt's attitude to Home Rule see Cooke and Vincent, *Governing Passion*, 353-4.
6. Morley, *Gladstone*, iii, 225.
7. Gladstone in the Commons, 13 Apr. 1886, in A. W. Hutton and H. J. Cohen (ed.), *The Speeches of W. E. Gladstone, 1886-8* (London 1902), 13;

Hammond, *Gladstone*, 56; Gladstone in the Commons, 7 June 1886, in Hutton and Cohen (ed.), op. cit., 127.

8. Gladstone in the Commons, 8 Apr. 1886, in Hutton and Cohen (ed.) *Gladstone's Speeches, 1886-8*, 13-15; ibid., 10 May 1886, 89-90.

9. Lord Thring, 'Home Rule and Imperial Unity' in Bryce (ed.), *Handbook*, 76; Gladstone in the Commons, 10 May 1886, in Hutton and Cohen (ed.), *Gladstone's Speeches, 1886-8*, 58; Lord Aberdeen on Gladstone, quoted in Sir Wemyss Reid, 'Mr Gladstone's Character and Career: A General Appreciation' in Reid (ed.), *Life of Gladstone*, 25-6. See also Selborne, *Memorials*, ii, 352.

10. Gladstone to Harcourt, 12 Feb. 1886, G.P. 44200; Gladstone's cabinet memo, 14 Mar. 1886, G.P. 44647; Morley, *Gladstone*, iii, 225; Gladstone, Irish government draft bill: two revised copies, 31 Mar. 1886, P.R.O., Cab. 37/18, no. 34; Cooke and Vincent, *Governing Passion*, 395-6; Morley, *Gladstone*, iii, 230; Hamilton diary, 26 Mar. 1886, H.P. 48643.

11. *A Bill to Amend the Provision for the Future Government of Ireland*, 3, H.C. 1886 (181), ii, 467 (hereafter cited as *Govt of Ire. Bill*); Gladstone in the Commons, 8 Apr. 1886, in Hutton and Cohen (ed.), *Gladstone's Speeches, 1886-8*, 35.

12. Lord Thring, 'The Irish Government and Land Bills' in Bryce (ed.), *Handbook*, 84.

13. J. H. Morgan, 'The Constitution: A Commentary' in Morgan (ed.), *The New Irish Constitution: An Exposition and Some Arguments* (London 1912), 32-3; Patrick Buckland, *Irish Unionism, 1: The Anglo-Irish and the New Ireland, 1885-1922* (Dublin 1972), 309-12.

14. Hamilton diary, 15 Feb. 1886, H.P. 48644; Lord Welby, 'Financial Relations', in Morgan, *New Ir. Constitution*, 132; Gladstone to Lord Granville, 15 Feb. 1886, in *The Political Correspondence of Mr Gladstone and Lord Granville, 1876-86*, ed. Agatha Ramm (Oxford 1962), ii, 431. Although having a lifelong interest in colonial affairs, Gladstone had only once held the post of Colonial Secretary, briefly in 1845-6. See Morley, *Gladstone*, iii, 466.

15. Gladstone's cabinet memo, 29 Mar. 1886, G.P. 44647; *Govt of Ire. Bill*, 467.

16. Thring, 'Ir. Govt and Land Bills', 88-90; *Govt of Ire. Bill*, 469-70.

17. *Govt of Ire. Bill*, 467-8; Thring, 'Ir. Govt and Land Bills', 89; Gladstone in the Commons, 10 May 1886, in Hutton and Cohen (ed.), *Gladstone's Speeches, 1886-8*. 94-5. Gladstone, though, did not envisage that the two orders would reflect rigidly opposed political views. In a letter to John Morley, referring apparently to Parnellite queries on the representation of the legislative body, he wrote: 'Surely it cannot be thought that a constituency of £25 occupiers could return a homogeneous body of Tories; and I should have thought one-fifth an excessive estimate of the anti-Nationalists on the other side to be chosen by the popular electorate.' See Gladstone to Morley, 22 Mar. 1886, G.P. 44255.

18. *Hansard 3*, ccciv, 1794 (16 Apr. 1886); Dunne, 'Political Ideology of Home Rule', 209-10; C.E. Lewis, *Hansard 3*, cccv, 675 (10 May 1886); Gladstone in the Commons, 10 May 1888, in Hutton and Cohen (ed.), *Gladstone's Speeches, 1886-8*, 96; *Daily News* on Gladstone's Home Rule bill, quoted in *P.M.G.*, 9

Apr. 1886; *Govt of Ire. Bill*, 468-9.

19. Harcourt to Gladstone, 7 Mar. 1886, G.P. 44200; Gladstone in the Commons, 8 Apr. 1886, in Hutton and Cohen (ed.), *Gladstone's Speeches, 1886-8*, 32-3. In his explanation of the Home Rule scheme in 1887 Lord Thring explicitly stated that a peer taking his place in the Irish assembly would 'cease to sit in the English parliament'. See Thring, 'Ir. Govt and Land Bills', 89.

20. K. O'Shea to Gladstone, 6 Jan. 1886, G.P. 44269; Hartington to Gladstone, 11 Mar. 1886, G.P. 56447.

21. Central News Agency report, quoted in *F.J.*, 11 Jan. 1886; Gladstone to Argyll, 27 Jan. 1886, G.P. 56447; Hamilton diary, 26 Mar. 1886, H.P. 48643.

22. Derby's diary entry, quoted in Vincent, *Gladstone and Ire.*, 223; Lord Kilbracken, *Reminiscences* (London 1931), 133; Selborne, *Memorials*, ii, 353.

23. *Govt of Ire. Bill*, 465-6; Thring, 'Ir. Govt and Land Bills', 85.

24. *Govt of Ire. Bill*, 466; Thring, 'Ir. Govt and Land Bills', 86; *Govt of Ire. Bill*, 477, 480-1; Gladstone in the Commons, 13 Apr. 1886, in Hutton and Cohen (ed.), *Gladstone's Speeches, 1886-8*, 54; Gladstone to Morley, 22 Mar. 1886, G.P. 44255; Spencer Childers, *The Life and Correspondence of H. C. E. Childers, 1827-86* (London 1901), ii, 249; Cooke and Vincent, *Governing Passion*, 394, 397-8. Gladstone's willingness to give the Irish the power to impose protective tariffs on British goods strongly influenced Joseph Chamberlain's decision to withdraw from the government. See Chamberlain, *A Political Memoir, 1880-92*, ed. C. H. D. Howard (London 1953), 198-9.

25. *Govt of Ire. Bill*, 471-7; *Sale and Purchase of Land (Ireland) Bill*, i, H.C. 1886 (193), v, 395-9 (hereafter cited as *Land Purchase Bill*); Morley, *Gladstone*, iii, 231.

26. McKenna to Redmond, 30 July 1893, N.L.I., Redmond papers, MS 15203(1); Thomas Lough, *England's Wealth, Ireland's Poverty* (London 1896), 7; Robert Giffen, 'The Economic Value of Ireland to Great Britain', *N.C.*, xix (Mar. 1886), 335, 337.

27. Welby, 'Financial Relations', 127. Gladstone originally proposed an Irish contribution of one-twelfth of imperial expenditure; however, this was argued against as being too high by Welby and Hamilton in a paper which had an important influence on the debate about Home Rule finance. See paper entitled 'Irish Finance', 17 Feb. 1886, G.P. 44771.

28. Gladstone in the Commons, 8 Apr. 1886, in Hutton and Cohen (ed.), *Gladstone's Speeches, 1886-8*, 40-1 (Thus it was not the case that Ireland was 'being asked to sign a blank cheque for an amount indefinitely expandable by wartime inflation', as has recently been implied by F. S. L. Lyons *(Parnell*, 344)); *Land Purchase Bill*, 394-5; Morley, *Gladstone*, iii, 459.

29. Gladstone in the Commons, 8 Apr. 1886, in Hutton and Cohen (ed.), *Gladstone's Speeches, 1886-8*, 44-6; Morley, *Gladstone*, iii, 459; Hamilton diary, 30 Mar. 1886, H.P. 48643.

30. Gladstone in the Commons, 8 Apr. 1886, in Hutton and Cohen (ed.), *Gladstone's Speeches, 1886-8*, 42-4; Hamilton diary, 30 Mar. 1886, H. P. 48643.

31. Home Ruler and Unionist criticism of financial provisions of Home Rule bill (ch. 4 below); Welby, 'Financial Relations', 129.

32. Sexton on Home Rule finance (p. 262 below); Welby, 'Financial Relations', 133: Sexton (p. 261 below); *Govt of Ire. Bill*, 470; Thring, 'Ir. Govt and Land Bills', 92-3.

33. Harcourt, Memorandum on the financial arrangement proposed in the Government of Ireland Bill, 16 Jan. 1893, P.R.O., Cab. 37/33, no. 4, 4-5. See also Vernon Bogdanor, *Devolution* (Oxford 1979), 28-9; R. J. Lawrence, *The Government of Northern Ireland: Public Finance and Public Services, 1921-64* (Oxford 1965), 11-12.

34. Morley to Gladstone, 2 Feb. 1886, G.P. 44255; Harcourt to Gladstone, 7 Mar. 1886, G.P. 44200; Ramm (ed.), *Gladstone-Granville Correspondence*, ii, 441 n. 4; Gladstone to Morley, 2 Feb. 1886, G.P. 44255; J. L. Garvin, *The Life of Joseph Chamberlain* (London 1933), ii, 192; Chamberlain, *Political Memoir*, 198-9; Hamilton diary, 26 Mar. 1886, H.P. 48643; *P.M.G.*, 9 Apr. 1886.

35. Gladstone in the Commons, 8 Apr. 1886, in Hutton and Cohen (ed.), *Gladstone's Speeches, 1886-8*, 21-2.

36. Ibid., 10 May 1886, 88; Morley to Gladstone, 19 Apr. 1886, G. P. 44255; Gladstone to Granville, 30 Apr. 1886, in Ramm (ed.), *Gladstone-Granville Correspondence*, ii, 445; *Govt of Ire. Bill*, clause 9, 484-5; Gladstone, 'Memorandum on Bill for Irish Government: *2nd Reading Division*', 5 May 1886, reproduced in Hammond, *Gladstone*, 507.

37. Hammond, *Gladstone*, 507-10.

38. Ibid., 535; Hutton and Cohen (ed.), *Gladstone's Speeches, 1886-8*, 92-4; Bogdanor, *Devolution*, 23.

39. Chamberlain, *Political Memoir*, 210-17; Hammond, *Gladstone*, 525-31. Chamberlain had wanted permanent Irish representation at Westminster.

40. Gladstone introducing the land purchase bill (*Hansard 3*, ccciv, 1779-80 (16 Apr. 1886)); *Return of Outrages Specially Reported ... throughout Ireland ... 1869-96*, S.P.O., C.S.O., R.P., 1897/3476; Gladstone to Harcourt, 12 Feb. 1886, G.P. 44200.

41. Thring, 'Home Rule and Imperial Unity', 75-6; Hamilton diary, 19 Mar. 1886, H.P. 48643; *Hansard 3*, ccciv, 1800 (16 Apr. 1886).

42. Vincent, *Gladstone and Ire.*, 227-9; Gladstone to Morley, 2 Feb. 1886, G.P. 44255; Morley, *Gladstone*, iii, 224. Parnell also wanted the land and autonomy issues tackled together. See Labouchere to H. Gladstone, 24, 26 Jan. 1886, B.L., Viscount Gladstone papers, Add. MS 46015.

43. Paper entitled 'Irish Land Purchase', 11 Mar. 1886, P.R.O. Cab. 37/18, no. 29, 1-3; *Land Purchase Bill*, 410-11; Chamberlain's memo of cabinet meeting, quoted in Garvin, *Chamberlain*, ii, 186.

44. Hamilton diary, 9 Mar. 1886, H.P. 48643; Harcourt to Gladstone, 7 Mar. 1886, G.P. 44200. Noting his tendency to give 'undue weight' to Labouchere's views, Hamilton described Gladstone as 'not a little' impressed by his letter (Hamilton diary, 23 Mar. 1886, H.P. 48643).

45. Robert Taylor, *Lord Salisbury* (London 1975), 92; B. L. Solow, *The Land Question and the Irish Economy, 1870-1903* (Cambridge, Mass. 1971), 187-8; Vincent, *Gladstone and Ire.*, 227; I.L.P.U., *A Critical Analysis of the Sale and*

Purchase of Land (Ireland) Bill (Dublin/London [1886]), passim. On the question of whether Gladstone's Home Rule scheme could have been enacted, Vincent's argument that there 'was no conceivable situation in the 1880s and 1890s in which the House of Lords would have passed a Gladstonian Home Rule bill' (*Gladstone and Ire.*, 224) is highly debatable. Indeed, Lord Salisbury, in a signed article in the *National Review* (Nov. 1892), accepted that the House of Lords would be bound to accept any measure from the lower house if the Commons enjoyed the obvious support of the people expressed at a general election. In this respect it is worth noting that his nephew A. J. Balfour expressed the belief at this time that were the House of Lords to reject his Home Rule bill, Gladstone would call a general election on the issue and return with a massive majority to enact it. See Taylor, *Salisbury*, 149; p. 282 below.

46. Gladstone's cabinet memo, 31 May 1886, G.P. 44647.
47. Gladstone to Harcourt, 12 Feb. 1886, G.P. 44200.
48. In 1885-6 the value of Irish agricultural output fell to £31,921,000, or 21 per cent below the 1881 figure of £40,374,000. See Solow, *Land Question*, 71-2; Robert Giffen, 'Home Rule and the Irish Landlords', reproduced in *F. J.*, 11 Jan. 1886.
49. Michael Davitt, 'Mr Giffen's Proposed Solution of the Irish Question', *C.R.*, xlix (Apr. 1886), 501-2.
50. Giffen's article in *The Statist* (6 Feb. 1886), quoted at length in Davitt, *Fall of Feudalism*, 510-12; John Dillon's memo of a conversation with Gladstone, 7 Mar. 1892, T.C.D., Dillon papers, MS 6296/27.
51. Currey to Hartington, 10, 13 Mar. 1886, G.P. 56447; Gladstone to Harcourt, 12 Feb. 1886, G.P. 44200; Hamilton diary, 24 Feb. 1886, H.P. 48643; ibid., 25 Feb. 1997. For the provisions to be made for determining the standard rental to be used as the basis of land sales on estates where no judicial rent existed see Gladstone's speech introducing the land purchase bill (*Hansard 3*, ccciv, 1798 (16 Apr. 1886)).
52. Gladstone's cabinet memo, 20 Mar. 1886, G.P. 44647; Granville to Gladstone, 21 Mar. 1886, in Ramm (ed.), *Gladstone–Granville Correspondence*, ii, 436; Spencer's minute to the memo circulated by Gladstone on 20 Mar. 1886, G.P. 44647; Morley's minute, ibid.; Gladstone to Granville, 22 Mar. 1886, in Ramm (ed.), op. cit., 437; Hamilton diary, 26 Mar. 1886, H.P. 48643; Gladstone's cabinet memo, 14 Apr. 1886, G.P. 44647; Gladstone introducing the land purchase bill (*Hansard 3*, ccciv, 1801 (16 Apr. 1886)).
53. While twenty years' purchase was to be the norm, Gladstone proposed that it could either be raised or reduced depending on the condit.on of an estate (*Hansard 3*, ccciv, 1799-1800 (16 Apr. 1886)); *Land Purchase Bill*, 384-5; I.L.P.U., *Analysis of the Land Purchase Bill*, 19 (On holdings valued above £4 it was usual for the tenant to share the payment of the poor rate with the landlord; however, the tenants, on becoming owners, would be liable for the total payment); *Land Purchase Bill*, 410-11 (The 'state authority' would be a body appointed by the Irish government to hold land and collect rents); Thring, 'Ir. Govt and Land Bills', 101-2; Caird's article and editorial in *The Times*, 22 Mar. 1886.

54. *Land Purchase Bill*, 387; Thring, 'Ir. Govt and Land Bills', 100; Gladstone's cabinet memo [early Mar. 1886], G.P. 44647; Hamilton diary, 12, 15 Mar. 1886, H.P. 48643; Trevelyan's views as described ibid., 20 Mar. 1886; Robert Hamilton's views as described ibid., 23 Mar. 1886; Chamberlain to Gladstone, 15 Mar, 1886, in Chamberlain, *Political Memoir,* 195-6. John Morley was to argue that he and Lord Spencer were the only members of Gladstone's cabinet wholeheartedly in favour of the land purchase scheme (*Gladstone,* iii, 227-8).

55. Chamberlain, 'Land Purchase', 15 Feb. 1886, P.R.O., Cab. 37/18, no. 22, 3; Gladstone introducing the land purchase bill (*Hansard 3*, ccciv, 1797-8 (16 Apr. 1886)); Morley, *Gladstone,* iii, 246.

56. Morley, *Gladstone,* iii, 246, 250; Selborne, *Memorials,* ii, 224.

Chapter 4: Political Opinion and the Home Rule Scheme: The Nationalist and Unionist Reaction (pp 95-122)

1. Davitt's presence at this meeting is denied by Healy. However, William O'Brien claims he was present, and Davitt writes of it as one who was there. See O'Brien, *Parnell and his Party,* 185; Davitt, *Fall of Feudalism,* 489.

2. *The Parnellite Split, or The Disruption of the Irish Parliamentary Party, reprinted from 'The Times'* (London 1891), 135-6, 146-7.

3. Morley, *Gladstone,* iii, 230; T. P. O'Connor, *Charles Stewart Parnell: A Memory* (London [1892]), 182; O'Brien's article on Irish Home Rule demands (pp 54-5 above); *B.N.L.*, 6 Jan. 1886.

4. Kettle, *Material for Victory,* facsimile of a letter between pp 82-3 (Parnell communicated the same view to Justin McCarthy (Justin McCarthy and Mrs Campbell Praed, *Our Book of Memories* (London 1912), 34)); Davitt, *Fall of Feudalism,* 489-90; *The Parnellite Split,* 145-6; O'Brien, *Parnell,* 406; McCarthy, *Story of an Irishman,* 287; O'Brien, *Parnell and his Party,* 186. Parnell's willingness to drop the land bill completely at this stage would seem to contradict the rather Machiavellian view recently argued (Paul Bew, *C. S. Parnell* (Dublin 1980), 83-4) that he used the Home Rule bill as bait to foist the land bill on his party.

5. *Hansard 3*, ccciv, 1130-2 (8 Apr. 1886), Parnell's anxiety on the financial clauses was heightened on the morning of 8 April when *The Times* carried a three-column report on the financial resources of Ireland. This provoked him to make a last-minute attempt to have Ireland's imperial contribution reduced from one-fifteenth to one-twentieth. See Cooke and Vincent, *Governing Passion,* 402.

6. *Hansard 3*, ccciv, 1132 (8 Apr. 1886).

7. Trevelyan's speech on the Home Rule bill (pp 116-17 below); *Hansard 3*, ccciv, 1132-4 (8 Apr. 1886). Sir J. N. McKenna informed Redmond in 1894 that Parnell was convinced that if the 1886 Home Rule bill had gone into committee, Gladstone would have included a clause, drawn up by McKenna, intended to limit the 'wholesale absorption of Irish revenues' proposed in the bill. See McKenna to Redmond, 25 Nov. 1894, N.L.I., Redmond papers, MS 15203(7).

8. Report of Davitt's speech on the Home Rule bill at Glasgow, in *Western News,* 24 Apr. 1886; *Times,* 17 Apr. 1886; O'Brien, *Parnell,* 396.

9. Hufford, 'Analysis of the Debates on the Home Rule Bill', 188; *Hansard 3*, cccv, 626-7 (10 May 1886).

10. *The Parnellite Split*, 147; *Hansard 3*, cccv, 960 (13 May 1886); Sullivan, ibid., 1348-9 (18 May 1886); McCarthy, ibid., 1667-79 (21 May 1886); Healy, ibid., cccvi, 112, 126 (25 May 1886); Sexton, ibid., 715 (1 June 1886); O'Connor, ibid., 848-9 (3 June 1886); Sir Henry James, ibid., cccv, 929 (13 May 1886); Parnell, ibid., cccvi, 1171-4 (7 June 1886).

11. Only John Dillon and J. F. X. O'Brien stressed the necessity of amending the bill on the lines of Parnell's speech on 8 April (*Hansard 3*, cccv, 997 (13 May 1886); ibid., 1706-7 (21 May 1886)); Morley, *Gladstone*, iii, 253-4; O'Connor, *Parnell*, 183; Morley, op. cit., iii, 252; Lyons, *Parnell*, 347.

12. It is interesting to note that neither Parnell nor John Dillon believed that Gladstone took up the Home Rule question primarily out of a sense of justice to Ireland. Both were of the view that Gladstone simply realised that the Irish question had to be dealt with, and was tackling it now on the best possible terms for England and the empire. See Kettle, *Material for Victory*, 83; Blunt, *Land War*, 139.

13. *Hansard 3*, cccvi, 77-8 (25 May 1886); Redmond, ibid., cccv, 963 (13 May 1886); ibid., 961-73 (10 May 1886); Dillon, ibid., 1000-8; T. D. Sullivan, ibid., 1350-1 (18 May 1886); J. F. X. O'Brien, ibid., 1706-14 (21 May 1886); Sexton, ibid., cccvi, 719-24 (25 May 1886).

14. Lord Fitzmaurice, 'Ireland, 1782 and 1912' in Morgan (ed.), *New Ir. Constitution*, 280.

15. Gladstone on the membership of the Home Rule parliament (pp 64-5 above); Blunt, *Land War*, 256-7; T. W. Moody, 'Michael Davitt' in J. W. Boyle (ed.), *Leaders and Workers* (Cork [1967]), 54; Blunt, op. cit., 322.

16. On Davitt's political views, especially his democratic vision of Ireland, see Moody, *Davitt and Ir. Revolution*, 555-7; Blunt, *Land War*, 311; McDonagh, *Home Rule Movement*, 26-7. Although Davitt appears not to have recognised at this time the role of nationalist agitation in revolutionising the consciousness of the farming population, he clearly acknowledged it later *(Fall of Feudalism*, 466).

17. Kettle, *Material for Victory*, 74; O'Day, *Eng. Face of Ir. Nationalism*, 26; O'Brien, *Parnell and his Party*, 33. O'Brien shows that of the Home Rule Party elected in 1880, only 5 were landowners of estates over 1,000 acres, and only 2 were from the farmer, small shopkeeper and wage-earning class.

18. *P.M.G.*, 10 Apr. 1886; Duffy to O'Brien, 26 Dec. 1881, N.L.I., O'Brien papers, MS 13424; O'Brien, *Parnell and his Party*, 187.

19. P. J. Walsh, *William J. Walsh: Archbishop of Dublin* (London 1928), 207-8; O'Brien, *Parnell and his Party*, 187; Blunt, *Land War*, 481.

20. Blunt, *Land War*, 481; Lord and Lady Aberdeen, *'We Twa': Reminiscences*, 2nd ed. (London 1927), i, 253, 255-63, ii, 190-1; McDonagh, *Life of William O'Brien*, 85.

21. *U.I.*, 17 Apr. 1886.

22. Ibid., 24 Apr. 1886; *F.J.*, 9 Apr. 1886.

23. *F.J.*, 20 Apr. 1886.

24. *Tuam Herald*, 2 Jan. 1886; *Western News*, 29 May 1886; *Connaught Telegraph*, 10 Apr. 1886.

25. *Limerick Chronicle*, 10 Apr. 1886; Davitt, *Fall of Feudalism*, 164. During the Cowper commission inquiry in October 1886 James Hamilton, Recorder of Cork, described how tenants on land owned by Lord Cunningham had been willing to pay 14 to 15 years' purchase before the introduction of the Home Rule bill, but only 6 to 7 years' purchase thereafter. G. A. Adamson, a land valuer under the Ashbourne act, gave similar evidence. See *Report of the Royal Commission on the Land Law (Ireland) Act, 1881, and the Purchase of Land (Ireland) Act, 1885*, Vol. II: *Minutes of Evidence and Appendices*, 87, 567 [C 4969-2], H.C. 1887, xxvi, 119, 597.

26. *Roscommon Herald*, 10 Apr. 1886; Appendix 1, p. 294 below. Of Ulster papers, 3 out of 4 gave the bill unqualified praise; of Leinster papers, 6 out of 8 accepted it subject to the modifications outlined by Parnell on 8 April.

27. For a full report on the committee's recommendations see *Ballymoney Free Press*, 29 Apr. 1886. On the Irish Protestant Home Rule Association see pp 190-1 below.

28. McCarthy, *Ir. Revolution*, 486-7. For another contemporary view corroborating McCarthy's see Sir Henry Robinson, *Memories: Wise and Otherwise* (London 1923), 86-7. For evidence of Irish opinion hardening against the bill as the Home Rule debate progressed see *Connaught Telegraph* (10 Apr., 12 June 1886): giving the bill unqualified praise in April, it reacted to its defeat in June by declaring that its loss 'need not be much deplored', since 'however well intended', it 'could scarcely be called a solution to the Irish difficulty'.

29. Kettle, *Material for Victory*, 71; Ribblesdale, 'A Railway Journey with Mr Parnell', *N.C.*, xxx (Dec. 1891), 969-74.

30. *Hansard 3*, ccciv, 116-19 (8 Apr. 1886).

31. Ibid., 120-1.

32. Ibid., 1330-2, 1338 (12 Apr. 1886). See also G. J. Goschen, ibid., 1467-82 (13 Apr. 1886).

33. [L. J. Jennings], 'Mr Gladstone and Ireland', *Quarterly Review*, clxiii (July 1886), 282; *Hansard 3*, ccciv, 1523-36 (13 Apr. 1886).

34. *Hansard 3*, ccciv, 1806 (16 Apr. 1886); I.L.P.U., *Analysis of the Land Purchase Bill*, passim. The charge that Gladstone distrusted the Irish would seem to have some element of truth in it. See his comparison of the merits of his land bill of 1886 with the Ashbourne act of 1885 (p. 215 below).

35. E. Ashmead-Bartlett, *Hansard 3*, cccv, 642-3 (10 May 1886); S. Hoare, ibid., 634; James, ibid., 912-30 (13 May 1886); E. A. Leathem, ibid., 1013; Wolmer, ibid., 1251-2 (17 May 1886); McCarthy, *Ir. Revolution*, 481. See also parliamentary report in *F.J.*, 21 May 1886.

36. O'Brien, *Parnell*, 399-400. Bright had similarly expressed his views on Home Rule in a letter to Gladstone on 13 May 1886 (Morley, *Gladstone*, iii, 247-8).

37. *Hansard 3*, cccvi, 686-96 (1 June 1886): Garvin, *Chamberlain*, ii, 222, 226. For the use made of the Ulster issue by leading Unionists see G. O. Trevelyan, *Hansard 3*, ccciv, 1115 (8 Apr. 1886); Lord Randolph Churchill, ibid., 1329 (12 Apr. 1886); G. J. Goschen, ibid., 1473-5 (13 Apr. 1886); Lord Hartington, ibid., cccv, 616-17 (10 May 1886).

Chapter 5: The Ulster Question (1): The Parnellite and Gladstonian Views (pp 123-152)

1. Moody, *Davitt and Ir. Revolution*, 424, 433-4; Parnell's speech in Derry, 30 Aug. 1881, explaining the reasons for Nationalist intervention in the Tyrone contest in *Parnell's Speeches, Letters, and Public Addresses (out of Parliament) in the United Kingdom, 1879-88* (Dublin 1889), 151; R. W. Kirkpatrick, 'The Origins and Development of the Land War in Mid-Ulster, 1879-85' in F. S. L. Lyons and R. A. J. Hawkins (ed.), *Ireland under the Union: Varieties of Tension. Essays in Honour of T. W. Moody* (Oxford 1980), 232.

2. Paul Bew and Frank Wright, 'The Agrarian Opposition in Ulster Politics, 1848-87' in Samuel Clark and J. S. Donnelly, jr (ed.), *Irish Peasants: Violence and Political Unrest, 1780-1914* (Manchester 1983), 217; O'Kelly to John Devoy, 21 Sept, 1882, in *Devoy's Post-Bag 1871-1928*, ed. William O'Brien and Desmond Ryan (Dublin 1948-53), ii, 142-3; Kettle, *Material for Victory*, 52.

3. Kirkpatrick, 'Land War in Mid-Ulster', 232-3.

4. Parnell, *Hansard 3*, ccclxxxiv, 323 (5 Feb. 1884); J. A. Taylor (ed.), *The Rossmore Incident: An Account of the Various Nationalist and Anti-Nationalist Meetings, held in Ulster in the autumn of 1883* (Dublin 1884), 11. For Unionist views of the Rossmore incident see ibid., passim; Patrick Buckland, *Irish Unionism, 2: Ulster Unionism and the Origins of Northern Ireland, 1886-1922* (Dublin 1973), 2-5.

5. *Hansard 3*, ccclxxxiv, 324-5, 335-6 (5 Feb. 1884); Parnell on demise of Ulster Unionism, in O'Brien, *Parnell*, 285; Ribblesdale, 'Railway Journey with Mr Parnell', 971. On the social composition of the Orange movement see Aiken McClelland, 'The Later Orange Order' in T. D. Williams (ed.), *Secret Societies in Ireland* (Dublin 1973), 130-1. Among leading Unionists embarrassed by the Orangemen's reputation for violence and religious bigotry were Hugh de F. Montgomery, Lord Carnarvon, Lord Ashbourne, Sir Stafford Northcote and Robert Knox, Protestant Archbishop of Armagh. See Patrick Buckland (ed.), *Irish Unionism, 1885-1923: A Documentary History* (Belfast 1973), 103-5; Carnarvon and Ashbourne in O'Day, *Eng. Face of Ir. Nationalism*, 100-1; A. B. Cooke (ed.), 'A Conservative Leader in Ulster: Sir Stafford Northcote's Diary of a Visit to the Province, Oct. 1883', *R.I.A. Proc.*, lxxv, sect. C, no. 4 (1975), 79; Knox to Ashbourne [1886], in A. B. Cooke and A. P. W. Malcomson (comp.), *The Ashbourne Papers, 1869-1913: A Calendar of the Papers of Edward Gibson, 1st Lord Ashbourne* (Belfast 1974), 57.

6. *Parnell's Speeches*, 134; ibid., 84; Religious statistics for Fermanagh in W. E. Vaughan and A. J. Fitzpatrick, *Irish Historical Statistics: Population, 1821-1971* (Dublin 1978), 58; Nationalist views on Ulster Orangeism in *Sligo Champion*, 27 Mar. 1886; *Limerick Reporter*, 18 May 1886; *Clare Advertiser*, 11 June 1886. Of course, despite their derogatory view of Orangeism, Nationalists representing marginal seats, such as William O'Brien in South Tyrone, were not above appealing to 'the honest Orangemen of Ulster' at election time. See *Weekly Examiner*, 5 July 1886.

7. *Report of the Commissioners of Inquiry, 1886, respecting the Origins and Circumstances of the Riots in Belfast, in June, July, August and September 1886*, 11, 15 [C

4925], H.C. 1887, xvii, 11, 15; Nationalist press reactions to the Belfast riots, in *Kilkenny Journal*, 9 June 1886; *Wexford Express*, 12 June 1886; *Anglo-Celt*, 3 July 1886; *Cork Daily Herald*, 10, 17 July 1886; T. M. Healy, *Letters and Leaders of My Day* (London 1928), ii, 262. On the lack of social contact between the two communities in Ulster see the following: J. A. Rentoul, *Stray Thoughts and Memories* (Dublin 1920), 202; Anon., 'The Riots in Belfast', *F.R.*, xl (Sept. 1886), 276; J. N. Richardson to the Bessbrook Spinning Company, 22 Feb. 1892, P.R.O.N.I., Richardson papers, D2956/1.

8. Gladstone on Saunderson's support for southern Unionists (*Hansard 3*, cccvi, 1219-20 (7 June 1886)); T. P. O'Connor, ibid., 862-3 (3 June 1886); Dillon at Cork, in *Cork Daily Herald*, 17 June 1886; T. D. Sullivan, *Recollections of Troubled Times in Irish Politics* (Dublin 1905), 348, 352; McCarthy, *Reminiscences*, ii, 395 (In this work, written in the late 1890s, McCarthy went on to state that he did believe that Saunderson would fight for his cause, but this view contradicts his opinion in 1886 (*Hansard 3*, cccv, 1675-6 (21 May 1886)) and 1892 (*Black and White*, 25 June 1892) that Ulster Unionist threats of violence were mere bluff); *W.N.W.*, 3 July 1886.

9 Parnell to Harrington, 9 June, 1886, N.L.I., Harrington papers, MS 858 (1); *Belfast Morning News*, 9, 10 June 1884 (the latter issue published Parnell's letter to Harrington); Parnell to Harrington, 2 Jan. 1885, loc. cit.

10. O'Connor, *Parnell Movement*, 522; T. M. Healy (*A Word for Ireland* (London 1886), 155) and O'Brien (*Home-Ruler's Manual*, 109) on the demise of Ulster Orangeism. For statistics given in Table 2 — apart from population — see J. J. Clancy, *Ulster* (Dublin 1886), 21-2. For the number of Ulster branches of the National League in 1883 see p. 31 above. The population statistics given in Table 2 are taken from Vaughan and Fitzpatrick, *Pop.*, 10-13.

11. Spencer quoted in Jeremiah McVeagh, *What Orangeism Means: An Object Lesson in Irish Politics* (London 1893), 1. On Spencer's derogatory opinion of Ulster Unionists see also Thomas McKnight, *Ulster As It Is, or Twenty-Eight Years' Experience as an Irish Editor* (London 1896), ii, 183.

12. *P.M.G.*, 13 Apr. 1886.

13. *Times*, 28 Dec. 1885.

14. Hammond, *Gladstone*, 346, on Chamberlain and Ulster; Malcolm McColl, 'The "Unionist" Position' in Bryce (ed.), *Handbook*, 108; Chamberlain to Labouchere, 26 Dec. 1885, in Thorold, *Labouchere*, 272; Labouchere to Chamberlain, 17 May 1886, ibid., 314.

15. Fisher, *Bryce*, i, 202-3; Bryce, Memorandum on the Ulster problem, 12 Mar. 1886, G.P. 56447, ff 1-10. See also Bryce, 'Alternative Policies in Ireland', *N.C.*, xix (Feb. 1886), 326.

16. McCarthy, *Reminiscences*, ii, 234-6; Russell, Memorandum on the Ulster problem, 17 Mar. 1886, G.P. 56447, ff 1-12.

17. Russell, Memorandum on the Ulster problem, 17 Mar. 1886, G.P. 56447, f. 13; Walker to Spencer, 10 Mar. 1886, ibid. See Sexton's reply to E. S. W. de Cobain's reference to anti-Home Rule resolutions passed at the Liberal convention (*Hansard 3*, ccciv, 35-6 (26 Mar. 1886)).

18. Duffin to his father, 28 Mar. 1886, P.R.O.N.I., Duffin papers, Mic. 127/3D; McGeogh to Gladstone, 7 Apr. 1886, G.P. 44496; Leaflet entitled *Nationalist Hostility to the Ulster Linen Industry,* ibid. The charges made in this leaflet were refuted in parliament by E. D. Gray, the owner of the *Belfast Morning News,* in which the offending articles originally appeared (*Hansard 3*, cccvi, 565-70 (31 May 1886)).

19. O'Brien, *Parnell*, 366-7; *The Ulster Liberal Unionist Association: A Sketch of its History, 1885-1914,* intro. J. R. Fisher (Belfast 1914), 27; Hutton and Cohen (ed.), *Gladstone's Speeches, 1886-8,* 18.

20. Gladstone to Hugh Childers, 28 Sept. 1885, in Morley, *Gladstone,* iii, 178; Gladstone's cabinet memo, 14 Mar. 1886, G.P. 44647.

21. Bryce to John Bryce, 17 May 1886, in Fisher, *Bryce,* i, 202-3; Bryce's memo on Home Rule politics in the 1880s, quoted ibid., 218 (As regards 'safeguards', Robert McGeogh put Bryce's ideas — on his behalf — to a meeting of Ulster Liberals in early March 1886, but the meeting 'found it impossible to suggest adequate guarantees' and also 'found it inconceivable how one section of the population would have special treatment' (McGeogh to Bryce, 13 Mar. 1886, in B. M. Walker, 'Parliamentary Representation in Ulster, 1868-86' (Ph.D. thesis, University of Dublin, 1976), 533)); Hutton and Cohen (ed.), *Gladstone's Speeches, 1886-8,* 19. Significantly even the call Gladstone made in a letter to Lord de Vesci in February 1886 for information on Irish opinions on Home Rule produced no suggestions for dealing with the Ulster problem. Representative sections of this correspondence were published as a parliamentary paper. See *Copy of Selections from the Representations made to the First Lord of the Treasury by Public Bodies, in response to the Invitation for Free Communication of Views on Ireland...,* 1-75, H.C 1886 (117), lii, 773-848. Interestingly, though, Robert Giffen suggested separate autonomy as the most acceptable way of dealing with the Ulster problem (*Statist* article reproduced in *F.J.,* 11 Jan. 1886); Hutton and Cohen (ed.), op. cit., 107.

22. Hutton and Cohen (ed.), *Gladstone's Speeches, 1886-8,* 107; Parnell's views on Ulster (*Hansard 3*, cccvi, 1170-81 (7 June 1886)) endorsed by Gladstone (Hutton and Cohen (ed.), op. cit., 107); O'Brien and Gladstone, *Hansard 3,* cccv, 629 (10 May 1886).

23. Hutton and Cohen (ed.), *Gladstone's Speeches, 1886-8,* 82-3.

24. Dillon in *Cork Daily Herald,* 17 June 1886, and *Hansard 3,* cccv, 1003 (10 May 1886); O'Brien, ibid., 630-1 (10 May 1886).

25. R. B. O'Brien, *The Irish Land Question and English Public Opinion* (London 1880), 44-5.

26. Redmond, *Hansard 3,* cccv, 967-72 (13 May 1886); Sullivan, ibid., 1352-3 (18 May 1886); O'Brien, ibid., 1704 (21 May 1886); McCarthy, ibid., 1668, 1676.

27. Sexton, ibid., cccvi, 676 (1 June 1886).

28. Ibid., 717-19; Parnell, ibid., 1168-84 (7 June 1886); Lyons, *Parnell,* 350.

29. *Weekly Examiner,* 15 July 1886.

30. See, for example, Lawrence, *Govt of Northern Ire.,* 4.

31. O'Brien, *Land Question,* 41; M. S. Crawford, 'Experiences of an Irish Landowner', *C.R.,* lii (Aug. 1887), 263.

32. *Hansard 3*, ccciv, 1473-4 (13 Apr. 1886).
33. Flynn, ibid., cccvi, 81-2 (25 May 1886); Parnell, ibid., 1176-7 (7 June 1886); Healy, ibid., 121-2 (25 May 1886); Sexton, ibid., 717-18; Thomas Sinclair, 'Ulster: Facts and Figures: A Reply', *C.R.*, lxiv (July 1893), 37. Sinclair's argument was partially and grudgingly admitted by Healy (*A Word for Ire.*, 155-6). Following the receipt of more statistical information from Adam Duffin, Goschen, in reply, noted the problem of apportioning to each province the amount of business each company conducted there, as an obstacle to countering nationalist statistics (Goschen to Duffin, 20 Apr. 1886, P.R.O.N.I., Duffin papers, Mic. 127/5).
34. *Return Showing the Population of 1871 and 1881; the Number of Electors in 1871 and 1881; the Area in Square Miles; the Number of Members; the Amount of Property and Income Tax Charged for the Last Year for which the Returns are made up, in each County and Parliamentary Division of a County in the United Kingdom... and Similar Returns for the Cities and Boroughs of the United Kingdom*, 23, H.C. 1882 (149), lii, 422; *Return Showing the Population in each County, City, and Borough in Ireland returning Members to Parliament; the Acreage... Number of Registered Voters... Valuation of Rateable Property in each of the same; the Number of Land Tenements, etc., in each County...*, 1, H.C. 1884 (164), lxii, 223 (hereafter cited as *Return Showing the Pop. in Ire. etc., 1884*). Nationalist statistics were drawn partly from the 1881 census, but mostly from these two returns.
35. The figures were: loyalist counties, 727,587; nationalist counties, 711,061 (*Return Showing the Pop. in Ire. etc., 1884*, 222). The poverty of western Ulster was underlined by its constantly falling population. T. W. Moody has shown that between 1841 and 1951 it fell by 67 per cent (Moody, *The Ulster Question, 1603-1973* (Dublin/Cork 1973), 16).
36. Goschen to Duffin, 15 Apr. 1886, P.R.O.N.I., Duffin papers, Mic. 127/4.
37. T. W. Russell, 'The Actual and the Political Ireland', *N.C.*, xxvii (Jan. 1890), 89-101. This division had earlier been made by the Cowper commission.

Chapter 6: The Ulster Question (2): The Problem of National Identity and the Loyalist Reaction to Home Rule (pp 153-171)

1. Dr Byrne, Dean of Clonfert, at Omagh, in *B.N.L.*, 15 Feb. 1886; Russell at Dungannon, ibid., 18 June 1886.
2. D. W. Miller, *Queen's Rebels: Ulster Loyalism in Historical Perspective* (Dublin 1978), 65-80. See also D. W. Miller, 'Presbyterianism and Modernisation in Ulster', *Past and Present*, 80 (Aug. 1978), 90.
3. Miller, *Queen's Rebels*, 71-2; Norman, *Anti-Catholic Prejudice in Victorian England*, 17 (For a discussion of anti-Catholic and anti-Irish riots and opinions see the following: Kevin O'Connor, *The Irish in Britain*, 2nd ed. (Dublin 1974), 13-71; J. E. Handley, *The Irish in Scotland, 1798-1845* (Cork 1943), passim; John Denvir, *The Irish in Britain from the Earliest Times to the Fall and Death of Parnell* (London 1892), 105, 117-296); G. D. Phillips, *The Diehards: Aristocratic Society and Politics in Edwardian England* (Cambridge, Mass./London 1979), 149-50.
4. Miller, *Queen's Rebels*, 157; *P.M.G.*, 10 May 1886 (Thomas Sinclair, leader

of the Ulster Liberal Unionists from 1886 to 1914, concurred in this view when he put it that if Home Rule was enacted, northern loyalists would wish to be exempted from its jurisdiction: they would wish 'to continue as an Irish Lancashire, or an Irish Lanarkshire' (Sinclair, 'The Position of Ulster' in Simon Rosenbaum (ed.), *Against Home Rule: The Case for the Union* (London 1912; reissued, New York/London 1970), 180)); Dr William Park at the jubilee assembly of the Presbyterian church in 1890, quoted in J. E. Davey, *1840-1940: The Story of a Hundred Years: An Account of the Irish Presbyterian Church from the Formation of the General Assembly to the Present Time* (Belfast 1940), 62-3; Anon., 'The Riots in Belfast', 286; Miller, *Queen's Rebels*, 118-19.

5. Miller, *Queen's Rebels*, 5, and passim.

6. W. L. Strauss, *Joseph Chamberlain and the Theory of Imperialism* (Washington 1942), 52 (See also the following speeches: Sir John Lubbock, *Hansard 3*, ccciv, 1235-8 (9 Apr. 1886); G. J. Goschen, ibid., cccvi, 1167-8 (7 June 1886)); Strauss, op. cit., 4, 60; Hufford, 'Analysis of the Debates on the Home Rule Bill', 5-6.

7. *Hansard 3*, cccv, 1365-6 (18 May 1886).

8. Peter Gibbon, *The Origins of Ulster Unionism: The Formation of Popular Protestant Politics and Ideology in Nineteenth-Century Ireland* (Manchester 1976), 136-7.

9. See A. C. Hume, 'Origin and Characteristics of the Population in the Counties of Down and Antrim', in *U.J.A.*, 1st series, i (1852), 9-26, 120-9, 246-54.

10. Davitt reported in *P.M.G.*, 10 May 1886; *B.N.L.*, 14 May, 15 Feb. 1886. It can also be added that many of the authorities Gibbon cites to support his theory do not in fact do so. For example, he cites Lord Ernest Hamilton's *The Soul of Ulster* (London 1917), but here Hamilton was merely repeating racist views he had held in 1886, as may be seen from a perusal of his speech in Fintona, noted in Appendix 2 below. He also cites James Logan, *Ulster in the X-rays*, (London 1923; 2nd ed., n.d.); but Logan, far from clarifying a type of distinctive ethnic 'Ulsterman', was concerned mainly to describe light-heartedly all aspects of Ulster life, and cited a long list of famous Ulstermen from John Mitchel and Lord Russell of Killowen to Lords Dufferin and Cairns (ch. 12). He also lists Rev. W. B. Woodburn, *The Ulster Scot: His History and Religion* (London [1914]). However, as D. W. Miller points out (*Queen's Rebels*, 109-10), this work was limited to a description of the Presbyterian community in Ulster.

11. Northcote on the conclusion of his tour of Ulster, 28-30 Oct. 1883, in Cooke (ed.), 'Northcote's Diary', 84.

12. McKnight, *Ulster*, ii, 116-17; D. C. Savage, 'The Origins of the Ulster Unionist Party, 1885-6', *I.H.S.*, xii, no. 47 (Mar. 1961), 191-2; Saunderson's reasons for re-entering politics, in North Armagh political papers, P.R.O.N.I., D1252/42/3/30; Saunderson to his wife, 18 Dec. 1885, P.R.O.N.I., Saunderson papers, T2996/2/B/87. For a detailed account of the emergence of organised Unionism in Ulster see Savage, op. cit., passim.

13. Froude's letter in *P.M.G.*, 10 Feb. 1886 (For the influence on Ulster

Unionists of Macaulay's *Eng.* — which emphasised the racial distinctiveness and superiority of the loyalist minority to the nationalist majority — see McKnight, *Ulster*, i, 10, 15, ii, 14); William Robinson to Saunderson, 3 Dec. 1885, P.R.O.N.I., Saunderson papers, T2996/4/7 (For similar opinions see *Portadown and Lurgan News*, 6 Mar. 1886; *Fermanagh Times*, 4 May 1886; *Down Recorder*, 22 May 1886; *Armagh Guardian*, 18 June 1886); Lynn Doyle, *An Ulster Childhood* (Dublin/London 1921), 48; *L.S.*, 26 Jan., 20 Mar. 1886; F. F. Moore, *The Truth about Ulster* (London 1914), 56; *L.S.*, 26 Jan. 1886; John Mogey, 'Social Relations in Rural Society' in T. W. Moody and J. C. Beckett (ed.), *Ulster since 1800: A Social Survey*, 2nd ed. (London 1958), 74 (See Lord Ernest Hamilton's claim that Protestant fears of being expelled from their farms were widespread in Ulster (*Hansard 3*, ccciv, 1498 (13 Apr. 1886)); *B.N.L.*, Jan.-Apr. 1886; *L.S.*, Feb.-Apr. 1886.

14. Leaflet entitled *Read What Was Done to the Protestants When the Rebels Had Home Rule*, together with another entitled *Bones of the Protestants Drowned in the Bann in 1641* and calling on Protestants not to employ Roman Catholics, in Saunderson papers, P.R.O.N.I., T2996/5/14; *B.N.L.*, 2 Jan. 1886; Doyle, *Ulster Childhood*, 48-9; Lord Ernest Hamilton, *Forty Years On* (London 1922), 66-7 (Hamilton notes that though several of his family's Catholic employees supported Home Rule, they nevertheless got on well with them; similarly, Lord Rossmore, though a strong Orangeman, was determined to show he was 'not bigoted' and did so by providing a site for a Catholic chapel (Rossmore, *Things I Can Tell* (London 1912), 38-40); E.J. Saunderson, *Two Irelands; or Loyalty versus Treason* (Dublin 1884), passim (also *L.S.*, 5 Jan. 1886, and *B.N.L.*, 2 Jan. 1886, for reports of several militant Parnellite speeches entitled 'What the Parnellites Really Aim At'); J. H. McCarthy, 'Home Rule', *Gentleman's Magazine*, lxxii (Feb. 1886), 132-4.

15. *B.N.L.*, 1 Feb. 1886; *U.I.*, 10 Apr. 1886; Speech of W. J. Hurst of Belfast Chamber of Commerce expressing fears of Nationalist intentions, in *B.N.L.*, 27 Apr. 1886; McKnight, *Ulster*, ii, 141-2.

16. *Hansard 3*, ccciv, 1086 (8 Apr. 1886); *B.N.L.*, 23 Apr. 1886.

17. *B.N.L.*, 14, 15, 18 June, 3 July 1886: *W.N.W.*, 19 June 1886; *L.S.*, 29 June 1886 (It is not unlikely that the Sligo riots helped prolong the Belfast disturbances, as the pro-Home Rule *Newry Reporter* (19 June 1886) noted: 'Just as the uproar at Belfast had begun to abate news was received that a serious riot had broken out at Sligo against the Protestant population of that place'); McKnight, *Ulster*, ii, 150-1.

18. *P.M.G.*, 8 May 1886.

19. *B.N.L.*, 8 Jan. 1886; Report of interview with William Johnston in *P.M.G.* (reprinted in *B.N.L.*, 6 Apr. 1886) admitting that to date no action to resist the imposition of Home Rule had so far been organised; Johnston diary, 28 Apr. 1886, P.R.O.N.I., Johnston diaries, D880/2/38; *P.M.G.*, 8 May 1886; Johnston diary, 8 May 1886, loc.cit.; *P.M.G.*, 17 May 1886.

20. McKnight, *Ulster*, ii, 145-7; Wolseley to Duke of Cambridge, 23 Apr. 1893, quoted in John Wilson, *C.B.: A Life of Sir Henry Campbell-Bannerman* (London 1973), 107; Patricia Jalland, *The Liberals and Ireland: The Ulster*

Question in British Politics to 1914 (Brighton 1980), 209; Morley, *Recollections*, ii, 341-2; *P.M.G.*, 31 May, 1 June 1886.

21. R.I.C. inquiry into advertisements for arms in *B.N.L.*, S.P.O., C.S.O., R.P., 1886/9609; Drilling at Richhill in Savage, 'Origins', 203-4; *Portadown and Lurgan News*, 5 June 1886; de Cobain and Saunderson in *P.M.G.*, 1 June 1886; McKnight, *Ulster*, ii, 147.

22. *P.M.G.*, 4 June 1886.

Chapter 7: Gladstone's Concept of Irish Nationality and the Moral Crusade for Home Rule, 1886-92 (pp 172-196)

1. Gladstone to Hartington, 11 Sept. 1885, in Hammond, *Gladstone*, 406.

2. *Graphic*, 16 Apr. 1881; Redmond, *Historical and Political Addresses*, 130; Lord Brabourne, 'Facts and Fictions in Irish History: A Reply to Mr Gladstone', *Blackwood's Magazine*, cxl (Oct. 1886), 5-6.

3. James Bryce, 'The Past and Future of the Irish Question' in Bryce (ed.), *Handbook*, 223-4; Walter Fitzpatrick to Gladstone on the poor market for Irish books in Britain, 12 Nov. 1886, G.P. 44699; Shaw Lefevre, *Peel and O'Connell* (London 1887); Shaw Lefevre to Gladstone requesting a recommendation for his *Peel and O'Connell*, 10 July 1887, G.P. 44151; O'Brien, *Parnell*, 365-6; Sir Algernon West, *Recollections, 1832-86* (London 1899; 2nd ed., n.d.), 425, on Gladstone's profound historical sense; Gladstone's view of history as the working out of Christian influence in world affairs (p. 58 above); Hamilton to Harcourt, 29 Jan. 1894, in Gardiner, *Harcourt*, ii, 254.

4. R. T. Shannon, *Gladstone and the Bulgarian Agitation, 1876* (London 1963), passim; Magnus, *Gladstone*, 237-42; Mansergh, *The Irish Question, 1840-1921*, 3rd ed. (London 1975), 136-7 (See also Hammond, *Gladstone*, 64-6); W. E. Gladstone, *Special Aspects of the Irish Question* (London 1892), 72-3. Gladstone claimed that this volume, consisting mainly of arguments on Irish history, was 'least associated with the angry polemics of the Irish question' (p. v); the quotation is from 'Notes and Queries on the Irish Demands' which first appeared in *N.C.* (Feb. 1887).

5. Mill on Irish nationality (*Eng. and Ire.*, passim); E. D. Steele, 'Gladstone and Ireland', *I.H.S.*, xvii, no. 65 (Mar. 1970), 82 (Steele argues that as early as 1866 Gladstone perceived the Irish problem in terms of an 'Irish nationality confronting an English nationality'); Gladstone, Memorandum entitled 'Notes on Irish Nationalism', 4 July 1888, G.P. 44773.

6. Steele, *Ir. Land and British Politics*, 252-4; Gladstone to Harcourt (p. 59 above).

7. Gladstone, 'Notes on Ir. Nationalism'.

8. Gladstone to Dicey, 12 Nov. 1886, G.P. 44499; Colin Campbell to Gladstone, 12 Nov. 1886, ibid.

9. *Edmund Burke: His Works and Correspondence,* 8 vols (London 1852); Gladstone's diary, quoted in Morley, *Gladstone*, iii, 211; Burke, *Reflections on the Revolution in France*, new ed. (London 1868), 101, 112-20.

10. Daniel O'Connell, *A Memoir on Ireland, Native and Saxon* (London 1842); Gladstone to Dicey, 12 Nov. 1886, G.P. 44499; Lecky, *Leaders*, ii, 213; O'Connell, op. cit., vii-xi (O'Connell declared British policy in

Ireland to be condemned before the bar of history); Harcourt to Glad-stone, 28 Dec. 1883, in Gardiner, *Harcourt*, i, 497.

11. Morley, *Gladstone*, iii, 320; Lecky *Leaders*, i, p. xiii.

12. W. E. Gladstone, 'Lessons of Irish History in the Eighteenth Century' in *Special Aspects of the Ir. Question*, 110; ibid., 88; Gladstone in the Commons, 8 Apr. 1886, in Hutton and Cohen (ed.), *Gladstone's Speeches, 1886-8*, 13 (Poynings' Law, introduced in the Irish parliament in 1494 by Sir Edward Poynings, Lord Deputy and emissary of Henry VII, was intended to, and effectively did, subordinate the Irish parliament to that of England; only by the most convoluted reasoning could it be described as Irish, in the sense of which Gladstone sought to describe the Irish par-liament as a national parliament enacting national legislation (see J. C. Beckett, *The Making of Modern Ireland, 1603-1923*, 3rd ed. (London 1973), 51; Patrick O'Farrell, *Ireland's English Question* (London 1971), 58); Gladstone at Liverpool, 28 June 1886, in Hutton and Cohen (ed.), op. cit., 174; Gladstone, 'Lessons of Ir. History', 111-13.

13. Gladstone, 'Lessons of Ir. History', 114, 117-26.

14. In his 'Notes on Ir. Nationalism', written in 1888, his views had developed somewhat on this matter. Here he described Irish nationalism from Henry II's reign down to the seventeenth century as having 'subsisted *germinally* as race feeling and was warred and hunted down. That it had the character of true nationalism was evinced strongly, perhaps namely, by its power of assimilation and of merging the English in the Irish element which, however, it largely modified.' However, I have not found that he expressed this view publicly. In any event, by 1888 his former view was well estab-lished in print.

15. Hirst, 'Gladstone and Home Rule, 1885-92', 710 (Smith's *Ir. History and Ir. Character* (1861), though critical of Grattan's Parliament in some respects, nevertheless praised its reforming intent and condemned not only the history of English oppression in Ireland in general, but particular phases of that oppression that were of special interest to Gladstone, such as the atrocities perpetrated by crown forces — especially Orangemen — during and after the 1798 rebellion, the corrupt methods by which the Act of Union was passed and the injustices suffered by the Catholic population thereafter); Lecky's concept of nationality, in McCartney, 'Lecky's *Leaders*', 130-3, and Anne Wyatt, 'Froude, Lecky and the "Humblest Irishman"', *I.H.S.*, xix, no. 75 (Mar. 1975), 285; Lecky, *Ire.*, i, 252; W. E. Gladstone, 'Kin Beyond the Sea' in *Prose Masterpieces of Modern Essayists* (London 1886), 381 (article first published in the *North American Review* in 1878): Lecky, *Ire.*, iv, 124.

16. Gladstone, 'Lessons of Ir. History', 133; Gladstone, 'Notes and Queries', 81.

17. Bew, *Parnell*, 82, on Gladstone's and Parnell's conservative vision; Kettle, *Material for Victory*, 58; R. F. Foster (*Charles Stewart Parnell: The Man and his Family*, 2nd ed. (Hassocks 1979), 167-8) and Magnus (*Gladstone*, 257) des-cribing Gladstone's and Parnell's views on the gentry as social leaders; Gladstone, 'Notes and Queries', 80-3; Morley, *Gladstone*, iii, 194-5.

18. *Two Hundred Years of Irish History, 1691-1870*, intro. James Bryce (London 1888), xii; W. E. H. Lecky, *The Political Uses of History* (London 1892), 16.

19. Bryce (ed.), *Handbook*, ix; Davitt, *Fall of Feudalism*, 116; William O'Brien, *Irish Ideas* (London 1893), 21.

20. Magnus, *Gladstone*, 315, on Gladstone's 'self-deception'; McCarthy, *Reminiscences*, ii, 451. See also Cooke and Vincent, *Governing Passion*, 53, noting Gladstone's contempt for the average Parnellite M.P.

21. James Loughlin, 'The Irish Protestant Home Rule Association and Nationalist Politics, 1886-93', *I.H.S.*, xxiv, no. 95 (May 1985), 341-60 (See also P. J. O. McCann, 'The Protestant Home Rule Movement, 1886-95' (M.A. thesis, N.U.I. (U.C.D.), 1972); Gladstone to C. H. Oldham, 9 Apr. 1887, *North and South*, 16 Apr. 1887 (*North and South* was the organ of the Irish Protestant Home Rule Association).

22. *Times*, 26 June 1886; *W.N.W.*, 26 June 1886; Gladstone, 'Notes and Queries', 61-2, Gladstone described the events surrounding the passing of the Act of Union as 'most important' to the historical argument for Home Rule (Gladstone to Dicey, 12 Nov. 1886, G.P. 44499).

23. Shaw Lefevre to Gladstone, 10 July 1887, G.P. 44151; J. G. S. McNeill, author of *How the Union was Carried* (London 1887), to Gladstone, 8 Nov. 1886, G.P. 44499 (See also Bryce to Dr George Sigerson, 29 Dec. 1886, N.L.I., Sigerson papers, MS 10904(2)); R. A. Cosgrove, 'The Relevance of Irish History: The Gladstone—Dicey Debate about Home Rule, 1886-7', *Éire-Ireland*, xv, 3 (autumn 1980), 21.

24. Dicey to Lecky, 10 Nov. 1886, T.C.D., Lecky correspondence, no. 405; J. D. Ingram, *A History of the Legislative Union of Great Britain and Ireland*, 2 vols (London 1887).

25. Marjoribanks to Gladstone, 9 May 1887, G.P. 44332; Bright's letter in *W.N.W.*, 20 Aug. 1887; W. E. Gladstone, 'Ingram's History of the Irish Union' in *Special Aspects of the Ir. Question*, 135-95; Marjoribanks to Gladstone, 7 Oct. 1887, G.P. 44332; Churchill to Marjoribanks, 6 Oct. 1887, ibid.; Lord Brabourne, 'A Review of a Review', *Blackwood's Magazine*, cxlii (Nov. 1887), 715-30.

26. Brabourne, 'A Review of a Review, 716, 722, 730; Gladstone to the editor, *Blackwood's Magazine*, n.d. [Nov. 1887?], G.P. 44499. Recent scholarship has tended to endorse Brabourne's view of Grattan's Parliament. Patrick O'Farrell has pointed out the illogical position of the parliament in claiming to speak for the whole Irish nation and being partially inclined to enact political reforms to benefit Catholics, while at the same time hoping to keep effective political control in Protestant hands. See O'Farrell, *Ireland's Eng. Question*, 63-6.

27. H. de F. Montgomery, *Correspondence with Mr Gladstone and Notes on the Pamphlet 'Gladstone and Burke'* (Dublin [1887]), 3-4, 5, 9.

28. Gladstone in the Commons on the Special Commission report, in Morley, *Gladstone*, iii, 309-11; Gladstone's disputes with Nationalists on Home Rule finance (pp 260-3, 269-71 below); Morley to Gladstone, 2, 5 Feb. 1894, G.P. 44257.

Chapter 8: The Home Rule Debate, 1886-92: The Search for an Irish Constitution (pp 197-219)

1. Hutton and Cohen (ed.), *Gladstone's Speeches, 1886-8*, 134-8, 148-51; Hirst,

'Gladstone and Home Rule', 709; Gladstone at Liverpool, in Hutton and Cohen (ed.), op. cit., 154-66.

2. Hirst, 'Gladstone and Home Rule', 716 (See also W. E. Gladstone, 'Daniel O'Connell' in *Special Aspects of the 'Ir. Question*, 263-302); Blunt to Walsh, 13 Aug. 1886, in Blunt, *Land War*, 167-70; Kettle, *Material for Victory*, 81 (See also D. A. Hamer, *Liberal Politics in the Age of Gladstone and Rosebery: A Study in Leadership and Policy* (Oxford 1972), 154); Donald McCormack, *The Incredible Mr Kavanagh* (New York 1961), 195-6 (Kavanagh was virtually without arms and legs).

3. *F.J.*, 16 June 1886; Walsh, *William J. Walsh*, 221, 224.

4. Walsh to Cardinal Manning, 13 Aug. 1886, in Walsh, *William J. Walsh*, 217; Gladstone to Walsh, 30 Oct. 1886, ibid., 222-3; ibid., 1 June 1887, 225-6. See also Gladstone to Morley, 28 May 1887, G.P. 44255.

5. Morley to Gladstone, 18 Dec. 1886, G.P. 44255; ibid., 19 July 1886.

6. Roundell to Gladstone, 9 Aug. 1886, G.P. 44499; Newspaper cutting of a letter from Gladstone to 'Mr Illingworth', 22 Nov. 1886, ibid.

7. *Times*, 20 Oct. 1886; Gladstone to Morley, 8 Dec. 1886, G.P. 44255.

8. Morley to Gladstone, 7 Dec. 1886, G.P. 44255; ibid., 12 Dec. 1886; Michael Hurst, *Joseph Chamberlain and Liberal Reunion: The Round Table Conference of 1887* (London/Toronto 1967), passim; Garvin, *Chamberlain*, ii, 276-9; Morley to Gladstone, 24 Dec. 1886, G.P. 44255.

9. Chamberlain to Harcourt, 20 Dec. 1886, in Chamberlain, *Political Memoir*, 235-6; Morley to Gladstone, 2 Jan. 1887, G.P. 44255 (See also Hamer, *Morley*, 216-17); Morley to Gladstone, 2 Jan. 1887, G.P. 44255; Gladstone to Morley, 3 Jan. 1887, ibid.

10. Chamberlain, *Political Memoir*, 238.

11. Chamberlain's memoranda on the first two meetings of the Round Table conference, ibid., 248-50.

12. Morley to Gladstone, 15 Jan. 1887, G.P. 44255; Gladstone to Morley, 21 Jan. 1887, ibid.

13. Garvin, *Chamberlain*, ii, 289; Chamberlain, *Political Memoir*, 252; *Times*, 18 Jan. 1887.

14. Garvin, *Chamberlain*, ii, 293; Chamberlain, *Political Memoir*, 258-61; A. V. Dicey, *England's Case against Home Rule* (London 1886) (See also *Times*, 18, 19, 28 Mar., 9 Apr., 2 May 1887, for letters of Sir John Lubbock, T. H. Huxley, Sir John Beddoe and the Duke of Argyll, arguing that the Irish were merely a part of the United Kingdom population and not a distinct nationality with a claim to independence); D. T. Dorrity, 'Monkeys in a Menagerie: The Imagery of Unionist Opposition to Home Rule, 1886-93', *Éire-Ireland*, xii, 3 (autumn 1977), 5-22.

15. Hutton and Cohen (ed.), *Gladstone's Speeches, 1886-8*, 238-54. However, feeling in the Liberal Party was growing steadily in favour of retention. See Morley to Gladstone, 26 May 1887, G.P. 44255.

16. Lord Salisbury also believed that coercion would win converts to Home Rule in England (Salisbury to Balfour, 24 Dec. 1887, 18 Jan. 1888, B.L., Balfour papers, Add. MSS 49688-9); Garvin, *Chamberlain*, ii, 310-16.

17. O'Brien, *Parnell*, 406-7; Morley to Gladstone, 14 Sept. 1887, G.P. 44255.

18. On the G.A.A. convention episode see Mark Tierney, *Croke of Cashel: The*

Life of Archbishop Thomas William Croke, 1823-1902, (Dublin 1976), ch. 10; Morley to Gladstone, 13 Nov. 1887, G.P. 44255; ibid., 30 Nov. 1887. For a range of hardline and 'disloyal' actions and statements by nationalists see the following: *Graphic*, 2 July 1887; *P.M.G.*, 22 Aug. 1887; W. J. O'N. Daunt, *Ireland since the Union* (Dublin 1888), 279; Leaflet no. 173, *Ireland: A Separate and Distinct Nation*, in L.U.A., *The Case for the Union: A Collection of Speeches, Pamphlets and Leaflets on Home Rule for Ireland* (London [1890]).

19. In the preface to his history of the tenant-right movement of the 1850s, which appeared shortly after the defeat of the first Home Rule bill, Duffy criticised the Parnellite party for failing 'to unite the four provinces in a common platform as your predecessors did. What signal results it might produce at this hour had you been able to' (Duffy, *The League of North and South* (London 1886), viii); Duffy, 'A Fair Constitution for Ireland', *C.R.*, lii (Sept. 1887), 304; ibid., 303. For Duffy's influence with Lord Carnarvon, the pro-Home Rule Tory viceroy of Ireland in 1885, see O'Day, *Parnell*, 50-1, 53, 74, 78, 91, 94.

20. Duffy, 'Fair Constitution', 303-4.

21. Ibid., 304-6, 308-11, 312, 315-17, 322-5, 326-7. See also Thomas Davis, *The Patriot Parliament of 1689*, ed. Sir C. G. Duffy (London 1895), 70-1.

22. Separate printing of Duffy's 'Fair Constitution' (London 1892), with additional material describing his attempts to promote an Irish debate on Home Rule, 1-3, 39-45, 104. See also Duffy to J. F. X. O'Brien, 29 Aug., 20 Dec. 1887, N.L.I., O'Brien papers, MS 13424.

23. Duffy, *Fair Constitution* (1892), 5-6; Walsh, *William J. Walsh*, 231; Walsh's action provoked William O'Brien's vehement denunciation of landlords (p. 189 above).

24. O'Brien, *Parnell*, 405, and O'Brien, *Parnell and his Party*, 267; E. J. C. Morton, 'The Home Rule Union', *J.H.R.U.* (July 1888), 73-4; Magnus, *Gladstone*, 375; A Liberal Woman, 'An Evening Stroll', *J.H.R.U.* (July 1888), 68-9, on working-class indifference to Home Rule; Liberal report on Irish politics in Daunt, *Ire. since the Union*, 296-8; Roundell's report of interview with Alfred Webb (pp 200-1 above)

25. W. E. Gladstone, 'Further Notes and Queries on the Irish Demands', republished in Gladstone, *Special Aspects of the Ir. Question*, 202; Daunt to Gladstone, 9 Mar. 1888, Gladstone to Daunt, 14 Mar. 1888, and Daunt to Gladstone, 29 Mar. 1888, in Daunt, *Ire. since the Union*, 287-9, 290-6; *First Report of Her Majesty's Commissioners appointed to Inquire into the Financial Relations between Great Britain and Ireland: Minutes of Evidence and Appendices up to 28 March 1895*, 52 [C 7720-1] H.C. 1895, xxxvi, 113.

26 Gladstone's notes for a meeting with Parnell, 8 Mar. 1888, G.P. 44773; Gladstone's memo of meeting with Parnell, 10 Mar. 1888, ibid. See also Lyons, *Parnell*, 440-2.

27. Lyons, *Parnell*, 443; Parnell interview with J. G. S. McNeill in *P.M.G.*, 10 July 1888; *W.N.W.*, 15 Dec. 1888; Balfour's memo on the Irish situation, early 1886, B.L., Balfour papers, Add. MS 49822. The source of Balfour's views about the effect of the crimes act in Ireland seem to have been a memorandum drawn up by C. K. Falconer, a member of the committee on Irish income tax which toured the south and west of Ireland in late

1887. See Falconer, Memorandum on the state of the south and west of Ireland, 16 Dec. 1887, B.L., Balfour papers, Add. MS 49688.

28. Chamberlain, *Political Memoir*, 279-82; Chamberlain at Huddersfield, 17 Sept. 1889, in L.U.A., *Case for the Union*, leaflet no. 126.

29. Gladstone at Birmingham, 7 Nov. 1888, in A. W. Hutton and H. J. Cohen (ed.), *The Speeches of W. E. Gladstone, 1888-92* (London 1902), 87-8; Morley to Gladstone, 27 Dec. 1888, G.P. 44255.

30. Morley to Gladstone, 15 Jan. 1889, G.P. 44255; Gladstone's notes for a meeting with Parnell, 18 Dec. 1889, G.P. 44773.

31. For Gladstone's discussion with his ex-cabinet colleagues, including Lord Ripon, Morley, Spencer and Harcourt, see Lyons, *Parnell*, 448-9; Gladstone's record of meeting with Parnell, 23 Dec. 1889, G.P. 44773; Lyons, op. cit., 457; Sullivan, *No Man's Man*, 60.

32. Chamberlain to Hartington, 21 Nov. 1890, in Chamberlain, *Political Memoir*, 291.

33. Morley to Gladstone, 13 Nov. 1890, G.P. 44255. See also a detailed memorandum of the meeting to which this letter refers in Morley, *Recollections*, i, 252-6.

34. Dicey to Balfour, 26 Apr. 1890, B.L., Balfour papers, Add. MS 49689; Balfour to Dicey, 30 Apr. 1890, ibid.; *Local Government (Ireland) Bill*, 1-46, H.C. 1892 (174), iii, 609-55; Blanche Dugdale, *Arthur James Balfour, First Earl of Balfour* (London 1936), i, 206; Morley to Gladstone, 21 Dec. 1890, G.P. 44256.

35. Sullivan, *No Man's Man*, 117; O'Brien, *Parnell and his Party*, 341-2; McDonagh, *Life of William O'Brien*, 136; Morley, *Gladstone*, iii, 342, on Gladstone's assurances to Nationalists regarding a future Home Rule bill.

Chapter 9: The Liberal/Nationalist Alliance and the Ulster Question, 1886-92 (pp 220-250)

1. B. M. Walker, *Parliamentary Election Results in Ireland, 1801-1922* (Dublin 1978), 133, 134, 137, 139.

2. Table 5, based on information in reports entitled 'Leading Nationalist Associations in Ireland (Open and Secret) with their *Approximate* Strength on 31 Oct. 1889', S.P.O., Police and Crime Records, Crime Branch Special files, 1890-1920, 6137/S; Samuel McElroy, *The Route Land Crusade* (Coleraine n.d.), 45, 57, 74-5; Jeremiah McVeagh on Catholic farmers in Ulster, in *F.J.* 2 May 1893; Woods, 'Catholic Church and Ir. Politics', 441; *W.N.W.*, 15, 29 Jan., 5, 26 Feb., 5, 12, 19 Mar. 1887. J. L. McCracken notes that while the National League was strong enough to affect the payment of rents, and to prevent the letting of farms from which tenants had been evicted on the Drapers' estate in Co. Londonderry, 'I can safely say that where there was a mixed Protestant and Catholic population the League made little mark. More common was what a police officer called "a silent resistance" — no boycotting, no intimidation, simply the determination not to pay a burdensome rent.' See McCracken, 'The Consequences of the Land War' in T. W. Moody and J. C. Beckett (ed.), *Ulster since 1800: A Political and Economic Survey*, 2nd ed. (London 1957), 65.

3. Newspaper cutting from *Belfast Morning News*,? Dec. 1886, entitled 'The Nationalist Cause in the North', P.R.O.N.I., Pinkerton papers, D1078/P/1; Report of *Daily News* article on 'Ulster and the Plan of Campaign' in *W.N.W.*, 1 Jan. 1887; *U.I.*, 24 Dec. 1886; Report of interview with William O'Brien on Plan of Campaign in *Dublin Evening Mail*, 28 Mar. 1887.

4. *W.N.W.*, 16 Apr., 31 Dec. 1887.

5. Leading article on Davitt's speech, in *W.N.W.*, 2 Apr. 1887; Gibbon (*Origins of Ulster Unionism*, 122), T. W. Russell (*Ireland and the Empire: A Review, 1800-1900* (London/New York 1901), 202) and Solow (*Land Question*, 189) on the sale of landed estates in Ulster; J. R. B. McMinn, 'The Reverend James Brown Armour and Liberal Politics in North Antrim, 1869-1914' (Ph.D. thesis, Queen's University of Belfast, 1979), ch. 9.

6. *W.N.W.* (6 Dec. 1886) and McKnight (*Ulster*, ii, 167-8) on Nationalist 'boycotting'; McCarthy, *Story of an Irishman*, 282 (Thomas Sexton had told McCarthy that to win Derry 'would be to wear the blue ribbon of the Irish national party'); *U.I.*, 30 Oct. 1886. In a variation on the theme of the essential 'Irishness' of Ulster Protestants, C. H. Oldham argued that by their heroism in 1689 the defenders of Derry had 'proved their right to live in this land' (Oldham, *The Record of Ulster Protestantism in the History of Irish Patriotism* (Belfast 1888), 8).

7. J. E. Redmond, *'Hugh O'Neill': A Lecture* (Naas 1887), 12 (For an example of this kind of rhetoric at local meetings in Ulster see Father McShane at Coalisland, Co. Tyrone, in *W.N.W.*, 23 Apr. 1887); Ronald McNeill, *Ulster's Stand for the Union* (London 1927), 6-7 (See also James Byrne to Hugh de F. Montgomery, 21 Mar. 1890, P.R.O.N.I., Montgomery papers, D627/428/134); Thomas Sexton on effects of the Belfast riots on Catholics in Belfast (*Hansard 3*, cccviii, 1614-27 (7 Sept. 1886)). See also *Riots Commission Report, 1886*, 11. It has been argued that the generation of rioting from mid-century up to 1886 established widespread segregation and discrimination in employment. See A. C. Hepburn, 'Catholics in the North of Ireland, 1880-1921: The Urbanisation of a Minority' in Hepburn (ed.), *Minorities in History* (London 1978), 89.

8. Nationalist demands for changes in the composition of the commission investigating the riots were given weight by the support given them by T. W. Russell, Liberal Unionist M.P. for South Tyrone (*Hansard 3*, cccviii, 1616-27 (7 Sept. 1886)); Saunderson to his wife, 25 Aug., 4 Sept. 1886, P.R.O.N.I., Saunderson papers, T2996/1/100, 105; *W.N.W.*, 21 Aug. 1886; *Riots Commission Report, 1886*, 17; *What the Loyal Minority Really Wants — Ascendancy*, in a collection of National Press Agency leaflets, N.L.I., Ir. 32341 n. 1; J. J. Clancy, *Six Months' Unionist Rule in Ireland* (London 1887), 80-2.

9. Andrew Commins, *Orangeism: What Is It? and What Will You Do About It? Facts and Considerations for the People of Great Britain* (London 1886), 19-21; McCann, 'Prot. Home Rule Movement', 60 (McCann, however, gives no source for this information); *Riots Commission Report, 1886*, 11, 16, 17.

10. Speech by Thomas Sinclair at Cambridge, 20 Nov. 188, in *W.N.W.*, 24

Nov. 1888; National Press Agency, *Shall Ulster Rule Ireland?*, N.L.I., Ir. 32341 n. 1.

11. Editorial comment on Nationalist attitudes to land reform in *W.N.W.*, 12 Feb. 1887; Debate on Belfast main drainage bill (*Hansard 3*, cccxiv, 186-206 (28 Apr. 1887); Johnston diary, 20 Feb., 12 Mar. 1888, P.R.O.N.I., Johnston diaries, D880/2/40.

12. Russell, *Ire. and the Empire*, 277; Blunt, *Land War*, 283 (Extracts from *U.I.*'s reaction to the news of Ulster Protestants being allocated vacant farms on 'Plan' estates, were compiled and made into a short pamphlet entitled *A Massacre of Protestant Farmers predicted by 'United Ireland'* (L.U.A., *Case for the Union*, leaflet no. 172)); O'Brien, *Home-Ruler's Manual*, 99.

13. Gladstone at Liverpool, 28 June 1886, in Hutton and Cohen (ed.), *Gladstone's Speeches, 1886-8*, 155.

14. Rosebery diary, 29 Oct. 1891, in Marquis of Crewe, *Lord Rosebery* (London 1931), ii, 375.

15. W. E. Gladstone, 'Plain Speaking on the Irish Union' in *Special Aspects of the Ir. Question*, 322; H. Gladstone, *After Thirty Years*, 20; Reginald Lucas, *Colonel Saunderson: A Memoir* (London 1908), 276; ibid., 145, 159; ibid., 125, 275; ibid., 187; H. W. Lucy, 'Mr Gladstone as an Orator' in Reid (ed.), *Life of Gladstone*, 523; Saunderson to his wife, 15 Feb. 1888, in Lucas, op. cit., 150; Johnston diary, 7 June 1886, P.R.O.N.I., Johnston diaries, D880/2/38; Sir John Ross, *The Years of My Pilgrimage* (London 1923), 84, 77; Editorial describing Gladstone's views on Orangemen in *W.N.W.*, 14 May 1887.

16. *W.N.W.*, 3 July 1886 (This paper blamed Saunderson, 'who looks at the question from the point of view of Cavan and not of Belfast', for planting the idea in Gladstone's mind that Ulster Protestants objected to being separated from the nationalist part of Ireland); Garvin, *Chamberlain*, ii, 285; Chamberlain's notes of conference discussion, 14 Jan. 1887, ibid., 286-7; Morley to Gladstone, 15 Jan. 1887, G.P. 44255; Morley, *Gladstone*, iii, 277; Morley to Gladstone, 17 Jan. 1887, G.P. 44255 (When the idea of excluding Ulster from the provisions of the Home Rule bill was first mooted during the 1886 Home Rule debate, Parnell firmly rejected it (Thorold, *Labouchere*, 290)); Chamberlain, *Political Memoir*, 267.

17. Parnell in the Ulster Hall, 29 May 1891, in *W.N.W.*, 30 May 1891; Garvin, *Chamberlain*, ii, 287.

18. McKnight, *Ulster*, ii, 189; H. Gladstone, *After Thirty Years*, 291; McKnight, op. cit., ii, 192; Bright to Gladstone, in *W.N.W.*, 18 June 1887; Gladstone to Bright, ibid., 25 June 1887.

19. H. Gladstone, *After Thirty Years*, 19-20 (Herbert Gladstone wrongly gives the period of this correspondence as 1889); *W.N.W.*, 17 Sept. 1887.

20. Quoted in Daunt, *Ire. since the Union*, 297. See also reports on the deputation in *W.N.W.*, 24 Sept., 8 Oct. 1887.

21. Hutton and Cohen (ed.), *Gladstone's Speeches, 1886-8*, 308 (See also his letter to the Belfast branch of the Young Ireland Society, in *W.N.W.*, 8 Oct. 1887); Chamberlain to Hartington, 27 Oct. 1887, in Garvin, *Chamberlain*, ii, 321.

22. *Ulster Lib. Un. Assoc.*, intro. Fisher, 57, 83; Joseph Chamberlain, *Speeches on*

the Irish Question, 1887-90 (London 1890), 48-71; Chamberlain in the Ulster Hall, 12 Oct. 1887, quoted in McKnight, *Ulster*, ii, 103; Morley to Gladstone, 15 Oct. 1887, G.P. 44255; Gladstone at Nottingham, in *W.N.W.*, 22 Oct. 1887 (In this speech he referred to the condemnation of separate treatment by Dr Kane and Colonel Saunderson following Chamberlain's speech of 12 October. Kane, however, was to argue that his views had been misrepresented on this point (McKnight, *Ulster*, ii, 211).).

23. Morley to Gladstone, 30 Nov. 1887, G.P. 44255; R. T. Reid, 'Ulster', *C.R.*, lii (Nov. 1887), 605-16.

24. Gladstone to the Dublin executive of the Irish Protestant Home Rule Association, in *W.N.W.*, 3 Nov. 1888; Gladstone at Birmingham, 7 Nov. 1888, in Hutton and Cohen (ed.), *Gladstone's Speeches, 1886-8*, 88-92; *B.N.L.*, 1 Feb. 1887, for extensive editorial reaction to Gladstone's historical charges; Robert McGeogh, vice-president of the Ulster Liberal Unionist Association, to Gladstone, 31 Oct. 1888 (published as pamphlet entitled *Ulster's Apology for Being Loyal* (Irish Question, no. 153), L.U.A. *Case for the Union*). See also A. T. Q. Stewart, *The Narrow Ground: Aspects of Ulster, 1609-1969* (London 1977), 164 (John Swanwick Drennan, son of the United Irishman, Dr William Drennan, became a Liberal Unionist and wrote verse celebrating Ulster Unionist resistance to Home Rule in 1892); J. J. Shaw, *Mr Gladstone's Two Irish Policies: 1868 and 1886* (Belfast 1888), 9-12; McKnight, *Ulster*, ii, 194, 231-2; Gladstone to the Belfast branch of the Young Ireland Society, urging Ulster Protestants to return to the patriotism of their forefathers, in *W.N.W.*, 8 June 1889.

25. In 1881 the total number of the three most important Protestant denominations (Episcopalian, Presbyterian and Methodist) was 865,856; the Catholics numbered 833,560 (Vaughan and Fitzpatrick, *Pop.*, 58-9); W. E. Gladstone, 'Home Rule for Ireland' in *Special Aspects of the Ir. Question*, 359, 361-2; Morley to Gladstone, 18 Nov. 1890, G.P. 44256.

26. Morley to Gladstone, Memorandum on the Irish crisis, 21 Dec. 1890, G.P. 44256; Clerical control of Nationalist politics in Ulster, in Gibbon, *Origins of Ulster Unionism*, 93; H. S. Kennedy, *The Irish News and Belfast Morning News, 1855-1935*, 11-13 (account privately printed for the shareholders to mark the paper's eightieth birthday in 1935 (Linenhall Library ref. N7798)).

27. Parnell in the Ulster Hall, in *W.N.W.*, 30 May 1891; Bew, *Parnell*, 127, 130.

28. Parnell's concept of Ulster Unionism (pp 125-6 above); Parnell in Ulster Hall, in *W.N.W.*, 30 May 1891.

29. Both these reactions are taken from a survey of Irish press opinions on Parnell's death in *F.J.*, 8 Oct. 1891.

30. O'Farrell, *Ireland's Eng. Question*, 199-207; Note by Inspector-General, R.I.C., to report on nationalist associations, 16 Feb. 1893., S.P.O., Police and Crime Records, Crime Branch Special files, 1890-1920, 6137/S; Captain Slack to Inspector-General, R.I.C., 23 Feb. 1893, in memo entitled 'Present Position of Political Parties in the Northern Division', ibid., 6364/S.

31. Captain Slack, 'Present Position of Political Parties in the Northern

Division', 23 Feb. 1893; Table 6 adapted from report estimating strength of nationalist associations in Ireland, Dec. 1892, S.P.O., Police and Crime Records, Crime Branch Special files, 1890-1920, 6137/S.

32. Notes on city of Belfast returns, 11 Feb. 1893, ibid.; Note attached to Northern Division returns, 23 Feb. 1893, ibid.; McKnight, *Ulster*, ii, 300, on Ulster convention.

33. Justin McCarthy, 'The Home Rule View of the Ulster Convention', *Black and White*, 25 June 1892; Editorial reaction, and Rosebery and Morley on Ulster convention, in *F.J.*, 18, 20 June 1892; Harcourt to Saunderson, 29 May 1892, P.R.O.N.I., Saunderson papers, T2996/3/23; Investigation into Belfast local government, 1891, highlighting discrimination against Catholics and cited extensively in McVeagh, *What Orangeism Means*, passim; Gladstone at Clapham, 18 June 1892, in *F.J.*, 20 June 1892.

34. Gladstone at Clapham, 18 June 1892, in *F.J.*, 20 June 1892; B. M. Walker, 'Party Organisation in Ulster, 1865-92: Registration Agents and their Activities' in Peter Roebuck (ed.), *Plantation to Partition: Essays in Ulster History in Honour of J. L. McCracken* (Belfast 1981), 209; Captain Slack, 'Present Position of Political Parties in the Northern Division', 23 Feb. 1893.

35. McCann, 'Prot. Home Rule Movement', 114-15; Mary Arnold-Forster, *Hugh Oakeley Arnold-Forster* (London 1910), 89; Ross, *Pilgrimage*, 73; Walker, *Parl. Election Results*, 147.

36. F. S. L. Lyons, *The Irish Parliamentary Party, 1890-1910* (London 1951), 133-4.

37. Saunderson, *Hansard 4*, viii, 268-70 (2 Feb. 1893); Redmond, ibid, 274. The new member for West Belfast, H. O. Arnold-Forster, moved the amendment to the Queen's speech in calling attention to the proceedings in Meath (Arnold-Forster, *H. O. Arnold-Forster*, 96).

Chapter 10: Liberals, Nationalists and the Struggle for Home Rule, 1892-3 (pp 251-283)

1. Hirst, 'Gladstone and Home Rule, 1885-92', 720, on the election result; Magnus, *Gladstone*, 397, and Morley, *Gladstone*, iii, 370-1; Gladstone to Morley, 26 Nov. 1892, ibid., 372.

2. Morley, *Gladstone*, iii, 371; Aberdeen, *'We Twa'*, i, 317-20 (Gladstone, though distressed at Morley's action, felt that at his age he could not press his views 'on those who undertook the charge of the various departments'); Morley, *Recollections*, i, 331-3; Jekyll to West, 25 July 1893, in *The Private Diaries of Sir Algernon West*, ed. H. G. Hutchinson (London 1922), 178-82; Bryce on Irish unfitness for self-government in L. P. Curtis, jr, *Anglo-Saxons and Celts* (New York 1968), 63; Morley, *Recollections*, ii, 322; Gladstone's cabinet memo, 21 Nov. 1892, G.P. 44648; Morley, *Gladstone*, iii, 374.

3. Redmond, Notes of meeting on Home Rule at Devonshire Club, 30 Mar. 1892, N.L.I., Redmond papers, MS 15206(1); Redmond to Mather, 28 Apr. 1892, ibid.; Redmond, Notes of meeting with Morley, 11 Oct. 1892, ibid., MS 15207(1).

4. Davitt to (?) Doherty, 30 July 1892, N.L.I., Davitt papers, MS 15347, acc. 2627; McCarthy to Mrs Campbell Praed, 4, 5, 24 Aug. 1892, in McCarthy

and Praed, *Our Book of Memories*, 325-7; Dillon, Notes of meetings with Gladstone, McCarthy and Sexton, 7 Mar., 21 June 1893, T.C.D., Dillon papers, MS 6796/27-8; McCarthy to Praed, 11 Aug. 1892, in McCarthy and Praed, op. cit., 327. To offset the prospect of Gladstone appealing to the Queen for permission to create new peers in the event of the Lords persistently rejecting a Home Rule bill, Lord Salisbury and Chamberlain agreed that it might be best to pass the bill at once 'with a clause requiring a referendum': Gladstone would have to accept the bill or take the responsibility for rejecting it, as he 'could not face an appeal to the country on this issue alone' (Garvin, *Chamberlain*, ii, 577).

5. Dillon, Notes of meeting with Gladstone, 3 Aug. 1892, T.C.D., Dillon papers, MS 6796/29; Gladstone's desire for appeal to country on Lords' rejection of his Home Rule bill (p. 273 below); Morley, Memoranda of meetings with Nationalists on Home Rule, 16, 17, 18 Nov., 1 Dec. 1892, G.P. 44774; McCarthy to Praed, 2 Nov., 10 Dec. 1892, in McCarthy and Praed, *Our Book of Memories*, 322, 337; Gladstone, Memorandum on the Government of Ireland Bill, 10 Dec. 1892, P.R.O., Cab. 37/32, no. 8, 1-2.

6. Margaret Banks, *Edward Blake: Irish Nationalist* (Toronto 1957), 11; Bryce to Blake, 10 Oct. 1892, N.L.I., Blake papers, Mic. p.4861; Blake to Bryce, 24 Oct. 1892, ibid.; Bryce to Blake, 18 Nov. 1892, ibid.

7. Bryce, Memorandum on foreign and colonial legislatures, 19 Nov. 1892, N.L.I., Bryce papers, MS 11009(4), 7-8.

8. Ibid., 8-9; Gladstone's cabinet memo, 21 Nov. 1892, G.P. 44648; McCarthy to Praed, 19 Dec. 1892, in McCarthy and Praed, *Our Book of Memories*, 339; ibid., 22 Dec. 1892, 341; Dillon to Blake, 22 Dec. 1892, N.L.I., Blake papers, Mic. p.4681.

9. Gladstone's cabinet memo, 24 Nov. 1892, G.P. 44648.

10. R. E. Welby, E. W. Hamilton and Alfred Milner, Memorandum on Irish finance, 14 Dec. 1892, P.R.O., Cab. 37/32, 1892, no. 51, 14, 15-18, 32, 33, 38-9. It is worth noting that in July 1891 Gladstone suggested to Morley that a future Liberal government should postpone a Home Rule bill for two years, in order to ascertain 'how the financial relations [between Great Britain and Ireland] really lie' (Morley, *Recollections*, i, 278); Hamilton diary, 21 Jan. 1893, H.P. 48659.

11. Morley to Gladstone, 14 Dec. 1892, G.P. 44648; Harcourt, Memorandum on the financial scheme of the Home Rule bill, 13 Apr. 1893, N.L.I., Bryce papers, MS 11009(4), 1-2. See also *Return Showing the Effect of the Financial Proposals in the Government of Ireland Bill... on the Basis of Estimated Revenue and Expenditure for 1892-3*, 3, H.C. 1893-4 (91), 1, 383.

12. Dillon to Blake, 11 Jan. 1893, N.L.I., Blake papers, Mic. p.4681.

13. Memorandum by the committee of the Irish Parliamentary Party on the contribution by Ireland to imperial charges, 13 Jan. 1893, P.R.O., Cab. 37/33, 1893, no. 7, 1-17.

14. Hamilton diary, 14 Jan. 1893, H.P. 48659; Gladstone to the Queen, 27-8 July 1893, in Philip Guedalla (ed.), *The Queen and Mr Gladstone* (London 1933), ii, 472.

15. Gladstone on Irish fiscal extravagance (p. 277 below); McCarthy to Praed, 13 Jan. 1893, in McCarthy and Praed, *Our Book of Memories*, 348

(also McCarthy to Dillon, 14 Jan. 1893, T.C.D. Dillon papers, MS 6733/49); Harcourt, Memorandum on the financial clauses proposed in the Government of Ireland Bill, 16 Jan. 1893, P.R.O., Cab. 37/33, 1893, no. 4, 6. See also Bogdanor, *Devolution*, 28-30.

16. Hamilton diary, 3 Nov. 1892, H.P. 48659. Harcourt to Morley, 18 Jan. 1893, in Gardiner, *Harcourt*, ii, 220. See also Gladstone, 'Disadvantages of Sir William Harcourt's Plan', 18 Jan. 1893, G.P. 44775.

17. *A Bill to Amend the Provision for the Future Government of Ireland*, 1-2, H.C. 1893-4 (209), iii, 255-6.

18. Ibid., 257-8.

19. Ibid., 258-60, 272, 259-60, 268-71.

20. Minutes of meeting of 13 Feb. 1893 in Irish Parliamentary Party minute book, T.C.D., Dillon papers, MS 6501; Banks, *Blake*, 51-2; Davitt, *Fall of Feudalism*, 666-7; Redmond, *Hansard 4*, viii, 1463-80 (14 Feb. 1893); General reaction to the bill in *Annual Register, 1893* (London 1894), 36, 39; Harold Spender, *The Story of the Home Rule Session* (London 1893), 92, on Unionist tactics on opposing the bill.

21. Spender, *Story*, 92-3; McCarthy to Praed, 14 Mar. 1893, in McCarthy and Praed, *Our Book of Memories*, 353-4; Morley, *Gladstone*, iii, 378.

22. Spender, *Story*, 36; Negative results of accepting changes to clause 1, in Morley to Gladstone, 15, 16, 17 May 1893, G.P. 44257; Spender, op. cit, 39; Morley, *Gladstone*, iii, 375-6.

23. Davitt to Dillon, Nov.-Dec. 1892, T.C.D., Dillon papers, MS 6728/18; Blake to McCarthy, 21 June 1893, in Banks, *Blake*, 64, 65; McCarthy to Praed, 10 June 1893, in McCarthy and Praed, *Our Book of Memories*, 362; Spender, *Story*, 56-7.

24. *Return Showing the Copy of the Report of the Commissioners of Inland Revenue to the Treasury, 6 June 1893, explaining an Error in the Computation of Ireland's Contribution to Spirit Duty as shown in the 'Financial Relations' Returns of 1891 and 1893*, 3, H.C. 1893-4 (248), 1, 345; Morley, *Gladstone*, iii, 374. For Harcourt's strong defence of the reformed financial scheme see *Hansard 4*, xv, 343-6 (24 July 1893).

25. Justin McCarthy, 'The Home Rule Bill', *N.C.*, xxxiii (Mar. 1893), 369-73; John Redmond, 'Second Thoughts on the Home Rule Bill', ibid. (Apr. 1893), 560-70; J. J. Clancy, 'The Financial Clauses of the Home Rule Bill', *F.R.*, lii (Apr. 1893), 619-24.

26. Morley to Gladstone, 26 May 1893, G.P. 44257; Redmond to Morley, 13 June 1893, N.L.I., Redmond papers, MS 15207(1) (also Sir Robert Meade to Sir Algernon West, 19 June 1893, in *Private Diaries of Sir A. West*, 166); Morley to Gladstone, 19 June 1893, G.P. 44257 (Morley may well have been influenced in his fears for Irish social order by a dynamite explosion at Dublin Castle on Christmas Eve 1892, which killed a policeman (McCarthy and Praed, *Our Book of Memories*, 342)); Gardiner, *Harcourt*, ii, 222; Welby 'Financial Relations', 136-8; *Statement Illustrating the Effect of the Amended Financial Proposals in the Government of Ireland Bill*, 1, H.C. 1893-4 (280), 1, 387; *Private Diaries of Sir A. West*, 168.

27. Blake to Morley, 10 July 1893, N.L.I., Blake papers, Mic. p. 4683; Hamilton diary, 18, 19 June 1893, H.P. 48660; Davitt to Doherty, 1 July

1893, N.L.I., Davitt papers, MS 15347, acc. 2627; *Private Diaries of Sir A. West*, 172-3, 174-6. In 1894 Sir J. N. McKenna informed Redmond that Gladstone's 'promise of a royal commission, saved the point of honour for our party' (McKenna to Redmond, 25 Nov. 1894, N.L.I., Redmond papers, MS 15203(7)). See also Lawrence, *Govt of Northern Ire.*, 188.

28. Lords' rejection of the Home Rule bill in F. W. Hirst, 'Mr Gladstone's Fourth Premiership and Final Retirement, 1892-5' in Reid (ed.), *Life of Gladstone*, 724, and Lord Eversley, *Gladstone and Ireland* (London 1912), 373; Ponsonby to Lord Houghton, 2 Sept. 1893, in Ponsonby, *Henry Ponsonby*, 221; Spender, *Story*, 91; Magnus, *Gladstone*, 414; R. C. K. Ensor, *England, 1870-1914* (Oxford 1936; 10th reprint 1968), 211-12.

29. Redmond to Mather, 23 Apr. 1892, N.L.I., Redmond papers, MS 15206(1); ibid., 28 Apr. 1892; Denis Gwynn, *John Redmond* (London 1932), 80-1.

30. Dillon, Memorandum of meeting with Gladstone, 21 June 1892, T.C.D., Dillon papers, MS 6796/27; Memorandum on the Home Rule Bill of 1886, 29 Oct. 1892, N.L.I., Bryce papers, MS 11009(4). (However, the Home Rule bill did, in clauses 18 and 34 respectively, forbid both the Irish legislative assembly from passing any vote or bill appropriating any part of the public revenue without the consent of the Lord Lieutenant, and Irish local authorities from borrowing money without the approval of the Irish government); *Commercial Ulster and the Home Rule Movement* (Belfast 1893), 55 (This argument against Home Rule was apparently compiled by the Belfast Chamber of Commerce); McKnight, *Ulster*, ii, 319.

31. John Greenhill, president of the Belfast Chamber of Commerce, to *The Times*, 13 Apr. 1893 in *Mr Gladstone and the Belfast Chamber of Commerce* (Belfast 1893), 38-9; Adam Duffin to 'Dearest', 20 Mar. 1893, P.R.O.N.I., Duffin papers, Mic. 127/10B (By 'closured' Duffin is referring to the parliamentary device for curtailing debate — generally known as the 'closure' — as a metaphor for describing Gladstone's tendency to stifle criticism during the interview); *Gladstone and Belfast Ch. of Comm.*, 3-9.

32. *Gladstone and Belfast Ch. of Comm.*, 9-13, 28, 17.

33. Ibid., 30-1

34. *F.J.*, 29 Apr., 2 May 1893. During this debate in the Commons Gladstone made the startling declaration that Parnell was prepared to accept separate treatment for Ulster in 1886. However, this was strongly objected to by both Nationalist factions.

35. Morley, *Recollections*, i, 355; McKnight, *Ulster*, ii, 341; *Gladstone and Belfast Ch. of Comm.*, 14; McKnight, op. cit., ii, 331, 344; Garvin, *Chamberlain*, ii, 540-1.

36. *Ireland As it Is and As it Would Be Under Home Rule: Sixty-Two Letters Written by the Special Commissioner of the 'Birmingham Daily Gazette' between March and August 1893* (Birmingham 1893), 16, 17-19, 28 (Thomas McKnight also informed Joseph Chamberlain that he had it 'positively on authority . . . he was able to trust that arms had been provided and stored' (Garvin, *Chamberlain*, ii, 541-2)); Lucas, *Saunderson*, 196-7; A. T. Q. Stewart, *The Ulster Crisis* (London 1967), 90; Thomas Sinclair, quoted in McKnight, *Ulster*, ii, 300; Gladstone on the Ulster convention (pp 248-9 above).

However, one resolution passed at the convention did warn of 'disorder, violence and bloodshed' if any attempt was made to place Ulster under a Dublin parliament (*Ulster Lib. Un. Assoc.*, intro. Fisher, 34); St Loe Strachey, 'Ulster and Home Rule', *N.C.*, xxxi (June 1892), 78-9.

37. Strachey, 'Ulster and Home Rule', 80-2; Rentoul, *Stray Thoughts*, 223-4, 225 (Rentoul argued that many Ulster Unionists thought the convention had killed Home Rule); Garvin, *Chamberlain*, ii, 541-2; McKnight, *Ulster*, ii, 238; Spender, *Story*, 24; Duffin to Hugh de F. Montgomery, 27 Aug. 1892, P.R.O.N.I., Montgomery papers, D627/428/193.

38. McKnight, *Ulster*, ii, 310; Ross, *Pilgrimage*, 64; Lucas, *Saunderson*, 194-5; *Ire. As It Is*, 15-16; Spender, *Story*, 24 (In fact the only fighting to take place between Nationalists and Unionists was on the floor of the House of Commons, when both groups were drawn into a brawl started by two English M.P.s (Ross, *Pilgrimage*, 78-80); Reid on Ulster (pp238-9 above).

Conclusion (pp.284-292)

1. Robert Kee, *The Bold Fenian Men: The Green Flag, Vol. 2*, 2nd ed. (London 1976), 92 (see also E. J. Feuchtwanger, *Gladstone* (London 1972), 232); Harrington on Nationalist Party support in 1885 (pp 30-1 above); For an important recent study arguing that local affairs rather than 'national' issues were central to Irish politics in the nineteenth century see K. T. Hoppen, *Elections, Politics and Society in Ireland, 1832-85* (Oxford 1984); O'Day, *Eng. Face of Ir. Nationalism*, 17-19, 27, 133-6; O'Farrell, *Ireland's Eng. Question*, 167.

2. Davitt and Healy on the need to educate British public opinion on Home Rule (p. 45 above); Morley to Gladstone, 25 Jan. 1894, G.P. 44257.

3. Cooke and Vincent, *Governing Passion*, 52 (also Vincent, *Gladstone and Ire.*, 228-9); Critique of Vincent, *Gladstone and Ire.* (pp 81-5 above).

4. Gladstone's intentions regarding the land bill (p. 85 above); Hammond, *Gladstone*, 72-3; What the Home Rule scheme of 1886 was intended to achieve (ch. 3 above, passim).

5. Curtis, *Anglo-Saxons and Celts*, 103, on anti-Irish prejudice; B. R. Mitchell and Phyllis Dean, *Abstract of British Historical Statistics* (Cambridge 1962), 398.

6. Lionel Tollemache, *Talks with Mr Gladstone* (London 1898), 59-60; Hammond, *Gladstone*, 711; Gladstone's fixity of opinion (p. 59 above).

7. Kettle on Gladstone's Home Rule scheme (p. 115 above); Weakness of historicist propaganda in Britain (pp 173-5 above).

8. Gladstone on the future of landlords in Ireland after Home Rule (pp 185-90 above); Gladstone and Nationalists on the Ulster problem (pp 224-5, 229, 249 above).

9. Ibid., Gladstone (pp 141, 249 above), Parnellites (pp 125-8 above); Unionist strategy in Patrick O'Farrell, *England and Ireland since 1800* (London 1975), 39-40, and L. P. Curtis, jr, *Apes and Angels: the Irishman in Victorian Caricature* (Newton Abbot 1971), 25-41; 'Evidence' to support Home Rulers' views on Ulster (pp 129-30, 133, 140, 143-52 above).

10. Stewart, *Narrow Ground*, 166-7; Beckett, *Mod. Ire.*, 424-6; Gladstone's cabinet memo, 9 Mar. 1893, G.P. 44648.
11. See pp 248-9 above.

Appendix 1 (pp 293-294)

1. For Irish Home Rule newspapers see *Newspaper Press Directory* (1887), 143-52. The nature of this study has been strongly influenced by the material on 'content analysis' in Clair Sellitz, Marie Jahoda, Morton Deutsch and Stuart Cook, *Research Methods in Social Relations*, revised ed. (London 1971), 335-42.
2. D. G. Boyce, *Englishmen and Irish Troubles: British Public Opinion and the Making of Irish Policy, 1918-22* (London 1972), 200.

Bibliography

The plan of this bibliography is based generally on that in T. W. Moody's *Davitt and Irish Revolution* (pp 579-80). Sections II-VIII comprise sources; sections X and XI secondary works; sections I and IX combine material in both categories. With reference to items in section IX, it is important, as Dr Moody notes, to distinguish between contemporary writings and later works by contemporaries, as the two can differ so greatly in value as historical evidence. Again, in regard to contemporary writings (section VI), many items could be classed in more than one category (for example, those in subsections 2 and 4); however, to avoid repetition I have entered items only in the category which appears best to describe their contents. This applies also to the bibliography as a whole, apart from materials in section X and works of major relevance to more than one category.

I PUBLICATIONS ON GLADSTONE

This section includes biographical works, studies of Gladstonian politics in general, and some other works important for an understanding of Gladstone's attitudes to Home Rule, Irish nationalism and Ulster Unionism.

Barker, Michael, *Gladstone and Radicalism: The Reconstruction of the Liberal Party in Britain, 1885-94* (Brighton 1974)
Bradley, Ian, *The Optimists: Themes and Personalities in Victorian Liberalism* (London 1979)

Cooke, A. B., and Vincent, John, *The Governing Passion: Cabinet Government and Party Politics in Britain, 1885-6* (Brighton 1974)

Cosgrove, R. A., 'The Relevance of Irish History: The Gladstone—Dicey Debate about Home Rule, 1886-7', *Éire-Ireland*, xv, 3 (autumn 1980), 6-21

Dunne, T. J., 'The Political Ideology of Home Rule' (M.A. thesis, N.U.I. (U.C.C.), 1972

——— '*La trahison des clercs*: British Intellectuals and the First Home Rule Crisis', *Irish Historical Studies*, xxiii, no. 90 (Nov. 1982), 134-73

——— Eversley, Lord [G. J. Shaw Lefevre], *Gladstone and Ireland: The Irish Policy of Parliament, 1850-94* (London 1912)

Eyck, Erich, *Gladstone*, trans. Bernard Miall (London 1938)

Feuchtwanger, E. J., *Gladstone* (London 1972)

Gladstone, Herbert, Viscount, *After Thirty Years* (London 1928)

Hamer, D. A., *Liberal Politics in the Age of Gladstone and Rosebery: A Study in Leadership and Policy* (Oxford 1972)

Hamilton, Sir E. W., *Gladstone* (London 1898)

Hammond, J. L., *Gladstone and the Irish Nation* (London 1938)

——— and Foot, M. R. D., *Gladstone and Liberalism* (London 1952)

Heyck, T. W., *The Dimensions of British Radicalism: The Case of Ireland, 1874-95* (Chicago 1974)

Hirst, F. W., *Gladstone as Financier and Economist* (London 1931)

Hufford, R. A., 'An Analysis and Criticism of the Rhetoric of the Debates on the Irish Home Rule Bill of 1886' (M.A. thesis, University of Durham, 1958)

Kilbracken, Lord, *Reminiscences* (London 1931)

Knaplund, P. A., *Gladstone and Britain's Imperial Policy* (London 1927)

Lubenow, W. C., 'Irish Home Rule and the Great Separation in the Liberal Party in 1886: The Dimensions of Parliamentary Liberalism', *Victorian Studies*, xxvi (winter 1983), 161-80

——— 'Irish Home Rule and the Social Basis of the Great Separation in the Liberal Party in 1886', *Historical Journal*, 28, no. 1 (1985), 125-42.

McCarthy, Justin, *The Story of Gladstone's Life* (London 1898)

Magnus, Philip, *Gladstone: A Biography* (London 1954); 2nd ed., corrected (1963)

Marshall, Peter, 'The Imperial Factor in Liberal Decline, 1880-85' in J. E. Flint and Glyndwr Williams (ed.), *Perspectives of Empire* (London 1972), 130-47.

Morley, John, *The Life of William Ewart Gladstone*, 3 vols (London 1903); 2nd ed. (1911)

Morton, Grenfell, *Home Rule and the Irish Question* (Seminar Studies in History) (London 1980)

Mr Gladstone and the Belfast Chamber of Commerce (Belfast 1893)

O'Day, Alan, *Parnell and the First Home Rule Episode, 1884-87* (Dublin 1986)

Ramm, Agatha, 'Gladstone's Religion', *Historical Journal*, 28, no 2 (1985), 327-40

Reid, Sir Wemyss (ed.), *The Life of William Ewart Gladstone* (London 1899) While the whole of this composite work is useful, the following articles are of particular interest:

Hirst, F. W., 'Gladstone and the Eastern Question' (pp 618-34)

———— 'Mr Gladstone's Second Premiership, 1880-85' (pp 635-81)

———— 'Mr Gladstone and Home Rule, 1885-92' (pp 682-720)

———— 'Mr Gladstone's Fourth Premiership and Final Retirement, 1892-5' (pp 721-36)

Lucy, H. W., 'Mr Gladstone as an Orator' (pp 502-27)

Reid, Sir Weymss, 'Mr Gladstone's Character and Career: A General Appreciation' (pp 1-52)

Selborne, Lord, *Memorials: Part 2, Personal and Political, 1865-95*, 2 vols (London 1898)

Shannon, R. T., *Gladstone and the Bulgarian Agitation, 1876* (London 1963)

———— *Gladstone*, Vol. I: *1809-65* (London 1982)

Steele, E. D., 'Gladstone and Ireland', *Irish Historical Studies*, xvii, no. 65 (Mar. 1970), 58-88

———— *Irish Land and British Politics: Tenant Right and Nationality, 1865-70* (Cambridge 1974)

———— 'Gladstone, Irish Violence and Conciliation' in Art Cosgrove and Donal McCartney (ed.), *Studies in Irish History presented to R. Dudley Edwards* (Dublin 1979), 257-78

Tollemache, Lionel, *Talks with Mr Gladstone* (London 1898)

Vincent, John, *Gladstone and Ireland* (Oxford 1978)

The Raleigh Lecture on History in the British Academy, 1977

West, Sir Algernon, *Recollections, 1832-86* (London 1899); 2nd ed. (n.d.)

II THE GLADSTONE PAPERS

The Gladstone papers in the British Museum (Add. MSS 44086-835) naturally constitute the largest and most important collection for any study of the Liberal leader, and Irish material for the Home Rule period has been extensively examined for the purpose of the present work. Of particular interest are the papers used by Morley when writing his biography of Gladstone (Add. MSS 56444-53) and only added to the collection quite recently. Additionally, the following printed documents have been consulted:

Carlingford, Lord, *Lord Carlingford's Journal: Reflections of a Cabinet Minister*, ed. A. B. Cooke and J. R. Vincent (Oxford 1971)

Gladstone, W. E., *The Gladstone Diaries, 1825-54*, ed. M. R. D. Foot and H. C. G. Matthews, 4 vols (Oxford 1968-74)

———— *The Gladstone Diaries, 1855-68*, ed. H. C. G. Matthews, 2 vols (Oxford 1978)

———— *The Gladstone Diaries with Cabinet Minutes and Prime-Ministerial Correspondence, 1869-74*, 2 vols (Oxford 1982)

———— *The Prime Ministers' Papers Series: W. E. Gladstone, IV: Autobiographical Memoranda, 1868-94*, ed. John Brooke and Mary Sorenson (London 1981)

———— *The Political Correspondence of Mr Gladstone and Lord Granville, 1868-76*, ed. Agatha Ramm, 2 vols (Oxford 1952)

———— *The Political Correspondence of Mr Gladstone and Lord Granville, 1876-86*, ed. Agatha Ramm, 2 vols (Oxford 1962)

———— *The Queen and Mr Gladstone*, ed. Philip Guedalla, 2 vols (London 1933)

———— *Gladstone to his Wife*, ed. A. T. Bassett (London 1936)

Hamilton, Sir E. W., *The Diary of Sir Edward Walter Hamilton, 1880-85*, ed. D. W. R. Bahlman, 2 vols (Oxford 1972)

West, Sir Algernon, *The Private Diaries of Sir Algernon West*, ed. H. G. Hutchinson (London 1922)

III PUBLICATIONS OF GLADSTONE

This section, consisting mainly of works by Gladstone in the period 1886-92 on Irish nationalism and Home Rule, includes both his own publications and collections of his speeches.

Gladstone, W. E., 'History of an Idea — Why I Became a Home Ruler' in T. P. O'Connor and Robert McWade, *Gladstone—Parnell, and the Great Irish Struggle* (Philadelphia 1886), 823-42

——— 'Kin Beyond the Sea' in *Prose Masterpieces of Modern Essayists* (London 1886), 349-95

——— *Special Aspects of the Irish Question: A Series of Reflections in and since 1886* (London 1892)

> This work consists of pamphlets and articles dealing particularly with the historical aspects of the argument for Home Rule, and published at different times in the period 1886-90. These are listed below in chronological order, with the year of original publication in brackets.

'The Irish Question' (pp 1-56) (1886)

'Notes and Queries on the Irish Demands' (pp 57-108) (1887)

'Lessons of Irish History in the Eighteenth Century' (pp 109-34) 1887)

'Ingram's History of the Irish Union' (pp 135-85) (1887)

'Dr Ingram and the Irish Union' (pp 187-95) (1888)

'Further Notes and Queries on the Irish Demands' (pp 197-234) (1888)

'Mr Forster and Ireland' (pp 235-62) (1888)

'Daniel O'Connell' (pp 263-302) (1889)

'Plain Speaking on the Irish Union' (pp 303-42) (1889)

'Home Rule for Ireland: An Appeal to the Tory Householder' (pp 343-72) (1890)

——— *The Speeches of W. E. Gladstone, 1886-8*, ed. A. W. Hutton and H. J. Cohen (London 1902)

——— *The Speeches of W. E. Gladstone, 1888-92*, ed. A. W. Hutton and H. J. Cohen (London 1902)

——— *Gladstone's Speches . . .* , ed. A. T. Bassett (London 1916)

The foregoing, however, do not contain all Gladstone's Home Rule speeches. These can be examined more fully in *The Times, Freeman's Journal* and *Hansard*. For a complete guide to Gladstone's speeches see Morley, *Gladstone*, iii, 463-95.

IV MANUSCRIPT SOURCES OTHER THAN THE GLADSTONE PAPERS

1 *BELFAST*
PUBLIC RECORD OFFICE OF NORTHERN IRELAND

North Armagh political papers: D1252/42/3/30

Rev. J. B. Armour papers: D1792

Adam Duffin papers: Mic. 127
Irish Loyal and Patriotic Union papers: D989
William Johnston diaries: D880/2/34-40
Jeremiah Jordan papers: D2073
John McElderry papers: Mic. 57
Hugh de F. Montgomery papers: D627/428/1-293; T1089
John Pinkerton papers: D1078
J. N. Richardson papers, 1868-94: D2956
Minute book of the Route Reform Club: D1426
Colonel Edward Saunderson papers: T2996; Mic. 281
Home Rule correspondence: Mic. 95
Newspaper cuttings on the anti-Home Rule campaign in Ulster, 1892-3: T1633
Anti-Home Rule printed material: T2917

2 *DUBLIN*

STATE PAPER OFFICE

Chief Secretary's Office, Registered Papers, 1886-90
Irish Crime Records, 1882-92
Police and Crime Records, Crime Branch Special files, 1890-1920
Irish National Land League and Irish National League papers, 1879-88 (10 cartons)

NATIONAL LIBRARY OF IRELAND

Edward Blake papers: Mic. pp 4681-3
F. S. Bourke papers: MS 10723
James (Viscount) Bryce papers: MSS 11009-10
   Contains many copies of cabinet papers and memoranda on the Home Rule bills of 1886 and 1893 and the devolution scheme of 1907-8.
Archbishop Croke papers: Mic. pp 6012-13
Letters of Michael Davitt to (?) Doherty: MS 15347, acc. 2627
E. S. W. de Cobain papers: MS 17729
T. P. Gill papers: MS 13478
William Haley papers: MS 3905
Timothy Harrington papers: MSS 8576-81
Minute book and notices of the Irish Protestant Home Rule Association: MS 3657
Michael McDonagh papers: MSS 11439-46
J. F. X. O'Brien papers: MS 13424
John Redmond papers: MSS 15191, 15203-7
George Sigerson papers: MS 10904
T. D. Sullivan papers: MS 8237
F. J. Tuohy papers: MSS 8882-3
Alfred Webb papers: MSS 1745-6
Minute book of the Young Ireland Society, 1885-6: MS 19158

LIBRARY OF TRINITY COLLEGE

Davitt papers: series 1: letters from and to Davitt, 1870-1906, and papers by
and relating to him
Dillon papers: MSS 6501-837
Rev. J. A. Galbraith papers: MS 3856
Lecky correspondence: nos 1-719

3 *LONDON*

BRITISH LIBRARY

Balfour papers: Add. MSS 49688-826
Viscount Gladstone papers: Add. MSS 46015-71
Edward Hamilton diaries: Add. MSS 48642-4, 48659-60

PUBLIC RECORD OFFICE

Cabinet papers, 1886, 1892-3

V PRINTED RECORDS

1 *PARLIAMENTARY PAPERS*

(a) HOME RULE AND RELATED PAPERS

*Copy of Selections from the Representations made to the First Lord of the Treasury by
Public Bodies, in response to the Invitation for Free Communication of Views on Ireland
contained in a Letter addressed by the First Lord of the Treasury to Viscount de Vesci on 12
February 1886*, H.C. 1886 (117), lii, 773
A Bill to Amend the Provision for the Future Government of Ireland, H.C. 1886 (181),
ii, 461
Sale and Purchase of Land (Ireland) Bill, H.C. 1886 (193), v, 395
A Bill to Amend the Provision for the Future Government of Ireland, H.C. 1893-4 (209),
iii, 255
————— [The foregoing as amended in committee], H.C. 1893-4 (428), iii, 287
————— [The foregoing as amended in committee and on consideration],
H.C. 1893-4 (448), iii, 323
*Return Showing the Effect of the Financial Proposals in the Government of Ireland Bill
as regards Ireland, on the Basis of the Estimated Revenue and Expenditure for 1892-3*,
H.C. 1893-4 (91), 1, 383
*Return Showing the Copy of the Report to the Commissioners of Inland Revenue to the
Treasury, 6 June 1893, explaining an Error in the Computation of Ireland's Con-
tribution to Spirit Duty as shown in the 'Financial Relations' Returns of 1891 and
1893*, H.C. 1893-4 (248), 1, 345
*Statement Illustrating the Effect of the Amended Financial Proposals in the Government of
Ireland Bill*, H.C. 1893-4 (280), 1, 387
*First Report of Her Majesty's Commissioners appointed to Inquire into the Financial
Relations between Great Britain and Ireland*, [C 7720], H.C. 1895, xxxvi, 1

———— *Minutes of Evidence and Appendices up to 28 March 1895* [C 7720-1], H.C. 1895, xxxvi, 5

Final Report of Her Majesty's Commissioners appointed to Inquire into the Financial Relations between Great Britain and Ireland, [C 8262], H.C. 1896, xxxiii, 59

(b) LOCAL GOVERNMENT

A Bill for the Better Government of Counties in Ireland, H.C. 1888 (6), ii, 377
    Introduced by John Dillon, Thomas Sexton, T. M. Healy and others.
Local Government (Ireland) Bill, H.C. 1892 (174), iii, 609

(c) POLICE AND CRIME

Report of the Commissioners of Inquiry, 1864, respecting the Magisterial and Police Arrangements and Establishment of the Borough of Belfast, [C 3466], H.C. 1865, xxvii, 1

———— *Minutes of Evidence and Appendices*, [C 3466-2], H.C. 1865, xxviii, 27

Report of the Commissioners of Inquiry, 1886, respecting the Origins and Circumstances of the Riots in Belfast, in June, July, August and September 1886, [C 4925], H.C. 1887, xvii, 1

———— *Minutes of Evidence and Appendices*, [C 4925-1], H.C. 1887, xviii, 25

Report of One of the Commissioners of Inquiry 1886, respecting the Origin and Circumstances of the Riots in Belfast, in June, July, August and September 1886, and the Action taken thereon by the Authorities; also in regard to the Magisterial and Police Jurisdictions, Arrangements and Establishment for the Borough of Belfast, [C 5029], H.C. 1887, xviii, 630

Report of the Special Commission 1888 (appointed to Inquire into Charges and Allegations made against Certain Members of Parliament in O'Donnell v. Walter), [C 5891], H.C. 1890, xxvii, 477

The Special Commission Act, 1888: Reprint of the Shorthand Notes of the Speeches, Proceedings and Evidence taken before the Commissioners appointed under the above-named Act, 12 vols (London 1890)

(d) POPULATION, VALUATION, ETC.

Census of Ireland, 1881: Preliminary Report with Abstract of the Enumerators' Summaries, [C 2931], H.C. 1881, xcvi, 159

Return Showing the Population of 1871 and 1881: the Number of Electors in 1871 and 1881; the Area in Square Miles; the Number of Members; the Amount of Property and Income Tax Charged for the Last Year for which the Returns are made up, in each County and Parliamentary Division of a County in the United Kingdom (exclusive of Cities and Boroughs) . . . and Similar Returns for the Cities and Boroughs of the United Kingdom, H.C. 1882 (149), lii, 397

Return Showing the Population and Electors in each County, City, and Borough in Ireland returning Members to Parliament; the Acreage in each of the same; the Number of Registered Voters in each of the same; the Valuation of Rateable Property in each of the same; the Number of Land Tenements, etc., in each County. . . ., H.C. 1884 (164), lxii, 221

Census of Ireland, 1891: Preliminary Report with Abstract of the Enumerators' Summaries, [C 6779], H.C. 1892, xc, 6

(e) LANDLORD/TENANT RELATIONS

Report of the Royal Commission on the Land Law (Ireland) Act, 1881, and the Purchase of Land (Ireland) Act, 1885, [C 4969-1], H.C. 1887, xxvi, 1
_____ Vol. II: *Minutes of Evidence and Appendices*, [C 4969-2], H.C. 1887, xxvi, 25

2 *RECORDS OF PARLIAMENT*

Hansard's Parliamentary Debates, 3rd series, cclxxv-ccclxiv (1882-92) (London 1882-92)
_____ *The Parliamentary Debates* (authorised section), 4th series, i-xvi (1892-3) (London 1892-3)
Lucy, H. M., *A Diary of Two Parliaments*, Vol. II: *The Gladstone Parliament, 1880-85* (London 1886)
_____ *A Diary of the Salisbury Parliament, 1885-6* (London 1886)
_____ *Diary of the Salisbury Parliament, 1886-92* (London 1892)
_____ *Diary of the Home Rule Parliament, 1892-5* (London 1896)
Spender, Harold, *The Story of the Home Rule Session* (London 1893)

3 *OTHER PRINTED RECORDS*

Irish Historical Documents, 1172-1922, ed. Edmund Curtis and R. B. McDowell (London 1943)
The Parnellite Split, or The Disruption of the Irish Parliamentary Party, reprinted from 'The Times' (London 1891)
Reports of meetings of the Dublin committee of the Irish Protestant Home Rule Association, June 1886 - Apr. 1893, in *Freeman's Journal*, June 1886 - Apr. 1893
Return of Outrages Specially Reported to the Constabulary Office, No. 10: Return of Agrarian Outrages Specially Reported throughout Ireland, during each of the years from 1869 to 1896 inclusive (C.S.O., R.P., 1897/3476)

VI PRINTED CONTEMPORARY WORKS OTHER THAN GLADSTONE'S

1 *GENERAL HISTORY*

Froude, J. A., *The English in Ireland in the Eighteenth Century*, 3 vols (London 1872-4)
Lecky, W. E. H., *A History of England in the Eighteenth Century*, 8 vols (London 1878-90)
_____ *A History of Ireland in the Eighteenth Century*, 5 vols (London 1892); new impression (1919)
Macaulay, T. B., *The History of England from the Accession of James II*, 5 vols (London 1848-61); Everyman's Library ed., 3 vols (1953)
Richey, A. G., *A Short History of Ireland down to the Plantation of Ulster*, ed. R. R. Kane (London 1887)

Two Hundred Years of Irish History, 1691-1870, with introduction by James Bryce (London 1888)

2 POLEMICAL WORKS

(a) BOOKS

Daunt, W. J. O'N., *Ireland since the Union* (Dublin 1888)

Davis, Thomas, *Prose Writings of Thomas Davis*, ed. T. W. Rolleston (London [1889])

Dicey, A. V., *England's Case against Home Rule* (London 1886); reissued with introduction by E. J. Feuchtwanger (1973)

———— *A Leap in the Dark or Our New Constitution* (London 1893)

Healy, T. M., *A Word for Ireland* (London 1886)

Ireland As It Is and As It Would Be Under Home Rule: Sixty-Two Letters Written by the Special Commissioner of the 'Birmingham Daily Gazette' between March and August 1893 (Birmingham 1893)

Jennings, L. J., *Mr Gladstone: A Study* (London 1887)

McCarthy, J. H., *The Case for Home Rule* (London 1887)

McNeill, J. G. S., *How the Union was Carried* (London 1887)

O'Brien, R. B., *The Home-Ruler's Manual* (London 1890)

O'Connell, Daniel, *A Memoir of Ireland, Native and Saxon* (London 1842)

O'Connor, T. P., and McWade, Robert, *Gladstone—Parnell, and the Great Irish Struggle* (Philadelphia 1886)

Sullivan, T. D., *Green Leaves: A Volume of Irish Verses* (Dublin 1879); 12th ed. (1888)

(b) PAMPHLETS AND COLLECTIONS OF LEAFLETS

Clancy, J. J., *Ulster* (Dublin 1886)

———— *Six Months' Unionist Rule in Ireland* (London 1887)

Commercial Ulster and the Home Rule Movement (Belfast 1893)

Commins, Andrew, *Orangeism: What Is It? and What Will You Do About It? Facts and Considerations for the People of Great Britain* (London 1886)

Counsell, E. P. S., *Our Orange Opponents* (Dublin 1886)

Fegan, Rev. H. S., *Irish Nationality – An Appeal to Educated Englishmen* (London 1886)

Home Rule Union, *'Protestant Ulster': Where Is It?* (London n.d.)

Houston, J. D. C., and Dougherty, Prof. (James), *Are Irish Protestants Afraid of Home Rule?* (London 1893)

Irish Loyal and Patriotic Union, *Home Rule in 1689* (Dublin/London 1886)

———— *The Real Dangers of Home Rule* (Dublin/London 1886); 3rd ed. (1887)

———— *'Irish Nationalism': Illustrated by Speeches of Parnellite M.P.s and Other Nationalists* (Dublin/London 1886)

———— *A Guide to the 'Eighty-Six': chiefly contributed by themselves* (Dublin/London 1886)

———— *The National League and Outrages* (Dublin/London 1886)

———— *The Way We Live Now in Ireland* (Dublin/London 1886)

Irish Protestant Home Rule Association, Collection of pamphlets and leaflets
on Home Rule (N.L.I., Ir. 32341 i. 27)
Laing, Samuel, *Boycotting* (London 1888)
Leech, H. B., *1848 and 1887: The Continuity of the Irish Revolutionary Movement*
(Dublin/London 1887)
Liberal Unionist Association, *The Case for the Union: A Collection of Speeches,
Pamphlets and Leaflets on Home Rule for Ireland* (London [1890])
    The following two pamphlets are to be found in this collection.
_____ *The Opinion of Irish Protestants on Home Rule* (London [1888])
_____ *A Massacre of Protestant Farmers predicted by 'United Ireland'* (London
[1888])
McVeagh, Jeremiah, *What Orangeism Means: An Object Lesson in Irish Politics*
(London 1893)
Mahoney, Pierce, *The Irish Land Crisis* (London 1886)
Montgomery, H. de F., *Correspondence with Mr Gladstone and Notes on the Pamphlet
'Gladstone and Burke'* (Dublin [1887])
National Press Agency, *Shall Ulster Rule Ireland?* (London n.d.)
_____ Collection of leaflets on Home Rule (N.L.I., Ir. 32341 n. 1)
Rolleston, T. W., *Boycotting: A Reply* (Dublin 1888)
Saunderson, E. J., *Two Irelands; or Loyalty versus Treason* (Dublin 1884)
Shaw, J. J., *Mr Gladstone's Two Irish Policies: 1868 and 1886* (Belfast 1888)
An Ulster Protestant, *Some Thoughts on Home Rule* (London 1886)
Webb, Alfred, *The Alleged Massacres of 1641* (London 1887)

(c) ARTICLES

Brabourne, Lord, 'Facts and Fictions in Irish History: A Reply to Mr
Gladstone', *Blackwood's Magazine*, cxl (Oct. 1886), 419-55
_____ 'Mr Gladstone and Lord Brabourne on Irish History', *Blackwood's
Magazine*, cxl (Nov. 1886), 681-98
_____ 'A Review of a Review', *Blackwood's Magazine*, cxlii (Nov. 1887), 715-30
A critique of Gladstone's review of Ingram's history of the Union (see above,
p. 337).
Bryant, Sophie, 'The Ripon and Morley Demonstration', *Journal of the Home
Rule Union* (Mar. 1888), 6-8
Colclough, J. J., 'Ulster: Facts and Figures', *Contemporary Review*, lxiii (June
1893), 261-81
Healy, T. M., 'Ulster and Ireland', *Contemporary Review*, xlviii (Nov. 1885),
723-31
_____ 'Jubilee Time in Ireland', *Contemporary Review*, li (Jan. 1887), 120-30
[Jennings, L. J.], 'Mr Gladstone and Ireland', *Quarterly Review*, clxiii (July
1886), 257-88
McColl, Canon Malcolm, 'The "Unionist" Position' in James Bryce (ed.),
Handbook of Home Rule (London 1887), 106-29
Morley, John, 'Some Arguments Considered' in James Bryce (ed.), *Handbook
of Home Rule* (London 1887), 246-62

Morton, E. J. C., 'Crimeless Ireland', *Journal of the Home Rule Union* (May 1888), 40-3

———— 'The Home Rule Union', *Journal of the Home Rule Union* (July 1888), 72-4

Murphy, J., 'Recent Protestant Historians of Ireland', *Irish Ecclesiastical Record*, xvii (Apr.-June, 1896), 289-305, 489-514

Reid, R. T., 'Ulster', *Contemporary Review*, lii (Nov. 1887), 605-16

Russell, T. W., 'The Actual and the Political Ireland', *Nineteenth Century*, xxvii (Jan. 1890), 89-101

Sinclair, Thomas, 'Ulster: Facts and Figures: A Reply', *Contemporary Review*, lxiv (July 1893), 29-40
   A reply to Colclough (see above).

3 *NARRATIVES AND REPORTS*

Bryce, James, 'How We Became Home Rulers' in James Bryce (ed.), *Handbook of Home Rule* (London 1887), 24 55

Crawford, M. S., 'Experiences of an Irish Landowner', *Contemporary Review*, lii (Aug. 1887), 262-74

A Liberal Woman, 'An Evening Stroll', *Journal of the Home Rule Union* (July 1888), 68-9
   On working-class indifference to Home Rule.

Mr Gladstone and the Belfast Chamber of Commerce (Belfast 1893)

Ribblesdale, Lord, 'A Railway Journey with Mr Parnell', *Nineteenth Century*, xxx (Dec. 1891), 969-74

'The Riots in Belfast', *Fortnightly Review*, xl (Sept. 1886), 276-99

Spender, Harold, *The Story of the Home Rule Session* (London 1893)

Strachey, St Loe', 'Ulster and Home Rule', *Nineteenth Century*, xxxi (June 1892), 78-82

Sullivan, A. M., *New Ireland: Political Sketches and Personal Reminiscences of Thirty Years of Irish Public Life* (London 1877); 10th ed., with a sequel on 1877-82 (Glasgow n.d.)

Taylor, J. A. (ed.), *The Rossmore Incident: An Account of the Various Nationalist and Anti-Nationalist Meetings, held in Ulster in the autumn of 1883* (Dublin 1884)

The Parnellite Split, or the Disruption of the Irish Parliamentary Party, reprinted from 'The Times' (London 1891)

Webb, Alfred, *The Opinions of Some Protestants regarding their Catholic Fellow-Countrymen* (Dublin 1886)

4 *STUDIES*

Acton, Lord, *The History of Freedom and other essays*, with introduction by J. R. Figgis and R. J. Lawrence (London 1907)

Anson, W. R., 'The Government of Ireland Bill and the Sovereignty of Parliament', *Law Quarterly Review*, ii (Oct. 1886), 427-43

Bagehot, Walter, *The English Constitution* (London 1867)

'Bagwell's *Ireland under the Tudors*', *Edinburgh Review*, clxiii (Apr. 1886), 436-65

Bryant, Sophie, 'The Truth of National Sentiment', *Dublin University Review*, ii (May 1886), 216-32

Bryce, James, 'Alternative Policies in Ireland', *Nineteenth Century*, xix (Feb. 1886), 312-29

––––––– 'The Past and Future of the Irish Question' in James Bryce (ed.), *Handbook of Home Rule* (London 1887), 214-46

Burke, Edmund, *Edmund Burke: His Works and Correspondence*, 8 vols (London 1852)

––––––– *Reflections on the Revolution in France* (London 1790); new ed. (1868)

Canning, A. S. G., *Revolted Ireland, 1798 and 1803* (London 1886)

Chamberlain, Joseph, *A Unionist Policy for Ireland* (London 1888)

Clancy, J. J., 'The Financial Clauses of the Home Rule Bill', *Fortnightly Review*, lii (Apr. 1893), 619-24

Courtown, Earl of, 'The Celts and Teutons in Ireland', *National Review*, lx (1887), 84-92

Davitt, Michael, 'Mr Giffen's Proposed Solution to the Irish Question', *Contemporary Review*, xlix (Apr. 1886), 501-12

Dicey, A. V., *The Law of the Constitution* (London 1885); 8th ed. (1923)

Duffy, Sir C. G., *The League of North and South* (London 1886)

––––––– 'A Fair Constitution for Ireland', *Contemporary Review*, lii (Sept. 1887), 301-32

––––––– *A Fair Constitution for Ireland*, with introduction (London 1892)

Giffen, Robert, 'The Economic Value of Ireland to Great Britain', *Nineteenth Century*, xix (Mar. 1886), 329-45

Grimshaw, T. W., *Facts and Figures about Ireland, Pts 1 and 2* (Dublin 1893)

Hamilton, Thomas, *History of the Irish Presbyterian Church* (Belfast/Edinburgh 1886); special ed. (1887)

Hume, A. C., 'Origin and Characteristics of the Population in the Counties of Down and Antrim', *Ulster Journal of Archaeology*, 1st series, i (1852), 9-26, 120-9, 246-54

––––––– *The Origins and Characteristics of the People in the Counties of Down and Antrim*, with introduction (Belfast 1872)

Ingram, J. D., *A History of the Legislative Union of Great Britain and Ireland*, 2 vols (London 1887)

Irish Loyal and Patriotic Union, *A Critical Analysis of the Sale and Purchase of Land (Ireland) Bill* (Dublin/London [1886])

Kennedy, Thomas, *A History of Irish Protest against Overtaxation from 1853-97* (Dublin 1897)

Lecky, W. E. H., *Leaders of Public Opinion in Ireland*, 2 vols (London 1861): new ed. (1912)

Lough, Thomas, *England's Wealth, Ireland's Poverty* (London 1896)

McCarthy, Justin, 'The Home Rule Bill', *Nineteenth Century*, xxxiii (Mar. 1893), 369-73

Mill, J. S., *England and Ireland* (London 1868)

O'Brien, R. B., *The Irish Land Question and English Public Opinion* (London 1880)

––––––– 'Federal Union with Ireland', *Nineteenth Century*, xix (Jan. 1886), 35-40

_____ 'The Study of Irish History', *Irish Ecclesiastical Record*, xviii (Dec. 1895), 399-407

O'Connor, T. P., *The Parnell Movement* (London 1886)

O'Curry, Eugene, *On the Manners and Customs of the Ancient Irish*, 3 vols (London 1873)

O'Donovan, John, *Ancient Laws of Ireland*, 6 vols (Dublin 1865-1901)

O'Leary, John, 'Some Guarantees for the Protestant and Unionist Minority', *Dublin University Review*, ii (Dec. 1886), 959-65

Prendergast, J. P., *The Cromwellian Settlement of Ireland* (London 1865); 2nd ed. (1875)

Redmond, John, 'Second Thoughts on the Home Rule Bill', *Nineteenth Century*, xxxiii (Apr. 1893), 560-70

Rolleston, T. W., 'The Archbishop in Politics — A Protest', *Dublin University Review*, ii (Feb. 1886), 92-103

Shaw Lefevre, G. J., *Peel and O'Connell* (London 1887)

Smith, Goldwin, *Irish History and Irish Character* (Oxford/London 1861); 2nd ed. (1862)

S.O.G., 'Imperial Government and the Irish National Schools', *Graphic* (20 Aug. 1887), 210

Spencer, Earl, Preface to James Bryce (ed.), *Handbook of Home Rule* (London 1887), vii-xix
    Brief but perceptive analysis of the Home Rule case.

Stephens, H. M., 'Modern Historians and their Influence on Small Nationalities', *Contemporary Review*, lii (July 1887), 108-20

Thring, Lord, 'Home Rule and Imperial Unity' in James Bryce (ed.), *Handbook of Home Rule* (London 1887), 55-79

_____ 'The Irish Government and Land Bills' in James Bryce (ed.), *Handbook of Home Rule* (London 1887), 79-106

5 *LETTERS, DIARIES AND SPEECHES*

Ashbourne: *The Ashbourne Papers, 1869-1913: A Calendar of the Papers of Edward Gibson, 1st Lord Ashbourne*, compiled by A. B. Cooke and A. P. W. Malcomson (Belfast 1974)

Blunt, W. S., *The Land War in Ireland* ((London 1912)
    Blunt's Irish diary, Dec. 1885 — June 1890

_____ *My Diaries, being a Personal Narrative of Events, 1888-1914*, 2 vols (London 1919-20)

Bright: *The Diaries of John Bright*, ed. R. A. J. Walling (London 1930)

Buckland, Patrick (ed.), *Irish Unionism, 1885-1923: A Documentary History* (Belfast 1973)
    Contains many letters on Unionist politics.

Burke, Edmund, *Edmund Burke: His Works and Correspondence*, 8 vols (London 1852)

Burke, T. N., *Ireland's Vindication: Refutation of Froude and other lectures* (Glasgow n.d.)

Chamberlain, Joseph, *Speeches on the Irish Question, 1887-90* (London 1890)

_____ *A Political Memoir, 1880-92*, ed. C. H. D. Howard (London 1953)

Crawshay, W. S., and Read, F. W., *The Politics of the Commons* (London 1886)

Daunt, W. J. O'N., *A Life Spent for Ireland*, edited by his daughter (London 1896)

Davitt, Michael, *Leaves from a Prison Diary*, 2 vols (London 1885); cheap edition in one volume (1885)

Devoy: *Devoy's Post-Bag, 1871-1928*, ed. William O'Brien and Desmond Ryan, 2 vols (Dublin 1948-53)

Esher: *Journals and Letters of Reginald Viscount Esher, 1860-1915*, ed. Oliver Esher and M. V. Brett, 3 vols (London 1934-8)

Granville: *The Political Correspondence of Mr Gladstone and Lord Granville, 1868-76*, ed. Agatha Ramm, 2 vols (Oxford 1952)

_____ *The Political Correspondence of Mr Gladstone and Lord Granville, 1876-86*, ed. Agatha Ramm, 2 vols (Oxford 1962)

Hamilton: *The Diary of Sir Edward Walter Hamilton, 1880-85*, ed. D. W. R. Bahlman, 2 vols (Oxford 1972)

Lecky, W. E. H., *The Political Uses of History* (London 1892) (a speech)

McCarthy, Justin, and Praed, Mrs Campbell, *Our Book of Memories* (London 1912)
    The correspondence of McCarthy and Praed.

McColl: *Malcolm McColl: Memoirs and Correspondence*, ed. G. W. E. Russell (London 1914)

Mitchel, John, *Jail Journal, or, Five Years in British Prisons* (New York 1854); new ed. (Glasgow n.d.)

Northcote: 'A Conservative Leader in Ulster: Sir Stafford Northcote's Diary of a Visit to the Province, Oct. 1883', ed. A. B. Cooke, *Proceedings of the Royal Irish Academy*, lxxv, sect. C, no. 4 (1975), 61-84

O'Brien, William, *Irish Ideas* (London 1893)
    Speeches delivered in the period 1886-92.

O'Curry, Eugene, *Lectures on the Manuscript Materials of Ancient Irish History* (Dublin 1861)

Oldham, C. H., *The Record of Ulster Protestantism in the History of Irish Patriotism* (Belfast 1888) (a speech)

Parnell, C. S., *Mr Parnell's Speeches, Letters and Public Addresses (out of Parliament) in the United Kingdom, 1879-88*, printed by R. D. Webb & Son for use before the Special Commission (Dublin 1889)

_____ Letters, in Katharine O'Shea, *Charles Stewart Parnell: His Love Story and Political Life*, 2 vols (London 1914)

Plunket, Archbishop, *Our Past Lineage and Present Duties* (Dublin 1891) (a speech)

Ponsonby: Ponsonby, Arthur, *Henry Ponsonby: Queen Victoria's Private Secretary: His Life from his Letters* (London 1942)

Redmond, J. E., '*Hugh O'Neill': A Lecture* (Naas 1887)

_____ *Historical and Political Addresses* (London 1898)

Rendel: *The Personal Papers of Lord Rendel*, ed. F. E. Hamer (London 1931)

Salmon, George, *The Infallibility of the Church: A Course of Lectures delivered in the Divinity School of the University of Dublin* (Dublin 1889); 2nd ed. (1890)

Seeley, Sir J. R., *The Expansion of England: Two Courses of Lectures* (London 1883); 18th ed. (1911)

Victoria: *The Queen and Mr Gladstone*, ed. Philip Guedalla, 2 vols (London 1933)

West: *The Private Diaries of Sir Algernon West*, ed. H. G. Hutchinson (London 1922)

VII CONTEMPORARY NEWSPAPERS AND MAGAZINES

1 *NEWSPAPERS*

Armagh. *Armagh Guardian*
Ballina. *Ballina Journal*
Ballinasloe. *Connaught People*
———— *Western News*
Ballymoney. *Ballymoney Free Press*
Ballyshannon. *Donegal Independent*
Belfast. *Belfast Evening Telegraph*
———— *Belfast Morning News*
———— *Belfast News-Letter*
———— *Belfast Weekly Telegraph*
———— *Northern Whig*
———— *Weekly Examiner*
———— *Weekly Northern Whig*
Boyle. *Roscommon Herald*
Carlow. *Nationalist and Leinster Times*
Castlebar. *Connaught Telegraph*
———— *Mayo Examiner*
Cavan. *Anglo-Celt*
Coleraine. *Coleraine Chronicle*
———— *Coleraine Constitution*
Cork. *Cork Constitution*
———— *Cork Daily Herald*
———— *Cork Examiner*
Downpatrick. *Down Recorder*
Dublin. *Dublin Evening Mail*
———— *Freeman's Journal*
———— *The Irishman*
———— *Irish Catholic*
———— *Irish Times*
———— *The Nation*
———— *North and South*
———— *United Ireland*
Dundalk. *Dundalk Democrat*
Ennis. *Clare Examiner*
———— *Clare Saturday Record*
———— *Independent and Munster Advertiser*
Enniskillen. *Fermanagh Mail*
———— *Fermanagh Times*
———— *Impartial Reporter*
Kilkenny. *Kilkenny Journal*

Kilrush. *Clare Advertiser*
_____ *Kilrush Herald*
Limerick. *Limerick Chronicle*
_____ *Limerick Reporter*
_____ *Munster News*
London. *Black and White*
_____ *The Graphic*
_____ *Pall Mall Gazette*
_____ *The Times*
Londonderry. *Derry Journal*
_____ *Derry Standard*
_____ *Londonderry Sentinel*
Maryborough. *Leinster Express*
Monaghan. *People's Advocate*
Mullingar. *Westmeath Examiner*
Naas. *Leinster Leader*
New Ross. *Wexford Express*
Newry. *Newry Reporter*
Parsonstown. *Midland Tribune*
Portadown. *Portadown and Lurgan News*
Sligo. *Sligo Champion*
_____ *Sligo Chronicle*
Tralee. *Kerry Sentinel*
Tuam. *Tuam Herald*
_____ *Tuam News*
Waterford. *Munster Express*
_____ *Waterford Daily Mail*
_____ *Waterford News*
Wexford. *The People*
Wicklow. *Wicklow People*

2 MAGAZINES

Blackwood's Magazine (London)
Contemporary Review (London)
Dublin University Review (Dublin)
Edinburgh Review (Edinburgh/London)
Fortnightly Review (London)
Fraser's Magazine (London)
Gentleman's Magazine (London)
Irish Ecclesiastical Record (Dublin)
Journal of the Home Rule Union (London)
Law Quarterly Review (London)
Liberal Unionist (London)
Methodist Times (London)
National Review (London)
Nineteenth Century (London)
Quarterly Review (London)
Ulster Journal of Archaeology (Belfast)

VIII CONTEMPORARY WORKS OF REFERENCE

Annual Register, 1882-93 (London 1883-94)
Dod's Parliamentary Companion, 1882-93 (London 1865-) (annual)
Newspaper Press Directory and Advertisers' Guide, 1880-93 (London 1846-) (annual)
Who's Who: An Annual Autobiographical Dictionary . . . (London 1897-)
Who Was Who, 1897-1916 (London 1920)
———— *1916-28* (London 1929)

IX LATER WRITINGS BY CONTEMPORARIES

1 *MEMOIRS AND AUTOBIOGRAPHIES*

Aberdeen, Lord and Lady, *'We Twa': Reminiscences*, 2 vols (London 1925); 2nd ed., 2 vols in 1 (1927)

Argyll: *George Douglas, Eighth Duke of Argyll: Autobiography and Memoirs*, ed. Dowager Duchess of Argyll, 2 vols (London 1906)

Asquith, H. H., *Fifty Years of Parliament*, 2 vols (London 1926)

Balfour, A. J., *Chapters of Autobiography*, ed. Blanche Dugdale (London 1930)

Campbell, T. J., *Fifty Years of Ulster, 1890-1940* (Belfast 1941)

Chamberlain, Joseph, *A Political Memoir, 1880-92*, ed. C. H. D. Howard (London 1953)

Denvir, John, *The Life Story of an Old Rebel* (Dublin 1910); reprinted with an introduction by Leon Ó Broin (Shannon 1972)

Doyle, Lynn [L. A. Montgomery], *An Ulster Childhood* (Dublin/London 1921)

Duffy, Sir C. G., *My Life in Two Hemispheres*, 2 vols (London 1898)

Dunlop, Andrew, *Fifty Years of Irish Journalism* (Dublin 1911)

Gwynn, Stephen, *Experiences of a Literary Man* (London 1926)

Haldane, Richard, *Richard Burdon Haldane: An Autobiography* (London 1929)

Hamilton, Lord Ernest, *Forty Years On* (London 1922)

Healy, T. M., *Letters and Leaders of My Day*, 2 vols (London 1928)

Holmes: Cooke, A. B., and Vincent, J. R., 'Ireland and Party Politics, 1885-7: An Unpublished Conservative Memoir [by Hugh Holmes]', *Irish Historical Studies*, xvi, no. 62 (Sept. 1968), 154-72; no. 63 (Mar. 1969), 321-38; no. 64 (Sept. 1969), 446-71

Kettle, A. J., *The Material for Victory*, ed. L. J. Kettle (Dublin 1958)

Lucy, Sir Henry, *The Diary of a Journalist* (London 1923)

MacBride, M. G., *A Servant of the Queen* (London 1938); 2nd ed. (Dublin 1954)

McCarthy, Justin, *Reminiscences*, 2 vols (London 1899)

———— *The Story of an Irishman* (London 1904)

McColl: *Malcolm McColl: Memoirs and Correspondence*, ed. G. W. E. Russell (London 1914)

McKnight, Thomas, *Ulster As It Is, or Twenty-Eight Years' Experience as an Irish Editor*, 2 vols (London 1896)

McNeill, J. G. S., *What I Have Seen and Heard* (London 1925)

Morley, John, *Recollections*, 2 vols (London 1917)

O'Brien, William, *Recollections* (London 1905)

———— *An Olive Branch in Ireland* (London 1910)

O'Connor, T. P., *Memoirs of an Old Parliamentarian*, 2 vols (London 1929)

Rathcreedan, Lord, *Memories of a Long Life* (London 1931)

Rentoul, J. A., *Stray Thoughts and Memories* (Dublin 1920)

Robinson, Sir Henry, *Memories: Wise and Otherwise* (London 1923)

Ross, Sir John, *The Years of My Pilgrimage* (London 1923)

Rossmore, Lord, *Things I Can Tell* (London 1912)

Sullivan, T. D., *Recollections of Troubled Times in Irish Politics* (Dublin 1905)

West, Sir Algernon, *Recollections, 1832-86* (London 1899); 2nd ed. (n.d)

2 *NARRATIVES AND STUDIES*

Davitt, Michael, *The Fall of Feudalism in Ireland: or The Story of the Land League Revolution* (London/New York 1904)

Fitzmaurice, Lord, 'Ireland, 1782 and 1912' in J. H. Morgan (ed.), *The New Irish Constitution: An Exposition and Some Arguments* (London 1912), 268-90

Hamilton, Lord Ernest, *The Soul of Ulster* (London 1917)

McCarthy, M. J. F., *The Irish Revolution*, Vol. I: *The Murdering Time, from the Land League to the First Home Rule Bill* (London 1912)

McDonagh, Michael, *The Home Rule Movement* (Dublin 1920)

MacDonnell, Sir John, 'Constitutional Limitations on the Powers of the Irish Legislature and the Protection of Minorities' in J. H. Morgan (ed.), *The New Irish Constitution: An Exposition and Some Arguments* (London 1912), 90-112

McDonnell, M. F. J., *Ireland and the Home Rule Movement* (Dublin 1908); 2nd ed. (1908)

McElroy, Samuel, *The Route Land Crusade* (Coleraine n.d.)

McNeill, Ronald, *Ulster's Stand for the Union* (London 1927)

Moore, F. F., *The Truth about Ulster* (London 1914)

Morgan, J. H., 'The Constitution: A Commentary' in J. H. Morgan (ed.), *The New Irish Constitution: An Exposition and Some Arguments* (London 1912), 3-50

O'Brien, R. B., *A Hundred Years of Irish History* (London [1902]) Lecture to Irish Literary Society.

O'Brien, William, *'The Party': Who They Are and What They Did* (Dublin 1917)

O'Donnell, F. H., *A History of the Irish Parliamentary Party*, 2 vols (London 1910)

Russell, T. W., *Ireland and the Empire: A Review, 1800-1900* (London/New York 1901)

Sinclair, Thomas, 'The Position of Ulster' in Simon Rosenbaum (ed.), *Against Home Rule: The Case for the Union* (London 1912; reissued, New York/London 1970), 170-82

Ulster Liberal Unionist Association, *The Ulster Liberal Unionist Association: A Sketch of its History, 1885-1914*, with introduction by J. R. Fisher (Belfast 1914)

Welby, Lord, 'Financial Relations' in J. H. Morgan (ed.), *The New Irish Constitution: An Exposition and Some Arguments* (London 1912), 112-56

X HISTORICAL WORKS AND RELATED STUDIES

1 *GENERAL HISTORY*

Beckett, J. C., *The Making of Modern Ireland* (London 1966); 3rd ed. (1973)

Cullen, L. M., *An Economic History of Ireland since 1660* (London 1972)

Ensor, R. C. K., *England, 1870-1914* (Oxford 1936); 10th reprint (1968)

Kee, Robert, *The Bold Fenian Men: The Green Flag, Vol. 2* (London 1976). First published as part of *The Green Flag* (London 1972)

Lee, Joseph, *The Modernisation of Irish Society, 1848-1918* (Dublin 1973)

Lyons, F. S. L., *Ireland since the Famine* (London 1971); 2nd ed. (1973)

MacDonagh, Oliver, *Ireland: The Union and Its Aftermath* (Englewood Cliffs, N.J. 1968); revised ed. (London 1977)

Mansergh, Nicholas, *The Irish Question, 1840-1921*, 3rd ed. (London 1975). First published as *Ireland in the Age of Reform and Revolution* (London 1940).

Moody, T. W., and Martin, F. X. (ed.), *The Course of Irish History* (Cork 1967)

Norman, E. R., *A History of Modern Ireland* (London 1971)

O'Farrell, Patrick, *Ireland's English Question: Anglo-Irish Relations, 1534-1970* (London 1971)

———— *England and Ireland since 1800* (London 1975)

Strauss, Emil, *Irish Nationalism and English Democracy* (London 1951)

2 *BIOGRAPHY AND STUDIES RELATING TO INDIVIDUALS*

Dictionary of National Biography, ed. Sir Leslie Stephen, 66 vols (London 1885-1901); reprinted with corrections, 22 vols (London 1908-9 etc.)

Boylan, Henry, *A Dictionary of Irish Biography* (Dublin 1978)

Crone, J. S., *A Concise Dictionary of Irish Biography* (Dublin 1928); 2nd ed. [1937]

Thom's Irish Who's Who (Dublin 1923)

Webb, Alfred, *A Compendium of Irish Biography . . .* (Dublin 1878)

Armour: Armour, W. S., *Armour of Ballymoney* (London 1934)

———— McMinn, J. R. B., 'The Reverend James Brown Armour and Liberal Politics in North Antrim, 1869-1914' (Ph.D. thesis, Queen's University, Belfast, 1979)

Arnold-Forster: Arnold-Forster, Mary, *Hugh Oakeley Arnold-Forster* (London 1910)

Asquith: Jenkins, Roy, *Asquith* (London 1964)

Balfour: Dugdale, Blanche, *Arthur James Balfour, First Earl of Balfour*, 2 vols (London 1936)

Blake: Banks, Margaret, *Edward Blake: Irish Nationalist* (Toronto 1957)

Brett: Brett, C. E. B., *Long Shadows Cast Before: Nine Lives in Ulster, 1625-1977* (London 1977)

Bryce: Fisher, H. A. L., *James (Viscount) Bryce*, 2 vols (London 1927)

———— Harvie, Christopher, 'Ideology and Home Rule: James Bryce, A. V. Dicey and Ireland, 1880-87', *English Historical Review*, xci, no. 359 (Apr. 1976), 298-314

Butt: Thornley, David, *Issac Butt and Home Rule* (London 1964)

Campbell-Bannerman: Spender, J. A., *Life of Sir Henry Campbell-Bannerman*, 2 vols (London 1924)

———— Wilson, John, *C. B.: A Life of Sir Henry Campbell-Bannerman* (London 1973)

Carnarvon: Hardinge, Sir Arthur, *The Life of H. H. Molyneux Herbert, Fourth Earl of Carnarvon*, 3 vols (Oxford 1925)

Chamberlain: Garvin, J. L., *The Life of Joseph Chamberlain*, Vol. II: *1885-95* (London 1933)

———— Strauss, W. L., *Joseph Chamberlain and the Theory of Imperialism* (Washington 1942)

———— Howard, C. H. D., 'Joseph Chamberlain, Parnell and the "Central Board" Scheme', *Irish Historical Studies*, viii, no. 32 (Sept. 1953), 329-55

———— Hurst, Michael, *Joseph Chamberlain and Liberal Reunion: The Round Table Conference of 1887* (London/Toronto 1967)

Childers: Childers, Spencer, *The Life and Correspondence of H. C. E. Childers, 1827-86*, 2 vols (London 1901)

Churchill: Foster, R. F., *Lord Randolph Churchill: A Political Life* (Oxford 1981)

Cowper: *Earl Cowper, K. G.: Memoir by his Wife* (London 1913)

Craigavon: Ervine, St John, *Craigavon: Ulsterman* (London 1949)

Croke: Tierney, Mark, *Croke of Cashel: The Life of Thomas William Croke, 1823-1902* (Dublin 1976)

Davis: Duffy, Sir C. G., *A Short Life of Thomas Davis* (London 1895)

Davitt: Sheehy-Skeffington, Francis, *Michael Davitt: Revolutionary Agitator and Labour Leader*, with introduction by Justin McCarthy (London 1908); reprinted with introduction by F. S. L. Lyons (1967)

———— Moody, T. W., 'Davitt' in J. W. Boyle (ed.), *Leaders and Workers* (Cork [1967]), 47-55

————Moody, T. W., *Davitt and Irish Revolution, 1846-82* (Oxford 1981)

Devonshire: Holland, B. H., *Life of Spencer Compton, Eighth Duke of Devonshire*, 2 vols (London 1911)

Dicey: Ford, T. H., 'Dicey's Conversion to Unionism', *Irish Historical Studies*, xviii, no. 72 (1972-3), 552-82

———— Harvie, Christopher, 'Ideology and Home Rule: James Bryce, A. V. Dicey and Ireland, 1880-87', *English Historical Review*, xci, no. 359 (Apr. 1976), 298-314

Dilke: Gwynn, Stephen, and Tuckwell, G. M., *The Life of Sir Charles W. Dilke*, 2 vols (London 1917)

———— Jenkins, Roy, *Victorian Scandal: A Biography of Sir Charles Dilke* (London 1958); revised ed. (New York 1965)

Dillon: Lyons, F. S. L., *John Dillon: A Biography* (London 1968)

Dufferin: Lyall, Sir Alfred, *The Life of the Marquess of Dufferin and Ava*, 2 vols (London 1905)

Freeman: Stephens, W. R. W., *The Life and Letters of E. A. Freeman* (London 1895)

Gonne: Cardozo, Nancy, *Maud Gonne* (London 1979)

Goschen: Elliot, A. D., *The Life of Lord Goschen*, 2 vols (London 1911)

Granville: Fitzmaurice, Lord Edmund, *The Life of Granville: George Leveson-Gower, Second Earl Granville*, 2 vols (London 1905)

Harcourt: Gardiner, A. G., *The Life of Sir William Harcourt*, 2 vols (London 1925)

Healy: Sullivan, Maev, *No Man's Man* (Dublin 1943)

Labouchere: Thorold, Algar, *The Life of Henry Labouchere* (London 1913)

Manning: Purcell, E. S., *Life of Cardinal Manning*, 2 vols (London 1896)

———— Leslie, Shane, *Henry Edward Manning* (London 1921)

Morley: Hamer, D. A., *John Morley: Liberal Intellectual in Politics* (Oxford 1968)

Morris: Wynne, Maud, *An Irishman and his Family: Lord Morris and Killanin* (London 1937)

O'Brien: McDonagh, Michael, *The Life of William O'Brien* (London 1928)

———— O'Brien, J. V., *William O'Brien and the Course of Irish Politics, 1881-1918* (Los Angeles/London 1976)

O'Connor: Fyfe, Hamilton, *T. P. O'Connor* (London 1934)

O'Grady: Marcus, P. L., *Standish O'Grady* (Lewisburg 1970)

Parnell: Bew, Paul, *C. S. Parnell* (Dublin 1980)

———— Foster, R. F., *Charles Stewart Parnell: The Man and his Family* (Hassocks 1976); 2nd ed. (1979)

———— Howard, C. H. D., 'Joseph Chamberlain, Parnell and the "Central Board" Scheme', *Irish Historical Studies*, viii, no. 32 (Sept. 1953), 329-55

———— Hurst, Michael, *Parnell and Irish Nationalism* (London 1968)

————Lyons, F. S. L., 'The Economic Ideas of Parnell' in Michael Roberts (ed.), *Historical Studies, II* (London 1939), 60-78

———— Lyons, F. S. L., 'The Political Ideas of Parnell', *Historical Journal*, xvi, no. 4 (Dec. 1973), 749-45

————Lyons, F. S. L., *Charles Stewart Parnell* (London 1977); 2nd ed. (1978)

———— Martin, Ged, 'Parnell at Cambridge: The Education of an Irish Nationalist', *Irish Historical Studies*, xix, no. 73 (Mar. 1974), 72-82

———— O'Brien, C. C., *Parnell and his Party, 1880-90* (Oxford 1957); corrected impression (1974)

———— O'Brien, R. B., *The Life of Charles Stewart Parnell*, 2 vols (London 1898); 2nd ed., in one volume [1910]

———— O'Connor, T. P., *C. S. Parnell: A Memory* (London [1892])

———— O'Day, Alan, *Parnell and the First Home Rule Episode, 1884-87* (Dublin 1986)

———— O'Shea, Katharine, *Charles Stewart Parnell: His Love Story and Political Life*, 2 vols (London 1914)

Ponsonby: Ponsonby, Arthur, *Henry Ponsonby: Queen Victoria's Private Secretary: His Life from his Letters* (London 1942)

Redmond: Redmond-Howard, L. G., *John Redmond* (London 1910)

———— Gwynn, Denis, *John Redmond* (London 1932)

Rhodes: Mitchell, Sir Lewis, *The Life of Cecil John Rhodes*, 2 vols (London 1910)

———— Taylor, G. F., 'Cecil Rhodes and the Second Home Rule Bill', *Historical Journal*, xiv, no. 4 (1971), 374-80

Rosebery: Crewe, Marquis of, *Lord Rosebery*, 2 vols (London 1931)

Salisbury: Cecil, Lady Gwendolen, *The Life of Robert, Marquis of Salisbury*, 4 vols (London 1921-31)

———— Taylor, Robert, *Lord Salisbury* (London 1975)

Saunderson: Lucas, Reginald, *Colonel Saunderson: A Memoir* (London 1908)

Tuke: Fry, Sir Edward, *James Hack Tuke: A Memoir* (London 1899)

Walsh: Walsh, P. J., *William J. Walsh: Archbishop of Dublin* (London 1928)

3 *THE ULSTER QUESTION*

Armour, W. S., *Armour of Ballymoney* (London 1934)

Baker, Sybil, 'Orange and Green: Belfast 1832-1912' in H. J. Dyos and Michael Wolff (ed.), *Victorian Cities: Images and Realities* (London 1973), 789-814

Bew, Paul, and Wright, Frank, 'The Agrarian Opposition in Ulster Politics, 1848-87' in Samuel Clark and J. S. Donnelly, jr (ed.), *Irish Peasants: Violence and Political Unrest, 1780-1914* (Manchester/Wisconsin 1983), 192-229

Boyd, Andrew, *Holy War in Belfast* (Tralee 1969)

Buckland, Patrick, *Irish Unionism, 2: Ulster Unionism and the Origins of Northern Ireland, 1886-1922* (Dublin 1973)

Budge, Ian, and O'Leary, Cornelius, *Belfast: Approach to Crisis: A Study of Belfast Politics, 1613-1970* (London 1973)

Burton, Frank, *The Politics of Legitimacy: Struggles in a Belfast Community* (London 1978)

Foster, R. F., 'To the Northern Counties Station: Lord Randolph Churchill and the Prelude to the Orange Card' in F. S. L. Lyons and R. A. J. Hawkins (ed.), *Ireland under the Union: Varieties of Tension. Essays in Honour of T. W. Moody* (Oxford 1980), 237-89

Gibbon, Peter, *The Origins of Ulster Unionism: The Formation of Popular Protestant Politics and Ideology in Nineteenth-Century Ireland* (Manchester 1976)

Harbinson, J. F., *The Ulster Unionist Party, 1882-1973* (Belfast 1973)

Harris, Rosemary, *Prejudice and Tolerance in Ulster* (Manchester 1972)

Hepburn, A. C., 'Catholics in the North of Ireland, 1880-1921: The Urbanisation of a Minority' in A. C. Hepburn (ed.), *Minorities in History* (London 1978), 84-102

Jalland, Patricia, *The Liberals and Ireland: The Ulster Question in British Politics to 1914* (Brighton 1980)

Kirkpatrick, R. W., 'The Origins and Development of the Land War in Mid-Ulster, 1879-85' in F. S. L. Lyons and R. A. J. Hawkins (ed.), *Ireland under the Union: Varieties of Tension. Essays in Honour of T. W. Moody* (Oxford 1980), 201-35

Logan, James, *Ulster in the X-rays* (London 1923); 2nd ed. (n.d.)

Lyons, F. S. L., *Culture and Anarchy in Ireland, 1890-1939* (Oxford 1979)

McClelland, Aiken, 'The Later Orange Order' in T. D. Williams (ed.), *Secret Societies in Ireland* (Dublin 1973), 126-38

McCracken, J. L., 'The Consequences of the Land War' in T. W. Moody and J. C. Beckett (ed.), *Ulster since 1800: A Political and Economic Survey* (London 1955; 2nd ed., 1957), 60-70

Miller, D. W., *Queen's Rebels: Ulster Loyalism in Historical Perspective* (Dublin 1978)

————— 'Presbyterianism and Modernisation in Ulster', *Past and Present*, 80 (Aug. 1978), 76-92

Mogey, John, 'Social Relations in Rural Society' in T. W. Moody and J. C. Beckett (ed.), *Ulster since 1800: A Social Survey* (London 1954; 2nd ed., 1958), 71-9

Moody, T. W., *The Ulster Question, 1603-1973* (Dublin/Cork 1973)

Murphy, Desmond, *Derry, Donegal and Modern Ulster, 1790-1921* (Culmore, Londonderry 1981)

Orangeism in Ireland and throughout the Empire. By a Member of the Order, 2 vols (London 1938)

Patterson, Henry, *Class Conflict and Sectarianism: The Protestant Working Class and the Belfast Labour Movement, 1868-1920* (Belfast 1980)

Savage, D. C., 'The Origins of the Ulster Unionist Party, 1885-6', *Irish Historical Studies*, xii, no. 47 (Mar. 1961), 185-208

Shannon, Catherine, 'The Ulster Liberal Unionists and Local Government Reform, 1885-98', *Irish Historical Studies*, xviii, no. 71 (Mar. 1973), 407-23

Stewart, A. T. Q., *The Ulster Crisis* (London 1967)

———— *The Narrow Ground: Aspects of Ulster 1609-1969* (London 1977)

Walker, B. M., 'Parliamentary Representation in Ulster, 1868-86' (Ph.D. thesis, University of Dublin, 1976)

———— 'Party Organisation in Ulster, 1865-92: Registration Agents and their Activities' in Peter Roebuck (ed.), *Plantation to Partition: Essays in Ulster History in Honour of J. L. McCracken* (Belfast 1981), 191-209

Woodburn, W. B., *The Ulster Scot: His History and Religion* (London [1914])

Wright, Frank, 'Protestant Ideology and Politics', *European Journal of Sociology*, xiv, no. 2 (1973), 213-80

4 STEREOTYPY AND ANTI-IRISH PREJUDICE

Best, G. F. A., 'Popular Protestantism in Victorian Britain' in Robert Robson (ed.), *Ideas and Institutions of Victorian Britain* (London 1967), 116-41

Bolt, Christine, *Victorian Attitudes to Race* (London 1972)

Curtis, L. P., jr, *Anglo-Saxons and Celts: A Study of Anti-Irish Prejudice in Victorian England* (New York 1968)

———— *Apes and Angels: The Irishman in Victorian Caricature* (Newton Abbot 1971)

Denvir, John, *The Irish in Britain from the Earliest Times to the Fall and Death of Parnell* (London 1892)

Dorrity, D. T., 'Monkeys in a Menagerie: The Imagery of Unionist Opposition to Home Rule, 1886-93', *Éire-Ireland*, xii, 3 (autumn 1977), 5-22

Handley, J. E., *The Irish in Scotland, 1798-1845* (Cork 1943)

Lebow, R. N., *White Britain and Black Ireland: The Influence of Stereotypes in Colonial Policy* (Philadelphia 1976)

McCartney, Donal, 'James Anthony Froude and Ireland: An Irish Historiographical Battle of the Late Nineteenth Century' in T. D. Williams (ed.), *Historical Studies, VIII* (Dublin 1971), 171-90

Norman, E. R., *Anti-Catholic Prejudice in Victorian Britain* (London 1968)

O'Connor, Kevin, *The Irish in Britain* (London 1972); revised ed. (Dublin 1974)

Wyatt, Anne, 'Froude, Lecky and the "Humblest Irishman"', *Irish Historical Studies*, xix, no. 75 (Mar. 1975), 261-85

5 *THE LAND QUESTION*

Bew, Paul, *Land and the National Question in Ireland* (Dublin 1979)

Clark, Samuel, 'The Social Composition of the Land League', *Irish Historical Studies*, xvii, no. 68 (Sept. 1971), 447-69

——— 'The Political Mobilisation of Irish Farmers', *Canadian Review of Sociology and Anthropology*, xii, 4, pt 2 (1975), 483-99

——— *Social Origins of the Land War* (Princeton 1979)

Curtis, L. P., jr, 'The Anglo-Irish Predicament' in *Twentieth-Century Studies, No. 4: Ireland* (Edinburgh 1970), 37-64

Dewey, Clive, 'Celtic Agrarian Legislation and the Celtic Revival: Historicist Implications of Gladstone's Irish and Scottish Land Acts, 1870-86', *Past and Present*, 64 (Aug. 1974), 30-70

Donnelly, J. S., *The Land and People of Nineteenth-Century Cork* (London/Boston 1975)

Kirkpatrick, R. W., 'The Origins and Development of the Land War in Mid-Ulster, 1879-85' in F. S. L. Lyons and R. A. J. Hawkins (ed.), *Ireland under the Union: Varieties of Tension. Essays in Honour of T. W. Moody* (Oxford 1980), 201-35

Marlow, Joyce, *Captain Boycott and the Irish* (London 1973)

Moody, T. W., 'The New Departure in Irish Politics, 1878-9' in H. A. Cronne, T. W. Moody and D. B. Quinn (ed.), *Essays in British and Irish History in Honour of James Eadie Todd* (London 1949), 303-33

———'Fenianism, Home Rule and the Land War, 1850-91' in T. W. Moody and F. X. Martin (ed.), *The Course of Irish History* (Cork 1967), 275-93

——— *Davitt and Irish Revolution, 1846-82* (Oxford 1981)

Palmer, N. D., *The Irish Land League Crisis* (New Haven/London 1940)

Pomfret, J. E., *The Struggle for Land in Ireland, 1880-1923* (Princeton 1930); reissued (New York 1970)

Solow, B. L., *The Land Question and the Irish Economy, 1870-1903* (Cambridge, Mass. 1971)

Steele, E. D., *Irish Land and British Politics: Tenant Right and Nationality, 1865-70* (Cambridge 1974)

Vaughan, W. E., *Landlords and Tenants in Ireland, 1848-1904* (Dublin 1984)

6 *NATIONALISM*

Banton, Michael, *Race Relations* (London 1967)

Berlin, Sir Isaiah, *Against the Current: Essays in the History of Ideas*, ed. Henry Hardy (London 1979)

Deutsch, Karl, *Nationalism and Social Communication: An Enquiry into the Foundations of Nationality* (Cambridge, Mass. 1953); 2nd ed. (1966)

Gellner, Ernest, *Thought and Change* (London 1964)

——— *Nations and Nationalism* (Oxford 1983)

Kedourie, Elie, *Nationalism* (London 1960)

Kohn, Hans, 'Nationalism' in Anthony De Crespigny and Jeremy Cronin (ed.), *Ideologies of Politics* (London 1975), 148-60

Minogue, Kenneth, *Nationalism* (London 1967)

Smith, A. D., *Theories of Nationalism* (London 1971)

7   IRISH-AMERICAN NATIONALISM

Brown, T. N., *Irish-American Nationalism* (Philadelphia/New York 1966)

Joyce, W. P., *Editors and Ethnicity: A History of the Irish-American Press, 1848-83* (New York 1976)

Moody, T. W., 'Irish-American Nationalism', *Irish Historical Studies*, xv, no. 60 (Sept. 1967), 438-45

8   THE HISTORICIST BACKGROUND TO THE HOME RULE MOVEMENT

Anderson, Olive, 'The Political Uses of History in Mid-Nineteenth-Century England', *Past and Present*, 36 (Apr. 1967), 87-106

Burrow, J. W., *The Uses of Philology in Victorian Britain* (London 1970)

Carr, E. H., *What Is History?* (London 1961); new ed. (Harmondsworth 1973)

Cullen, L. M., 'Irish Economic History: Fact and Myth' in L. M. Cullen (ed.), *The Formation of the Irish Economy* (Cork 1969); reprinted (1976)

———— 'The Cultural Basis of Modern Irish Nationalism' in Rosalind Mitchison (ed.), *The Roots of Nationalism: Studies in Northern Europe* (Edinburgh 1980), 91-107

Curtis, L. P., jr, Introduction to Lecky, W. E. H., *A History of Ireland in the Eighteenth Century*, abridged (Chicago/London 1972), ix-l

Dewey, Clive, 'Celtic Agrarian Legislation and the Celtic Revival: Historicist Implications of Gladstone's Irish and Scottish Land Acts, 1870-86', *Past and Present*, 64 (Aug. 1974), 30-70

Gooch, G. P., *History and Historians in the Nineteenth Century* (London 1959)

Hale, J. R., *The Evolution of British Historiography from Bacon to Namier* (London 1967)

McCartney, Donal, 'The Writing of History in Ireland, 1800-30', *Irish Historical Studies*, x, no. 40 (Sept. 1957), 347-62

———— 'Lecky's *Leaders of Public Opinion in Ireland*', *Irish Historical Studies*, xiv, no. 54 (Sept. 1964), 119-41

———— 'James Anthony Froude and Ireland: An Irish Historiographical Battle of the Late Nineteenth Century' in T. D. Williams (ed.), *Historical Studies, VIII* (Dublin 1971), 171-90

Mulvey, Helen, 'The Historian Lecky: Opponent of Irish Home Rule', *Victorian Studies*, i, no. 4 (June 1958), 337-51

Roach, John, 'Liberalism and the Victorian Intelligentsia', *Cambridge Historical Journal*, xiii, no. 1 (1957), 58-81

Sheehy, Jeanne, *The Rediscovery of Ireland's Past: The Celtic Revival, 1830-1930* (London 1980)

Wyatt, Anne, 'Froude, Lecky and the "Humblest Irishman"', *Irish Historical Studies*, xix, no. 75 (Mar. 1975), 261-85

9   IRISH NATIONALISM AND HOME RULE

Boyce, D. G., *Nationalism in Ireland* (Dublin 1980)

Brasted, H. V., 'Irish Nationalism and the British Empire in the Late Nineteenth Century' in Oliver MacDonagh, W. F. Mandle and Pauric Travers (ed.), *Irish Culture and Nationalism* (London/Canberra 1983), 83-103

Cronin, Seán, *Irish Nationalism: A Study of its Roots and Ideology* (Dublin 1980)

Garvin, Tom, *The Evolution of Irish Nationalist Politics* (Dublin 1981)

Lyons, F. S. L., *The Irish Parliamentary Party, 1890-1910* (London 1951)

———— 'The Two Faces of Home Rule' in Kevin B. Nowlan (ed.), *The Making of 1916: Studies in the History of the Rising* (Dublin 1969), 99-127

———— *Charles Stewart Parnell* (London 1977); 2nd ed. (1978)

McCaffrey, L. J., *Irish Federalism in the 1870s: A Study in Conservative Nationalism* (Philadelphia 1962) (*Transactions of the American Philosophical Society*, new series, liii, pt 6)

McDonagh, Michael, *The Home Rule Movement* (Dublin 1920)

MacDonagh, Oliver. 'Ambiguity in Nationalism — The Case of Ireland', *Historical Studies* (Melbourne), 10, no. 26 (Apr. 1981), 331-52

Morton, Grenfell, *Home Rule and the Irish Question* (Seminar Studies in History) (London 1980)

O'Brien, C. C., *Parnell and his Party, 1880-90* (Oxford 1957); corrected impression (1974)

O'Brien, R. B., *The Life of Charles Stewart Parnell*, 2 vols (London 1898); 2nd ed., in one volume [1910]

O'Day, Alan, *The English Face of Irish Nationalism: Parnellite Involvement in British Politics, 1880-86* (Dublin 1977)

———— *Parnell and the First Home Rule Episode, 1884-87* (Dublin 1986)

Thornley, D. A., *Issac Butt and Home Rule* (London 1964)

Wolleston, E. O. M., 'The Irish Nationalist Movement in Great Britain, 1886-1906' (M.A. thesis, University of London, 1958)

10 *PROTESTANT HOME RULERS*

Armour, W. S., *Armour of Ballymoney* (London 1934)

Loughlin, James, 'The Irish Protestant Home Rule Association and Nationalist Politics, 1886-93', *Irish Historical Studies*, xxiv, no. 95 (May 1985), 341-60

McCann, P. J. O., 'The Protestant Home Rule Movement, 1886-95' (M.A. thesis, N.U.I. (U.C.D.), 1972)

McMinn, J. R. B., 'The Reverend James Brown Armour and Liberal Politics in North Antrim, 1869-1914' (Ph.D. thesis, Queen's University, Belfast, 1979)

11 *SOUTHERN IRISH UNIONISM*

Buckland, Patrick, *Irish Unionism, 1: The Anglo-Irish and the New Ireland, 1885-1922* (Dublin 1972)

Curtis, L. P., jr, 'The Anglo-Irish Predicament' in *Twentieth-Century Studies*, no. 4: *Ireland* (Edinburgh 1970), 37-64

D'Alton, Ian, 'Southern Irish Unionism: A Study of Cork Unionists, 1884-1914', *Transactions of the Royal Historical Society*, 5th series, xxiii (1973), 71-88

360   *Bibliography*

12 *THE CHURCHES AND IRELAND*

Bowen, Desmond, *The Protestant Crusade in Ireland, 1800-70* (Dublin 1978)

Davey, J. E., *1840-1940: The Story of a Hundred Years: An Account of the Irish Presbyterian Church from the Formation of the General Assembly to the Present Time* (Belfast 1940)

Hurley, Michael (ed.), *Irish Anglicanism, 1869-1969* (Dublin 1970)

Larkin, Emmet, 'The Devotional Revolution in Ireland, 1850-75', *American Historical Review*, lxxvii, no. 3 (June 1972), 625-52

———— *The Roman Catholic Church and the Creation of the Modern Irish State, 1878-86* (Philadelphia/Dublin 1975)

Megahey, A. J., 'The Irish Protestant Churches and Social and Political Issues, 1870-1914' (Ph.D thesis, Queen's University, Belfast, 1969)

Miller, D. W., 'Presbyterianism and Modernisation in Ulster', *Past and Present*, 80 (Aug. 1978), 76-92

Whyte, J. H., 'The Influence of the Catholic Clergy on Elections in Nineteenth-Century Ireland', *English Historical Review*, lxxv, no. 295 (Apr. 1960), 239-59

Woods, C. J., 'The Catholic Church and Irish Politics, 1879-92', (Ph.D. thesis, University of Nottingham, 1968)

13 *OTHER SPECIAL STUDIES*

Bleakley, David, 'Trade Union Beginnings in Belfast, with special reference to the period 1880-1900' (M.A. thesis, Queen's University, Belfast, 1955)

Bogdanor, Vernon, *Devolution* (Oxford 1979)

Boyce, D. G., *Englishmen and Irish Troubles: British Public Opinion and the Making of Irish Policy, 1918-22* (London 1972)

Curtis, L.P., jr, *Coercion and Conciliation in Ireland, 1880-92: A Study of Conservative Unionism* (Princeton/London 1963)

Droz, Jacques, *Europe between Revolutions, 1815-48* (London 1973)

Ensor, R. C. K., 'Some Political and Economic Interactions in Late Victorian England', *Transactions of the Royal Historical Society*, 4th series, xxxi (1949), 17-28

Farwell, Byron, *Queen Victoria's Little Wars* (Newton Abbott 1974)

Green, W. J., *Methodism in Portadown* (Belfast 1960)

Haxey, Simon, *Tory M.P.* (London 1939)
    A study of the Conservative Party.

Hooton, E. A., and Dupertuis, C. W., *The Physical Anthropology of Ireland* (Cambridge, Mass. 1955); reprinted (1974)

Hoppen, K. T., *Elections, Politics and Society in Ireland, 1832-85* (Oxford 1984)

Hufford, R. A., 'An Analysis and Criticism of the Rhetoric of Debates on the Irish Home Rule Bill of 1886' (M.A. thesis, University of Durham, 1958)

Jalland, Patricia, 'Irish Home Rule Finance: A Neglected Dimension of the Irish Question, 1910-14', *Irish Historical Studies*, xxiii, no. 91 (May 1983), 233-53

Kaartvedt, Alf, 'The Economic Basis of Norwegian Nationalism' in Rosalind

Mitchison (ed.), *The Roots of Nationalism: Studies in Northern Europe* (Edinburgh 1980), 11-19

Kennedy, H. S., *The Irish News and Belfast Morning News, 1855-1935* (Belfast 1935)
    A privately printed account to mark the paper's eightieth birthday. Linenhall Library ref. N7798.

Lawrence, R. J., *The Government of Northern Ireland: Public Finance and Public Services, 1921-64* (Oxford 1965)

Malcolm, Elizabeth, 'Temperance and Irish Nationalism' in F. S. L. Lyons and R. A. J. Hawkins (ed.), *Ireland under the Union: Varieties of Tension. Essays in Honour of T. W. Moody* (Oxford 1980), 69-115

Phillips, G. D., *The Diehards: Aristocratic Society and Politics in Edwardian England* (Cambridge, Mass./London 1979)

Short, K. R. M., *The Dynamite War: Irish-American Bombers in Victorian London* (Dublin 1979)

Walker, Brian, 'The Irish Electorate, 1868-1915', *Irish Historical Studies*, xviii, no. 71 (Mar. 1973), 359-406

XI LATER WORKS OF REFERENCE AND TECHNICAL WORKS

(a) REFERENCE

Bibliography of British History, 1851-1914, compiled and edited by H. J. Hanham (Oxford 1976)

Brown, S. J., *The Press In Ireland: A Survey and a Guide* (Dublin 1937)

Carty, James, *Bibliography of Irish History, 1870-1911* (Dublin 1940)

Mitchell, B.R. and Deane, Phyllis, *Abstract of British Historical Statistics* (Cambridge 1962)

Vaughan, W. E., and Fitzpatrick, A. J., *Irish Historical Statistics: Population, 1821-1971* (Dublin 1978)

Walker, B. M., *Parliamentary Election Results in Ireland, 1801-1922* (Dublin 1978)

(b) TECHNICAL

Sargent, S. S., and Saenger, Gerhart, 'Analysing the Content of Mass Media', *Journal of Social Issues*, 3 (1947), 33-8

Sellitz, Claire, et al., *Research Methods in Social Relations*, 2 vols (New York 1959); revised ed., in one volume (London 1971)

Index